# THE MESSAGE BEYOND WORDS

## The Illusion of Death and the Reality of Living

*Talks on the Kathopanishad*

Extemporaneous talks given by Osho
at a meditation camp in Mount Abu, India.

# THE MESSAGE BEYOND WORDS

## The Illusion of Death and the Reality of Living

*Talks on the Kathopanishad*

OSHO

JAICO PUBLISHING HOUSE

Ahmedabad Bangalore Chennai
Delhi Hyderabad Kolkata Mumbai

Published by Jaico Publishing House
A-2 Jash Chambers, 7-A Sir Phirozshah Mehta Road
Fort, Mumbai - 400 001
jaicopub@jaicobooks.com
www.jaicobooks.com



THE MESSAGE BEYOND WORDS
ISBN 978-93-48098-67-2

First Jaico Impression: 2025



The material in this book is a translation of the book originally published in Hindi under the title: *Kathopanishad*.
The complete text archive
can be found at www.osho.com/library



Page design and layout: Yogesh Typesetting, Pune

Printed by
Thomson Press India Limited, New Delhi

# Contents

# Preface

The mind can understand everything that is outside you. All that is objective is available to the mind: science and technology, philosophy and theology – all are mind-oriented. But that which is within you is behind the mind, beyond the mind. It opens itself in your meditations when you start dropping your thoughts and relaxing deeper and deeper, when only a witness is left. The body is far away and no longer you; the mind is just an echo in the valleys and is no longer you. In the innermost core of your being, there is no thought, no cloud, a great silence. In that silence arises authentic understanding. In that silence you are closest to the divine. That silence is a way, a bridge, a path, a connection to the ultimate.

Once you know the ultimate, the difficulty arises: How do you convey it? And there is a tremendous urge to convey it because millions of people are living in darkness, in blindness, stumbling, finding no way out. Millions of people are born in the night and die in the night; there is no dawn in their lives. When one comes to the dawn, when one realizes the sunrise and his whole being becomes full of light and beauty and blessings, he wants to share it. This desire to share comes autonomously.

But how do we share that which is beyond words? All masters have been struggling to find some way to communicate, to commune. That's why you find differences in their statements. Rather than thinking about their statements, it will be better to go within yourself and find the truth. Nobody can help you. The masters can only show the way; you have to walk. Nobody can come inside you. That is the dignity of man, a great privilege: nobody can interfere in your inner life. You are alone there, the supreme most sovereign.

Osho

*Christianity: The Deadliest Poison, and Zen: The Antidote to All Poisons*

# A Note about Language

Spoken Words: Osho's books are not "written" but rather are transcribed from recordings of his talks. These talks are extemporaneous, without reference to notes other than copies of questions, stories or scriptures he has been asked to comment upon, or jokes he might use to drive home a particular point. He has asked his editors to preserve that quality of the spoken word in his printed books.

Pronouns: When hearing him speak, it is quite clear to the listener that generally when Osho talks about "man" he is referring to "human beings." His use of "he" as a default pronoun simply serves an ease and flow of speaking – in no way does it imply that "she" (or "they") is being dismissed or disregarded.

Osho's unique vantage point is good to keep in mind:

*A meditator is neither a man nor a woman,*
*because meditation has nothing to do with your body;*
*neither does it have anything to do with your mind.*
*In meditation you are simply and purely consciousness.*
*And consciousness is neither male nor female.*

Osho

# 1

# Death Is the Master

*Om.*
*We enter this Upanishad with the remembrance of godliness – the abode of truth, consciousness, bliss.*

*It is well known that Uddalaka, the son of Vajashrava, desiring to possess the fruits of vishvajit yagna, the fire ritual for world conquest, gave all his riches away to the brahmins. He had a son named Nachiketa.*

*When Uddalaka's cows were being taken to be given to the brahmins as gifts, Nachiketa could see that they were very old. Their bodies were worn out: they had eaten their last, they had drunk their last water and given their last milk. Nachiketa was filled with trust and sincerity – he started thinking that it was not right to donate such useless cows: "The person who donates these nearly dead cows will surely go to hell, to the lower dimensions of existence, where there is no possibility for happiness or joy." He thought, "I must discourage my father from doing such a thing."*

*Nachiketa then asked his father, "And to whom will you give me as a gift?" Uddalaka remained silent.*

*When asked the same question a second and a third time, his father became angry and said, "I give you to death!"*

*Hearing this, Nachiketa started thinking within himself, "About most things, I have followed the highest conduct. About some things I may be a little remiss, but I have never fallen into any bad behavior. So why does my father say that he is giving me to death? What work of Yama, the Lord of Death, does my father want to accomplish through me?"*

*Nachiketa said to his father, "Consider how your forefathers behaved and how otherwise people now behave, then decide what is the right thing for you to do.*

*"Like the crops, mortal man ripens, withers and then is born again. So in this transitory life, man should not waver from goodness and engage in wrong actions. Do not be sad, father. Honor your word now and allow me to go to Yama, the Lord of Death."*

*When he heard these words from his son, Uddalaka became very sad; but feeling Nachiketa's dedication to truth, he allowed him to go to Yama.*

*When Nachiketa reached the abode of Yama he found that Yama was not at home, so he waited for him for three days without food or water.*

*When Yama returned home his wife said to him, "When a brahmin comes to a home as a guest, know that a divine being has come – so it is our duty to prepare for his rest, to give him our hospitality. The son of a brahmin has been sitting here; he has not eaten for three days. Go and receive him with reverence."*

*Yama went to Nachiketa and said, "O brahmin! You are an honored atithi, an honored guest. You have stayed at my house for three days without food. Therefore, you can ask three wishes from me, one for each night."*

*Nachiketa said, "O Yama! As the first of the three wishes, I ask that my father, Uddalaka, may become peaceful, joyous and free from sorrow and anger. And when you send me back to him, may he receive me lovingly as his son."*

*Yama replied, "Seeing you returning from the mouth of death, your father Uddalaka, inspired by me, will receive you and recognize you as his son. He will be freed from anger and grief and will spend the rest of the days and nights of his life in peace and joy."*

*Having had his first wish granted, Nachiketa said, "O Lord, there is no fear in heaven. Even you, Death, are not there. There, none are afraid of old age. Those living in heaven are beyond hunger and thirst. Free from all suffering, they are in bliss.*

*"O Lord of Death, you know the inner fire which is the path to heaven. So tell me, a sincere seeker, the science of the inner fire, the science by which those who are in heaven attain deathlessness. This is my second wish."*

*Yama said, "O Nachiketa, I know the science of the inner fire which bestows heaven. I will tell it to you so that you may understand it completely. Know that this science will give boundless heavenly joy. This fire is hidden in the innermost sanctum of your heart."*

*Yama then explained the science of the inner fire to Nachiketa, the science which bestows heaven. He explained in detail all the processes involved. Having understood it, Nachiketa repeated the details back to Yama, and Yama was satisfied.*

*Seeing Nachiketa's extraordinary intelligence, Yama was well pleased. He said, "Now I will grant you an additional honor – that the science of the inner fire be known by your name, as Naachiket Fire. Please also accept this beautiful necklace of jewels."*

*Yama then said, "One who ignites this inner fire three times and desirelessly practices the fire ritual, practices sharing and practices austerity in accordance with the three Vedas, will become free from birth and death. By knowing this sacred fire and by choosing it with sincerity, he will attain to eternal peace, the peace which I know."*

*Yama continued, "One who ignites and attains this inner fire will cut the snares of death while still in the body. He will go beyond sorrow. He will experience the joys of heaven.*

*"Oh Nachiketa, this is the science of the inner fire that will lead to heaven. You have asked this as your second wish. From now onward this fire will be known by your name.*

*"Now, what is your third wish?"*

The Upanishads are unique scriptures about the mysteries of life, and the Kathopanishad is unique among all the Upanishads. Before we enter this Upanishad, it will be good to understand the inner current that underlies it.

The first thing is that in this world, a person who wants to know life must go through the experience of death. Except for this there is no other way.

To know life you have to learn the art of dying. And someone who is afraid of death will also remain unacquainted with life because death is the innermost and the most mysterious center of life. Only those who enter death consciously, with awareness and a welcoming heart, can know this life.

Everyone dies, but not everyone is able to know life just by dying. You have also died many times, and there is the fear that you will still die many more times. But death happens to you involuntarily: you do not want to die but you have to die. That is why death is a sorrow, a pain, an anguish. And the pain of death is so intense that the only way to bear it is to become unconscious. Hence, just before dying you become unconscious, you go into a coma. Surgeons have discovered only recently that becoming unconscious is a way to avoid feeling intense pain, but nature has always known it. The mind goes into unconsciousness; consciousness is lost because of this fear and the pain of death.

You all die in unconsciousness. Many times you have died unconsciously, hence you have no memory of it. You have also been born many times, but unconsciously; and you have no memory of your birth either, so there is no question of remembering past births. This much is certain, that you have been born this time! But you also have no memory of this birth.

For someone whose death happens in unconsciousness, his birth will also happen in unconsciousness because death and birth are simply two sides of the same coin. Someone who is unconscious on one side will be unconscious on the other side also. A person who dies unconsciously is born unconsciously. That is why you have no memory of your birth. You have heard that you were born – your parents say so, your family says so. It is you who have been born, but you don't have any memory of your own birth. And everybody dies, but unconsciously. Hence you remain deprived of what can be learned from death.

Religion is the art of dying consciously. Religion is the science of entering death in total understanding and awareness. And death disappears forever for the person who enters death consciously because by dying consciously, he knows that he is not dying at all. Dying consciously, he knows that what is dying is the body; it is no more than when you discard old clothes. But his inner flame of consciousness is burning bright even in death; even the storm of death is unable to blow it out.

For the person who is awake and fully aware in death, death does not exist. Death exists only for someone who dies unconsciously. There is no death for someone who dies consciously; for them, death becomes a door to the deathless, to the eternal.

A person who dies consciously is born consciously. And for someone who is born consciously, the whole quality of his life is different. Then he also lives consciously. Every fiber of his being, every part of his consciousness, becomes filled with light, with wisdom, with buddhahood.

For someone who is born consciously, there will no longer be any death. There will be no new birth for him either. Then he will simply leave the body, merging with the cosmic consciousness. The seers have called it nirvana, moksha, *kaivalya*: the merging with the ultimate reality.

A person who has known death consciously and realized the deathless, the eternal, has no longer any reason to be bound to the body. You become identified with the body because you are unconscious. Your unawareness is the bridge, the connection with the body. With awareness, the identification is broken – you become separate from the body. As the realization of this separation deepens, death disappears because it is the body that dies and it is the body that is born. The one who is hidden in the body, the bodiless one, is neither born nor dies. It is life itself. How can life die? And the person who dies, his life was only a deception, an illusion, something borrowed. His life does not mean anything.

It is very interesting that man is a combination of two entities: one is the mortal body which is already dead, and the other is the immortal soul which is life itself. It is only because of the proximity of the soul that the body appears to be alive. But the aliveness of the body is borrowed; it is a reflected phenomenon. It is as if you stand before a mirror and see yourself in it: the reflection that appears in the mirror is a borrowed phenomenon, it is not real. The moment you step away from the mirror, the image will disappear. It is just a reflection, it is not a reality. It is an indication of the real, and it also hints toward the real – but the person who takes it to be real will go astray. He will be disconnected from the real forever.

The body only gives a hint of the life that is hidden within. The body appears alive only because of its closeness, its proximity, to the soul. The aliveness of the soul is so profound that even the material body seems to be alive. But if you take the life of the body to be life itself, you will never know the soul.

To enter death means to move away from the mirror and to enter the original reality. This is the essence of this Upanishad. The rest is a story – but the story is also very beautiful because it shows many unique mysteries of life.

You may have read the Kathopanishad many times and heard many statements about it, but it is not as simple as it seems. Remember that mystics have always tried to say very complex things in a very simple way. The reason is that these things are so difficult that even when said in a simple way, they will not be understood. If they are told as they are, there will be no contact at all between you and these truths.

The Kathopanishad is a narrative, a story, but this story has everything in it that is hidden in life. We will begin unfolding it layer by layer.

> *Om.*
> *We enter this Upanishad with the remembrance of godliness – the abode of truth, consciousness, bliss.*

We begin with the remembrance of godliness. In life, you also begin many things, but you begin them all with the remembrance of the ego. Whatever you do, your "I" is always present in it. In fact, you do things so that your "I" will become stronger, more intense and more crystallized. All your activities are efforts to strengthen your "I." All your sense of doing is an effort to fulfill your ego. Hence in the world everything else can begin with the ego, but the spiritual search cannot begin with the ego. It can begin only in a state of egolessness.

Remembrance of godliness is the remembrance of the truth: "I am not, only godliness is. My existence is equal to nonexistence." When I begin with the remembrance of godliness, it means, "I am removing myself, my ego, from the center." Now godliness is the center and "I" becomes the periphery. "I" becomes secondary and godliness becomes the priority.

If your remembrance of godliness is real, then everything can happen just through this remembrance. Perhaps with this remembrance there will be no need to go any further into the Upanishad. Just by remembering that godliness is all and you are nothing, if this remembrance becomes real and alive, if it becomes an experience – if your whole being is filled with this one feeling, if every breath, every heartbeat starts resonating with the remembrance of godliness – then there may be no need to go any further.

Everything that has been said after this has been said by those who were filled with the remembrance of godliness. Those who experienced this remembrance, all the mysteries of life were revealed to them. For them there were no veils left; for them life became an open book.

The sage says: *Om. We enter this Upanishad with the remembrance of godliness...* I also say to you, do not begin this meditation camp with your ego, with your self; begin with the remembrance of godliness. Anyone who begins with the ego will end up empty-handed; they will have come in vain. In fact they will not have come because meditation begins from the point when you disappear. Until *you* are not, there can be no meditation. Your death, your disappearance, is meditation.

Remembering godliness means: I am not worth remembering. I step aside, I give way. And when you give way, it is as if you open the door and the sun which was waiting outside enters in. The moment you step aside, the eternal light starts filling you. Except for you, there is no other hindrance.

People come to me and ask, "What is the hindrance? What is the obstacle?" They try hard to meditate but it does not happen. They pray but it remains incomplete. They try to remember but remembrance slips away. They move their prayer beads but the prayer remains just in the hand: within them, something else is happening. They go to the temple, but really they never reach it. They read scriptures but their hearts are never touched. What is the hindrance? What is the obstacle? If there were something on the outside that was a hindrance, you would have removed it. But *you* are the hindrance! And nobody else can remove this hindrance except you.

Remembering godliness means: I remove myself. I forget myself and I remember godliness. But we are very strange people; when you are remembering godliness, *you* are remembering it. And where *you* are present, godliness cannot be present. There is no way for you both to meet. There will never be any kind of meeting between you and godliness; it has never happened before with anybody. Only when the person disappears does godliness start appearing.

Kabir has said, "It is very strange. I used to search for the divine. Seeking and searching, I lost myself. Now the divine has come, but I am no more. The man who had begun the search is no more." He has said, "When I was wandering in search of the divine, calling for the divine, the divine was nowhere to be found. And now, wherever Kabir goes, the divine follows him, calling out, 'Kabir, Kabir!' But now *I* am not there."

Up to now no one has ever met godliness, and it will never happen. This meeting is impossible, just as there cannot be any meeting between light and darkness. When there is darkness there is no light, and when there is light there is no darkness.

You are the darkness. Even when you remember godliness, you remember it within this darkness. You make even this remembrance a part of the darkness. Your religion is smaller than you. Your prayer also is smaller than you. And in the same way as you carefully manage other things, you manage your prayers. But the ego remains the master.

Remembrance of godliness means: "I am no more." And if this feeling of "I am no more" comes from the totality of your heart, then you become the all, the everything. Then nothing else is left to be achieved.

Remembrance of godliness means to forget your own self, your own ego. And to think about yourself is to forget godliness. The potential that is hidden within you will remain hidden as long as your ego, your I-feeling, remains alive. The moment the *I* disappears, the hidden inner potential appears. That potential hidden within you is godliness.

Godliness is not somebody sitting somewhere in the sky, so if you are addressing your prayers to the sky, it is pointless. And it is not hidden in the temples either. If you are searching for it in some temple, you are wasting your time and your life. Godliness is hidden within you. But as long as *you* are, the godliness hidden within you cannot manifest.

It is just like when a seed breaks, sprouts, and becomes a tree: it is the shell of the seed that is hiding the tree. Unless you perish and dissolve into the earth, unless you die and disappear, what is hidden in you will not manifest. You are the hindrance – this is why the Upanishad begins with the remembrance of godliness.

> *It is well known that Uddalaka, the son of Vajashrava, desiring to possess the fruits of the vishvajit yagna, the fire ritual for world conquest, gave all his riches away to the brahmins. He had a son named Nachiketa.*

We have to unfold each layer of this story: *It is well known that Uddalaka, the son of Vajashrava, desiring to possess the fruits of the vishvajit yagna, the fire ritual for world conquest, gave all his riches away to the brahmins.* Much is hidden in these lines. The first thing is that people desire to possess the world even in the name of religion. *Vishvajit yagna* – performing the fire ritual to possess the world: "I want to conquer the world, I want to possess the world." People even renounce to acquire, but then that renunciation is false. Renunciation is not worth anything if it is made with the intention of acquiring more luxuries to indulge in. What is the point of a renunciation that is followed by desire and greed for more? Then it is a bargain, not renunciation.

This is how you also renounce: this is how everybody renounces. If you want to buy something from the market you have to empty your wallet, but you don't call it renunciation; you call it a deal, a bargain. When you want to gain something you have to give something, but nobody will call it renunciation.

Renunciation simply means that you give without any expectation of getting anything in return. There is giving, but there is no demand. You simply give and you don't make any condition for some return. You don't say, "Therefore I will give." You don't say that you will give to get something in return. This giving is true charity: otherwise your charity is a deception. If you are donating to get into heaven then you are only expanding your business. You are simply making an investment. You are trying to purchase heaven – but whatever can be purchased will only be hell. Whatever can be bought will only be of the world.

Godliness cannot be purchased. So if you are giving something in order to achieve godliness, you will never meet it. You may renounce the whole world, but if the desire to achieve is in you, then the whole world is present inside you. Desiring *is* the world.

Buddha has said that desire, lust and longing are the world. The world which is on the outside is not the question; it will always remain outside. It was there before you were born, it will be there even when you are gone. The world remains even when a man like Gautam Buddha becomes free from all his desires; this world continues to be as it is. But this world is not the question. The inner world is born out of your desires, the desires which flow from inside you toward the physical world. The hands and the wings of your desire spread out to possess the whole world.

In this Upanishad the sage says that Uddalaka performed a fire ritual, *vishvajit yagna*, so that he could become a world conqueror. Now someone who wants to conquer the whole world, what connection can he have with religion? This is the desire of an Alexander, a Napoleon, a Hitler. All mad people have this desire.

Jesus has said that you may attain the whole world, but if you lose your own being then all your attainments are useless. Uddalaka is filled with the ambition to conquer the whole world, but there is no sign of any longing to attain his own being. He has no idea about his own being.

Uddalaka has nothing to do with religion. He is born into a noble family, his family lineage is very famous. He is an intelligent and learned man and he is performing a fire ritual – but to conquer the world. He is an experienced man, but he is not a man of wisdom. He is quite an old man, but the experiences of many years have not brought him any maturity. So whatever he does in the name of religion will be just a formality, inside there will be no soul. He gave all his wealth to the brahmins, but out of the desire to conquer the world. The desire is for fame and prestige, the desire is to feed his ego.

The ego can drop everything provided you do not drop the ego itself. If you are ready to protect your ego, then the ego will be ready to renounce everything – palaces, thrones, wealth, family, everything. The ego is afraid of only one thing, and that is that you should drop the ego itself.

Whatever you renounce, the ego is very cunning: it fulfills itself even through renunciation. The ego is not fed only by wealth, it is also fed by renunciation. The mathematics of the ego is very clear. It does not make any difference to the ego whether you live in a palace or in a hut. You can renounce the palace and start living in a hut, and the ego will feel strong and boast that it has let go of the palace: "What value is there in a palace? It means nothing to me." The ego can make you stand naked and say, "I have even renounced clothes!" The ego can nourish itself with any kind of action.

Uddalaka has donated everything, there is no doubt about it. Hence you should not be concerned about your small donations – Uddalaka has given everything, renounced all. He has renounced everything, but even so, his intelligence is not as clear as his son's intelligence. His own son, Nachiketa, who does not know anything, is purer and more innocent than he is. The little son can see that his father is making a great mistake.

Try to understand this: often something that is not visible and clear to a father is clear to a son because often the intelligence of the father is covered with dust. The passing of time and the many bitter and sweet experiences do not necessarily refine the intelligence. Rather, they make it duller; intelligence becomes rusty. So don't think that just by growing older you become intelligent. You simply become old, but not intelligent.

The truth is that a child has a clearer and cleaner intelligence. A child has more innocent eyes, he can see things directly. He has an honest heart – not because he has cultivated honesty but because he has no acquaintance yet with dishonesty. Soon he also will become dishonest because you are all so busy teaching him. The parents, the family, the society, the university, the gurus – everybody is busy teaching the child. Before the child becomes capable of protecting his innocence, you teach him all kinds of diseases. He is useful to you only when he has become sick and perverted.

Your whole education system exists to destroy the innocent intelligence each child is born with. The child has a clean heart without any stains, but the stains are bound to come. This clean heart is not an achievement: this clean heart will soon become dirty because it has to go into the world. Nachiketa's father also had the same clean heart as a child. But childhood is simply a natural state, it is not something to brag about. However, when an old man regains the innocent eyes of a child, then it is really an achievement. When an old man does not let his heart become old but allows it to remain fresh and innocent, then it is really something to be proud of.

That is why Jesus has said that only those who are like small children will be able to enter the kingdom of God – like small children. If Jesus had known about Nachiketa he would have mentioned Nachiketa's name because in all of history, it is difficult to find such a pure heart as Nachiketa's.

All children have such hearts; don't think that your child does not. Uddalaka could not understand, and you will also not be able to understand. Listen attentively to the talk of your children. Uddalaka did not listen, and you also will not listen because you think that your child is unintelligent and that you are intelligent. People think that growing in age is synonymous with growing in understanding. If we would pay attention to the words of children, if we could hear what they say and put aside our own understanding, then millions of Upanishads like this Kathopanishad would be born.

Some sage, some mystic was able to conceive this story, but an Uddalaka could not understand it. What happened? What happens every day? This is what happens every day – you lose your childlike innocence, you sell your heart. You have bought things of the world and to buy them, inevitably, you have to sell your innocence. You have increased your bank balance, you have built a big house, bought some land – but you have lost your childlike qualities.

When a child says something to you, the first thing is that you don't understand each other's language because the child speaks from some other world. For the child other things are valuable, and you speak from another world. There is a great distance between you and the child. You have lost your childlike innocence. There is an abyss between you.

When a child speaks you don't understand. And when you speak then there is no way for a child to understand. If the child is running after butterflies you think he is mad. And when you count your money every night behind a closed door, the child cannot conceive what has happened to this old father who is counting dirty papers when there are so many beautiful butterflies in the world! The child will throw away those papers, he will tear them up. And if the child tears up your money your very soul will be torn away. You cannot even imagine that for a child there is no value in money. To create value out of money, a sick mind like yours is needed; only then money has value. But the value is just an imposed idea.

Once, when I was staying with a family, I saw that the father was angry with his son and was saying, "I have told you twenty times that you should not hit your younger brother, and you have hit him again! I have explained to you many times never to beat anybody who is younger than you." As he was saying this, the father slapped the boy. The boy saw this and in a shock he said, "But I am very small, and you are older than me." But the father did not understand at all that he had done something wrong.

The child is seeing that if he beats his younger brother it is a mistake, but when his father is beating him – and beating him because he has beaten the younger brother – then it is not a mistake! What is the child learning from this? He is learning only that beating someone younger is not wrong as long as you are a grown-up. This child will become an adult soon, and the father will slowly grow old, weak and dependent – then this child will beat his father in many ways.

Every child beats his father; only the ways of beating differ. And then fathers feel pain and they suffer, but they don't realize that it is their own voices that are bouncing back in response. The seeds they have sown they are now reaping. Now the time has come to reap the crop. What every father does to his son in childhood, the son does the same to the father when he becomes old because by becoming old, the father becomes weak and vulnerable like a child.

If you understand the language of children, then it will be very easy to understand the language of the sages. Mostly, the sages become just like children; not exactly children, but *like* children. The experiences of a whole lifetime are with the sages. They have passed through the area of life where it was possible to be corrupted, but they have remained unaffected.

Kabir has said, "I have been wearing the cloak given to me by the divine, and I am returning it in its utter, original purity. It has no stain on it. I am returning to the source as innocent as a child." Kabir is saying to the divine, "You had sent me to the world as an innocent child. Now, as death approaches, I come back to you with the same childlike innocence."

If a person still has the innocence and simplicity of a child as he dies, then there is no hindrance to his moksha, to his ultimate liberation.

> *He had a son named Nachiketa.*
>
> *When Uddalaka's cows were being taken to be given to the brahmins as gifts...*

Nachiketa could see the truth and his father could not see.

> *...Nachiketa could see that they were very old. Their bodies were worn out: they had eaten nearly for the last time, they had drunk water and had given their milk for the last time. Nachiketa was filled with trust and sincerity – he started thinking that it was not right to donate such useless cows...*

But people usually donate such cows, when their last milk has been taken. It is not only true about cows but about everything you donate: they have already become useless to you.

There is a small but unique sect of Christians, the Quakers. They have a rule that every week each member has to donate one thing, but it should be something which is loved by him.

You should donate only what you would not like to give away; otherwise there is no sense in your donation. You also make donations, but only of what has become a collection of junk in your house. You donate things only when they have become utterly useless to you.

You may wonder why rich people give so many donations. But they do it only when they no longer have any use for their money, when they have squeezed all possible juice out of it. There is a point at which wealth ceases to give you any further benefit. Just think, what can an Andrew Carnegie or a Ford or a Rockefeller or a Birla buy with their money that they don't already have? Whatever can be bought with money, they have already bought. Now the money has become useless to them. Now what to do with all this money? Then the effort to buy heaven begins. Then Birla erects temples. The "cow" does not give "milk" – nothing new can be bought with this money; whatever could have been bought has already been bought. Now this money is useless, so people donate their useless money to religion. They don't give their hearts, only their junk.

This started becoming clear to Nachiketa. The sage of the Upanishad says that a deep trust arose in Nachiketa's heart. In fact, innocence is trust, simplicity is trust.

Nachiketa could not argue, but there was no need of argument. Even a small child could see that when these old cows don't give milk, why are they being donated? The father was bound to become angry because this simple truth would hurt his ego, would touch a wound. Children often touch your wounds. This comment was bound to touch his father's wound. The father also knew that these cows did not give milk – but that is why he was donating them! If there had been any milk left he would not have donated them. The father was not as "ignorant" as Nachiketa. For pure eyes, a certain ignorance is needed. The intellect is cunning: this is why the more intellectual the world becomes, the more cunning it becomes.

People ask me, "So many people are coming out of the

universities, completing their education – the cunningness in the world should have decreased, but instead it has become more!" I am saying that it is bound to increase because along with intellect, cunningness also will grow. As a person becomes more clever in calculation, more articulate in argument, then his cunningness will not become less, but more. The more humanity becomes universally educated, the more it will become universally clever and cunning. It has already happened. Educate a person, and if he can still remain innocent and simple-hearted, then know that he is a sage. Through education, innocence is usually lost.

Nachiketa's father also knows this. He is clever, he knows the mathematics. He knows that when a cow stops giving milk, it is time to donate her. Then by giving the cow away nothing is lost, and by donating the cow some virtue can even be earned. Charity is done, so when he faces God in heaven he can say that he has donated a thousand cows. But he cannot deceive even a small child, so how can he deceive God?

Nachiketa felt, "What is happening?" Seeing those old and useless cows a certain feeling arose in him, an innocence, a simple-heartedness arose in him, not a cunningness.

In my understanding, atheism is part of mathematics and theism is a kind of innocence. An atheist says he can prove that God does not exist – he has logic and calculation. And when a theist also says that he can prove that God exists, then you can take it for granted that he is not a theist, he also is an atheist. The authentic theist will say, "Though I cannot prove that God exists, God does exist. Even if you prove that God does not exist, even then I say that God exists because the existence of God is not based on my calculation, logic and intellect. It is a deep experience of my heart." The theist will say that however much you may try to prove, all your arguments will simply prove that you are clever, efficient, a mathematician, a logician – but the existence of God will not be disproved.

Keshavachandra, a brilliant scholar, went to Ramakrishna and tried to prove to him that God does not exist. He expected that Ramakrishna would answer him. But when Keshavachandra started arguing, on every point Ramakrishna would get up and give him a hug. Keshavachandra was in a difficulty: he was disproving the existence of God, and this strange man did not understand the situation! He was expecting that Ramakrishna would get upset and angry, that he would answer in response. But not getting any response, Keshava was lost. The people accompanying him were also in a difficulty because they had thought that this Ramakrishna, who was a rustic, an uneducated man, would be in a difficulty. Many people had gathered to see the embarrassment of Ramakrishna.

But it is difficult to embarrass a man like Ramakrishna. How can you embarrass such an innocent man? You can only embarrass an intellectual man.

Keshavachandra became tired and sad. He asked, "Won't you give me an answer?"

Ramakrishna said, "What answer can I give? Seeing you, I am even more convinced that God exists."

Keshavachandra said, "Seeing me?"

Ramakrishna said, "Yes, seeing you, because an intelligence such as yours cannot exist in this world without God." Then Ramakrishna said, "Who but God himself can prove that God is not?"

Now *this* man is a theist.

The sage says that a feeling of sincerity arose in the heart of Nachiketa and he felt, "What is my father doing by donating these old, useless cows?" *Their bodies were worn out: they had eaten their last, they had drunk their last water and given their last milk.* Their senses had almost stopped functioning…

> *"The person who donates these nearly dead cows will surely go to hell, to the lower dimensions of existence where there is*

> *no possibility for happiness or joy." He thought, "I must warn my father against doing such a thing."*

Nachiketa felt that it was cheating, dishonest – and not just an ordinary cheating, but trying to cheat existence itself.

If somebody steals your wallet he is deceiving you. One man is deceiving another man: it is understandable. But when somebody is trying to deceive existence itself, then naturally the result is going to be great misery because how can you deceive existence?

The ultimate existence abides in the deepest core of your heart. What Nachiketa is saying, Uddalaka also knows because the innocence of childhood is hidden somewhere within him also. Even the most dishonest man knows deep inside that he is dishonest. The thief knows that he is stealing and the cheat knows somewhere within that he is deceiving. It is not possible to destroy the inner child, the inner innocence completely. At whatever depth it may be hidden, howsoever we may have repressed it, it is there. It is alive and kicking from there.

Listening to Nachiketa, the father became angry because the child within him, the Nachiketa within him, must have been awakened by this hit. Uddalaka must have felt inside that what Nachiketa was saying is true.

Try to understand it: when somebody is lying to you, you don't get angry; anger only arises when somebody is telling the truth. If you are not a thief and somebody says that you are a thief, then you can laugh: there is no reason to be angry. But if you *are* a thief and somebody says you are a thief, you start burning with anger because they have touched a wound in you. You were hiding some wound and they have brought it to the surface. They have pressed some sick spot in you and pus has started oozing. So whenever you get angry, know well that some truth has really come close to your wound; your anger indicates that a wound has been touched.

Buddha and Mahavira don't get angry because they don't have any wounds for you to touch. They are not hiding anything which you can expose. Everything is out in the open. If you abuse a sage and he laughs, it does not mean that he is enjoying your abuse. The reason is that what you are saying is absurd, ridiculous. You are making yourself ridiculous because your abuse is meaningless; it does not touch the sage at all, he has no connection with it.

If somebody abuses you, you are immediately on the defensive. What are you defending? You are hiding something that could be exposed by the abuse. Something is hidden within and the abuse brings it to the surface. Something is hidden in you and the abuse will also make you aware of it, will wake you up.

Nachiketa's father became angry because it seems that Nachiketa touched the right wound. He had put his finger on the right spot. Nachiketa wanted to alert his father, but it is a difficult matter. Whenever a son tries to make his father aware of something, the father is going to feel bad about it because a father cannot accept that his son can be more intelligent than he is; it is impossible.

The father of Jesus could not accept that his son was intelligent. Buddha's father also did not accept that Buddha was intelligent. Even after Buddha had become enlightened, Buddha's father told him, "Stop being so stupid. Enough is enough! Now come back home! After all, I am your father – I can still forgive you. I have the heart of a father. Stop being a vagabond. In our family lineage, nobody has ever begged. And you – becoming a beggar, begging in the capital of my kingdom? Don't hurt my pride, don't destroy my prestige."

Just think, Buddha's father was not an uneducated man, he was a king. He was well-educated and cultured. He had read the scriptures, he had listened to wise men. Great scholars used to go to him, learned people were around him. But it is difficult to recognize a Buddha. The ego of a father cannot accept that his own son has become enlightened before he has. Buddha said, in humbleness, "You rightly say that nobody has ever begged in your family lineage. But as far as I know, I am an ancient beggar, an old monk. I have begged many times before."

Buddha's father answered, "Do you think you know yourself better than I know you? My blood is flowing in your blood. My bones are in your bones. I have given life to you. I know you very well."

Buddha said, "You are making a small mistake – I have been born through you, but not by you. You are a passage through which I have come but you are not my creator."

Naturally, when a son tells his father "you are not my creator" it will be painful, the ego will be hurt.

Buddha said to his father, "You were a crossroads through which I passed, but my journey is an ancient one. I have been here before. I existed even before being born through you."

Once Jesus was standing amidst a crowd and someone said, "Your mother and father have come to meet you."

Jesus said, "Who is my mother? Who is my father? I existed before I had these parents. Before Abraham was, I am."

The wisdom of the son disturbs the ego of the father. So if a son wants to make his father aware, then he should do it very carefully. It is risky. It is okay to make somebody else alert, but to make your own father alert is risky because his ego will be deeply hurt. The father thinks, "My own son is trying to correct me. The one who is born out of me, who has come after me, is trying to make me alert!"

Nachiketa made the same mistake. Similar mistakes are often made by innocent minds. It is bound to be so. Nachiketa felt that his father was getting involved in a wrong act, that his charity was false, that it was cheating and dishonest, and that it would result in great misery.

Pondering over this…

> *Nachiketa then asked his father, "And to whom will you give me as a gift?"*

The father had said that he would give all his possessions away to charity, and Nachiketa thought, "I also belong to my father, and when everything else is being donated, then I too will be donated!"

Fathers assume their children to be their possessions; husbands take their wives as their possessions. You turn even people into things: you say "mine." In this world where even things don't belong to you, how can people belong to you? The effort to possess people is sheer madness. But a father feels that his son is his possession.

Nachiketa thought, "My father says, 'Nachiketa, you are mine.' And he says that he will donate all his belongings, so it is clear that I will also be given away as a donation. So I should ask him, 'To whom will you give me?'" This is a question which has arisen from an innocent heart. When you are giving everything else away, then would you not also give away your personal attachments? Would you not give away this, "my son"?

Nachiketa has asked a right question – it is true that the real thing to be dropped is attachment. There is no sense in dropping things or people: the real thing to be dropped is the feeling of "mine," of possessiveness.

"You are donating old, useless cows, but who are you going to give me to? Where am I supposed to go?" This must have hurt his father deeply: the father felt that the son was going beyond the limit. The father had not thought that when he said he would donate all his belongings it would also include donating his son. There was no reason to think so because he was renouncing his wealth but not his attachments. But his son provoked a deep irritation, the hurt went deep.

> *"...to whom will you give me as a gift?" Uddalaka remained silent.*

When somebody remains silent it does not mean they are not angry. Often a person remains silent because he is angry. If the son were clever he also would have remained silent; he would have understood his father's anger. But Nachiketa was a very simple and innocent child. He asked his father a second and then a third time, "*...to whom will you give me as a gift?"*

> *...his father became angry.*

And as any father would naturally have said, Uddalaka said:

> *"I give you to death."*

Usually, whenever any father becomes angry with his son, he says, "I wish you had never been born!" When the mother is angry she says, "Get lost! Go to hell! Disappear!" Uddalaka said, *"I give you to death!"*

It is a very natural thing. If the person who has given birth to you becomes really angry, he will give you to death. Hence, if the father becomes angry he wants to kill his son: "What I have created, I will destroy." This tendency has a deep psychology behind it.

In a father's mind there is the idea of having given life: along with that is also hidden the idea of giving death. These two feelings come together. This is why no son can ever forgive his father; it is very difficult. And whenever a son does forgive his father, a flower of nobility opens in his being. Otherwise, sons remain resentful toward their fathers.

Turgenev has written a very wonderful book, *Fathers and Sons.* He has created a complete novel based on this fundamental and essential theme. Turgenev feels that the struggle between fathers and sons is very ancient. It has been happening since the beginning, always: the father is fighting with the son, the son is fighting with the father. And when this struggle spreads it becomes a struggle between generations; the generations start fighting with each other.

Today this struggle is happening throughout the world – the

generation of sons is saying one thing and the generation of fathers is saying something else. There is a vast gap between them; there exists no communication between them. And the more a country becomes affluent, the greater the gap between fathers and sons. The poorer the country, the less this gap between the generations. Because as a country becomes richer, the children will become more educated: they will remain in school for a longer time. In poor countries, children begin to work from the time they are ten or twelve years old; then they get into child marriages and become fathers themselves. Before he is grown-up enough to start fighting with his father, he becomes a father himself. Child marriage may be an ancient invention of fathers! Before the poor son starts creating trouble, it is necessary that he become a father. The moment he becomes a father he becomes a part of his father's generation; he becomes a co-conspirator with his father.

You will be surprised to know that you will remain young until you have become a father. The day you become a father, you become old; a deep transformation happens in the mind. As long as a man is unmarried and does not have a child, his whole behavior is different. Until then he remains a wanderer, a vagabond. Until then he does not bother about security; until then he does not care about money; until then he can fight with the society, he can be rebellious. As soon as he is married he becomes tied to a post: the home surrounds him from everywhere. The moment a child is born to him he becomes old; he starts thinking like a father. Then he feels that what his father used to say to him was right.

This is a very interesting point: unless you become a father you will not feel that what your father used to say to you was right. Before that you will feel that your father is senile, that he is crazy, that he is talking such old rubbish. But when you become a father yourself you start talking the same old rubbish.

In America a large number of people are hippies, but as soon as they get married and have a child, the hippie disappears.

They return to society. They start feeling that what their fathers were saying is right. In fact, there is no other way unless you experience it: until you become a father you cannot understand what your father was saying.

The reason for this constant struggle between the young and the old is that the father thinks because he has given birth to the child, he can possess him completely. He doesn't want even a little rebellion from his child. He wants his son to be a replica, a shadow, an echo of his own voice. Whatsoever the father says, the son must agree with it totally. But this is difficult because the son has his own ego. As the son grows older his own ego becomes stronger. The son wants to be free: on many occasions when the father says something the son insists on just the opposite because there is no other way for his ego to become stronger except by rebelling against his father. As the son starts fighting with his father, the father starts repressing him. In the unconscious mind of the father is hidden this idea that because he has given birth to his son, he can also give him death.

> *When asked the same question a second and a third time, his father became angry and said, "I give you to death!"*

Nachiketa's father said that he will give him to death and Nachiketa took it to be literally true. A son cannot argue at such a young age. A trusting heart does not doubt; innocence does not argue. He believed with no doubt that he would be given to death. He simply accepted it.

This quality of acceptance is very revolutionary – this was no ordinary acceptance. He did not ask, "Why will you give me to death?" He did not say, "Have you gone mad!" He did not ask, "What evil thing have I done that you are giving me to death?" He did not argue or feel bad about being given to death. He thought, "If my father is giving me to death, it must be the right thing. If my father is giving me to Yama, the Lord of Death, Yama must need me." He simply accepted it. This acceptance is the basis of this whole Upanishad because someone who accepts death will transcend death; he will attain to the deathless.

There is still another secret meaning in what Uddalaka has said. There is an esoteric meaning in his statement. The ancient scriptures have a saying: they say that death is the master, the guru. They also have another saying: the master is a form of death because when a disciple goes to the master, the master destroys, erases, his ego. The master erases the disciple's ego so much that it dissolves completely. Within the disciple a pure emptiness is born, samadhi is born. And in that samadhi the union with the ultimate happens.

There is a difference between a master and a teacher. The teacher gives you something, the master takes something away from you; the teacher fills you, the master empties you; the teacher gives you information, the master takes away the so-called knowledge that your ego has collected; the teacher gives you a livelihood, the master gives you life.

To give you a livelihood something has to be taught to you: you have to be taught mathematics, geography, history, science, physics, chemistry and all these things. But if you are to be given the ultimate knowledge, then whatsoever you have learned needs to be unlearned; it has to be thrown away, discarded. You will find teachers in the schools, colleges and universities. But in this century the guru, the master, is missing.

The guru was the person you would go to when you were totally fed up with knowledge and learning, when you wanted to be unburdened. This is why in the scriptures it is said that the master is a death. He kills you, he makes you disappear. And when you return you have gone through a transformation. You have returned new; you are *dwij*, twice-born. So there is one womb, that of the mother, and there is also another womb – that of the master.

Death is the guru, the master: this is the hidden mystery, the hidden meaning of this story. For Nachiketa, death proved to be the master – and for you also it will prove to be the master.

If you can learn how to die you will gain everything that is worth gaining. Then nothing else will remain to be achieved.

I have called you here so that you can also become a Nachiketa. Here, I also want to give you into the hands of death. I would like death to surround you from all sides and that whatsoever can die in you should die. And what cannot die because there is no way for death to kill it – only that should remain within you in its crystal clarity. All the junk, the rubbish inside you should burn and only the pure gold should remain, cleaned and refined. You also have to pass through this fire.

Later in the sutras Yama will say to Nachiketa, "This fire will be known by your name" – the fire which renews the person who passes through it, through which he attains the deathless.

> *Hearing this, Nachiketa started thinking within himself, "About most things I have followed the highest conduct. About some things I may be a little remiss, but I have never fallen into any bad behavior. So why does my father say that he is giving me to death? What work of Yama, the Lord of Death, does my father want to accomplish through me?"*

It will be good to go more deeply into this. Naturally, when someone tells you that he gives you to death, then the first thought that will arise in you will be, "I must have done something wrong and this is why I am being punished."

But Nachiketa thought, "I have not done anything wrong, I have done only what is good. And if sometimes I forget, I don't do anything *really* wrong; I always manage to stay in the middle. So this decision could not be because of my faults. The only reason for this must be that Yama, the Lord of Death, has some work to accomplish through me. This must be why my father is handing me over to death."

It is very significant that it does not occur to Nachiketa that his father is giving him to death because he is angry. This is an indication of a true religious mind: it always thinks, "Perhaps it is my own fault." Nachiketa thinks that Yama must have some work to accomplish through him but he cannot understand what the work might be. He cannot even imagine that his father is just angry. "My father is displeased," or "My father is to blame" – this idea does not arise in him.

When a person looks for the fault in himself, then religiousness begins in his life. Most people are busy finding fault in others. When somebody abuses you, you will immediately think that he is doing you some mischief – you never think that you may deserve the abuse. His abuse may be appropriate, but this thought does not occur to you. The idea does not arise that there must be some purpose behind the abuse. The only idea that comes is that this man is cruel, that this man is a devil. And this is the difference between a religious mind and an irreligious mind.

*Hearing this, Nachiketa started thinking within himself...* Nachiketa started thinking, but he did not think at all about his father's anger, although his father had spoken out of anger. It is not that when somebody is abusive to you, he must have done it because of his own inner madness, that he abused you because he is crazy inside, is burning with the fire of anger, is a devil. The question is how you take it. If you think you are responsible for it, then you will start trying to transform your life. But if you think that the fault is with the other, then you will not pay any attention to what is inside you.

And if this idea that the fault is always with the other becomes a pattern in your life – as it has become – then your life will remain untransformed. Then how can there be any transformation, any revolution? It is not a question of whether the other person is right or wrong. If my attention is constantly focused on myself, then slowly, slowly I will change and a new life will begin within me.

> *Nachiketa said to his father, "Consider how your forefathers behaved and how other wise people now behave, then decide*

> *what is the right thing for you to do.*
>
> *"Like the crops, mortal man ripens, withers and is born again."*

"*Like the crops...*" this metaphor, used by a small child, is worth contemplating. In fact, all the races still living like innocent children – the aboriginals living in the forests – think like this. So, don't think that it is impossible for a small child to speak so wisely, saying that crops ripen and die, again sprout, ripen and die, and that it is the same with the cycle of birth, life and death. This sounds to us like a statement of great wisdom and we wonder how a small child like Nachiketa could have said it. But try to understand that for the people who are still primitive, who are still living in the old way – close to nature, who have not created any scientific civilization – this is their way of thinking.

If we observe life, we will find that it is circular: the sun rises in the morning and sets in the evening; again it rises in the morning and sets in the evening. A circle is created. The summer comes, then it rains, then comes winter; again the same circle is repeated. A circle is created; the seasons move in a circular way. The crops grow, the seeds ripen and fall, then again they sprout, ripen and the seeds fall back to the ground – this is a circle.

Societies which have innocent ways of thinking do not believe humans to be an exception to this natural cycle. They say that just as the seed ripens and falls to the earth, then sprouts and grows, then ripens and falls again, so is it with human birth and death. Man is born, grows up and dies and then again he is born, grows up and dies: the whole of life is circular. The moon and the stars move in circles, the seasons move in circles, and in the same way the life of man is also circular. Small children can understand this easily: when everything is circular man cannot be linear, man is also circular.

There is a vast difference between Western and Eastern

thought. The West thinks that life is linear: everything is moving in a line, like railway lines. The East thinks this is not so, that everything in life moves in circles – childhood, youth, old age, death, rebirth and childhood again. It ends where it began and again it begins from that same point. For this reason we have the concept of the cycle of birth and death.

The Sanskrit word for the world is *sansara*, which means the wheel, a wheel which is moving. On the national flag of India we have a wheel. This wheel is very ancient: it had been carved in the pillar made by the Indian king, Ashoka. It was made according to the teachings of Buddha because Buddha says that life moves like a wheel, it does not move in a straight line.

So the small child said to his father, "It is not something to worry about, that you are giving me to death because man dies and is reborn. Death is not the end, birth and death will happen again and again. That you are giving me to death is not a problem. The only thing I ask is that you reflect on it and tell me if you are saying it in anger."

This has to be understood. Nachiketa is not saying, "Don't give me to death," or "It is wrong to give me to death." What he is trying to say is that if you are doing it out of anger, then because of your anger you will suffer unnecessarily. "You can give me to death because nobody dies – everything returns to its original source." From its Himalayan source at Gangotri, the Ganges starts flowing, and in the end it falls into the ocean. Then, evaporating, it starts rising to the sky. Then the clouds rain at Gangotri and this water again flows into the Ganges. "I will return just as the crops return. There is no harm in giving me to death. But think it over, see if you are saying it because of some inner pain, anger, misery, anguish."

Remember, if you look at anger even for a moment, the anger will disappear. If you become conscious, aware, even for a moment, then anger will disappear. There is only one way, only one remedy, only one antidote for anger – that you become full of awareness. If anger arises, close your eyes, become aware, and you will find that as the awareness increases the anger will start diminishing. The very energy that was anger is transformed into awareness, into consciousness.

Buddha has said, "Do not be angry." I am not saying this. I say, be angry, but with awareness – and no one can be angry with awareness. Buddha has said, "Do not steal." I do not say this. I say, steal with awareness – and nobody can steal with awareness.

The evil that happens in life happens in unawareness, the good that happens in life happens in awareness. If the unawareness is deep then whatever happens out of it is bad.

Acts in themselves are neither good nor bad; it depends on the awareness of the actor. It is possible that if you are doing a good deed in unawareness, you may feel you are doing something good but the result is bound to be bad. And it is also possible that if somebody is doing something with awareness and you feel it is wrong, even then, the outcome will be good. The ultimate deciding factor is how aware you are, how aware the person is. Unawareness is sin, awareness is virtue.

Nachiketa said to his father, "Whatsoever you do, be aware before you do it. First be full of awareness."

> *"So in this transitory life, man should not waver from goodness and engage in wrong actions. Do not be sad, father; honor your word and allow me to go to Yama, the Lord of Death."*

Certainly, hearing what Nachiketa was saying, Uddalaka must have felt very sad. He must have become aware and felt very hurt. He must have realized what he had said. Even when a father tells his son to go away and die, he does not really mean it. A moment later he must have thought, "What have I said?" A moment later the attachment to his son must have returned. And what Nachiketa said to his father is very valuable: it contains the essence of the whole of life. It must have touched the father's heart, although it is rare that this happens. The father must have realized that what Nachiketa was saying was right; he must have been very disturbed.

Nachiketa also must have seen the sadness in his father's face and eyes. Hence he says to him, "Please don't be sad. But honor what you have said – don't go back on your word."

> *When he heard these words from his son, Uddalaka became very sad…*

…but now there was no going back…

> *…but feeling Nachiketa's dedication to truth, he allowed him to go to Yama.*
>
> *When Nachiketa reached the abode of Yama, he found that Yama was not at home, so he waited for him for three days without food or water.*

There was no other way: Uddalaka had given his word and Nachiketa was emphasizing to his father that he should not feel distressed: "What has happened, has happened. It cannot be undone. Your word has been given, so send me to death." So Nachiketa was sent to death.

This is a story, a myth. There is no Lord of Death sitting somewhere to whom Nachiketa is being sent – but the story is very beautiful and also gives many hints and signs.

*When Nachiketa reached the abode of Yama, he found that Yama was not at home.* Now it will be helpful to understand two things. The first is that except for Nachiketa, never before had anybody knocked at the door of death. It is always death that knocks at your doors, and you will always be found inside the house. You are never outside the house. Where else can you be? There is no way to be outside. The body is a house, so whenever death knocks it finds you there. But Nachiketa went to the door of death; the whole phenomenon was reversed because it is always death that comes to man; man does not go to death. When a man goes to death, everything is reversed. This story is only symbolic of that reversed process.

Nachiketa found that Yama was not at home. The whole process was reversed. The moment a person becomes ready to encounter death, his whole life is reversed: where life – what seemed to be life – was visible, it now appears as death, and what seemed to be death appears as life. Everything that had seemed so essential before becomes worthless. And the things that had been given no attention, there all the treasures of life appear. This story is only symbolic, that everything has been reversed.

When a person has the courage to go to death and knock at his door, then he will find that death is not there. When you go to death, you will find that there is no death; death does not exist. It appears to exist only because you escape from it. The more you escape, the more real it is; the more you avoid it, the more real it is. The more you desire that death should not come, that you should not die, the more death-oriented you will become.

It is said that a courageous man dies once but a coward dies a thousand times. After all, what is the difference between a coward and a courageous man? The coward constantly tries to escape from death so he dies every day, and the courageous man says that whenever death comes, let it come, so he dies only once.

But someone like Nachiketa, who knocks at the door of death, finds that there is no death. He finds that death is not at home. Whoever has knocked at the door of death has never found it to be there. Death is an illusion. And illusion has this unique quality: if you move away from it, it grows; as you come closer to it, it starts disappearing.

For example, a rope is lying in a street in the dark. You are passing by, and seeing the rope you create the illusion that it is a snake. You start running, you start perspiring – but your perspiration has nothing to do with whether the snake is actually real or not. Your heart starts beating faster, your blood pressure rises, the veins in your head begin to pulsate. You start running – and the more you run, just by running, the more panicky you become.

William James, a psychologist from the West, used to say that people don't run out of panic, they become panicky because of their running. They don't run because of fear, they become afraid because they run. There is some truth in what James says. The more you run, the more panicky you will become: your running gives energy to your nervousness, to your fear. And the more you run from the rope, the more certain you will feel that the snake is there. Then there will be no way to see that the snake is just a rope. The only way to know is to go close to the rope. If you had brought a light and gone near the rope you would have found that there was no snake.

An illusion is something that increases by running away from it and decreases by moving closer to it. It is very interesting, and if you can understand this definition then you will see that in your own life there is nothing but illusions.

A woman looks very beautiful, and she will always seem beautiful as long as you are not allowed to meet her. If you are allowed, then everything will change. If you marry her she will no longer seem so beautiful. You used to go crazy seeing her, you would start dancing; but after marriage nothing vibrates in you, nothing moves in you. The truth is that a husband stops looking at his wife; he doesn't see her at all. Even if his eyes fall on her, he does not see her. Only other people's wives are seen, his own wife is never seen. It is very difficult because there are no more illusions. All illusions have been shattered and everything has been revealed as it is.

Whatever you don't have looks very valuable, but the moment it becomes available its value is lost on you. That is why wise people like Shankara have said that this world is an illusion, a lie; it is unreal, it is maya. Maya is whatever disappears when you move closer to it and becomes more real when you move away from it.

You think that millionaires are very happy in their palaces, but it is just your imagination. No millionaire is happy. But you will not realize this until you yourself become very rich and live in a palace. Living in the palace you will realize, "What am I doing here? It is nothing!" But this will be your personal realization. Those who pass by your palace will think you are very blissful.

Did you know that all the twenty-four tirthankaras of the Jainas are the sons of kings? Buddha is also the son of a king. All the avatars of the Hindus are the sons of kings. What is the reason for this? The reason is that for a king, all the illusions of the world are shattered. A king means someone who has everything. When you have everything, the feeling comes that it is all simply useless. Only the son of a king can be a tirthankara. It is very difficult for the son of a poor man to become a tirthankara because how will the illusions be shattered? Faraway illusions cannot be shattered if they remain far away from you; only the illusions which are close to you can be shattered.

In the West, they have dropped nearly all the limitations and restrictions in male-female relationships. One man can have relationships with hundreds of women and a woman can relate with hundreds of men. It is very interesting that illusions which have not been shattered in the whole history are now being shattered in America. There, people are now saying that there is nothing in sex; something more than sex is needed. So now they are hoping that LSD, mescaline, marijuana – that if you take some drugs or inject some chemical into the body – maybe that will give some happiness.

The old, traditional people were very clever: they created so many hindrances for men and women to meet so that the attraction between them would never end. In India, a man's attraction for his even own wife never dies because the husband is not allowed to see his wife in the daytime. In the night, the husband and wife have to meet secretly because there is no privacy in the large, extended families. The husband and wife cannot meet openly with all those other people around, so the attraction between them continues for their whole lives. The elders have been very clever. There is no question of divorce because their meeting is never complete. Divorce is a consequence of familiarity, of meeting all the time.

The more deeply you experience life, the more meaningless it becomes. Know well that anything that becomes meaningless through experience is an illusion, and whatever becomes more significant through experience is real. If something is becoming more and more real as you move closer to it, then it is beyond the web of illusion. And that which becomes more and more real as you go closer to it, I call godliness. What becomes more and more unreal, illusory, as you get closer to it is *sansara*, it is of the world.

This is a very sweet story – Nachiketa went and knocked at the door of death and found that death was not at home. You also have to knock at that door. In the coming days of this meditation camp, my effort will be to bring you to a point where you can knock at the door of death. And I assure you, you will also find that death is not there.

Death does not exist, death is an absolute lie. Death is the greatest fiction in the world. But you are so afraid of death, you try so hard to escape from it, that for you it has remained a reality.

Nachiketa was sitting and fasting for three days. He would not eat unless he met with death – but death was not there. Death was not at home. This is how it is described in the story: *...he found that Yama was not at home, so he waited for him for three days without food or water.*

Try to understand this: in fact, what you call life is sustained through food. If you want to experience death, you have to stop eating food. This is why fasting has become such a great phenomenon. Fasting means that you stop what nourishes life for a period of time so that death can come closer. The flow of life stops, and you can know whether you will survive or die when the flow of life has stopped.

Mahavira has taken the science of fasting to its peak. It is said that in the twelve years of his seeking, Mahavira ate food on only three hundred and sixty-five of those days. Sometimes he did not eat for a month or two, or even for three months. He experimented with what happens when there is no food in the body. Fasting for ninety days is the limit – a very healthy person can live without food for ninety days. But after ninety days, a moment will come when the life energy of the body will be in limbo. It will not be able to move, it will be ready to stop. In that moment you can watch and see if you are still alive or not. When the body is almost dead and you find that you are still alive, then the purpose of fasting is fulfilled. Then you have experienced deathless through fasting.

Nachiketa continued to sit for three days without eating or drinking. He said that he would not eat until he met Yama. And this is the purpose of the science of fasting: I will not eat until I see death. It is a process, it is one of thousands of methods. But now people who are fasting don't know what they are doing.

Fasting is a very subtle process. When the life force of the body is shrinking, awareness should simultaneously go on growing within you. While the life force is shrinking in the body, if there is sadness and depression within you, then the experiment has failed because as awareness grows within you your aliveness should also grow. A moment comes when the body is almost dead but you are totally alive. Now you have understood that food is not the ultimate source of life, it is only a fuel for the body. Life does not come from food, food only keeps the body functioning. If food is totally stopped, then the body will die because the body is made of food. But *you* will not die.

This story has many clues. Nachiketa was sitting there for three days without food.

> *When Yama returned home his wife said to him, "When a brahmin comes to a home as a guest, know that a divine being has come – so it is our duty to prepare for his rest, to give him our hospitality. The son of a brahmin has been*

> *sitting here; he has not eaten for three days. Go and receive him with reverence."*

When a seeker enters the world of spiritual exploration through the process of fasting, a moment will come when death will appear because the body cannot survive for very long without food. As I have told you, the body can survive for ninety days if it is completely healthy because it has a reservoir of food. The flesh and the marrow you have, are just collected food; you have collected it for an emergency. It is accumulated and the body can eat that reserve of food for three months.

There is a double process going on in your body: if you stop eating food from the outside, then for three to five days you will be in difficulty. But after the fifth day, the pain and uneasiness will disappear. You will not be hungry anymore because now the body will start digesting its own flesh and marrow. This is why when you fast you lose around one or two pounds every day. Where do these two pounds go? You are digesting them, you are eating yourself. The body has this double process. You are digesting the reserve of food that is stored in your body, but within three months the reservoir will be finished and only the bones will remain. Then death will happen, death will be present.

These three days were symbolic. If someone has a heart full of innocence like Nachiketa, then the presence of death can come even in three days. The body can be seen lying dead and only your consciousness will remain.

> *Yama went to Nachiketa and said, "Oh brahmin! You are an honored atithi, an honored guest..."*

An *atithi* is someone who arrives at your home unexpectedly, without giving any date or warning of their arrival. "You are a guest, and a brahmin."

> *"You have stayed at my house for three days without food.*

> *Therefore, you can ask three wishes from me,*
> *one for each night."*

This is a story, so try to understand its symbolism. If a person fasts properly, before death happens he will experience psychic powers which are lying dormant within him. For someone who fasts for a long time, before death happens many psychic powers will arise. These powers are called *siddhis*. There is every possibility that the person will get caught up in these psychic powers and forget his search. Then those blessings will prove to be curses. Just before the arrival of death, which could have given you enlightenment, the last temptations come as a trick of the mind.

All the psychic powers, the *siddhis* which Patanjali has talked about, start arising inside someone who is on a long fast. Yama is saying to Nachiketa that because he has been fasting for three nights, he will grant one wish for each of the nights; he need only ask for them. This happens within each seeker on the path. And those who become satisfied with just these ordinary gifts on the path will be denied the ultimate blessings.

But Nachiketa was not going to be satisfied with small gifts: he went on inquiring further and further. He wanted to unveil the ultimate mystery.

> *Nachiketa said, "Oh Yama! As the first of the three wishes, I ask that my father, Uddalaka, may become peaceful, joyous and free from sorrow and anger. And when you send me back to him, may he receive me lovingly as his son."*

He has asked the first wish for his father, the one who sent Nachiketa to death! The first wish he has is for someone you would have wished the first curse. The person who sends you to death, you would want to give them a double death. If you had been there in place of Nachiketa you would have asked: "The first thing I want you to do is that, wherever my father is, finish him right now!" To you, someone who wishes your death is an enemy.

But Nachiketa's first wish was for the enemy! "May my father be peaceful, may his anger disappear and may he accept me lovingly as his son."

There are many things to be understood in this. The first thing is that happiness has been asked for someone who has done wrong to you.

Buddha has said that if you don't also pray for your enemy, then your prayers are meaningless. And Jesus has said that if you have even one enemy, then go to him and ask his forgiveness; make him a friend and then return to the temple. Otherwise, no prayer can be fulfilled. If there is any psychological wound within you, lying like a thorn, you first need to remove it. Otherwise, the flowers of life cannot bloom.

Nachiketa said, "May peace come to my father. And when I return from here may my father accept me lovingly as his son." This will be very difficult because he will be returning to his father after having known death. To receive this transformed Nachiketa as his son will be very difficult for the father.

> *Yama replied, "Seeing you returning from the mouth of death, your father, Uddalaka, inspired by me, will receive you and recognize you as his son. He will be freed from anger and grief, and will spend the rest of the days and nights of his life in peace and joy."*
>
> *Having had his first wish granted, Nachiketa said, "Oh Lord, there is no fear in heaven. Even you, Death, are not there. There, none are afraid of old age. Those living in heaven are beyond hunger and thirst. Free from all suffering, they are in bliss.*
>
> *"Oh, Lord of Death, you know the inner fire which is the path to this heaven. So tell me, a sincere seeker, the science of*

> *the inner fire, the science by which those who are in heaven attain to deathlessness. This is my second wish."*

Nachiketa is saying that his second wish is to transcend death and attain deathlessness! Now, this wish can only be fulfilled by death itself. Those who want to know what is beyond death can do it only by passing through death.

> *Yama said, "Oh, Nachiketa, I know the science of the inner fire which bestows heaven. I will tell it to you so that you may understand it completely. Know that this science will give boundless heavenly joy. This fire is hidden in the innermost sanctum of your heart."*

The fire through which you will attain immortality is hidden within you. You will find the great joy which has no sorrow, you will attain the ultimate freedom which is liberation – but that fire is hidden in the inner sanctum of your own heart. You don't have to go somewhere else to find that fire, you don't have to ignite that fire somewhere outside you. It is always burning within you and it belongs to you. You are immortal – but you don't know it, you are not aware of it.

> *Yama then explained the science of the inner fire to Nachiketa, the science which bestows heaven. He explained in detail all the processes involved. Having understood it, Nachiketa repeated the details back to Yama, and Yama was satisfied.*
>
> *Seeing Nachiketa's extraordinary intelligence, Yama was well pleased. He said, "Now I will grant you an additional honor – the science of the inner fire be known by your name, as Naachiket Fire. Please also accept this beautiful necklace of jewels."*

How to ignite this fire that is hidden in the heart? There is a complete process for it: how to make the fire pit, how to create the fire by friction of the firewood, with what bricks to create the fire pit, how you will be burned in it and how your impurities will be destroyed in the flames so that you become pure gold. Yama told all of this in detail to Nachiketa, but no details are given here.

In the next eight days I will give you all the details, the whole process. In this Upanishad, deliberately, knowingly, it has not been given. In the Upanishads, the methods which a master would give directly to a disciple have been kept secret. It is dangerous to mention them in a book because many mistakes are possible. If somebody experiments with them just by reading about them, it can end in disaster. To play with the inner fire is far more dangerous than playing with any outer fire.

The meditations we will be practicing here are the processes for igniting the inner fire. In these next eight days it will become very clear to you how your heart can become aflame and how death can disappear for you – you can experience the immortal. But this can happen only through experience.

My whole effort will be to take you through the complete process. We will try so that this does not remain just a verbal communication, but becomes your action and your direct experience.

> *Yama then said, "One who ignites this inner fire three times and desirelessly practices the fire ritual, who practices sharing and practices austerity in accordance with the three Vedas, will become free from birth and death. By knowing this sacred fire and by choosing it with sincerity, he will attain to eternal peace, the peace which I know."*

What Yama, the Lord of Death, has attained, you can also attain. Death is immortal because death never dies. You will die, but death cannot die. How can death die? So death is the key to deathlessness. If you learn to die consciously you also will attain to immortality.

*Yama continued, "One who ignites and attains this inner fire will cut the snares of death while still in the body. He will go beyond sorrow. He will experience the joys of heaven.*

*"Oh, Nachiketa, this is the science of the inner fire that will lead to heaven. You have asked this as your second wish. From now onward this fire will be known by your name.*

*"Now, what is your third wish?"*

In our meditations, we will pass through this inner fire. Rather than just talking to you, I will lead you into that fire. I will take you to the door of death where you can also knock at Yama's door.

Now listen and understand this process clearly because from tomorrow morning we will begin the experiment.

Tonight, before going to sleep, lie down on your bed for ten minutes. Turn off the light and close your eyes. Exhale totally through the mouth; begin with the exhalation, not with the inhalation. Exhale deeply through the mouth and while exhaling, make the sound *o…o…o…o*. As your intoning of the sound becomes clearer, it will automatically create the sound om. You intone only the sound *o…o…o…o* and let the sound *m…m…m* arise by itself. You don't say "om." You have only to say "o" and allow the "m" to come on its own.

Exhale the whole breath, then close your mouth and allow the body to inhale; don't *you* inhale. You have to intone *o…o…o* with the exhale and allow the body to inhale.

Usually we do the inhalation and the body does the exhalation. There is a reason for this – the incoming breath is connected with life and the outgoing breath is connected with death. When a child is born, the first thing it does is inhale. In the beginning it has no breath to exhale so first it inhales. The incoming breath is the first action of life. And the last action of a dying person is to exhale because if the breath remains inside, death cannot happen.

Death is the outgoing of breath, life is the incoming of breath. Every moment, you are born when you inhale and you die when you exhale.

Here, in this meditation camp, we are preparing to become Nachiketas, so the emphasis will be on the exhalation. Don't be concerned with inhalation. And don't be afraid that you will die. The body will take care of inhalation; there is no need to hold your breath. You have to do nothing at all while the inhalation is happening. You have neither to inhale nor to control; you have only to exhale.

You have to do this experiment for just ten minutes before you fall asleep because sleep is also part of death. Sleep is a small death. If you fall into sleep with an exhalation, then your whole sleep will become a deep death.

Do this experiment for ten minutes: exhale through the mouth while intoning the sound *o…o…o*, and then let the nose inhale; again exhale through the mouth and let the inhalation happen through the nose. Fall asleep as you repeatedly intone the sound *o…o…o*. This will be your night meditation.

There is another method for the morning that I will explain to you tomorrow, at our morning session.

[*Osho now gives the following explanation in English for the benefit of the Western seekers present at the meditation camp.*]

In this camp I will be speaking only in Hindi. Those who cannot understand Hindi are very fortunate because their intellect will not be involved at all. You can leave your heads off, your head will not be needed. And this is good! This is a great opportunity because intellect is the problem. It never solves anything; it cannot. It can only puzzle and confuse.

So people who cannot understand Hindi should not feel they are missing something. No, they are not missing anything.

They are missing only a certain intellectual confusion. They will not be confused.

While I am speaking in Hindi, just listen to the sound of my voice. That carries more than any words can carry. Just listen to my sound – meaningless – and the very sound will become a meditation for you.

I will tell you about the technique we are going to do. Tonight you have to start the first technique, and you have to do it every night.

Just before going to sleep, lie down on your bed and turn out the light. Close your eyes and exhale deeply. Start with exhalation. And while exhaling, make the sound *o…o…o…o*. Exhale through the mouth, not through the nose. While exhaling, make the sound *o…o…o…o*. Exhale with the sound and your mind will be exhaled through it. And don't inhale: allow the body to inhale. Inhale through the nose but don't make any effort to inhale. You simply exhale, close the mouth, and let the body inhale.

Remember this: make every effort to exhale deeply but don't make any effort to inhale. And remember, there is a very deep relationship between life, death and breathing.

The first thing a newborn child will do is inhale. Life begins with inhalation. And the last thing a person will do when he dies, when he is old, will be to exhale. Death begins with exhalation.

Meditation is a death. And here we will be trying to die completely so that something which is eternal can come, can be born.

Throughout this whole camp, whenever you remember, exhale deeply.

This is for the night. You have to do it; it is a must. For ten minutes in the night, every night, exhale deeply through the mouth with the sound *o…o…o…o*; then close the mouth and let the body inhale through the nose. And then fall into sleep. The whole sleep will become deathlike, deep, silent. You may never have known such a deep sleep before. Dreams will disappear. Dreams belong to life, they don't belong to death.

At other times also, during the day – while walking, while sitting, whenever you remember – exhale deeply. If you want, you can make the sound o…o…o at any time, and that will be helpful. If you feel any anger, if you feel any lust, any desire, any sex, anything in the mind which you want to throw out, immediately exhale with the sound *o…o…o* and you will feel that it has gone out. It is no longer inside you.

In this camp, exhale more and more. And don't inhale, let the body inhale. This is the first technique for tonight.

Tomorrow morning we will start our first meditation. I will explain it to you in the morning. We will meet in the morning.

# 2

# The Thirst for the Deathless

*Of his third wish, Nachiketa said, "There is so much uncertainty about death. Some say that the soul lives on after death and others say that it does not. I want to finally understand this through your teaching. This is my third wish."*

*Yama thought, "It is harmful to teach the secrets of the soul to one who is unworthy of the teaching." Seeing the need for a test, Yama tried to dissuade Nachiketa by telling him of the complexity of the matter. He said, "Nachiketa, on this matter, even the gods have had their doubts; they also could not understand because this subject is so very subtle and difficult to understand. You may ask for something comparable as your third wish. Do not insist on this. You must let go of this desire to know the secrets of the soul."*

*Nachiketa was not discouraged by hearing of the difficulties; his enthusiasm was not affected. Rather, he said even more strongly, "Yama, you say that the gods have also thought about this but even they could not decide, and that it is not easy to understand. But there is no one who can explain this matter as well as you. As I understand it, no other wish can be compared to this one."*

*Nachiketa was not dissuaded by the difficulty of the subject:*

*he remained firm in his wish to know. He succeeded in passing this test.*
*As a second test, with the intention of exposing Nachiketa to many temptations and allurements, Yama said to him, "You may ask for sons and grandsons with life spans of hundreds of years; you may ask for many cows and other cattle, for elephants, horses and gold. You may ask for an empire with vast boundaries. You may ask to live for as long as you wish.*

*"Nachiketa, if you consider a wish for wealth or a means for living a long life as equal to your wish for the knowledge of the soul, you may ask for that. You could be the greatest emperor on this earth! I can make the greatest pleasure of all pleasures available to you!"*

*When Nachiketa did not waver from his decision even at this, Yama then tempted him with the heavenly pleasures of the gods. Yama said, "Ask for all the pleasures which are rare in the world of mortals. Take these celestial women with you, along with chariots and musical instruments. Such women are surely not available to mortals. You can enjoy these women and be served by them. But Nachiketa, do not ask to know what happens to the soul after death."*

*But Nachiketa had a firm will and was truly worthy: he knew that even the greatest pleasures in heaven and earth could not be compared with the tiniest portion of the bliss that comes through enlightenment.*

*Nachiketa, supporting his decision with reasoning, said these words of non-attachment to Yama: "Yama, the pleasures that you are describing are ephemeral; they exhaust the sensitivity and sharpness of all the senses. Furthermore, a life span, howsoever long it may be, is brief: it will end sooner or later. You can keep those celestial women, the chariots, those songs and dances – I don't want them.*

*"A man can never be fulfilled through wealth. Now that I have set my eyes on you, I have already attained abundant wealth. As long as your compassion rules there can be no death for me. It is meaningless to ask for those other things. The only wish that is worth asking for is the one that I have already said: the knowledge of the soul.*

*"Man is subject to decay and death. Knowing this reality, where is the man living in this world who, after having met you, an immortal and noble being, would continue to long for the beauty of women, for the pleasures of the senses and to yearn for a long life?*

*"O Lord of Death, reveal to me the ultimate truth of this most wondrous and otherworldly subject – the destiny of the soul. Man does not know if the soul lives after death. I wish only for this most mysterious knowledge."*

There is one thing to keep in mind about little Nachiketa, only then will we be able to understand his exploration of death: as young as Nachiketa may be, as young as his body may be, the age of his soul is eternal.

No child is just a child. No child is merely like a blank slate. The story of his innumerable lives is recorded in his mind. A child has also been an old man many times. Hence, children have to be treated with deep reverence. The body is new, but the consciousness hidden within the body is not new. The age of this consciousness is the age of this world. For thousands of times this consciousness has been born into bodies and has left them. The pleasures and pains, the problems and comforts of life, the miseries and joys of life, the illusions and realities of life – all this has been experienced by this consciousness.

This is why Nachiketa's deep search is not puzzling to the

Indian mind. But Western thinkers will certainly wonder how such a small boy can raise such profound questions. Christianity, Islam and Judaism, these three religions have been born outside India; the other important religions have been born in India. The three religions which were born outside India believe that there is only one birth and one death, and that afterward there is no reincarnation. Hence, according to their conception, children cannot raise such questions and a child cannot contemplate so deeply. According to their understanding such contemplative thoughts are only possible in old age. But this story of Nachiketa is not merely a story: many thousands of other children have shown this amount of maturity. In the West there are also many instances of this.

At the age of seven, Mozart, the great Western musician, became proficient at playing extremely complex music, music which even a man of seventy could not play. It is astonishing because how can music which needs seventy years of practice be created by a child of seven? Mozart had started showing signs of being a great musician by the age of three! He certainly must have had some sort of preparation in a past life – past life experiences that he could not remember, past life treasures that he may not have been aware of, but they were within him.

Even at the age of two children have given thousands of signs which cannot be explained except by the concept of past lives. Nachiketa is no exception. What Nachiketa has asked shows the fact that his search is very old; that this child is a very ancient soul.

It is said about Lao Tzu that he was born an old man. This Nachiketa is also such a one: his search is connected with his past lives. He may not actually be aware of what he is asking, but he has inquired about these things many times, in many lives. He has knocked on many, many doors. He has been sitting at the feet of many masters. This stream, which only became apparent on that day, has been flowing in the past as an undercurrent.

Keep this in mind because only then will Nachiketa's questions seem natural to you; otherwise they may seem unnatural. Otherwise it will seem to you that the sage is imposing, in the name of Nachiketa, things which even old people don't ask. But many other children have also asked such questions.

Shankara died when he was just thirty-three years old. By then he had completed his great commentaries on *Brahmasutra*, the Upanishads and the *Gita.* Somebody else even at the age of three hundred would not have been able to compete with Shankara. There would be no possibility of somebody accomplishing all this writing in thirty-three years or even in three hundred years.

Shankara started writing his commentaries when he was seventeen. He had expressed the intention of becoming a sannyasin at the age of nine – this depth of longing at the age of nine! The age of nine is not much: you remain childish even at the age of ninety. Even at that age, your mind does not mature. Even in old age your mind remains like that of a stupid, ignorant man. How was it possible that a longing to become a seeker could arise in Shankara at the age of nine, even though he had not yet seen and experienced life? How could the issue arise of renouncing a life that he had yet to experience? He had not yet known misery, so what was the meaning of his longing to go beyond misery? He had not yet experienced the pleasures of life so what could be the meaning in his renouncing them?

He has certainly known many pleasures because it is a consequence of entering deeply into the pleasures of life for many lifetimes that a boy of nine years of age can experience a longing to become a sannyasin.

Many times people come to me and ask me why I sometimes give sannyas even to small children. Nobody is a small child, and the age of the body is not the real age.

In the West, the concept of "mental age" has evolved. It will be good to understand it in relation to Nachiketa's story. Binet, a French scientist, developed the concept of mental age for the first time. He said that there is one age, that of the body, and another age, that of the mind. There is no connection between the age of the body and the age of the mind. You can be seventy years old and it may be that your mental age is only seven years. And it can be just the reverse, that your mental age is seventy and your physical age is only seven.

After the Second World War, the United States wanted to find out the mental age of their soldiers. The results were very surprising: the average mental age of a soldier was thirteen years old! Their minds had stopped growing at the age of thirteen.

Usually the mental age of the majority of people never goes beyond thirteen or fourteen years. As soon as a man becomes sexually mature, his mental growth stops. The mental age of women stops even earlier than that of men. Because women become sexually mature one or two years before men, their mental growth stops there. The age of the body goes on increasing but the mind stops growing.

Binet may have discovered mental age, but the Eastern mystics have talked about three dimensions of human age: the age of the body, the age of the mind and the age of the soul. The age of the soul is beyond all limits. The soul of a one-day-old child is as old as the soul of an old man. As far as the age of the soul is concerned we are all of equal age.

So Nachiketa's questions belong to his ancient soul. His mental age must also be very high because the questions he is raising show that they are coming out of deep experiences.

Observe old people and observe children. In children sometimes you can see an old man and in old people you will often find just children. With aging, differences come, but these differences are only superficial. Small children are arranging marriage celebrations with their dolls and grown-ups are playing *Ramaleela*, enacting the story of Rama, one of the Hindu incarnations. Somebody is acting as Rama and somebody else is acting as Sita, Rama's bride; the marriage is happening as a procession moves along – but the mental age has not changed, it is still stuck at thirteen. Now the dolls have become life-sized and the names of the dolls have become Rama and Sita, but the game of marriage, the joy of playing with the dolls, is the same: a procession and a pageant are arranged.

Right now, it is happening all over India. These are the games of the old children: they are enjoying marriage rituals, they are enjoying arranging marriages and they are all participating in marriage processions. Of course when old people do something childish they rationalize it, they create logic around it; otherwise they will feel ashamed, they will feel uneasy. Small children fight over trivia but old people don't seem to be fighting over something very great either. Their fights are also about petty things, but because of their age they glorify their petty actions.

Just a few days ago I was passing by Chowpatti, a sea beach in Mumbai, and I saw that some prominent politicians and many schoolchildren were gathered there. They were all singing: "May our national flag always fly high!" This is so childish! What is a flag, after all? – just a piece of cloth tied to a stick with ideology attached to it. But people can sacrifice their lives for it. If somebody lowers your national flag then a massacre can take place. You think that your flag should remain higher and other flags should not as high as yours.

Small children stand on chairs near their fathers and say, "I am taller than you!" This is another form of keeping the national flag high. If the father is intelligent he will smile. Otherwise he may feel hurt; he may also stand up high and say that he is taller than the child.

The very search to prove that you are great is childish. But old people have rationalizations for their childish ideas. They say it in a roundabout way; they don't directly say, "I am a great man." That would sound too egoistic. They say, "My country is great." But why is *my* country great? – because I have been born in this country, because of me! If I had been born in Pakistan then Pakistan would be the great country. If I had been born in Afghanistan then Afghanistan would be the great country. Wherever I am, that country is great. My religion is great – my scriptures, my *Gita*, my *Purana*, my tirthankara, my God, my incarnation – they are the greatest. Behind these facades *you* become great. This madness is prevalent all over the world, in everybody.

It seems that humanity has not yet become mature. The average mental age of humanity at present is only about ten years old. This is why there have been so many wars, so many stupid incidents. The whole behavior of the world is full of just sheer ignorance.

Just as old people behave childishly, sometimes a child behaves with the dignity and wisdom of an old man. This second possibility is at the core of this story of Nachiketa.

Now we will enter the sutras.

> *Of his third wish, Nachiketa said, "There is so much uncertainty about death. Some say that the soul lives on after death and others say it does not. I want to finally understand this through your teaching. This is my third wish."*

This is the search of all religions. The innermost core of all religions is focused on this one point: is the death of the body also the death of the person? Does everything die after death or does something remain? This is such a profound question that everything depends on it.

All the values of life, the whole meaning and purpose of life; all the dignity, the poetry, and the glory of life, everything depends on one thing: whether or not all is finished with the death of the body. If everything ends with the death of the body then being moral has no meaning, being religious has no meaning. Then nothing is virtuous and nothing is evil because after death good people dissolve into the earth and bad people also dissolve into the earth. There is no qualitative difference in their bones. There is no difference between the dead body of a thief and that of a saint. And if a thief and a saint both end up in the same place, in the dust, they both become the same.

Then the differences between their lives were just illusions because death has exposed all the differences as illusory. Whether you were good or bad did not really matter at all.

If everything ends with death, then in this world there is no meaning in any moral or religious values. Then dishonesty and honesty are the same; then committing a murder or saving a life are not any different; then there is no difference between violence and nonviolence. Then what is the difference between truth and untruth? If everything becomes the same in the end and if good and bad both dissolve into the earth and disappear, then the whole foundation of being virtuous collapses.

The whole of spiritual endeavor depends on the idea that the death of the body is not the end. The meaning of life depends on the premise that when the body dies, something remains which survives death; that when the body disappears into dust everything does not dissolve with it, something remains, some flame continues on another journey; that in some sense, "I remain." Only if I continue does the way I live now have significance. If I don't remain, then what is the sense? Then perhaps those we call "evil" people are more intelligent, and those we call "virtuous" are just fools.

If the soul also is mortal then the saints are fools and the meditators are simply misguided. Then only mad people are gathering in the temples. Then the people who are doing their *namaj*, their prayers in the mosques, are crazy because what they are doing has no meaning. Then whether they pray or whether they gamble, it makes no difference.

If the soul exists after the death of the body, only then do the temples, mosques and gurdwaras, the Koran, the Bible and the Vedas have some meaning; only then are Mahavira, Buddha, Krishna, Christ and Mohammed special: they have some secret with them. They have been searching for the key to a greater life. But if everything finishes with death then what is the need for a key? And what is the search for? Then the whole of life is just a futile effort.

There is a very significant statement of Shakespeare's: "Life…is a tale told by an idiot, full of sound and fury, signifying nothing."

Nachiketa raises all these questions: the immortality of the soul, the existence of the soul beyond the body, and the transcendence of the body by the soul – the lamp being destroyed but the flame remaining. Nachiketa says, "In this there is much confusion. Some say that the soul remains after the death of the body. Some say that the soul does not survive death. What happens after death? To know this is my third wish. This is what I want to know."

This is what everybody wants to know because only if something remains after death can there be something within you right now. And if nothing remains after death, then even now there is nothing within you. Right now you are empty, blank, mechanical; you are nothing more than a mechanism. Right now you don't exist if you will not exist beyond death; you are simply in a deception. If you are just a combination of matter, if you are only a chemical system moving like a machine, then all you have is the idea that you are.

A car is moving, a watch is ticking, a machine is functioning – but we cannot say that a machine is alive, that a machine exists." A machine is just a combination of parts: if we take out all its parts nothing will remain behind. Is man also such a mechanical combination that if we separate all his parts, nothing will remain behind? Death will separate the mechanical parts and if you are just a mechanical combination and nothing remains inside, then you don't have a being; you don't exist, you are just an idea, you only have a false notion that you exist.

Your intellect does not prove that there is a soul within you. Computers have been invented which can work with greater efficiency than your intellect. So the efficiency with which you work is no indication that you have a soul, a consciousness. You cannot become as efficient as a computer; in fact, computers are far more efficient. That is why, whenever greater efficiency is needed, people cannot be trusted. In such situations we have to trust the machines.

What is special about you? – that you can do mathematics, that you can speak a language? Machines also can do all of these things. Compared to computers, man's intellect is not special. The work that Einstein has done can be done by a computer with even more efficiency. Your intellect is nothing more than a computer; you also are a machine.

Man gives birth to children – but now scientists have invented certain machines that can create other machines. A machine can create another machine of its own kind, so a man creating a child is nothing very great: these machines can automatically produce other identical machines. They have even been designed so that machines can improve themselves when they create their new generation. And then all the successive machines that are produced in the future will go on becoming better and better than the originals.

There is no guarantee that your son will always be better than you are. Usually it is not the case. Often, good fathers give birth to bad sons. With machines, arrangements have been made so that the new machines that they create are better than the previous ones. The same faults will not be found in the next machines that are produced; the machines just go on becoming better and better than the previous ones. In this way it is possible for a machine to create a new machine which is without any faults. Man has not been able to accomplish this.

Feelings of pleasure and pain are also mechanical. B. F. Skinner, a great psychologist, has done many experiments where he has discovered that our pleasures and pains are just mechanical. The greatest pleasure that man knows is that of lovemaking, but the findings of the research done by Skinner, Delgado and others are very surprising.

Skinner and his colleagues were working with rats. They found areas in the brain that caused the rats to experience pleasure; they called these the "pleasure points." They also found points that cause the experience of pain. They connected the pleasure points to an electric wire, an electrode, and if the points were stimulated with an electric current the rat would feel pleasure. If the pain points were connected to an electrode then the rat would feel great pain.

In Skinner's experiments with rats, he worked with the part of the rat's brain that experiences sexual pleasure. He connected that part to an electrode and showed the rat how to press the right button. As soon as it pressed the button it became ecstatic. And then the rat learned to press the button by himself. You will be surprised to know that in one hour, the rat pressed the button five thousand times. Five thousand times! He did not stop until he collapsed unconscious.

Skinner says that in the coming century we can give people a small machine that they keep in their pockets. Whenever they want to experience sexual pleasure they can press the button and the pleasure point in their brain will be activated. Then a man will have no need for a woman or a woman for a man. Just walking along the road you can go on pushing the button and having orgasms – and nobody will know. All those troubles that you have to put up with for sexual pleasure – creating a household, suffering the misery that is created by a woman or a man – will become unnecessary. You can be completely independent.

There are also pain centers in the brain. Skinner says that those centers can be cut off and then there will no longer be any experience of pain. If you think that you experience misery because misery really exists, then you are mistaken. You simply have a pain center, and if it is removed then you will not experience any misery. When you are given an injection of morphine the center of suffering in the brain becomes dulled. Then if your hands or feet are cut you will not feel any pain. Even if someone kills you, you will not be able to know it. All these centers are mechanical.

You will be surprised to know that this new research will lead man to a very dangerous point. Delgado has done experiments to control the mind from a distance, by remote control. He inserted an electrode in the brain of a bull. If something is put into your brain you cannot feel it because there is no sensitivity in the brain. If you undergo surgery and a piece of iron is put inside your brain, you will never know that it is there inside because there are no nerves in the brain to feel the sensations.

It is very interesting that although the brain is the base of all experiences it feels no sensation from within itself. This is why you cannot feel what is happening inside the brain. Great work is going on, it is a huge factory. There are billions of cells in the brain; around the clock there is a great rushing of electricity – but you know nothing about it.

Delgado inserted an electrode connected to a remote control into the brain of a bull, and then he started controlling the bull through it. When he would press a certain button that was connected to the anger-point in the brain of the bull, the bull would become enraged. There was not even a wire connection between Delgado and the bull, just a wireless connection. Delgado could be in the United States and the bull could be here in India, but Delgado could make the bull angry even from thousands of miles away. It was only a matter of pressing a button and the bull would become enraged and would attack anybody who was nearby.

When he gave a demonstration of this experiment in Spain, the observers were amazed. A few thousand people had gathered to watch. When the button was pressed the bull became furious and ran toward Delgado, who was standing there with his radio in his hand. The bull came very near to him, almost in front of him! It was a moment of panic. At any moment the bull could have pierced Delgado's stomach with his horns. But then Delgado pressed another button and the bull suddenly became quiet. It was only a foot away from Delgado but the bull stood still, as if he had suddenly gone into meditation.

This discovery is very dangerous because sooner or later the politicians will want to use it. Electrodes can be put into the brains of babies in the hospital as soon as they are born. They will never know about it. Then you only need to press a certain button from the capital of a country and everybody will shout, "May my national flag fly high!"

Dictatorships will certainly use this. Even if a whole country is dying of hunger, there is no need to worry: if the pleasure centers of people can be activated, then even starving people will be filled with happiness. And no matter how happy you may be, if your suffering center can be activated then you will immediately become miserable.

So not even pleasure and pain can give you any proof that you have a soul within. They only prove that you have a mechanical brain.

There is only one thing in man which is not mechanical. The body is a machine, but the one who is residing within this body is not a machine. Of course, the body is a very complicated, very subtle and delicate machine – but the master is hidden within it.

Nachiketa is asking, "For my third wish, I want to know if I remain even when this body-machine dies or not? There is much doubt about this. Some say that something lives after death and others say that nothing lives after death."

> *Yama thought, "It is harmful to teach the secrets of the soul to one who is unworthy of the teaching."*

It will be good to understand this point: to teach the secrets of the soul to an unworthy and unprepared person is harmful. In fact, an unworthy person will use even the truth for harmful purposes. And a worthy person will use even a lie for a good purpose. How educated you are is not important – your worthiness or unworthiness is the deciding factor. And unworthy people have misused all kinds of teachings.

In India, you have been taught about reincarnation. The intention behind these teachings was to remind you that your search for happiness is in vain. You had searched for happiness many times, in many lives, and you had even found it – but nothing was attained. How many times have you fallen in love with a woman or become entangled in a love affair with a man? How many palaces have you built? How much wealth have you accumulated? And in each life, you have died a miserable person. And still you are doing the same things again. If you were able to remember that you had done these things many times and did not achieve anything and that you are doing the same things again, realizing this, you would stop.

But what did the unworthy people do with this teaching? They said, "If there are many lives, then what's the hurry? We will search for the soul some time in the future. Pleasures are momentary, so if we don't have them now we will miss something. The soul is eternal; it will never die. It is reborn again and again, so if enlightenment is not attained in this life then it can be achieved in the next life. There is no hurry at all." This is the interpretation of an unworthy mind. The sages have spoken about reincarnation so that you can more easily become disillusioned with trivia, but the unworthy interpreted that there is no hurry!

You will be surprised to know that in Eastern countries people have no time consciousness; they have no sense of time. A man can promise to come and see you at five o'clock and he may not turn up until ten! There is no consciousness about time because there is so much time. Awareness of something enters only when it is scarce. For example, a poor man is bound to be very concerned with money. Even if he loses a small coin he will be aware of it because money is scarce. A millionaire will not be concerned about losing a coin; for him, nothing much is lost. Even if millions are lost it does not matter because he still owns an inexhaustible treasure.

Eastern countries have no concept of time. This is why they could not have invented the watch. The West had to do it because they are very time conscious. Time moves quickly, time is short because Jesus, Mohammed and Moses have taught that there is only one life. It is interesting that they taught this concept, considering the unworthiness of their listeners. The East had already made the mistake from the other end, of teaching reincarnation to unworthy people, with the result that these teachings were misused. In the East, hearing a teaching about infinite lives, the ignorant people feel very good.

The religions of the West were born later than the religions of the East. Hence in the West they tried to avoid the mistakes that were made in the East – but they did not realize that unworthy people are also very clever. You cannot save them. If you save them from falling in a ditch, they will fall into a well. So Jesus, Mohammed and Moses have taught that there is only one life and that reincarnation is wrong.

The theory of reincarnation is not wrong. But these Western mystics wanted to avoid what had been done in the East by unworthy people. This is why Jesus has insisted that there is only one life: "Whatever you want to do – meditation, prayer, worship, transformation – do it now! There is no time in the future. Don't postpone! Each moment is valuable because you will never get it back. The treasure of time is limited." The unworthy person heard this and thought "If the treasure of time is so limited, then why drop this material world for some imaginary one and for empty ideas of a soul and a God of which he had no experience? And if there is only one life, once missed it will be missed forever."

So in the West they say that half a loaf of bread in the hand is better than a whole one in a dream. Maybe those dreams of faraway things exist, maybe not. And life is not going to repeat itself, so they say, "Enjoy life completely!" What the West understood from the teachings of Jesus, Moses and Mohammed was to indulge because time is short. Enjoy and indulge as much as possible, as quickly as possible because who knows what happens after death? It is better not to renounce that which is visible in the light for the unknown things in the darkness.

Because of this, the mistake which was made in the East

because of the teachings of Buddha, Krishna and Mahavira, was now repeated in the West – in spite of the teachings Jesus, Mohammed and Moses. The East indulges because there are so many lives, so what's the hurry? The West indulges because time is so short and pleasures should not be missed – who knows if all those teachings about reincarnation can be trusted? It is strange that whatsoever the teaching, the unworthy person will always misuse it to harm himself.

Yama thought, "Nachiketa is so young, he is not yet mature. He is pure and innocent but he has had no experience of life. If I tell the reality of the soul to this unprepared boy, there may be danger. He may draw his own meaning from my words."

Many enlightened people have remained silent because of this fear about you. It is not because what they wanted to say could not be said – it is difficult to say, but it *can* be said – but because of their fear about you, because you will give a meaning to whatsoever is said to you that will lead you to hell! Many enlightened people have remained silent – but even their silence makes no difference. Even from their silence you draw a meaning which was never meant. That is also the reason why many enlightened people have spoken: so that you might not draw a wrong meaning from their silence, which would be far worse.

Buddha sometimes remained silent. He did not answer many questions just because the answers to those questions could lead the unworthy into great troubles. As soon as Buddha died, twenty-five different sects arose from his teachings; the unworthy people gave different meanings to his silence. If Buddha had answered their questions it would have been better. Now there was no base: "Why has Buddha remained silent?" became the subject of discussion. Someone would say, "Buddha has remained silent because nothing can be said about the soul." Someone else would say, "Buddha has remained silent because there is no soul, so what is there to say?"

You are bound to project some meaning onto silence. This is why some enlightened people have continued to speak because you might misinterpret their silence. But you also give wrong meanings even to what is being said. So the mystic is in a great dilemma because whatsoever he does, the listeners can interpret it wrongly.

Yama thought, "Should I tell this to Nachiketa or not?" First, he tried to avoid the issue. Any master would do the same. And if a master does not avoid answering, then know well that he is not worthy of being called a master. A master will try to avoid answering because if you are easily satisfied with trivia, then it shows that you were not ready. You are asking for a diamond, you are asking for the Kohinoor, and the master picks up a piece of stone and gives it to you and you are satisfied believing it to be the Kohinoor diamond. This indicates that you are not worthy of receiving the Kohinoor; it would be a mistake to give it to you. And the person who mistakes a piece of stone for the Kohinoor might at some other time take the Kohinoor for a piece of stone. He has nothing: he is unable to discriminate, he has no understanding, no ability to distinguish – no touchstone.

Yama said:

> *"Nachiketa, on this matter, even the gods have had their doubts; they also could not understand because this subject is so very subtle and difficult to understand. You may ask for something comparable as your third wish. Do not insist on this. You must let go of this desire to know the secrets of the soul."*

Many significant things have been said here. One is that even the *devas*, the gods, have doubts about this. Those who are in heaven, who are living in bliss every moment, even they are doubtful. Yama is saying, "You are living on this earth; you should not get involved in this complicated matter. The *devas*, the ones who have become virtuous in every way and who have accumulated the virtue of their good deeds – even they are in doubt, even they do not know for certain. So it is better if you do not concern yourself about it."

When Buddha became enlightened, it is said that Brahma, the god of creation, went to his feet and said, "Please tell me the secret. Although I have created the world, even I don't know what will be left after the whole world is finished." Brahma is the greatest engineer, very powerful; he is the creator of the whole world, but even he asks, "Does anything remain after *pralaya*, the end of creation? And what is hidden in me? Is it immortal or will it die?"

There are stories about the life of Mahavira, that there were many different beings in his audiences. There were human beings, animals, birds, and even *devas*. Why did the *devas* go to listen? At least the *devas* are supposed to know.

It will help you to understand the concept of *devas*. Hell is for those who have lived their lives in unawareness. Hell belongs to those who have only sinned, to those who have experienced happiness only by creating misery for others. Heaven is for those who have found happiness by making others happy, for those who have lived in virtue. But remember, heaven and hell both have one thing in common: both are other-oriented. Hell belongs to those who enjoy creating misery for others and heaven belongs to those who are happy by creating happiness for others – but the attention of both is focused on the other. The *devas* who live in heaven are as deluded as the beings who live in hell because their attention is focused only on the other.

The wise man is one whose attention is no longer focused on the other. He is neither interested in making the other happy nor is he interested in making the other unhappy. He is interested in awakening himself. Hence we have three words: *hell*, *heaven* and *moksha*, absolute freedom.

*Moksha* is not another name for heaven; moksha happens when a person has become completely free from the other, when a person is completely centered in his own being, when someone is fulfilled. When someone experiences and attains to the wholeness of his own being, then he is liberated.

So the *devas* are not liberated. The beings that are in hell are bound in misery: their chains are made of iron. Those who are in heaven are bound in virtue: their chains are made of gold – but both are in chains. *"...even the gods have had their doubts; they also could not understand because this subject is so very subtle and difficult to understand."* In fact, the secrets of the soul will never be grasped by the intellect. As long as the intellect is dominant, it will never be understood. Only when the intellect is dropped, when thinking ceases, when your trust in the intellect is gone, will it be understood. This is the complexity and the demarcation line between worthiness and unworthiness. As long as you are thinking and brooding, as long as you are guided by logic, as long as the intellect is still the ultimate thing for you, you cannot understand what is beyond death.

Matter is the realm of the intellect. The intellect can know the object but it cannot know the subject. The intellect can see outward but it cannot see within. You can put on glasses and it will help you to see outward, but they are of no use when you are dreaming. Spectacles are useless for looking within.

The intellect is the right faculty for looking outward. If I want to look at you I have to do it with the intellect. If I want to search in the world I have to do it with the intellect. For this reason, science is dependent on the intellect. But if I want to see my own being, the intellect is not needed at all. Hence religion is a search beyond the intellect.

Religion is going *beyond* the intellect, and science is going *into* the intellect through the intellect. That is why religion and science are standing diametrically opposite to each other. Science cannot understand what religion is saying and religion cannot understand what science is saying. It is natural because the very medium of religion is the transcendence of intellect and the medium of science is the practice of the process of thinking. The methodologies of religion and science are so contrary that even their languages are foreign to each other.

Yama is saying that this subject is very difficult, very subtle, that it is not easy to understand. It can be understood only if you go beyond your ordinary understanding.

The process of thinking is natural and easy. For those who live through the intellect, to drop that habit and enter meditation is very unnatural. Once someone has entered meditation, for him, meditation becomes natural and the intellect becomes unnatural. But as long as we are living from the intellect, to enter meditation is very difficult. Yama is saying that this subject is subtle, that it is not easy to understand.

> *"You may ask for something comparable as your third wish. Do not insist on this. You must let go of this desire to know the secrets of the soul."*
>
> *Nachiketa was not discouraged by hearing of the difficulties; his enthusiasm was not affected. Rather, he said even more strongly, "Yama, you say that the gods have also thought about this but even they could not decide, and that it is not easy to understand. But there are none who can explain this matter as well as you. As I understand it, no other wish can be compared to this one."*

Certainly, because who else besides the Lord of Death can say whether the soul survives after death or not? Yama is the right one to ask because he is the one who knows the secret. And only one who asks death itself can know.

That is why I have told you that until you learn the art of dying consciously, you cannot know whether or not something survives after death. The art of dying means to stand face-to-face with death. Ask directly to the one who is always standing at the door; ask the one through whom all beings must pass again and again.

But people pass through death unconsciously. If you can pass through death consciously, only then can the question be asked of Yama, the Lord of Death.

Nachiketa asks with even more resolve and firmness about something which is so difficult that even the gods don't understand it: "I will not drop this quest! And where will I find a better person than you to answer me? Who else can answer me? The gods cannot answer, they themselves are in doubt. It cannot be grasped by the intellect – and I only have the intellect, which cannot understand. To search with my intellect would be meaningless. I will not find a person like you again who can answer me. Hence I cannot drop this third wish."

Nachiketa did not become discouraged. Because he has remained as firm as he was before, he has passed through another of Yama's tests. Yama saw that Nachiketa was determined: he was not going to escape from the difficulty, he could remain firm. He was ready to enter the fire.

Yama gave him a second test: he tried to allure him, to shake his resolve.

> *Yama said to him, "You may ask for sons or grandsons with life spans of hundreds of years; you may ask for many cows and other cattle, for elephants, horses and gold. You may ask for an empire with vast boundaries. You may ask to live for as long as you wish.*
>
> *"Nachiketa, if you consider a wish for wealth or a means for living a long life as equal to your wish for the knowledge of the soul, you may ask for that. You could be the greatest emperor on this earth! I can make the greatest pleasure of all pleasures available to you!"*

This has to be understood. When someone enters into meditation, a moment comes when his capacity to enjoy this world becomes very intense and deep. So this is not only a story. When a meditator makes love, the pleasure hc feels is greater than that of a non-meditator because the sensitivity of a meditator becomes very profound.

When a meditator smells a flower he perceives a fragrance that a non-meditator can never experience. When a non-meditator is with a flower he is not present, he is somewhere else. Hence the nose receives the fragrance but the mind does not receive it deeply. The mind continues to wander. The meditator comes so close to the flower that the fragrance which he can detect is not available to the non-meditator.

As meditation deepens, the capacity for enjoyment also deepens. At the last moment, when the meditator can take a leap into the beyond if he wants, he can also dive deeply into experiences of the body. In those moments the capacity for enjoyment becomes so profound that the question arises whether to stop there or to move ahead.

This is why meditators can sometimes fall from even the highest rung of the ladder of meditation. In that state there is a great temptation to fall – a temptation which is not experienced by ordinary people. There is no way to fall lower than the state where you ordinarily are because you are standing at the lowest rung. There is no lower place to fall to, you are already at the lowest level of your sensitivity.

As meditation goes on becoming deeper the senses will go on becoming more and more pure, pleasures will become more profound. This is why before enlightenment the temptations of the world become much stronger. One moment before enlightenment, the whole world becomes a heaven: if a meditator falls from there and starts indulging in it, we call that person a *deva*, a god. It is very difficult for someone to resist the temptation to fall because the whole of life becomes filled with such music: all misery disappears from life, all anguish; every fiber of his being starts throbbing with bliss. In that moment, to turn back to the world of dreams and desires has a great gravitational pull – as if the gravity of the whole world is pulling you.

This is not just a story; what Yama is saying is symbolic of reality. Yama is saying, "I will make you a king. You can ask for a long life, as long as you want. You can ask for as many riches as you want – but drop this third wish."

> *When Nachiketa did not waver from his decision even at this, Yama then tempted him with the heavenly pleasures of the gods. Yama said, "Ask for all the pleasures which are rare in the world of mortals. Take these celestial women with you, along with chariots and musical instruments. Such women are surely not available to mortals. You can enjoy these women and be served by them. But Nachiketa, do not ask to know what happens to the soul after death."*

These are the temptations which come just before moksha, enlightenment…

> *But Nachiketa had a firm will and was truly worthy: he knew that even the greatest pleasures in heaven and earth could not be compared with the tiniest portion of the bliss that comes through enlightenment.*

All that is of this world will be taken away. It will be taken away in a few years or in a few million years, but it will certainly be taken away. Nothing in this world is eternal. The duration can be prolonged but it cannot be prolonged forever. Finally, everything will be taken away.

Yama is not saying that he will make Nachiketa immortal. Yama is saying, "I can delay your death – you will not die for thousands of years – but one day you will die. And I will give you every pleasure." But Nachiketa has understood that all those pleasures would be given instead of his third wish, so what he has asked for must certainly be greater than all the pleasures he is being offered. Those allurements cannot be compared to what he has asked for.

And as Yama continues trying to tempt him, Nachiketa only becomes more and more resolute.

As you start going deeper into meditation and the world of

pleasures begins to become more intensely attractive, then know well that the moment is coming when great ecstasy can arise. These are the last temptations from *prakriti*, from nature: *prakriti* is casting its final nets. If you can resist these temptations, your suffering will be transcended forever, your misery will cease. But if you fall victim to those temptations then you will achieve happiness, pleasure – but all the pleasure in this world will eventually come to an end. There is nothing of this world which can remain forever, which is eternal.

> *Nachiketa, supporting his decision with reasoning, said these words of non-attachment to Yama: "Yama, the pleasures that you are describing are ephemeral; they exhaust the sensitivity and sharpness of all the senses."*

Consciousness is not awakened through pleasure; on the contrary, it becomes more asleep. The inner light does not grow through experiencing pleasure, the darkness only deepens. Remember, all pleasures blunt your senses. Whatever pleasures you are indulging in, at the same time your sensitivity will decrease, it will not increase.

This is a very significant point: with meditation your sensitivity will increase and with sensuous pleasures it will decrease. It is good to understand that with meditation your sensitivity increases and with indulgence in sensuous pleasures it decreases. Today you have eaten delicious food, but if you eat the same food tomorrow it will be a little less delicious. If you eat the same food the day after tomorrow it will become even less delicious. If you have to eat the same food even for a fourth day you will simply suffer; and if you have to eat it for a fifth day you will throw the plates against the wall. On the first day you experienced great pleasure through the food, but on the fifth day it will have become a hell. If you have to eat the same food for your whole life, you will commit suicide!

If you listen to some music today and again listen to the

same music tomorrow and then again the day after tomorrow, your ears will become insensitive to it. The senses will stop receiving it because the senses have become less sensitive.

Nachiketa is making a very important point. He is saying, "All those sensuous pleasures will shrink my consciousness and blunt my sensitivity. I will become simply dull and stupid." This is why a man of indulgence slowly, slowly becomes more and more dull. A meditator will slowly become more alive and alert.

> *"Furthermore, a life span, howsoever long it may be, is brief: it will end sooner or later. You can keep those celestial women, the chariots, those songs and dances – I don't want them.*
>
> *"A man can never be fulfilled through wealth. Now that I have set my eyes on you…"*

Nachiketa is saying that now that he has seen death itself, he cannot be satisfied with mere wealth. A man who is not aware of death may have the illusion of satisfaction through riches, but one who is aware that he will eventually die cannot feel fulfilled with wealth. One who is aware that he will have to die cannot be satisfied with love. And one who is aware that he will have to die, nothing in this world can satisfy him because he knows that death is standing there, waiting.

If somebody tells you that you are going to die within a few minutes, then all your pursuit of enjoyment will disappear. If while you are sitting here a message comes that within a few minutes an atom bomb will fall on Mount Abu, then all your enjoyment will simply disappear. The most beautiful woman will not be seen by you. Food may be in front of you but all your hunger will disappear. If somebody were to tell you that he will make you the emperor of the whole world you will just say, "Are you mad? In a few minutes an atom bomb will be dropped!"

In reality, the moment of death is not far away; it is never very distant. An atom bomb may or may not drop, but death is always standing just behind you. Whether it comes in the next moment or in a year or in seventy years, the difference of time is not important.

If your intelligence is not very far-reaching, then you will feel that death is not close by. Because of time, there appears to be a difference. A death which is only a few moments away becomes visible to you because your intelligence can reach only that far; it cannot perceive something which may be seventy years away. The length of time functions as a thick barrier to your perception. But there are people whose intelligence is such that it can perceive things which are even thousands of years away.

Nachiketa is saying, "Howsoever long it may be, our life span is always too short. A life span that comes to an end cannot be called long. Keep those things for yourself because what you are offering me so easily has no value now that I have seen you."

> *"Now that I have set my eyes on you, I have already attained abundant wealth. As long as your compassion rules there can be no death for me. It is meaningless to ask for those other things. The only wish that is worth asking for is the one that I have already said: the knowledge of the soul."*

Nachiketa is saying that once death has been seen, then nothing else has any value anymore. Now there is only one thing that is valuable: to know that which is beyond death. Without this understanding, all becomes futile.

> *"It is meaningless to ask for those other things. The only wish that is worth asking for is the one that I have already said: the knowledge of the soul."*

> *"Man is subject to decay and death. Knowing this reality, where is the man living in this world who, after having met*

> *you, an immortal and noble being, would continue to long for the beauty of women, for the pleasures of the senses, and to yearn for a long life?"*

Nachiketa is saying a beautiful thing: "After having met you, a great sage; after having seen death, who can still think of spending his time in the pursuit of sexual pleasures or of acquiring luxuries and enjoying beautiful women? After having seen you, now these things are no longer possible. Now only one longing arises within me: the longing to know if there is anything beyond you. Seeing you, the things of the world have become empty. All pleasures have become meaningless."

And whosoever remembers death, for him, everything becomes futile…

Have you heard the story of Buddha?

Once Buddha saw a dead man, so he asked his charioteer, "What has happened to this man?"

The charioteer said, "He has died."

Buddha was looking at a dead body for the first time. Then he immediately asked, "Am I also going to die?"

At that time, Buddha was a young man and was at the peak of his youth. The charioteer said, "It is not for me to say, but I also cannot tell a lie. One who is born will die. You will also die."

Buddha had been on his way to participate in a youth festival. He said to his charioteer, "Turn the chariot around. If I am going to die, then that death has already happened. I have no interest in going to a youth festival. I have already become old."

With the realization that death is a certainty, everything became meaningless. Now what was the point in entertainment? On that same night, Buddha left his home.

Realizing that death is there, the search for the immortal begins. Death is the great awakener. One who sees death begins the search for that which is deathless.

You all hide the fact of death. You avoid facing it. If you see death somewhere you divert your attention to somewhere else. If somebody dies you say, "The poor fellow" – as if he has died and you will remain alive forever. You show pity by saying, "That poor fellow has died an untimely death." You are avoiding an indication, a hint, which reminds you that you will also die.

Every death is a declaration of your own death. Whenever somebody is dying, if you are even a little aware, you will realize that you too are dying. But man lives in the illusion that everybody else will die but he is an exception: "I am not going to die." Nobody ever thinks that he has to die. So many people die, but man goes on believing in his immortality.

This belief in immortality is dangerous. It is better to have an encounter with Yama, the noble being of death, because with this encounter the search will begin.

> *"O Lord of Death, reveal to me the ultimate truth of this most wondrous and otherworldly subject – the destiny of the soul. Man does not know if the soul lives after death. I wish only for this most mysterious knowledge."*

To stand before death and seek the immortal, this is the state of samadhi.

Now we will begin our journey toward this ultimate state.

Now, understand a few things about the morning meditation.

This meditation has four stages. In the first stage, for ten minutes, breathe in and out with total energy. Let it be chaotic and unrhythmic, as if your whole body has become an ironsmith's bellows. Forget everything; let there be only one thing happening: breathing in, breathing out, breathing in, breathing out. Let the whole energy become involved in breathing in and breathing out, bringing your whole body to a storm-like state. This will hammer at and activate your inner fire, *naachiket-agni,* the Naachiket Fire. In this hurricane, the fire hidden within you will be ignited.

In the second stage, for ten minutes throw everything out that is suppressed within you – your madness, your repressed emotions, your perversions – everything. If you feel like crying, cry; if you feel like screaming, scream; if you feel like dancing, dance. Whatsoever you feel like doing, allow it to be expressed.

Don't control anything. Put aside your intellect and let your mind do whatsoever it feels like doing. Every person has accumulated much madness, and until it is thrown out nobody can become free of it. So this second stage is a catharsis.

In the third ten minutes, a *mahamantra* is to be used: that *mahamantra* is *hoo.* Jumping, dancing, shouting loudly, make the sound *hoo! hoo!* This loud sound *hoo* will set your inner fire ablaze. If done rightly, in these three steps *you* will disappear.

In the fourth stage, remain absent. The fourth step is of silence, of not being. Suddenly stop, whatsoever posture and gesture you are in – lying down, standing up, sitting. After the third stage when I say "Stop!" you should stop then and there. Do not make yourself comfortable by making space and lying down comfortably. In arranging for this comfort, your ego will return. After all that work done in the three steps, when I say stop, stop immediately, as if you are dead. If your hands were raised, let them remain raised; if a foot is off the ground, let it be so. You may think that you will fall down: if you fall down let it be so, there is no problem. But don't rearrange anything from your side. When I say stop, then stop. Then nobody is here, only corpses are lying here. This fourth stage is also ten minutes.

After these four stages there will be a few minutes for expressing your bliss. In all these previous stages, bliss and peace have been gathering within you – express it, as if you have become a small child again. Dance, laugh, jump!

Now, get ready for meditation.

[*Osho now gives the following explanation for the benefit of the*

*Western seekers present at the meditation camp.*]

Now something about the morning meditation.

This meditation has four steps. The first is chaotic breathing. For ten minutes you have to breathe and forget everything; just take the breath in and throw it out, take the breath in and throw it out. Let your whole body be involved in it.

In the second step you have to pass through a catharsis: for ten minutes go completely mad. You can scream, you can jump, you can dance, you can weep, cry, laugh. Whatsoever comes to your mind, do it – but do it totally, with no inhibitions, with no suppressions.

And in the third step, for ten minutes you are to use a *mahamantra*, *hoo! hoo!* Go on jumping, dancing with this *mahamantra*. Go on shouting *hoo! hoo! hoo!* Bring your total energy to it.

These three steps will erase you completely, you will be no more.

And after the third step, when I say "Stop!" you have to stop totally. Then don't move, don't make any noise. The moment I say "Stop!" stop dead. Don't try to make arrangements for the body; don't try to sit down. Stop as you are. If you are standing, remain standing. Even if your posture is inconvenient, don't make any arrangement for your convenience because the moment you start thinking about convenience the ego has come back.

So when I say "Stop!" it means stop.

And after the fourth step I will give you a few minutes to express your ecstasy, your bliss. Then you can dance and laugh and jump; be just like small children.

Now, get ready. Close your eyes and use the blindfold. If you don't have a blindfold, then close your eyes and keep them closed.

Create space around you because you are going to be completely mad.

Start the first step...

# 3

# The Science of the Soul

*Having tested Nachiketa, Yama was convinced of his determination, his desirelessness, fearlessness, and worthiness to be taught the science of the soul.*

*Before he spoke on the science of the soul Yama elaborated on its significance. He said, "The way to shreya, all that moves one toward the ultimate goodness, is different from the way to preya, all that moves one toward the pleasures of the world. Both of these ways bring different fruits and both attract and catch the human mind. But the one who chooses the way to ultimate good is blessed and the one who accepts the ways to immediate pleasure will remain empty.*

*"In life there are opportunities for both shreya and preya. The intelligent man discriminates between the two, and upon contemplating their nature, he understands the difference. He then chooses the way to ultimate good over the way to immediate pleasures. Concerned for his worldly welfare, the unintelligent one follows the way to immediate pleasures.*

*"Nachiketa, you are free from desire. Having considered and understood, you have renounced the objectives of pleasure and sensuous enjoyment, both in this world and in the next. You have not fallen prey to the lure of riches by which most men are seduced.*

*"What is known as vidya, true learning and avidya, false learning, bring very opposite fruits. Nachiketa, I can see that you have the longing for vidya because no amount of temptation for the pleasures of the senses has deceived you.*

*"The foolish continue to believe themselves to be intelligent and learned; they will continue to suffer and to pass through the life forms of many species in the same way that the blind man who is led by other blind people will wander, suffer, and never reach his destination."*

Man grows in two ways. One way is when his comforts, his wealth and his possessions grow but his consciousness does not grow. The other way is when his inner consciousness grows.

Whatsoever you gain in the world, you don't grow through it. Your power may increase, your palaces may become bigger, your wealth may grow, you may accumulate much knowledge, your memory may increase, your degrees, honors and respect may become greater and greater, but the inner consciousness, the inner soul, your being, will remain as unevolved as it was at the time of your birth. This desire for things of the outer world takes possession of humanity, but the longing to go on the inner journey rarely takes hold of people. And there are many reasons for this.

The desire for external things grips you very easily because it is the outer world that you experience through the senses. You see things with your eyes, you hear sounds with your ears, your nose gives you the experience of fragrance and your tongue gives you taste. All your senses bring you the news of the outer world but they cannot give you any hint of the inner. The body is meant to give you information about the outer world; the body is a bridge between the outer and the inner, the soul. Hence the body gives you information about the outer and naturally, receiving these messages from without, consciousness starts moving and focusing outward.

The eyes see out, not in. And whatsoever you can see, you naturally assume that it is the same way to see within. All your senses are outgoing. They are bound to be because the senses are not needed for going inward. I can experience that which is within me without the senses, but there is no way to know the external world without the senses.

All the senses of man have developed because of his desire to know the outer world. My hands can touch you; I can touch everything outside with my hand but I cannot touch inside my own hand. My eyes can see everything else but they cannot see themselves. For this reason, consciousness flows naturally to the outside. You become involved with acquiring more and more possessions. Man becomes rich in things but he remains poor within. Man can become very powerful in the outer world but remain very weak, very poor in the inner world. And as long as there is inner poverty, no outside power or ability is of any worth.

Secondly, all around you are people who are focusing on the outer – and the mind of man is a great imitator. We learn everything by imitation. A child learns the language which is spoken in the home; naturally, there is no other way to learn a language. A child will believe in the religion that his parents believe in; he will start visiting the temples where his parents go to worship. Wherever his parents, his family, his town, and his country are going, he will also join the same game.

You flow with the crowd. And everybody is running on the outside, so you also start running with them. All your education is for the outer journey but there is no education for the inner journey.

In ancient times India tried this. At the time that these Upanishads were written, the attempt to educate for the inner journey was at its peak. Before a child could become entangled in the outer world, he was sent to the *gurukul*, the mystery school of a spiritual master where people were focused on the inner search. Before someone could become lost in the outer, we wanted to give him a taste of the inner.

And when someone has had a taste of the inner even once, then nothing of the outer world will be of more value to him. Once a person has had even a taste of the inner journey then the mad race for the outer will lose all color for him. The outer will look dull. When someone who has tasted the inner moves into the outer world, it is only out of care, out of concern, and not out of ambition and desire. Then even if he becomes engaged in the outer world he will remain a witness, he will not be a doer.

Only in India has this unique experiment occurred that before a person could begin to pursue the outer and be caught by the crowd, we would send him away to the forest university of a spiritual master. There he would be in the company of those who were focusing on the inner world. In that atmosphere, he too would start moving inward. When he had become a little aware of the inner world, when he had heard the music of his inner being, only then would he be sent into the world – and then there would be nothing to fear.

In India we had divided life into four stages. The first stage of life we called brahmacharya. This word is unique: it means living in a godly way, behaving as in a godly way. This word does not mean what people have ordinarily understood it to mean. Ordinarily, people think that brahmacharya is the conservation of semen. This is a very limited definition. The conservation of semen happens spontaneously: if life is lived in godliness then the conservation of semen follows like a shadow. This control is not in any way fundamental. When one moves outward his semen will also start moving outward. If one starts entering within the movement of his semen will also become introverted.

To live a divine life means that consciousness is constantly turning inward. And brahmacharya happens when the consciousness starts moving toward the center. A consciousness that is moving outward, toward the other, is called *abrahmacharya*, non-*brahmacharya*. When consciousness moves toward the other it becomes sexuality. Only when consciousness is moving toward oneself is it brahmacharya.

We would send our young children to the *gurukul* for the first twenty-five years of their lives so that they could learn how to turn their focus within. So before they experienced the pleasures of the outer world, they would taste godliness. Then there would be no fear that they would become lost in the world. The memory of that glimpse of godliness would remain with them forever. Then the inner call would persist, that inner music would continue. Then howsoever strong the pull of money might become, it would be very difficult to suppress their inner voice totally. Then howsoever strong the attraction between a man and a woman, it would remain only shadowy. For all men and women on the outside become like shadows, just forms, with nothing real for the one who has seen his inner woman or her inner man even once. Then the pull of outer attraction has disappeared. Only at that point was a person considered ready to go out into the world.

It is such a beautiful idea to first experience the inner and only then go into the outer world. It is a very valuable insight. Then even when the person has gone into the world, the world will not enter in him because one who has acquired some understanding of the inner will be able to pass through the world untouched. He will pass through this river of life but the water will not touch his feet. He will pass through all the same places that you are passing through but he will pass through them as if he were just a guest. For him, his house is an inn, a caravanserai. For him, the family has no more importance than a drama. He can do all the necessary things but there will not be a craving that can become like a madness. And in the second stage, the man becomes a householder.

Such a unique experiment has never happened again on this earth. And unless this experiment happens again this earth will continue to be full of pain and misery.

Before going out into the world you should have a strong grounding within. Before your hands touch money the inner treasure should be experienced. Then money will be only a means:

then you will use money but it will not become your master.

In this second stage, after brahmacharya, we ask the person to become a *grihastha*, a householder. Now he can get married and have children. Now he can experience life, but such a person will be living in a different way. The quality of his living will be totally different because he is capable of being a witness.

You are unable to be a witness – you become identified, you become the doer. To be a doer is painful and to be a witness is absolute bliss. Even if you throw a person who has become a witness into hell, you cannot make him miserable. And even if you take a person who is not a witness to heaven, you will not be able to bring him out of his misery.

The indulgent mind will always be in misery because it has certain particular qualities. Its first quality is that whatsoever it has is never enough. The second quality is that what it has looks meaningless and what it does not have yet appears to be very meaningful. The third quality of the indulgent mind is that its desires are infinite. The ways in which you can fulfill your desires are always limited; that is why it is impossible to ever make such a mind happy. It will remain miserable whatever the situation because the misery is arising from within. And anyone who comes in contact with such a mind will be soaked in its misery.

And it is impossible to make one who is a witness unhappy because the witnessing consciousness also has certain qualities. The first quality of being a witness is that one always feels oneself to be separate from whatever is happening. One who has become a witness finds himself distanced from whatever is happening; he knows that he is just a witness. If misery is happening, then he is also a witness to that. He cannot become identified with it – and unless you become identified with misery you cannot be miserable.

The second characteristic of the witnessing consciousness is that it feels gratitude for that which is. It feels whatever it receives to be a blessing from existence. Whatever is available is not taken to be a result of the person's effort but a blessing from the existence.

The witness never becomes a doer; hence one who is a witness can never say that he has achieved through doing something. He always feels that he has not done anything and yet he has received everything. That is why he feels gratitude. His gratitude has no limit; his thankfulness, his feelings of being grateful are infinite.

Try to understand this: to witness means to know that you have never done anything, you are just an observer. Whatever has happened has not been done by you; you are not a doer of it. Hence whatsoever happens is by the grace of existence.

It is impossible to take away the witness's happiness. And the witness knows the art of spreading happiness all around itself. Just as a spider creates a web, the doer creates a web of misery all around and the witness a web of happiness.

The witness has no desire because if one is not the doer then the desire to do something becomes meaningless. One who has no desire and no expectation cannot be made unhappy. Misery comes only when expectations and desires are not fulfilled.

I have heard about a man who was sitting, looking very sad and unhappy. He owned a big hotel and it was doing a good business. So a friend asked him, "Why have you been so unhappy for the last few days? Is there some problem with the business?"

The owner said, "There are many problems! The hotel is running at a loss."

The friend exclaimed, "I cannot understand that because so many guests are coming and going. Whenever I pass through your hotel in the evening I always find a 'no vacancy' sign on the front door. So business must be going very well."

The hotel owner said, "You don't know! Fifteen days ago, when we were putting the 'no vacancy' sign up in the evening, a minimum of fifty customers always had to be turned away. But now, for the last few days, only fifteen people are turned away every night. The business is running at a great loss!"

A mind full of expectations is bound to be unhappy…

I was a guest in a house. The wife said to me, "Please find out what is happening to my husband. He is always worrying that he has lost half a million rupees. I wonder how there could be such a loss – I don't see any loss."

So I asked the husband and he said, "There is a loss: I was expecting a profit of one million rupees and instead I only got a profit of half a million rupees, so I have suffered a loss of half a million rupees!"

A mind that is full of expectations experiences loss even when there has been gain. A mind full of witnessing experiences gain even though there may have been loss because it knows that it has not been the creator of it. Whatsoever has been given is a gift from existence; it is a blessing.

So a man would become a householder only after he has had a few glimpses of witnessing. Then he would have a wife but he would never become a dominating husband. Then he would have children, taking care of them, but not becoming an authoritarian father. He would build a house, run a shop, but he would do everything as if he were an actor in a theater play. He would wait with a patient longing for the day when he would be able to continue the unfinished inner journey that he had left at the age of twenty-five. And at the age of fifty he would become a *vanaprastha*.

*Vanaprastha* means "one whose eyes are turned toward the forest." The life's journey that had begun in a spiritual master's forest school would again point toward the forest. He would not actually return to the forest because his children would now be returning from the *gurukul*, and if the father were to leave his children immediately to go to the forest, the children would be in a difficulty.

The children have experienced some inner tranquility, but now they need to learn about the ways of the world. For this reason the father would remain at home for another twenty-five years. He would live in the house until he was seventy-five years old, but with his vision turned toward the forest. He would slowly be uprooting himself from family life. When his children returned from the *gurukul*, the mystery school in the forest, he would teach them about the world out of his own experiences.

And when he would become seventy-five years old he would renounce the world, become a sannyasin, a monk, and return to the forest. By then his children would be about fifty years of age; now it would be their turn to enter *vanaprastha*. These people who went to the forest as sannyasins at the age of seventy-five would take on the role of spiritual teachers, teaching the children who would be coming to the mystery school.

This was the cycle of life. We would send the children to the guru, to the people who had finally returned to the forest after experiencing the first three stages of life. In the mystery school the children would imbibe the essence and the mysteries of life so that at the age of twenty-five they would be ready to enter life full and enriched.

And there should always be this much of an age difference between the teacher and the student. Because of the absence of a feeling of respect between the teacher and the student, there is much difficulty in the world today. Sometimes it even happens that a student is wiser and more experienced than the teacher. When there is a very small age difference, it does not create respect.

When children approach a teacher who is seventy-five years of age and who has already experienced the three stages of life and is moving into the fourth, they feel as if they are near a snow-capped Himalayan peak touching the sky. Respect is naturally there.

People say that a teacher, a guru, should be respected. But I say that only one who is respected is a guru. It is not a question of "should be respected." Whenever respect is a "should" it is not there. Respect is not something that can be imposed from the outside or that can be demanded.

Thus there are two dimensions to the journey of life: one is the inner and the other is the outer.

Now let us enter the sutras.

> *Having tested Nachiketa, Yama was convinced of his determination, his desirelessness, fearlessness and worthiness to be taught the science of the soul.*

> *Before he spoke on the science of the soul Yama elaborated on its significance. He said...*

Yama saw that Nachiketa was rooted in a state of desirelessness. And only one who is rooted in desirelessness can enter inward. A person who is full of desires will move outward because he will only go where the outer desires can be fulfilled. And all desires, all passions, all lust can be satisfied only in the outer world. Whether these desires will actually be satisfied or not is another thing – but at least there is the semblance of fulfillment on the outside.

Yama became sure of Nachiketa's desirelessness; he felt that now he could transmit the science of the soul.

*Brahmavidya*, the science of the soul, means the ultimate inner journey to the state where only the inner remains and the outer has simply disappeared. The outer is no longer there, nothing remains as an outer phenomenon. All becomes inner: the whole of existence is merged with the inner, the whole life energy converges at the inner center. But this becomes possible only when your life energy is not scattered, when it is not moving toward desires on the outside. This state of desirelessness, *vairagya*, means that the very inclination to go outward has disappeared. Only then can one be allowed entry into the science of the soul.

Yama could see that Nachiketa was truly determined and that he had reached to this state of desirelessness, he could not be shaken from that state.

A seeker of truth has to have an attitude of absolute decisiveness, but mind is very shaky, always wavering. If someone says something against your opinions, your opinions will simply collapse. Even if someone tries to create a small doubt, you immediately start doubting. Believers are afraid to listen to the talk of non-believers. These believers are very weak people. What is there to be afraid of? The believer's fear is that the talk of the non-believer will disturb his beliefs. And a belief which can be shaken just by talk is worthless. Then what is its value? It is worse than being a non-believer.

At least the non-believers are not afraid of the believers. I have never seen a non-believer afraid of a believer, or one who could be shaken just by listening to his talk. The non-believer is not afraid; rather, he is in search of a believer whose belief he can try to disturb.

It is a very strange situation. Atheists have not said in any of their writings that an atheist should not listen to the talk of a theist. But the theists have said in their scriptures: Don't listen to the atheists and don't read what they write because it will disturb your mind and your faith!

But remember, the mind can be shaken only if it is already in a shaky state. When you are available to being shaken, only then can you be shaken. And I say unto you that if you are a theist, then make arrangements for atheists to be all around you. They will go on trying to shake you, and this will give you opportunities to find out if you can still be shaken or not. And if the atheists succeed in shaking you out of your theism, then know well that the real theism has not yet happened to you. Then don't go on carrying your false theism.

My feeling is that most of the theists we see in the world are false. Otherwise, the whole world would have been transformed by now! There are so many theists in the world – only one out of a hundred people are atheists, ninety-nine are theists. And even your ninety-nine percent theists have not been able to bring religiousness to this earth, and the one percent atheists have made the whole earth irreligious. It is very surprising!

But these ninety-nine percent of theists are false, they are not true: there is no experience and no trust in their hearts. They have somehow adopted and maintained a false appearance of theism. These theists are full of fear. And fear arises only when doubt is hidden in you. Nobody can make you doubtful unless you are already carrying doubt within you. You have created an outer mask of determination; hence whenever someone expresses their doubt, the doubts within you are reactivated. They have been hidden there, dormant, within you.

Only what is already hidden within you can be provoked in you. Understand this to be an ultimate principle: no one can create in you what is not already there within you. If you already have a doubt within then anybody can trigger it. And if you have trust in your heart, only then can somebody create trust in you. There is no way to create anything in you that is not already there.

Yama tried hard to make Nachiketa waver. It seems as if Yama is overdoing it on such a small boy, because he is creating all sorts of temptations for such an innocent child. If you think about it you will feel that Yama was being very hard with this boy who was only about seven years old. To tell him, "I will give you heavenly women" – this is simply too much! But Yama was trying hard to pervert his innocence. To tell a small boy that he can be the emperor of the whole world, that he can ask for anything he wants – when such a small child could have been tempted with just a toy… But by offering him the whole world Yama was creating a difficult test for Nachiketa. Even old men become entangled and caught with these toys.

Once a young man came to see me. Just by the way I asked him if his father had ever come to listen to my talks.

He said, "No, my father has no time. He is busy all the time washing his car. He does not even drive the car because he is afraid that it will be spoiled! He goes on improving it, changing this part and changing that part, putting in new things, decorating it. The whole day he's busy with his car so he has no time to come to your talks. My mother wants to come to listen to you, but because my father is home for twenty-four hours a day she cannot come."

The car has become a toy. It is no longer a means for transportation, there is no question of going anywhere. Because of his fear that the car will be damaged, it will never be driven. But even sitting unused, the car will begin to deteriorate, so the father goes on cleaning and servicing it.

For small children to play with toys is understandable, but even "old children" go on playing with toys. Just see how much you worry about your things; your whole life passes in worrying about things.

But to tell such a small boy that he will be given the whole earth as his empire, to tell him that he can live as long as he wants, that his children and grandchildren will live for thousands of years and his own life can also be as long… Remember, a small child has no awareness of death. Even old people, very rarely and with much difficulty, become aware of death because if the awareness of death happens, then one will become a sannyasin, a seeker. The awareness of death brings you to sannyas, to detachment.

But until they take their last breath, people cling to life. Even if you tell someone who is breathing his last breath that he is dying, he will look at you as if you are his enemy.

I have heard that a young man returned home after having studied astrology.

His father was an old, experienced astrologer. He told his son, "Never be in a hurry to divulge too much because astrology is a profound art. It is not necessary to always tell the truth. Many times you will even have to avoid telling the truth. And even if the truth has to be told, it should be told in such a way that it is vague. In this business you even have to tell lies. It is a very delicate and subtle art; the knowledge of books is not enough. So wait, and don't start displaying your knowledge of astrology to everyone."

But the young man said, "I have just returned from Kashi, the greatest seat of learning, and I know everything about astrology. I cannot wait now – I am going to the king. Because of what I have studied I can tell the king what is going to happen."

The father said, "Well, it's up to you. But I am also coming. Let me read the king's hand first. I will tell him some things first and then you can follow me."

The father looked at the king's hand and said to him, "Your kingdom will expand! In your life, a sunrise is very near."

The son was surprised to hear this because the lines of the king's hand were showing something different: the lines indicated that the king was about to die.

The father was highly honored by being given much money and valuable gifts. Then the son looked at the king's palm and said, "One thing is certain, and that is that you will not be alive for longer than seven days more." And the king ordered that the son be taken and whipped! The father just stood there laughing.

Later on, when he took his son home he said to him, "Do you see? What has been written in the books is for intelligent people – but where to find intelligent people? I also could see that the king was going to die within seven days, but to say it means to die even before the king dies! It is not enough just to tell the truth: the astrologer must know what his customer wants, what his desires are. It is more important to know the lines of his desires than to know the lines on his palms."

This is why when you go to an astrologer he looks at the lines of your desires. He tries to understand where your desires are running, then he supports them as far as he can.

Up to the very last breath of life, man does not want to hear that he is dying or that he is going to die. And to a small child who has not yet seen anything of life, it is totally absurd to tempt him with a long life. But Yama did all this because if Nachiketa could be shaken, then let him be shaken. And remember, in the face of death everybody is a small child. Up to the very end of life temptations go on shaking you and doubts make you waver. Anyone can put you in difficulty – anyone! There is no need even for a powerful sage like Yama to do it.

People come to me and say, "We were meditating and as a deep joy started to happen, somebody remarked, 'What are you doing? Do you call this meditation?' Now a doubt has entered." You were enjoying the meditation, so why has doubt entered you so easily? At least try to see whether this doubt is bringing you any joy, then go in the direction from where the joy is coming. Because if a man goes on choosing bliss he will ultimately reach to truth, to godliness.

That is why we have said that godliness is truth, consciousness and bliss. We have called it the ultimate state of bliss. If you go on checking to feel if the direction you are choosing brings you more bliss, then howsoever much you may go astray you will not remain lost for long.

But when bliss is arising in you, even then you can be disturbed because doubt is lying there deep within you; someone has only to activate it and it will surface. Deep down you are afraid, saying, "I don't know what I am doing. I don't know if this is madness." Your own fear becomes the doubt – the other is only an excuse.

Yama tried his best to tempt Nachiketa to waver from his decision, but he found that there was no possibility. He found that Nachiketa was firm in his determination; he was desireless, fearless. Hence he was completely worthy of receiving *brahmavidya*, the science of the soul.

There are three qualities which prove a seeker to be worthy: first, there should be a state of total desirelessness where consciousness is ready to move inward; second, there should be a firm resolve to do whatsoever has to be done with totality; and the third is fearlessness, where nothing can make you waver from the path.

Remember, as long as there is fear there will be greed. Fear and greed are two sides of the same coin. Whosoever is fearful can immediately be caught up in greed and whosoever is greedy can be made fearful. Remember, both are interconnected. Often people try to become fearless but they don't know that as long as there is greed they cannot be fearless – because greed is the root of fear. As long as you desire things you will be afraid to lose them.

I have heard that Chuang Tzu, a great Chinese mystic, was once a minister to an emperor. After some time he resigned from the ministry and became a sannyasin, started living in a forest under a tree.

Once the emperor went to the forest to hunt and his friends told him, "Chuang Tzu, your ex-minister, lives under a tree nearby. If you are interested we can go and see him."

The emperor replied, "Certainly, it would be worth seeing him. What has happened to Chuang Tzu? How has he changed after becoming a sannyasin?"

Chuang Tzu had been minister to the emperor for many years and the emperor knew him well. He also remembered how cultured a man Chuang Tzu was.

So the emperor went there. He got down from his chariot and stood near Chuang Tzu. Chuang Tzu was sitting with his legs outstretched, playing on his tambourine, and as the emperor approached he remained in the same posture. This was disrespectful! The emperor was standing in front of him and he was sitting with his legs stretched out. The king said, "Chuang Tzu, it is alright to be a sannyasin, but don't forget your culture. Why do you continue to keep your legs stretched out in my presence?"

Chuang Tzu said, "On the day my greed disappeared, my fear also disappeared. Now I want nothing from you so I have no fear of you. In the past I used to fold my outstretched legs not because I was cultured but because of my greed. I was afraid that you would deny me your favors. Now that I myself have left behind all that you could have deprived me of, there is no longer any fear of you. You think that you are an emperor, but to me you are the same as any person passing by on this road. Once you were an emperor for me, but that was because of my greed: I could get many things from you which were not possible to get from anybody else. But now? – now you are just a passerby, just like anyone else. Now I don't need to fold my outstretched legs to please you. Now there is no fear in me."

As soon as greed disappears, fear also disappears.

When Yama saw that all these temptations had not shaken Nachiketa, he naturally concluded that Nachiketa was fearless, that he had attained to a state of fearlessness; hence he was worthy of receiving the science of the soul.

> *Before he spoke on the science of the soul Yama elaborated on its significance, He said, "The way to shreya, all that moves one toward the ultimate goodness, is different from the way to preya, all that moves one toward the pleasures of the world. Both of these ways bring different fruits and both attract and catch the human mind. But the one who chooses the way to ultimate goodness is blessed and the one who accepts the way to immediate pleasure will remain empty.*
>
> *"In life there are opportunities for both shreya and preya. The intelligent man discriminates between the two, and upon contemplating their nature, he understands the difference. He then chooses the ways to ultimate good over the ways to immediate pleasures. Concerned for his worldly welfare, the unintelligent one follows the ways to immediate pleasures."*

These two words, *shreya* and *preya,* are very significant.

*Shreya* means the noble, the truthful, the sacred, the good. *Preya* means the appealing, the pleasing, that which cheers the mind and gives hope for the fulfillment of some passion. *Preya* is that through which desires are fulfilled and *shreya* is that through which the soul is nourished. *Preya* gives the mind the illusion that something will bring happiness, but one will never attain to happiness through it because just your wishing for something will make no difference. You may wish that you could squeeze oil from the sand, but what is the point in this desire? You may be able to see a garden in the desert at a distance, but seeing it will not necessarily have anything to do with the reality. When you go near it you will find that it was all a play of light rays. There was no oasis, it was only a mirage. Your seeing it does not mean that it is actually there.

*Preya* is when you feel something will give satisfaction, but when you have it, it does not satisfy you. For example, a man dreams of having a particular woman or a woman desires to have a particular man. As long as you don't get the one you desire, all your dreams will continue to revolve around that person. But as soon as you get what you desire you find a mirage in your hands.

No love has ever succeeded. If you want to be in love forever then it is necessary to never be near your beloved.

Rabindranath Tagore has written a novel out of very deep experience. In the novel the hero is in love with a young woman and he tells her that they should not marry because marriage always destroys love. The young woman cannot understand this because she feels that when there is love, marriage should follow. It is understandable. But the hero says, "Even if we marry, you should live on the other side of the lake and I will live on this side. Sometimes we may meet by accident or sometimes we can invite each other over – but we should not live together."

And the young woman answers, "Are you mad? The purpose of getting married is to live together for twenty-four hours a day!"

But the hero replies, "Then our love will die."

It is the story of thousands of love affairs. Majnu must still be in love with Laila, wherever he is, because he was not able to live together with her. If he had he would have been free of her forever. It is a mirage.

*Preya* is when you are far away from things, people, and relationships – and it appears that they will give you great joy, but as you approach closer to them all the joy simply disappears and misery takes its place.

The state of *shreya* is just the reverse. With *preya*, happiness seems to be there in the beginning, but later on unhappiness follows; with *shreya*, in the beginning you feel unhappiness arising, but later on happiness follows. So in the beginning *shreya* is very arduous; it means choosing the uncomfortable and the difficult out of your own understanding. Thus the seeker who chooses *shreya*, the means to the ultimate good, is bound to go into *tapashcharya*, efforts toward his own transformation.

It is very interesting to see that whenever there is happiness in the beginning, in the end there is misery. And this is everyone's experience. You have all in some way experienced that whenever there seemed to be happiness, it really turned out to be misery. But you have not learned anything from it; you did not learn the law of life, that when there is happiness in the beginning it is dangerous, it is an allurement. The appearance of happiness at the beginning is like a sugar coating on a bitter pill. And all bitter pills have a coating of sugar.

If you want to catch a fish you first have to put bait on a fishhook. Don't think that people sit there to feed fish with the bait – they sit there to offer the hook. In reality, they sit with a hook, but if people sit there with an exposed fishhook the fish won't bite it. Hence the simple strategy is to hide the hook inside the bait. And for your whole life you are doing the same. This needs to be understood because it is deeply connected with the psychology of your life.

In the West they are doing much research into this. The West has made a great mistake in making love the basis for marriage. Before this, all marriages were arranged. It was not any concern of the boy or the girl – as if it were not their marriage – it was the concern of the parents. The priest and the astrologers would consult their horoscopes, the parents would investigate the other family, and in this way the marriage was decided. The boy and the girl were not involved in the decision making. The marriage was a deal between two families; there was no question of love.

In the West, during the last two or three hundred years, they have tried a new experiment: they have said that an arranged marriage is not a marriage at all, that marriage must be based on love. It is a good idea, but in fact love marriages are breaking down. The divorce rate is increasing every day. In America, out of one hundred marriages, at least fifty end up in divorce. And don't think that the remaining fifty couples are living in great happiness! They simply don't have enough courage to get divorced because there are so many difficulties to do with it.

Only in stories or in the movies – particularly in Indian movies – after the marriage, couples live happily ever after. But it never happens this way. The movie shows that the prince and the princess get married and they live happily ever after and the story ends there. In reality the story begins there, the whole struggle starts from there. Before this everything was an introduction, a preparation, just the bait. Later on, when both people start living together, the fishhook reveals itself.

In the West, marriage is collapsing because it is based on love. And a marriage that is based on love is bound to fail. There is a reason for this: whenever two people fall in love, both of them present what is beautiful in themselves to the other – and hide the ugly. When you fall in love, whether you are a man or a woman, you show your most beautiful face to the other, but it is not your reality, it is not your totality. It may be just one facet of your personality, or it may not even be a facet but only a pretense. You can show this false face with no problem when you meet sometimes on a sea beach, sometimes in a garden, sometimes under the moon and the stars, but when you really start living together then the reality starts surfacing. The real person is a hell and all that sweet talk that had happened under the stars becomes just lies.

When two people move closer their inner realities start to show. The miseries of both become obvious, their pretensions and masks fall away because to wear a mask for twenty-four hours is not that easy. What I am trying to tell you is that even lovers show the outer bait and hide the fishhook. This is why all those marriages that are based on love affairs fail.

Love marriages can succeed only if the two people who love each other gather the courage to show their fishhooks. Both lovers need to expose their inner hell totally before the marriage. And if they both agree to live with each other's hell, only then should the marriage happen. Then there will be no divorce because the reasons for the divorce have already been exposed.

But usually, both people show only their sweet faces. Both show their beautiful dreams, but as they come closer the dreams start disappearing, just as when you get closer to a rainbow it disappears. A rainbow is visible only from a certain distance; don't make the mistake of going too close to it.

And this is the case in all dimensions of life. It is not only true between husbands and wives; it is also true between friends, between teachers and students, between the leader and the follower. Wherever there is a relationship, there is a bait. Soon the layer of bait will be torn away and the hook will be revealed like a thorn because that is the reality; the bait was only on the surface, an outside layer.

Those things which are initially pleasurable, which at first give a hope that happiness will be coming, but which end in unhappiness, we call *preya*. We have all had the experience of *preya*.

*Shreya*, the way to the ultimate good, is just the opposite. When it is possible for something to begin with a glimpse of happiness and end with unhappiness, then just the reverse is also possible: something can begin with unhappiness and end with happiness.

With this concept as a base, India had attempted to create a different type of life. In this country we started the lives of our children with intense difficulties. To send children to *gurukuls* in the forest was difficult for them because there were no facilities or amenities of a civilized life. The child had to grow up right in the middle of the forest, with all the difficulties and hardships it entailed. The gurus were very hard. Hard work had to be done: wood had to be cut for fuel, cows had to be taken out for grazing, grass had to be cut. The small children were doing all that hard work and afterward they would learn some lessons. When they returned to a social life after twenty-five years of such an austere life, then even very simple and plain food made them feel so happy.

India was a happy country for a long time not because it had everything but because its education and training began with a very hard life. Today, education begins with all sorts of conveniences and comforts; hence the whole country – the whole world – is unhappy.

The conveniences and comforts that a student experiences in the university and the hostel cannot be provided at home by his father. And when the son returns from the university after having enjoyed all those conveniences, he will get married and get a job that pays only a few hundred rupees per month. Then the difficulties will begin and his life will become a great misery because in fact what begins with happiness ends in unhappiness and what begins with unhappiness ends in happiness.

If early education and training begins with hardship and unhappiness, then there is every possibility of contentment in the later years of life. But all parents think that they have to make their children happy, and in that way they are only creating a basis for the child's whole life to be miserable.

Austerity means that you yourself choose hardship or inconvenience; it is out of your own choice. The direction of *shreya* is just the opposite to the direction of *preya*, so it is better to accept the hardships that happen in the beginning. Don't escape from pain and don't hide from it. Don't be afraid of pain – go through it so that you are no longer afraid of it. And as you accept pain and it no longer makes you miserable, then there is the possibility for great happiness to arise.

This is why to live a life of integrity is uncomfortable and to truly do good is very arduous. Evil has a certain appeal. If you find a hundred thousand rupees lying around, your mind will become divided into two parts. One part will say to take it because with the money will come a possibility of happiness, a chance to build a dream palace. The other part of the mind will say to leave it – but leaving it will make you unhappy. If you take the money and choose to steal then you have chosen *preya*, the pleasurable, but your whole life will be affected by this choice.

If you have the courage to just leave the money and go then you have chosen unhappiness because you will be giving up the hope for happiness through that money. But by making this choice not to steal you have chosen *shreya*, and this will take you toward happiness. Stealing has never made anybody happy. Howsoever many riches a thief may accumulate, he will remain a thief and he will remain unhappy. His soul will always feel burdened and the flower of his being cannot blossom in this way.

To choose *shreya* means to choose what is not so easy at first for the ultimate good. When someone goes through pain, anguish, hardship and trouble for the ultimate good, his soul will become stronger. His being will become more integrated and whole. When you voluntarily choose hardship for the sake of inner growth, it will become a fire. As you pass through this fire your soul will blossom in its utter purity. But the one who chooses momentary pleasures will find that slowly, slowly his soul has become divided into fragments. Because of his desires and the struggle to fulfill them, he will accumulate a big pile of things, but his inner being will slowly be lost.

Nachiketa also had to make a choice. Yama said to him that there are two possible ways: one is *preya*, the way to pleasure, and the other is *shreya*, the way to the ultimate good.

> *"Nachiketa, you are free from desire. Having considered and understood, you have renounced the objectives of pleasure and sensuous enjoyment, both in this world and in the next. You have not fallen prey to the lure of riches by which most men are seduced.*
>
> *"What is known as vidya, true learning and avidya, false learning, each bring very opposite fruits. Nachiketa, I can see that you have the longing for vidya because no amount of temptation for the pleasures of the senses has deceived you."*

Once again, it is important to understand these two words, *vidya* and *avidya*. *Avidya* does not mean ignorance as it is defined in dictionaries, and *vidya* is not just knowledge as it says in the dictionaries. *Avidya* is the kind of knowledge that makes you open to *preya*; *avidya* is the means to immediate gratification. *Vidya* is the knowledge which opens you to *shreya*, the means to ultimate good. *Avidya* and *vidya* are both knowledge, but *avidya* is knowledge that brings *preya*, immediate pleasure.

Both a thief and a yogi need knowledge. Not only does a man of Yoga, of meditation, have knowledge, but a man of *bhoga*, of indulgence, also has a certain kind of knowledge. A sinner also has a system, an efficiency, an expertise, a certain art.

All knowledge which ends in temporary pleasure is called *avidya*. If you understand this deeply, it will create much trouble for you. It will mean, for example, that all scientific knowledge is *avidya* because it brings you immediate pleasure and not the ultimate good. With science, at the most, you can achieve the pleasures of life but you will not attain to your own being. Science is part of *avidya*.

And knowledge that helps you experience your soul, your

inner being, is called *vidya*. *Vidya* is that which supports detachment from pleasures and helps you on the search for truth, for the sacred. You renounce the sweetness of immediate gratification and become ready to drink of truth, howsoever bitter it may be. From this readiness, a new life will arise.

Yama is telling Nachiketa that these are two different ways. Nachiketa has been very courageous; he has proved his worth. He did not become trapped in the web of desire for immediate gratification that binds most people.

*"What is known as vidya, true learning and avidya, false learning, each bring very opposite fruits. Nachiketa, I can see that you have the longing for vidya because no amount of temptation for the pleasures of the senses has deceived you."* Yama is saying, "You are in search of the essence, the wisdom, the realization, the meditation, the Yoga, the alchemy by which the seeker can achieve the ultimate benediction, the ultimate truth. You are not in search of pleasure. I have presented you with many temptations but you have come out of it untouched. Nothing has made your mind waver."

> *"The foolish continue to believe themselves to be intelligent and learned; they will continue to suffer and to pass through the life forms of many species in the same way that the blind man who is led by other blind people will wander, suffer, and never reach to his destination."*

Yama is saying a great thing: that there are so many scholars and intellectuals who consider themselves to be knowledgeable, but all their knowledge is rooted in wrong knowledge and centered in the desire for instant pleasure.

Seen in this way, our schools and universities are still not places of right knowledge. They are places of *avidya*, because only *preya* can be the result of what is being taught there. And even that much is not happening. Education gives only empty promises, nothing more.

If we ask the mystics of the Upanishads, they will say that you have given a wrong name, *vidyalaya*, to your educational institutions. Rather, they should be called *avidyalaya*, a place where *avidya* is taught. *Vidyalaya* is a place where the individual can learn how to attain to his own inner being, how to realize the truth. It is a place where he will learn the art of living life rather than gain the knowledge for earning a livelihood.

Yama is saying, "Nachiketa, you are longing for *vidya* in your quest for the science of the soul because you are desireless, detached, fearless; you are not wavering or indecisive. The winds of passion cannot disturb the flame of your awareness. You are ready. You are worthy. I will teach you the right knowledge of the science of the soul."

You also have much knowledge, but it is not *vidya*. *Vidya* is not what an engineer, a doctor, a professor, a shopkeeper, a carpenter, a sculptor or a painter knows. With their knowledge they can have pleasure but they cannot have the ultimate truth.

And as long as man does not know the art of how to find the ultimate good, he is not a real man of knowledge. Yama is telling Nachiketa that if someone thinks himself to be intelligent without knowing the art of *shreya*, he is simply a fool. Not only do those so-called wise men go astray, but they also mislead many other people – just as when a blind man tries to lead another blind man, saying that he will show him the way. He will only wander aimlessly for many lives and make many others suffer the same fate.

It is interesting that even a blind man wants to show others the path because even if one does not know the path, to guide others gives a deep satisfaction to the ego.

Kahlil Gibran has written a small story…

There was a guru who was traveling from village to village telling the people that he knows where God lives, and anyone who wants to reach to God should follow him. He warned that whosoever followed him would have to do it with determination.

He said that nobody should go only halfway or be indecisive because, he said, "The path is difficult and the journey is long."

He was creating greed in people, and at the same time he was making them afraid by telling them that the path was arduous and that it was very difficult to move on it: "Out of a hundred thousand seekers, maybe one will reach the goal. But if someone is an authentic seeker he can follow me; I will lead that seeker to the goal."

People would tell him, "We want to search for God, but at the moment it is not convenient. Later, when we have more time and when we are free of family problems, we will come to sit at your feet."

The guru became bolder because nobody was ever ready to follow him. So he exaggerated his claims by saying, "I can take you to God right now if you are willing! – but the path is very, very arduous."

But in one village he came across a madman. The madman said, "I am ready. There is no need to delay."

The guru became a little afraid. For the first time he thought, "Where will I lead him to?" He had forgotten about his lie because nobody had ever agreed to follow him. But he tried to frighten the man by saying, "The path is long and arduous…"

But the madman said, "Stop talking! It's no good wasting time. Let's go! Why waste any more time talking? We've decided to go, so let's go!"

The guru said, "But you won't be able to turn back."

The madman said, "I'm not going to leave you. But please, don't leave me in the middle. Now I won't be going anywhere. Wherever you go, I will follow you like a shadow."

The guru became very worried but he thought, "How long can this man keep up his courage?"

One year passed and the man continued to follow the guru and the guru was starting to get nervous. Now, whenever he would arrive at a new village, he was not as emphatic as he had been before because his disciple was standing right behind him.

The disciple would say, "I've been following this guru for a year now, but still we have not reached anywhere. We are simply going from village to village."

The guru was losing courage. He tried hard to make the seeker run away, to get rid of him, but that crazy man was a sincere seeker. He must have been like Nachiketa: he was following his guru totally. Six years passed but the seeker did not even say, "We have not reached yet!" He just thought that the path was arduous, but that some day they would reach the goal. He was determined to follow the guru.

One day the guru gave up, and with folded hands said to him, "Look, because of you I have also forgotten the path. I used to know it! Now please be kind enough to leave me alone."

Even blind people sometimes think that they can lead others on the path. There are certain reasons for this: if a blind man can have a couple of followers – even if they are blind – he thinks, "Two people are following me so I can't be blind and they cannot be blind. I must have eyes." That is why, as the crowd of followers grows, the guru becomes more and more confident that he must certainly be going somewhere.

All these so-called gurus need followers. Because of the followers, they feel certain that they are gurus and that they have eyes. Ninety-nine out of a hundred gurus are blind themselves, but somehow they lead other blind people. And there are great difficulties because if a blind man wants to know whether or not the man leading him has eyes, how can he know it? If he had eyes he could see for himself, but he has no eyes. Hence a seeker is in great difficulty: he goes on groping from one master to another master, but how can he be certain?

But as it happened in the story I told you, if you latch on very tightly to a guru, if he is blind, he himself will confess with folded hands and say that he is blind; he will ask your forgiveness and tell you to go somewhere else.

Remember one thing: to wander cannot be avoided. It is

impossible to meet the master immediately; it is almost impossible. But if you go on searching with courage – fearlessly, desirelessly – then even a blind guru cannot deceive you for long. A blind guru can tempt you only because you are so full of desires, because there is no detachment. So you become impressed when somebody shows you a miracle, gives you an amulet or materializes holy ash from somewhere. You are full of desires and greed so you feel that a man who can materialize an amulet from the sky can do anything for you; he can fulfill your desires. You think that a man of miracles can cure your diseases, grant you a wish for a son, make you wealthy by winning a case in court – and this is how your desiring mind is seduced.

If a master is fulfilling your desires in any way, then you can be sure that he is blind and that he knows only the art of seducing other blind people.

A real master will not fulfill your desires; he will help you to move toward desirelessness. He will guide you toward the ultimate death where you will be free from the miseries of life, where your outer wandering will end and your inner silence will happen. The authentic master will guide you toward *shunyata*, inner emptiness. He will not give you hope that you will get rich, that you will attain to power, prestige, fame, that you will win a political election.

In Delhi, the capital of India, you will not find a single political leader who does not have a guru because these gurus bless them to win elections! As soon as a leader loses an election, if he has not approached a guru earlier, he will immediately rush to one. You will find that those who have had to leave their political posts have immediately gone to some so-called ashram and are sitting in the holy company of some so-called religious leader. Ironically, they will remain in his company only until they win an election again. Actually, they are seeking only the so-called blessings of the guru. And there are gurus making all kinds of promises, saying, "Everything will be taken care of, all will be gained. Just surrender, come to my feet, and you will get everything."

People who are full of desires are attracted to the blind. It is just as Yama is saying: blind people are following the blind. When the leader falls into a ditch, all the followers also fall into the ditch. Nanak has said, "The blind are leading the blind and the blind are guiding the blind."

Yama is saying, "Nachiketa, you cannot be led by a blind man. To guide you, a real master will be needed because you cannot be seduced."

If your greed has disappeared then no one can lead you astray. Only greed leads you astray. Therefore, do not search for the master; find out how to drop your greed. On the day when there is no longer any greed, the master will be found. On the day when there is no longer any greed within you, a wrong person cannot mislead you on the path. Then you will come into contact and communion with the right one.

Now, understand two things about the night meditation.

The night meditation is an experiment called *tratak,* eye-gazing. It is a very unique and powerful meditation. In the first step, for fifteen minutes you will be looking at me without blinking your eyes. Even if tears start flowing, don't allow your eyelids to blink. Your eyes have to be totally fixed on me. While doing this, remain standing and raise both your hands.

When I give the signal with my hands, start jumping with your total energy so that the dormant energy within becomes active. You have to keep your eyes on me so that a contact happens with me – a bridge, a circuit is created. Keep on jumping with your hands raised toward the sky and go on shouting the *mahamantra*, the mystic sound, *hoo*, *hoo*, *hoo*... This mantra *hoo* will hammer you from within, the gesture of my hands will give you more intensity and the eye contact will create a deep communion. If this experiment is done with total intensity, within fifteen minutes you will have jumped into another world.

After fifteen minutes I will ask you to stop: then you have to freeze, eyes closed, like a corpse. Then for fifteen minutes remain silent and unmoving, just standing, or lying down if you have fallen down.

Then there will be a third step of fifteen minutes to express what is inside you – your joy from the whole day, your gratitude to existence dancing, singing. And remember, the more you express your joy, the more it will go on growing. So don't be a miser, and don't be afraid of what other people may say. Express your joy like small children.

[*Osho now gives the following explanation for the benefit of the Western seekers present at the meditation camp.*]

This meditation has three steps. The first fifteen minutes, you have to stare at me without blinking. Even if tears come out of your eyes, you have to go on staring at me. You will be standing and staring at me. Your hands will be raised toward the sky, so the cosmic force can come down to you and you are receptive to it. I will be making gestures with my hands all the time for you to jump. When you see my hands moving upward, you have to jump so that your energy starts dancing within. And for the whole time, for the first fifteen-minute step, you have to use the mantra *hoo, hoo*. You are to jump with raised hands with the mantra *hoo, hoo, hoo*! And then I will say to stop. Then you have to stop for fifteen minutes, completely frozen. In this second step close your eyes and remain as you are.

In the third step, for fifteen minutes, you will be requested, invited to express your ecstasy and bliss as madly as possible. Be totally festive. And remember one ultimate law: the more you express your bliss, the more it increases – so don't be a miser.

4

# Alight with the Inner Fire

*"Beguiled by their greed for wealth, the unaware cannot see any other world. They believe that this visible world is all there is, that there is nothing more. In their arrogance, they fall again and again into my clutches.*

*"Many never know that there is a science of the soul, and many cannot understand it even after having heard it. The noble one who can describe the profound science of the soul is a miracle, and the wise one who can receive the truth of the soul is rare. But the one who knows the science of the soul and who has been taught by one who has known truth, is even more miraculous and rare.*

*"Explained by the unenlightened, even when contemplated upon in many ways, the science of the soul is almost impossible to grasp. One cannot enter this subject unless it is taught by an enlightened one because it is the most subtle of the subtle. It is beyond logic.*

*"Beloved, your intelligence has not been acquired through logic: you can intuit self-realization just by being told. Nachiketa, you have true patience. If only I were always to come across such sincere seekers.*

*"I know that the fruits of accumulated past actions are*

*transitory and the eternal cannot be attained through the transitory. This is why, from the transitory, I have distilled the Naachiket Fire. In this way, through the unique power of choicelessness, I have found the eternal.*

*"Nachiketa, I can see that you have so courageously forfeited the heaven where all the pleasures of the senses are available – the heaven which is revered by the world; the heaven which is the gift of the lasting fruit of the yagnas; the heaven which is the place of no fear; the heaven which is noble and whose praise the Vedas have sung in numerous ways; the heaven which is endowed with eons of existence – and I acknowledge your profound intelligence.*

*"By understanding godliness – the godliness hidden behind the veil of Yogamaya, the elusive creative energy of existence; which is omnipresent; which dwells in the inner sanctum of the hearts of all beings; which lives in the dark and dense jungle called the world; which is ancient; which is seen only with great effort; which is attainable through Adhyatma yoga, the discipline of the science of the soul – the patient seeker will go beyond joy and sorrow.*

*"When mortals realize the subtle science of the soul through their own experience, have heard and grasped this teaching of religiousness and have attained to the supreme brahman, which is the abode of bliss, they themselves become imbued with bliss.*

*"For you, Nachiketa, the doors to the ultimate abode are open."*

Before we enter into the sutras, it will be good to understand a few introductory points.

First, we can see only what is already hidden within our own desires. The truth is not visible to us because our eyes can see only what we want to see. There is choice in seeing and there is choice in hearing. We hear only what we want to hear and what we don't want to hear our ears will miss. And what we don't want to see our eyes will not see. Hence every man lives in his own world, the world of his own desires.

Many people are present here and you will all give your own meaning to what I am saying. Everyone will hear what he wants to hear: he will choose whatsoever is meaningful for him and the rest he will discard. Or he will interpret a meaning which fits with, which is in accord with, his desires. In this world we are able to see only what is hidden in our desires.

People ask me, "Where is God?" Now this is a wrong question. The right question would be, "Do I have a longing for godliness?" And unless there is a deep longing for godliness, a deep thirst for godliness, it cannot be seen – not because it does not exist but because your eyes do not *want* to see it. Even if godliness were in front of you, you would miss it. Even if godliness were to knock at your door, you would give some other meaning to it. You would not be able to recognize it.

A river may be flowing nearby, but if you have no thirst you will not take any notice of the river. If there is thirst, only then will you see the river. Only when you have the longing can a thing become visible to you. This phenomenon is so complex that if your thirst is strong, then many times you will even see things which don't exist. And if your thirst is weak, then even that which is will not be visible to you.

We live in the world of our desires and we see and recognize only things which will allow the expansion of our desires. In the East, Yoga has known this truth for a very long time. Now the psychologists in the West are also accepting this truth.

In the last fifty years Western psychologists have discovered many things. One of them is that we are able to see only two percent of the things that exist around us. If one hundred things happen, we are able to see only two of them and we miss ninety-eight of them because our eyes are choosing, our ears are choosing, our hands and our minds are choosing.

So whatsoever you know, it is your own choice, you have chosen it. You don't know the reality. And if your choice is very strong then you will create a world of imagination around you which does not exist in reality. What is happening to people who are locked inside insane asylums? They have projected a world which does not exist anywhere except in their own minds. In their own minds, it exists: if you go to a madhouse you will find someone talking loudly to somebody, but he is alone. The person he is talking to does not exist for you, but he absolutely exists for the madman. He is receiving answers, he is quarreling, and he has no doubt about the presence of the other person. He has created the other man out of his own imagination. Possessed by some deep desire, this imagining has become crystallized.

Thus, in this world, two things are happening: people are seeing things which are not there, and missing things which are really there. This is the first point to be understood.

If you are not able to perceive godliness it simply shows that there is no thirst for it within you. Otherwise, only godliness exists. And on the day the thirst happens within you, all things will start receding and will become transparent and godliness will be visible within them. A tree will be visible then, but only as a form of godliness. There will still be clouds floating in the sky, but only as forms of godliness. There will still be people all around – wives, husbands, children, friends – but all will be but reflections of the splendor of godliness. Godliness will become the center and all else will become its shadow, its reflection. Only godliness will be and all else will go on becoming secondary, more and more irrelevant.

To describe this phenomenon, enlightened people like Shankara have called this world maya, illusion. On the day that godliness becomes real, the world becomes unreal, illusory, maya. But as long as the world seems real to you godliness will seem to be unreal. People who consider this world to be very real ask, "Where is godliness?" They have no idea that their way of seeing, of living, of thinking, their very gestalt, is such that godliness cannot become real for them.

A new school of psychology, Gestalt Psychology, has emerged in Germany based on this concept. It is worth understanding. For example, people look at the floating clouds in the sky and then imagine that they are seeing things in the clouds – but there is nothing in the clouds. Someone might see Lord Krishna playing on his flute: this is a gestalt. It is within the person and it is being projected onto the clouds. Someone else might see a movie actress in the clouds, but there are only clouds. Children can see horses or elephants or fighting demons or fairies flying. Each person will see different things in the same clouds, and everybody is projecting from within. The clouds are functioning as a screen and everybody is projecting his own imagination on them.

You have spread this projection of your imagination all around you. A person may look beautiful to you and nobody else agrees that that person is beautiful – but for you that person is beautiful. You may feel that somebody is very disgusting but he may be very lovely for someone else. So you are not living in the world of facts, you are living in the world of imagination. You are creating your own individual subjective worlds around you out of your imagination. It continuously surrounds you: you think, sit, stand and walk according to this subjective world. And people surrounded by these individual, subjective worlds ask, "Where is godliness?" but there is no longing within them to experience it.

Remember, godliness will be present for you only on the day that you have a deep longing for it. Then there will not even be a single moment's delay. On that day, godliness will become visible to you and all else will become maya, illusion. You see only that for which you are thirsty; your thirst will create godliness. It is not right to say create; rather, it is better to say that you will discover that which is hidden within you.

Godliness is a discovery. And it is not present for you unless you are ready to realize it. Until then it is nonexistent; until then it will be neither seen nor heard nor touched. Although all touch is of godliness, all visions are of godliness and all sounds are of godliness, to recognize this, a deep longing and enormous patience are needed.

Now we will enter into the sutras.

Yama said to Nachiketa:

> *"Beguiled by their greed for wealth, the unaware cannot see any other world."*

The one who finds meaning in wealth cannot conceive that there is any meaning in the soul, in being. The two are opposites. If money is very valuable to you, then the soul, the being, cannot be valuable at all. One who feels the journey into worldly fame, pride and ego to be of value will find meditation to be worthless because the adventure into meditation is a totally opposite dimension; its whole process is different.

With ego you have to spread your influence over others, whereas in meditation you dissolve and disappear to such an extent that you cannot be found as a separate entity. With the ego, you have to accumulate things and the power that comes with them, and in doing this you will become filled with tension, anxiety and restlessness. Then restlessness will become your destiny. In meditation you will have to drop tensions and worries completely and become so tranquil, as if you no longer exist. You become nonexistent; you exist as if you are nobody.

The dimensions of ego and meditation are diametrically opposite. This is why if the outer journey is still significant to someone, then the higher dimension of consciousness will have no significance for him. He will not be ready to perceive it; rather, he will be busy with just the opposite.

You may have seen in some children's book a line drawing in which there are two faces, one of an old woman and the other of a young woman, and both are in the same sketch. The interesting thing is that when you see the old woman you cannot see the young woman because the lines of the old woman's face will catch hold of your attention and you will not be able to see the face of the young woman which is hidden in it. If you see the young woman first then you will find it difficult to see the old woman. But if you continue to look at the picture, the young woman will disappear and the old woman will appear because your perception is constantly changing.

Nothing in the world is fixed. Or if you were seeing the old woman first, she will disappear and the young woman's face will appear – but the strange thing is that you cannot see both faces at the same time. You can see both faces, but only one at a time. Even if you have seen both figures and you know that both figures are hidden in one drawing, still you will not be able to see both figures simultaneously. When you see one, then in this very choice the lines of the other picture will be lost; when you see the other picture, then in that very choice the lines of the first picture will be lost. You know that the other face is hidden there all the time, but there is no way to see both faces at the same time.

If you see a friend in a person, you cannot see an enemy in him. You can see an enemy in him tomorrow, but then there will be no way to see the friend in him. You can find a friend in the morning and an enemy in the evening in the same person. Then you know that the friend and the enemy are both hidden in him – but in any one moment you cannot see both at the same time.

In the morning you fight with your wife and you feel that she is an enemy, a poison, but by the evening love has returned. Then you totally forget that she is poison, then she becomes nectar. Tomorrow morning she may become poison again, but it is impossible to see both together. You can see only one face at a time. It is not possible to see opposites together.

The other world is hidden in this world. Godliness is hidden in matter. Godliness is hidden in every particle of matter, but as long as you are obsessed with the material, you have chosen one picture and the other picture will not appear to your eyes.

And this is not so only with you: even for the enlightened ones there is the same difficulty. When they begin to see the *brahman*, the divine, then they cannot see the transitory, the material world. They *cannot* see it. That is why they call the world maya, illusion.

You will find this difficult to understand because when Shankara says that this world is an illusion, you feel that it must be a philosophical statement because if you hit Shankara's foot with a stone, blood will flow. If a stone is rolling toward his feet, Shankara will pull his leg away to save it from the stone. He feels hunger and thirst. He has to drink water – to drink existence is not enough; he has to eat food, to eat the divine is not enough. You feel a difficulty when you hear Shankara saying that the world is an illusion, unreal. You think, "Then why is he using unreal things? Then why is he living with these unreal, illusory things? If the world is unreal then who is Shankara talking to? There is nobody to listen to him."

You feel this difficulty because you feel that this world is real. Godliness does not look real to you. But Shankara also has his own difficulty: he is seeing the reality of godliness because for him, the world has disappeared. If you throw a stone at his foot he will feel that something divine is being thrown at him. But it is difficult for you to understand that when Shankara pulls his foot away he is not saving his foot from the stone, he is saving godliness within the stone from touching his insignificant foot.

There is an old Buddhist anecdote:

A Buddhist monk told his disciple that only godliness resides in everything. The disciple understood it rationally and became convinced because the master was charismatic and the young disciple was deeply impressed by him. He believed whatsoever his master said.

One day, he was walking along a road when a mad elephant came rushing toward him. The elephant driver shouted at everybody to get out of the way, but the young disciple thought that godliness, the *brahman* which is everywhere, was also in the elephant, so he was not afraid and he did not move out of the way. But the elephant was mad, and it had none of this philosophy or wisdom. And the elephant also did not know that this young man was a disciple of a famous spiritual master. So the mad elephant caught hold of the young man with his trunk and threw him down and the disciple was badly wounded.

Tattered and dirty, he went crying to the master saying, "You taught me something that wasn't true. Your *brahman*, which is everywhere, didn't take care of me at all today!"

The master said, "The godliness in the elephant was mad and godliness in the elephant driver was shouting to get out of the way, so why didn't you listen to him and move? And why didn't you listen to the godly voice of within you that was telling you to get out of the way?"

It will be difficult for you to understand this. When you are engaged in seeing the mundane world, it will be very difficult for you to understand the language of the inner world. The possibility for misunderstanding is always greater than the possibility for understanding.

For Shankara, it is godliness that is falling in a stone, it is godliness that wants to move away; it is godliness that will be hurt and it is godliness which hurts. For you, everything is material: the stone is matter and the foot is also matter, and one piece of matter is hurting another piece of matter. For Shankara, both are godly: for him matter has disappeared and godliness is hurting godliness. And if matter can hurt matter, there is no reason why godliness cannot hurt godliness. But the whole gestalt has changed: wherever there was matter, now there is godliness. Matter has disappeared and only godliness is.

The difficulties that unconscious people and the enlightened ones have are not much different; it is actually one difficulty. The eyes of unconscious people are focused on the world and to them godliness is not visible, and the eyes of the enlightened ones are focused on godliness and the material world does not exist for them. This is why the worldly man says that God does not exist. This is the declaration of the atheist, and the atheist is the totally worldly man. He is just the opposite of the awakened man: he is saying that godliness is unreal, an illusion. And the enlightened one is just the opposite of the atheist: he says that the world is unreal and godliness is real, and the real can only be one because he sees only godliness.

Yama said to Nachiketa:

> *"Beguiled by their greed for wealth, the unaware cannot see any other world. They believe that this visible world is all there is, that there is nothing more. In their arrogance, they fall again and again into my clutches."*

A person who is totally lost in the world of desires and who is obsessed with *sansara*, the material world, will die again and again. He will die and be reborn again and again because he is clinging only to the visible.

The body is visible but the soul is not visible. The soul will never be visible because the soul is the very seer. It can never become an object that can be seen; it is always the seer, it is always the one who sees. The soul itself cannot become an object to be seen. The body is not an observer, it is the observed. The body is an object, it is matter. The soul is awareness, it is the knowing watcher, consciousness – and there is no way to see the watcher.

The body is visible to you. For the person who believes that what is visible to the eyes is the only truth, then the seer which is beyond the eyes will be the untruth. But remember, the eyes are in between: on the outer side of the eyes is the world and behind the eyes is godliness. The one who says that he can trust only what is in front of his eyes will not be able to see what is hidden behind his eyes, it will not be visible. Such a man will trust everything else but he will not trust his own being.

Science also makes the same mistake in thinking that what is visible is real and what is not visible, the consciousness hidden within us and which can see everything, is unreal. This is absurd! The whole conclusion of science is that science is the truth and the scientist is not: the scientist is an untruth. It is a very strange conclusion. We can agree and believe in what Einstein says as well as with his experiments. And Einstein also believes in what he has experimented with in the laboratory. But with the one who is conducting the experiments, with the one who is sitting within and doing all the research, by and by, the relationship with that one is broken. The eyes become fixed on the outside reality, and any fixation is a disease. Your vision becomes used to only looking outward. Then you forget to close your eyes, you forget that there is also something within you.

Yama is saying to Nachiketa that the man who takes matter, the visible, as the only reality will miss that which is invisible, hidden, mysterious, subtle; that which is but which is not apparent – because it is the very seer itself. For this reason, there is no way for it to be an object.

*"In their arrogance, they fall again and again into my clutches."* Only the irreligious person dies, the truly religious person cannot die. You will be surprised to hear this because you see a religious person also dying, his dead body is also taken to the crematorium. But he really cannot die because he has known the seer, the witness which is immortal. Only the body of a religious person dies. But the irreligious person feels that *he* is dying in his totality. Although he too cannot die, he feels that his body is all there is. This is why when his body is dying he feels as if *he* is dying.

Only the irreligious man dies. And if you are afraid of death, then know well that you are irreligious. What you say does not reflect who you are. It does not matter how much you may shout that you are a religious man. It is of no importance how much you may say that you believe in the soul and that you trust in existence. You may be going to the temples and mosques to pray, but that also does not matter. If you are afraid of death, then you are irreligious. This is the real criterion.

The true man of religion will not be afraid of death. There is no question of fear because he knows there is no death.

When Ramakrishna was dying, his wife, Sharda, started to cry and he asked her to stop. His death was certain: the doctors had told him that he was suffering from cancer, and in those days there was no treatment for cancer. Ramakrishna asked his wife not to cry. But Sharda said, "You are leaving me, I am going to become a widow. You are dying and you ask me not to cry?"

Ramakrishna said, "You will not become a widow! I am not dying, because I cannot die. Only this body is dying. If you were a wife only to this body, if you had a relationship only with the body, then it would be okay, you could weep. But if you have a relationship with *me,* then I will be only changing my clothes."

Perhaps there has been no other woman in the whole history of India who even after the death of her husband did not become a widow. Sharda was such a woman.

When the other women gathered after the death of Ramakrishna, they asked Sharda to break her bangles and change her clothes to the clothes of a widow. Sharda refused to do it. She said to the women, "Ramakrishna has told me that he will not die, so there is no need for me to live like a widow by breaking my bangles and changing my clothes."

Ramakrishna said that he was only changing his "clothes." For the man of religion, death is nothing more than a change of clothes. It is just like shifting into a new house from the old, dilapidated one. It is as if you are casting off old clothes and putting on new ones, or taking all the clothes off and remaining naked.

An irreligious man will repeatedly fall into the clutches of death – and it is not because of death but because of him. But actually, you are not afraid because of death; you are only afraid because of your ignorance about death.

Yama is revealing an important fact: that only the irreligious man comes into his clutches. The real religious man does not because he trusts in that which is deathless. The irreligious man trusts only in the mortal.

> *"Many never know that there is a science of the soul, and many cannot understand it even after having heard it. The noble one who can describe the profound science of the soul is a miracle, and the wise one who can receive the truth of the soul is rare. But the one who knows the science of the soul and who has been taught by one who has known truth, is even more miraculous and rare."*

Yama is saying that there are many who never even hear about the science of the soul. And even if they do hear about it, they are unable to listen and understand it. Even if they do come across a Buddha, they manage to escape; they try to save themselves. Even when a Mahavira is present and speaking, the words do not reach their ears, their ears are tightly plugged.

Jesus has said in the Bible many times, "He who has eyes will see me, he who has ears will hear me." But everyone has eyes and ears: was he always speaking to the blind and the deaf? No, he was speaking to people like you, with eyes and ears. He was not addressing blind and deaf people – but this whole humanity is a crowd of blind and deaf people.

It is difficult to see a Jesus. There is the body of Jesus which is visible to everyone, and then there is the soul of Jesus which is visible only to those who are in deep silence, in emptiness – who are in a state of meditation. For them, the outer, physical form of Jesus recedes and his luminous being, which is full of splendor and wisdom, becomes clear.

This is why there are bound to be two opinions about Jesus. One opinion is of the blind people, who crucified Jesus. They said that he is an ordinary man and he is claiming to be the only begotten son of God. As far as they could see, what they were saying was not wrong, it was true. They knew that he was the son of Joseph and Mary, so how could he be the son of God? But the one who was speaking was certainly the son of God. And that divine being does not end at Jesus: the son of God is also present within you.

Once a Christian priest came to see me and said, "Jesus is the only begotten son of God."

I told him, "Everybody is the only begotten son of God."

He asked me, "But how is it possible?"

Whosoever experiences godliness will know that he has come from the same existential source. This is the real meaning of being the son of God: one feels, "I am a spark of the same divine flame, I am a ray of the same divine light." One who experiences godliness will feel, "I am alone, I am the only one" because he will feel himself to be utterly alone. Nobody else will be there. In that moment the whole universe will disappear: you will remain all alone, just you and existence. The distance between you and existence will also disappear. If existence is the supreme sun and you are its ray, in that moment of experiencing, you will be the only ray.

What was godly in Jesus was not visible to all, only to a few. And it is strange that the few who could see were all uneducated, rustic people. It was not visible to the scholars; rather, they crucified Jesus – the scholars who were full of knowledge, the scholars who were the knowers of scriptures, the scholars who could illustrate the scriptures. They were the high priests who held the authority in the temples. The high priest and the council of priests of the great temple of Jerusalem had also given their consent for the crucifixion of Jesus. Actually, these are the people who tried their best that Jesus should be crucified.

The people who could see the godly, luminous form of Jesus were simple weavers, fishermen, farmers, simple and innocent villagers. They were not men of words or scriptures. They trusted Jesus. They could see. It happens many times that the more layers of knowledge gather on your intellect, the less is your capacity to see. The world is less religious today – and it is not because there are more irreligious people, it is because of the increase of knowledge. The more knowledgeable you are, the more difficult it will be to have a contact with existence.

Yama is saying: *"Many never know that there is a science of the soul..."* Even if it reaches your ears, it is not heard. And even if it enters your ears, it is in vain.

*"...many cannot understand it even after having heard it."* You may hear it, but to hear it and to understand it are two totally different things. Some people think that just hearing is equal to understanding. Some people have read the Gita and think that reading it is understanding. But even if they have memorized the Gita it makes no difference because understanding is a very different matter.

Understanding means experiencing. Understanding means realization. What you have heard should also become your realization.

For example, you have heard that a roseflower has a fragrance; you may have heard it and memorized it. Now even if somebody were to wake you from sleep and ask you about the rose, you will say that there is a fragrance in the roseflower. But if this fragrance has never touched your nostrils, if it has never entered your heart, if this fragrance has not touched your breath and if you have in no way experienced the fragrance, then the words "the roseflower has a fragrance" will be your knowledge but not your understanding, your realization.

Knowledge and understanding are not synonymous. Understanding is a totally different dimension. Understanding means you have also realized what you have heard through your own experience. You have also lived it. What you have heard has become your realization and your experience.

Knowledge can be stolen, knowledge can be destroyed, contrary arguments can be given against your knowledge. But there is no way to take away your understanding. No logic can destroy your understanding; understanding rises above all arguments.

You touch fire and find that your hands get burned: now if all the scholars of the world were to tell you that fire is cool and give arguments for it, you would say, "Keep your arguments to yourself. I have touched fire and I have experienced that my hands were burned."

Nobody can influence you against your own experience, but anybody can influence you against your knowledge because knowledge has no roots within you.

In many Indian forests there is a particular yellowish creeper called *amarbel.* This creeper has no roots of its own, but it spreads over the other trees. It depends totally on them for its food and nutrition. It exploits them. It has no life source of its own, it has no contact with the earth. Knowledge is like the *amarbel.* What you call scholarship is also like the *amarbel*: it has no roots of its own, it has no connection with the sources of life energy. It has no penetration into experience.

Understanding is like a tree whose roots have reached very deep into the earth and have found the hidden sources of water. Such a tree can live on its own, it is not dependent on others. A scholar always lives on the authority of others. He says, "It is written in the Gita, therefore it is true. It is written in the Koran, therefore it is true." He says, "Mohammed has said it, therefore it is true" – but he does not have any treasure of his own experience.

The enlightened one says, "This is my experience, hence it is true. And if the Bible, Gita and Vedas are against it, then they must be wrong. There is no way for my experience to be wrong. My own realization is above all scriptures."

That is why it is said that the ultimate Veda, the ultimate knowledge, is hidden within. Only the people who have no experience, no realization of the inner, depend on the outer knowledge. The ultimate master is hidden within. One has to depend on the outside master only as long as one has not yet come into contact and communion with one's own inner master.

Yama says: *"...many cannot understand it even after having heard it. The noble one who can describe the profound science of the soul is a miracle..."* It may be difficult for you to understand this statement of Yama's because all around you there is no shortage of gurus. There is no scarcity of people who teach. In fact, there is a shortage of disciples but there is no shortage of gurus! That is why there is so much mischief going on: gurus are trying to pull the followers of other gurus into their own fold. If a disciple goes to a guru he is asked not to go elsewhere, even by mistake, because he will be led astray. The disciples are very few and there is great struggle and competition among the gurus. It is just like a bazaar where there are many shops and very few customers: each shopkeeper will be against all the other shopkeepers. There is a shortage of goods. There is also a shortage of disciples: disciples are very few and gurus are many.

The truth is that nobody wants to be a disciple. Nobody wants to go through the trouble of becoming a disciple when he can just immediately become a guru! It is trouble to become a disciple, because to be a disciple means to dissolve, to disappear, to surrender, to efface yourself. Only then can you learn. But it is a great joy to become a guru because there is no need to surrender and dissolve. On the contrary, there is joy in making others surrender. A guru can save his ego and the surrender of disciples can strengthen his ego. The more numerous the disciples, the greater the ego becomes. This is why the gurus go on counting and remembering how many disciples they have: "How many hundreds of thousands have come?" Every new disciple's arrival becomes food for his ego. Everybody wants to be a guru but nobody wants to be a disciple.

But unless one has passed through the stage of disciplehood, there is no possibility of becoming a guru. Then the whole thing is a deception. One who has not ceased to be himself cannot help others to drop their ego. He can kill but he cannot create surrender. He can destroy but he cannot create emptiness in the other.

That is why near the so-called gurus, disciples become crippled; their hands and feet are cut, their intelligence is destroyed. They become dull and mediocre. Their stupidity is deepened and there is no opening toward ultimate illumination. So surrendering does not mean becoming crippled or paralyzed; but a so-called guru whose ego is still there can do only that with his disciples.

A master is one who has ceased to be. In his presence you can also cease to be; otherwise it is not possible.

Yama is rightly saying that a man who can make you understand the truth is rare. He is rare for two reasons: one, it is very difficult to find a man who has disappeared as an ego. Even if you were to meet such a man, he may not be one of those who can communicate his experience. Out of one hundred people who become enlightened, only one will be able to say what has happened to him.

Many people become enlightened, but they are not many in comparison to the great number of unconscious people. In that sense, they are very few. Out of millions of men one becomes enlightened, and out of hundreds of enlightened people one happens to be a master. All enlightened people cannot be masters.

The Jainas have defined it very systematically. According to them all *kewalgyanis*, all enlightened people, do not become tirthankaras, masters. To attain to enlightenment is one thing, but it is much more difficult to help someone else to experience it. Truth can never be defined in words and to express, to explain, to make others understand and realize what has been experienced, is a matter of great expertise.

That is why in the Jaina terminology those who, over many lives, have accumulated the necessary conditions and desires to become a master, those who have created a *tirthankara bandha,* an energetic intention and inclination to become a master; those who have learned over many lives the art of expressing their experiences in words – when these individuals finally experience the inner truth, then a rare one out of these becomes capable of expressing and communicating it to others. Sometimes it is centuries before someone is able to put his inner experience into words and give it the right shape and form. It takes centuries for someone to be able to translate his experience into a living teaching. It is really very difficult.

The sun rises in the morning, but rarely does anyone see it because he is going to the factory or to the office, or going to drop the children off at school. It is very difficult to see the morning sun. And even if the sunlight is falling on your eyes it is not certain that you will see the sun because if your mind is wandering somewhere else and you happen to see the sun rising, then the beauty of the rising sun does not blossom within you. You will simply keep going as if you have not seen the sun. Among thousands of men, sometimes one man stops, and sees the beauty of the rising sun, and he finds that something is rising within him which feels the beauty of the sunrise. Out of thousands of people who experience the beauty of the sunrise, one person may be able to paint a picture of the sunrise because only one may be a painter. Or among them, one may be a poet who will be able to describe his experience in a poem.

But the beauty of the sun is very earthly, very mundane. The beauty of the ultimate truth is unearthly. There can be no painting of it, no poetry can be created about it. How to give a form to it? When the experience of the formless, the ultimate truth, happens, then out of thousands of these enlightened mystics, only rarely does one happen to be a master.

That is why such a big crowd of the so-called gurus can continue to operate in the world. A *satguru,* an authentic master, happens once in centuries. And it is a strange fact that whenever a real master appears all the so-called gurus go against him.

If Jesus were here then all the phony gurus would go against him; if a Mahavira were to appear all the so-called gurus would be against him; when buddhas appear the so-called gurus are against them. All the contemporary so-called masters will turn against him because a man who brings his authentic experience of truth will destroy the business of all the phony gurus who are trading on their borrowed knowledge. So whenever all the so-called gurus gather against one master, then you should consider that master carefully.

All the so-called gurus fight with each other and don't agree on any point – but they all join together against a *satguru*, a true master. On this matter they all agree. They drop all their disputes and totally agree to join together to fight against the true masters because the true master will collectively cut the very roots of their exploitation.

Rare and wonderful is the man who can describe the profound science of the soul. And even the one who has found such a man is not less skilled because although it is difficult to express it, it is also not an easy thing to listen to it. It is difficult to listen and even more difficult to understand it than to express it. For these reasons it is not only rare to find a real master, but it is equally rare to find a true disciple. And whenever the meeting of a true master and a true disciple happens, the nectar showers.

This is why Yama says,

> *"Nachiketa, you have true patience. If only I were always to come across such sincere seekers."*

This meeting was a moment of bliss not only for Nachiketa, the disciple, but also for Yama, the master. When a Buddha meets a Sariputta or a Mahavira meets a Gautama or a Jesus meets Peter or John, the nectar showers.

Yama continued:

> *"Explained by the unenlightened, even when contemplated*

> *upon in many ways, the science of the soul is almost impossible to grasp. One cannot enter this subject unless it is taught by an enlightened one because it is the most subtle of the subtle. It is beyond logic."*

A very deep meaning is hidden in this sutra. Yama is saying that it is not possible to become enlightened without a master. This is a very controversial issue. Most of the traditions say that enlightenment is not possible without a master. But in some traditions there have been very unique people who have said that enlightenment can never happen through a master. Buddha is the foremost among them. Just before dying Buddha said to Ananda, "*Appa deepo bhava*: be a light unto yourself. He is saying that nobody else can give you enlightenment.

In this century Krishnamurti has been constantly declaring that a master is a hindrance and that enlightenment cannot happen through a master. He has constantly been telling people around him for the past forty years to beware and to keep away from masters. On the other hand, there are the rishis of the Upanishads, the eighty-four *siddhas* and a long tradition of Indian mystics such as Nanak, Kabir and Dadu who have been declaring to the whole world that enlightenment is not possible without a master.

The most interesting thing is that both statements are true. Anybody who takes only one to be true will go astray. This is my own statement. I say this because both views are true simultaneously, but to choose one of the two will lead you astray. A man who clings to the idea that enlightenment is not possible without a master will go astray because of his clinging too much to the master. And a man who strongly clings to the belief that the master is a hindrance will also go astray in the absence of a master.

To cling to the master and then to let go of the master are two stages of one single process. There is a stage when one has to hold on to a master because without a master there is no beginning. Then later on comes another stage when one has to let go of the master because one cannot grow any further with the master. A master is like a ladder: one has to climb it and then one has to let go of the ladder too.

But there are some who say that one can only reach the goal through a ladder and without a ladder one cannot reach. They are right because how can you go up without climbing a ladder? But these people emphasize it so much and then you become so attached to the ladder that you do not want to let go of it even after you have climbed up to the last rung. You say, "The ladder brought us up to here and any talk of letting go of it is wrong." So you stay on the ladder, and to stay on the ladder is not an achievement of any sort. Just as you had climbed the ladder from the first step, so must you let go of it at the last step.

But some people argue that if a ladder has to be left behind in the end, why should one bother to climb it at all? Those people will remain on the ground. One has to climb the ladder but one has to let go of it also. One has to come close to a master but a time will come when one has to go beyond the master. The *satguru*, the real master, is one who allows you to remain with him as long as you are climbing up the ladder. But before any attachment or clinging to the ladder happens, the real master will break the ladder; he will remove the bridge that is in between.

Buddha told Ananda to be a light unto himself – but this was told to Ananda, who was standing on the very last rung of the ladder. This context has been completely forgotten because Ananda became enlightened only one day after the death of Buddha – just the next day! He was standing on the last rung of the ladder and the ladder had become an obstacle.

Ananda said to Buddha, "I could not become enlightened while you were in the body. Now you are leaving me, so what will happen to me?"

Buddha told him, "Maybe it is because of me that you are not becoming enlightened – and now it is right for me to leave."

On the very next day, Ananda became enlightened.

The same thing happened to Gautama, the chief disciple of Mahavira. Gautama could not become enlightened during the life of Mahavira.

At first it is difficult to be with a master, but once you have been with a master it is even more difficult to let go of him. In the first place it is difficult to come close to a master because it implies dropping the ego; it is very difficult and painful. The ego looks for ways to avoid the master.

Most of Krishnamurti's listeners are egoists who want some rationalization to keep themselves away from the master. They are very satisfied with Krishnamurti. They want to avoid a ladder because in going up the ladder they will have to transform themselves. They are reassured by listening to Krishnamurti that they themselves are sufficient, that a master is not necessary, that they can find enlightenment alone. Because of Krishnamurti – although he was right – thousands of people have been harmed because of that true statement. And Yama is saying the same thing: that unconscious people create many problems.

But this has not happened only with Krishnamurti: because of Nanak, Kabir and Dadu, all of whom have said that enlightenment cannot happen without a master, millions of people have been harmed. But in fact, the harm has not happened because of these masters. There are people who will always cause themselves harm no matter what the master does.

This last category of people catch hold of their masters and say, "Now nothing more is needed to be done on our part." They cling to the feet of the master because they believe that there will be no possibility of enlightenment without a master, as if the master is the end. The master is not the end, he is a means; he is just an indication.

For example, I point my finger at the moon and instead of looking at the moon you catch hold of my finger! The finger is not the moon. The one who catches hold of my finger will never look at the moon, he will remain stuck with my finger.

Forget my finger, let go of the indicator. The finger is needed only so that your eyes can look at the moon. After that the finger will not be needed. But still, people have got stuck with their masters.

A friend has been coming to me for many years. He is a great devotee of Meher Baba. About thirty years ago he surrendered everything to Meher Baba and after that he did nothing. He would say, "Now there is nothing to be done. Now when Meher Baba wants, it will happen."

It is a very beautiful idea. But that friend continued to tell lies and to indulge in drinking alcohol. He continued to live as before, but now he had this excuse to hide his weaknesses: "Now, whenever Meher Baba wants, it will happen. I have left everything to the master."

Nothing has changed. Only the words are there and they have become an excuse, a hiding device – nothing has changed even a bit. If really everything had been left to the master, his whole life would have been totally transformed. It is bound to be so. But his life is the same as it was when he was living for his ego; his ego has remained the same.

An egoless person cannot abuse alcohol. He cannot abuse it because people drink to forget their ego problems. When there is no ego there is nothing left to forget – so the egoless person has no reason to drink alcohol. The egoless person is never angry because you become angry only when your ego is hurt.

So I used to tell that friend, "You become angry, you are a drunkard, you are doing everything exactly the same as before – stealing, cheating, lying. You are exactly the same as you were before meeting Meher Baba!" But again and again he would say that he has surrendered everything to the master and that now whatever the master wills is good for him.

So there are people who surrender everything to the master and there are also people who escape from the master. But I say unto you that you have to hold on to the master and later on you need to remember to also let go of the master.

A master is a great help in the beginning of your journey and he is a great obstacle at the end of your journey – but a master is essential in the beginning.

This is what Yama is saying to Nachiketa: *"One cannot enter this subject unless it is taught by an enlightened one..."* This has to be noted, that Yama too is only saying that one will be unable to *enter*. Initiation is not possible without a master – but the end of the journey always happens in aloneness, never with anyone else. On the first step, the first push, the first inspiration is like a lighted lamp coming close to an unlit lamp: just one jump of the flame and the unlit lamp will be lit. Then the first lamp from which the spark has come is no longer needed because now the second lamp will burn on its own. Once a lamp is lit then its own flame will go on giving light. Now its own journey has begun.

As long as a disciple's inner lamp is not lit, a master is needed. But as soon as it is lit the master is no longer needed.

You can understand it in this way: nobody can be born by himself, on his own, a mother is needed. But also, nobody can stay in the womb indefinitely. If someone were to decide that because the mother has conceived him in her womb, has given him life, he will remain in it, then both the mother and the child would die. But for the nine months, the initiation will continue. For nine months the lamp of the child will burn through the mother's light; for nine months the mother's breath will be the child's breath; for nine months the mother's blood will function as the child's blood. Because for these nine months the child is not separate from the mother – she is the child's heartbeat. But as soon as the child's body has developed to a certain point, as soon as the lamp is ready to be lit with its own oil and wick, as soon as the body's mechanisms are ready and the lungs of the child are ready to breathe on their own, then the baby has to come out of the womb.

But then because of her ignorance the mother also wants to keep the child in her womb, just as the child wants to remain inside the womb. This is why there is so much pain in the birth process; otherwise there is no reason for any pain during the delivery.

Scientists say that the process of labor can be an experience of bliss as much as it is an experience of pain. In France, many experiments have been done which prove that pain can be totally eliminated from a delivery. It is a very easy method: the mother should be willing for the child to come out. Normally she is preventing it and contracting; her whole system withdraws. Nature pushes the child out and she tries to prevent it. But the baby also wants to remain inside because the mother's womb is very peaceful. It is almost like nirvana, the lotus paradise: there are no worries, no work, no responsibility, no pain, no inconvenience.

Science has developed so much, but we have not been able to create anywhere as comfortable as a womb. A child in the womb is as happy as the god Vishnu floating in *kshirasagar*, an ocean of milk. Actually, there is no difference because in the womb the child also floats in a certain fluid and this fluid has exactly the same proportion of salt and other chemicals as that which is found in ocean water.

Scientists say that because man has evolved from the fish, in the early stages of development the human child requires the same type of environment as a fish. Hence the womb has a similar environment to that of the ocean. That is why pregnant women start eating more salt, and also clay. The salt in her body is being drawn away continuously by the womb because the womb needs to have a similar kind of water to that of the sea. The child in the womb floats in this fluid – the child is in a *kshirasagar*, an ocean.

But in nine months the child's body will be ready to come out of the womb. If by accident the child comes out of the womb before nine months, it is dangerous for his life because his body is still underdeveloped. It will be half dead. A premature delivery can be fatal for the child; he should complete the full nine months.

But the child also wants to remain in the womb. This is why psychologists say that when a child is born, the greatest pain of his life happens. They call it "birth trauma." The child goes through a great shock because life in the womb has been so comfortable; now suddenly it comes out into an uncomfortable life. Its first task is to breathe, which is very painful for the child. For someone who has never breathed by himself, to breathe for the first time is painful. And out of the womb the child feels insecure, incomplete and helpless. The child wants to stay inside the womb and the mother also wants to keep the child in her womb while nature is pushing the child out – hence the pain, the labor pains.

Many scientific experiments have been done with birth. Hypnotherapists have hypnotized many pregnant women and given them suggestions that the delivery process is not painful but is very blissful, that they should let the child come out, that they should be in a let-go, relaxed, not resisting but allowing the child to come out of the womb smoothly. They found that then there was no pain during the delivery process.

In France, this new method has been developed in which hundreds of thousands of women have given birth to children without pain. This new method is a first step in this direction: when this method is further developed a woman will experience a great orgasmic joy in giving birth to a child. She will never experience such great joy from anything else because it is a great creative phenomenon. When the burden and the tensions of nine months of pregnancy are suddenly released in a moment, there comes such a deep peace and weightlessness within, like the experience after a storm.

But most mothers are deprived of this joy. The mother not only wants to hold on to the child in her womb, but later on in life she will also try to possess her son until he marries and brings his young wife home.

The real cause of the endless conflict between a mother-in-law and the daughter-in-law begins in the mother's womb. The wife tries to make her husband totally independent from his mother, so the struggle which had started in the womb is being brought to its culmination by the daughter-in-law. She tries to make her husband totally free of his mother by demanding his total attention. Hence it is difficult to reduce the enmity between the mother-in-law and the daughter-in-law because the problem has started in his mother's womb.

If a mother can give birth to her son spontaneously and joyfully, then no conflict will arise with her daughter-in-law because she will be happy that her son is becoming more and more free and independent of her.

Just the same as these foolish mothers, there is also a crowd of pseudo-masters who want to keep and possess their disciples. They are just like ordinary mothers. Then the separation of a disciple will become painful for both the master and the disciple. These pseudo-masters create all kinds of difficulties, all kinds of fear and greed to prevent the disciple from leaving them.

But these pseudo-masters have not known the truth. If they did, as soon as the disciple matures and is ready to go on his own, the first work of an authentic master will be to tell him, as Buddha did, "Be a light unto yourself. Now leave me. Go ahead on your journey alone. And now forget me, as if I were not here at all."

A true mother will always try to make her son independent, and a true master will try in every way to make the disciple free of him as soon as the disciple is mature.

The disciple must enter the womb of the master. To become a disciple means to enter the womb of the master – not into any physical womb, but into the womb of the master's energy field. And when a certain maturity happens then there is the courage in the disciple to come out of the womb.

Yama said,

> *"Beloved, your intelligence has not been acquired through*

> *logic: you can intuit self-realization just by being told. Nachiketa, you have true patience. If only I were always to come across such sincere seekers."*

The trust that Nachiketa has cannot be attained through reasoning. Howsoever much you may think and reason, you cannot become innocent through thinking. By thinking you become clever and cunning. You become innocent and simple only when you are tired of thinking, when you become aware that by thinking you can only go mad. Then you will put aside all thinking. On that day, you become innocent; trust is born.

Remember, to know the outer world reasoning is needed. Matter can be known by reasoning. But to know the existential the search begins through trust. The two journeys are in opposite directions. To know the material world you have to move outward and for this, the more you think, the better. To know yourself you have to move inward, the direction changes. And to go within, the less reasoning there is the better.

Innocence will take you inward, complexity will take you outward. Hence the thinking of a scientist becomes very complex. As the education in the various sciences goes on growing, people will lose their peace of mind and their contact with their inner being will be cut off more and more. *"Beloved, your intelligence has not been acquired through logic…"* But the intellect can do one job: it can be useful in understanding the words of the enlightened one; it has this much use. And as soon as you have understood the words, the intellect should be put aside.

> *"I know that the fruits of accumulated past actions are transitory and the eternal cannot be attained through the transitory. This is why, from the transitory, I have distilled the Naachiket Fire. In this way, through the unique power of choicelessness, I have found the eternal."*

Yama is saying that by passing through the process of inner

fire and being burned in it, he has come to the realization of godliness. In honor and in memory of Nachiketa, Yama gives the name "Naachiket Fire" to this inner fire.

A few things need to be understood about this inner fire. Firstly, as Yama has said, this fire is hidden in the innermost core of your heart; it is within you. In fact, you are alive because of this fire. This is why if the heat of your body drops below ninety-eight degrees, death will start approaching. If the body temperature rises above one hundred and ten or twelve degrees, death will also start approaching. If the body heat is maintained between ninety-eight and one hundred ten degrees, you can remain in the body; otherwise your connection with the body will be broken.

Out of the fire that is burning in your heart, a certain amount of it reaches to your body; the body can live only within that range of temperature. If the heat goes below a certain point your connection with your body will start falling away. If the heat rises above a certain point the body will begin to die. And this fire is within you.

You know only one use for this fire and that is just to continue to live in the body. There is another use for this fire, and that is to go beyond the body. This fire is energy: it can become a vehicle to go beyond the body. Just as this fire keeps you in the body, it can also take you to the bodiless reality.

Always remember one thing: the path on which you go out also has to be used to go in. Only the direction will change but the path will be the same. Right now this inner fire is flowing toward the body. One has to learn the alchemy for making the fire flow toward the soul.

The first step in working with this Naachiket Fire is that the direction of its flow has to be changed. At present it is flowing outward and downward. This flow has to move inward and upward. This is the first task.

The second thing is that you are continuously breathing to keep this inner fire burning. Science also agrees with this –

without oxygen you cannot live. When a candle is burning what is happening? What is a flame? In fact, when a candle is burning, the oxygen that is present in the surrounding atmosphere is what is burning. If strong winds start blowing you may become worried about protecting the flame and you may put an empty jar upside down over the candle to protect it. It was possible that the wind may not have blown the candle out, but the jar over it will certainly put it out very quickly because as soon as the oxygen in the jar is burned the flame will be extinguished.

You have to breathe constantly for twenty-four hours. If your breathing stops for a few minutes, you will die because your breathing takes in oxygen and keeps the inner fire burning. Your life will be only as dynamic as the depth of your breathing. The deeper your breathing, the healthier and more alive you will be. As your breathing becomes shallower, your life will become more and more dull and dead because the fire will be burning less. And you all are breathing in a very shallow way. There are reasons for this shallow breathing.

Scientists say, and for centuries Yoga has also been saying, that until man is taught to breathe deeply, he cannot live fully. And one who is not fully alive does not have enough energy to move. This is why Yoga has invented many breathing techniques. The breathing techniques are devised to make your inner fire burn more intensely, so that the excess fire created can be used for the inner journey. This fire is fuel, energy. It is like putting petrol in a car so that it can run. Petrol is a dormant fire, a dormant energy, but you also cannot live without fire, without fuel.

All life is because of this inner fire. The trees are alive through taking fuel for their fire from the air. The birds and the animals are alive through consuming oxygen. The whole of life is this fire.

The amount and intensity of this inner fire is in direct proportion to the depth of your breathing. But only children breathe deeply. Watch a child sleeping: his stomach moves up and down, his breathing goes right down to the navel. Watch an adult sleeping: his chest moves up and down but his breathing does not go to the navel, it remains shallow. There are several thousand pores in a person's lungs out of which less than half absorb oxygen. The remainder are filled with carbon dioxide, which can cause death. It is a dead gas with no fire in it. Thousands of diseases grow in our bodies simply because of this dead gas. Deep breathing makes the inner fire burn more intensely.

So understand the second sutra and the second key: if you want to ignite the inner fire, the Naachiket Fire, then the deeper you breathe, the better. When your breathing is deeper you become aflame with aliveness. That is why in the first step of Dynamic Meditation you are trying to breathe deeply for ten minutes. Your inner fire will burn intensely in this first step of deep breathing and this fire can then be taken inward. Otherwise you don't have enough energy to move inward.

The third thing is that this inner fire is ordinarily flowing outward toward the physical body, and its flow has to be turned inward. But there are two obstacles to this inward flow: one, whatsoever you have suppressed inside you is in the way, like stones blocking the inward flow of energy. These stones have to be removed; otherwise the energy will hit against them and then return outward. This is why in the second stage of Dynamic Meditation you have to throw out all your suppressed emotions without any hesitation. You have to throw out all your suppressions, putting your intellect aside. How many times have you repressed your tears? – you did not weep and cry and it is all lying there like a stone. Until you weep totally those blocks cannot be removed.

Your whole life has passed and you have not yet laughed totally and loudly because civilization does not allow you to laugh totally. If you were to burst out in uninhibited laughter, you would suddenly find that there was some blockage within you that has broken and dissolved. You have not jumped and danced because from your very childhood you have been told to be quiet. Because of this there is so much tension in this world. If children were allowed to jump, dance and totally enjoy themselves, there would not be so much tension in this world.

But you are asking children to sit silently! The child will sit silently but within him there will be much noise because the child is so alive. People sit silently when they are dead, but the child is alive. Life is simply fresh in him. His life energy wants to dance, jump and run around like a deer and we have asked him to sit silently. He will try to sit silently but the energy within him will go on vibrating. When a child is forced to sit silently his dynamic energy will stop and become static. Blocks will be created in the way of his energy flow.

Now you will have to go back to the day in your childhood when your father told you to sit quietly and you will have to release those blocks. As soon as those blocks are removed your childhood will come back in all its freshness. The energy will again become dynamic and intense. Hence the second step of Dynamic Meditation is for removing the blocks.

The third step of Dynamic Meditation is for hammering the energy so that it can move inward and upward. Remember, water flows downward, that is its nature. If you want water to flow upward you will have to force it up by pumping it. Your energy also is naturally flowing downward. In the third step, shouting *hoo! hoo!* is not any ordinary sound: this sound hammers deeply on the area below your navel center. This is the place where your sex energy is born and flows downward.

After your blocks have been removed and the inner fire has been kindled, this sound *hoo* hammers the energy and makes it move upward through the spine, through the channel of the kundalini. The stronger the hammering of the sound *hoo*, the more intense will be the upward flow of the inner fire from the sex center. It is just like the swift movement of a snake straightening its coiled posture and moving upward. Yoga calls this inner fire, the life energy, kundalini.

The day this energy reaches to the seventh center, the

*sahasrar,* at the top of your head, the lotus of your life will bloom.

This sutra is about the Naachiket Fire.

> *"Nachiketa, I can see that you have so courageously forfeited the heaven where all the pleasures of the senses are available – the heaven which is revered by the world; the heaven which is the gift of the lasting fruit of the yagnas; the heaven which is the place of no fear; the heaven which is noble and whose praise the Vedas have sung in numerous ways; the heaven which is endowed with eons of existence – I acknowledge your profound intelligence.*
>
> *"By understanding godliness – the godliness hidden behind the veil of Yogamaya, the elusive creative energy of existence; which is omnipresent; which dwells in the inner sanctum of the hearts of all beings; which lives in the dark and dense jungle called the world; which is ancient; which is seen only with great effort; which is attainable through Adhyatma yoga, the discipline of the science of the soul – the patient seeker will go beyond joy and sorrow.*
>
> *"When mortals realize the subtle science of the soul through their own experience, have heard and grasped this teaching of religiousness and have attained to the supreme brahman, which is the abode of bliss, they themselves become imbued with bliss.*
>
> *"For you, Nachiketa, the doors to the ultimate abode are open."*

Wherever there is trust and patience, wherever there is a longing and readiness to experience, Yama is saying, "There, Nachiketa, the doors to the ultimate abode are open to you."

That door can also be open for you. Except for you, nobody else is responsible for the door being closed. With perseverance, patience and desirelessness you have to put all your efforts into making your energy move inward. Perhaps the door is already open, and in the moment when you move toward the door, your entry into the temple will happen.

Now get ready for the morning meditation.

# 5

# Never Born, Never Dies

*Hearing Yama's words, Nachiketa said, "Knowing one, tell me of that which is experienced beyond religion or irreligion, which is outside the world of cause and effect, which is separate from past, present and future and from all that is related to it."*

*Yama said, "I will tell you the ultimate sound of which all the Vedas have spoken, the sound toward which all spiritual practices approach, the sound that is the reason for which seekers practice brahmacharya, celibacy – that sound is om.*

*"This eternally resonating sound is the ultimate reality, is the absolute. Having experienced it, one finds what one wishes.*

*"It is the greatest support. It is the ultimate refuge. By experiencing this sound the seeker will enter brahmaloka, the dimension of godliness.*

*"The eternally all-knowing soul is never born and never dies. It is neither a cause nor an effect. It is ageless, unborn, permanent, eternal. Nothing can be added to it or taken away from it. Even when the body has died, the soul cannot die.*

*"If a murderer believes that he can kill, and if the one to be killed believes that he can be killed, both are deluded.*

*Neither can the soul kill nor can it be killed.*

*"The soul, which resides in the inner sanctum of the heart of all living beings, is subtler than the subtle and greater than the great. The glory of the soul can only be seen by the rare, desireless and tranquil seeker through the grace of the supreme brahman, the sustainer of all."*

First, it will be good to understand an original discovery of the Indian spiritual search; only then will you be able to enter these sutras.

By deeply analyzing matter, modern science has come to the conclusion that if we go on breaking down and dividing a particle of matter, what finally remains cannot be further divided. Right now, the ultimate unit or particle is electricity; it is called the atom. That is why, according to science, whatever is visible in the world is made of electricity in various combinations. Matter is only solidified electricity and electricity is only unsolidified matter; electricity is the fundamental element.

Eastern mystics have also discovered a fundamental element but their discovery is from another dimension. Western science went on dividing matter from molecule to atom and from atom to electron, and they ended with electricity. Eastern mystics have gone deeply into it and reached to the very core of consciousness. They have called that deepest point "the sound."

Eastern mystics discovered that the whole existence is a materialized form of sound, of *shabda*. Hence we have said that the Vedas are the divine because they are *shabda*. And this has not only been discovered by the mystics of the East. Anyone who has searched in the dimension of being has found the same thing. The Bible says that in the beginning of creation there was the word, *logos*. From that sound, *shabda*, everything has been created.

Whosoever has searched for the foundation of life by entering his own being has found "the sound" to be the most basic element of all. Those who have looked into the core of matter have found electricity to be the basic element. However, it is interesting to note that Western science says that sound is a form of electricity, and in the East, Yoga says that electricity is a form of sound. Science and Yoga both agree on this point, that sound and electricity are not two different things. So it is only a matter of interpretation whether we call electricity a form of sound or we call sound a form of electricity. But science and Yoga both agree about one thing: that the smallest unit of life is either electricity or sound; there is no difference between them. They have both approached it from completely different directions and found the two forms of the very basic element of existence.

If you start looking into matter, in the end you will certainly stumble upon electricity. Matter is inanimate; electricity is also inanimate. If the search begins from consciousness then the basic elements of consciousness are found to be sound, words, thought, mind, reasoning. Howsoever deep we may go, the purer forms of sound will remain. And the ultimate form of sound we have called *omkar,* "om."

This om is not confined only to the Hindus. The Jainas do not agree with the Hindus on the fundamentals of philosophy, but both agree on the fact that the sound of the ultimate inner happening is om. Buddhists do not agree with Hindus or Jainas on fundamental principles, but they do agree on the fact that when samadhi comes to its culmination, when enlightenment happens, the sound that is experienced within is om.

Mohammedans use the word *ameen* at the end of their prayer; Christians and Jews also use the word *amen*. Etymologists say that the word *amen* is just another form of *om* because the inner sound may be understood by some as om and by others as amen. As far as sound is concerned, you can easily decode and interpret as you want. For example, when you listen to the sound of the wheels while traveling on a train, you can interpret them in any way you want. If you want you can hear them as the tune of a song, and someone who is a lover of movie songs will hear it that way. If someone is a devotee of Rama he will start hearing "Rama, Rama" in the sound of the wheels.

But the ultimate sound is very subtle. The mystics in the East have experienced it as om. Jewish and Mohammedan mystics have grasped it as *omen*, which later on became *amen*.

In the English language there are words such as *omnipresent* and *omnipotent*. Etymologists are not able to trace the origin of these words, but those who understand the science of om would say that these words are born out of it. *Omnipotent* means one whose potency of being is as universal as om. *Omnipresent* means one who is present everywhere and eternally, just as om is.

Almost all the refined languages of the world have been born from Sanskrit. Sanskrit is the ancientmost language. Whether it is English, Lithuanian, French, Slavic, Russian, German, Italian, Spanish, Swiss or Danish, in all of these languages you will find many words with Sanskrit roots.

Om is the essential sound of Sanskrit; all the basic sounds are included in om. In Sanskrit, om is made up of three phonetic sounds: *a*, *u* and *m*; these three are the basic sounds. From these three sounds the whole of language has been born, all the words are created from it. Om is the base, *a*, *u* and *m* are its three branches, and then the whole network of sounds and words is created. In the Jewish language om is described as *logos*; in Christian terminology it is called the word.

These sutras are about om.

You will have to understand these sutras very deeply because anyone who wants to go inward can do so very easily with the help of the sound of om. This sound is already resounding within; in every moment this sound is resonating. This sound is your very life; the moment it disappears from inside you, you will die. This sound is the source of your very existence. But you are full of so many words, sounds and noises that you cannot hear the subtle sound of om within you. It is very subtle and very deep within, and you are so engaged in the marketplace which is full of hectic activity and noise that your ears are laden with them. You are unable to hear this small, silent, basic sound.

To hear the sound om it is necessary that your mind become totally silent. You have to get rid of all outside noise; your mind should become totally unoccupied. If you can become free of the outside noises and there are no thoughts within you, then slowly, slowly you will start experiencing the sound om.

However, there is one danger which has led India into a deep decline: the moment unconscious people heard that om is the ultimate, divine sound, they began sitting down on one spot and chanting and repeating it. This chanting of om is not the basic sound. Om, the ultimate sound, is already there within you without your having to chant it. Whatever sound you pronounce with your throat or within your mind is your own creation; it is superficial. That which comes spontaneously from within you, without any effort on your part, is the basic sound om. This sound surges up, breaks out, removes your inner layers and spreads over you. The sound om is a pure happening within you, it is not your doing. The person who experiences om becomes one with the very foundation of life. He enters into communion with the ultimate reality, he attains ultimate freedom.

But no sooner did the East come to know the significance of om than they began just to sit and repeat it. If you go on repeating, "Om, om, om," slowly, slowly your mind will become filled with the sound om, but this is a created sound. You have created this sound, and whatsoever you can create cannot be bigger than you.

How can you create anything bigger than you? Whatsoever you can create is just like the dirt on your hands. You cannot give birth to the one who has given birth to you, to the one from where you have been given life. Nobody can give birth to his own father; there is no way. But those who think that they can reach the cosmic sound by chanting it are trying to give birth to their fathers. It is impossible, there is no way for this to happen. Continuously chanting "Om, om, om," there is a danger that it may become so mechanical that you will forget that this sound is not real, it is false.

You have created imitations of everything. You have even created false mantras. Man is such an expert at imitation that no sooner does he come to know of the original than he immediately makes an imitation of it. Not only have you made paper and plastic flowers, you have also made great mantras on paper. Then you go around showing these paper mantras in the hope that perhaps with their help you may get the real flowers of life.

The danger is that by repeating and chanting om you may create so much noise inside you that you may never hear that subtle, innermost sound. Your chanting of om will become the barrier.

The rishis, the Upanishadic seers, say that om is the *anahat nad*, the unstruck sound. *Anahat nad* means a sound which has not been created by striking two things together. For example, clapping my hands is *ahat nad*, a created sound. When two things clash a sound is created: these sounds are not *anahat nad*. When the lips move and the tongue touches the palate, sound is created: these sounds are not *anahat nad*.

Om is *anahat nad*, the sound which is not created by the impact of two things. It is the very nature of existence. It has never been born. And remember, whatsoever is born will die. That which is created by the impact of two things, how long can it remain? No sooner is it created than it will die. No sooner is the sound of clapping heard than it will vanish. How long can the small energy created by the sound of clapping both palms together last? But om is eternal, ever existing. It is not created by striking two things. It is not being created, it is there.

In search of *anahat nad*, one can use the help of the mantra om, but much care has to be taken. This is why in the meditation experiment that I have given you for the night, before you go to sleep, I have asked you to intone the sound *o...o...o* and not to make the sound *m...m...m*. You simply go on humming the sound *o...o...o*: one day, suddenly, you will find that om has started arising. And you were only making the sound *o…o…o*; you were only tuning yourself so that the inner music could arise. When one day, suddenly, to your surprise, when you were only intoning the sound *o…o…o*, you will find that om has begun to arise from within you.

Understand that a new breakthrough has happened within you. Then do not be in a hurry, just wait. Go on making use of the sound *o…o…o* and leave the other half for the inner happening. When the current flows they will be connected.

And on the day you find that something has arisen from within and has become united with your pronounced *o…o…o* sound, stop intoning *o…o…o*. From that day, sit silently with closed eyes and try to listen to the mantra; don't make the sound *o…o…o*. Don't intone the mantra, but try to listen to the mantra which is happening. Don't make use of your lips, tongue and throat, but make use of your inner ears. Listen to what is happening inside and you will find that the sound om is continuously happening within. It is not created by you. It was there when you were not born, it will be there when you cease to be. Your being is like a wave and om is like an ocean hidden underneath.

Sometimes, out of impatience, a seeker is in a hurry. This is why I have given you only half of the mantra and half of it has been kept aside, so that when the other half is completed from within you will realize that something new is happening now which you are not doing. When this happens you should stop chanting *o…o…o* and begin to listen.

The rishis, the Upanishadic seers, have heard the mantra om, they have not chanted it. But for you as you are, something has to be started by first pronouncing so that the stone block is removed and the stream can start flowing.

This chanting of *o…o…o* is only meant for removing the stone block. As soon as the stone is removed the spring of om will begin to flow. Then you have to become silent. Then do not pronounce *o…o…o*; then don't create the *ahat nad* because the happening is very near. If your ears are attuned to that sound you will begin to hear. Then you will be surprised to find that this sound has always been resonating within you. But why did you not hear it? – you were somewhere else, your mind was occupied with something else.

Remember one law of the mind: the mind is aware only of that which is the focus of its attention, and when the mind is totally occupied with something it becomes oblivious to everything else. For example, a young man is playing hockey: his foot gets hurt, it starts bleeding, the spectators sitting around the grounds see that his foot is wounded and it is bleeding, there are some bloodstains on the field, but the young player does not know that his leg is hurt. He has no pain, he has no idea of any bleeding because his attention is totally focused on playing hockey. Then the whistle sounds and the playing stops: he immediately becomes aware that his foot is hurt, that it is bleeding and that there is much pain there. His foot had been hurt long before but his attention was elsewhere.

If your house is on fire and if somebody greets you, you will not see the person or hear his greetings. Although your eyes will see, you will not see. Your ears will hear but you will not listen because your whole attention will be focused on the fire that is destroying your house. Every day you walk on a certain road. You go on reading the signs and the posters on the walls, you go on walking and looking into various shops. But on the day your house is on fire, then these things will not be visible to you on that road. Your eyes will be open but your mind will not be present behind those eyes. And unless the mind is related with the eyes you will not experience anything.

You are too occupied on the outside, hence your attention is not available for the inner. The whole effort of Yoga is to make you a little free from the outer so that your attention can flow inward. And everything that can be longed for is available within you. What you go on desiring and still don't get is present, just within you. That which you have been seeking for lifetimes is there within you.

When Buddha became enlightened somebody asked him,

"What have you achieved?" Buddha said, "I have not achieved anything. I have simply realized what was already within me. It has always been there!"

Om is continuously resonating within you. It is the sound of your very being. It *is* your very being. Keeping this in mind, we will now enter the sutras.

> *Hearing Yama's words, Nachiketa said, "Knowing one, tell me of that which is experienced beyond religion or irreligion, which is outside the world of cause and effect, which is separate from past, present and future and from all that is related to it."*

Nachiketa wants to know the ultimate truth, which is neither born nor dies, which is beyond past, present and future, which is eternal, beyond time. He wants to know that which has no beginning and no end. Nachiketa has asked Yama to explain the ultimate truth that is beyond this whole world, which transcends all that can be seen or heard.

> *Yama said, "I will tell you the ultimate sound of which all the Vedas have spoken, of the sound toward which all spiritual practices approach, the sound that is the reason for which seekers practice brahmacharya, celibacy – that sound is om."*

Om is like a physics or chemistry formula. The whole search of the Indian mystics is included in om. In this one word, we have put the essence of all that is. Don't think that this word is just a small word – a key may be small but it can open the door to huge palaces. With a small key the door to the whole existence can open. But one should know how to use the key rightly. You may have the key in your hand and you may be standing before the door but not putting the key in the right place in the lock, or you may not find the lock itself and the key may remain in your hand.

I have heard…

One night Mulla Nasruddin went home completely drunk. He tried his key for a long time but the door would not open.

His wife called from upstairs, "Are you so drunk? Or have you lost the key?"

Mulla said, "No, I have the key."

His wife said, "If you have lost the key should I drop you another one?"

Nasruddin said, "I have the key, but if you have another lock then drop it down to me because I can't find the lock."

To only have the key in your hand is not enough – you must also know where the lock is; you should also know the right way to turn the key because you can go on turning the key in the opposite direction. Just a little mistake and everything will go wrong. The more subtle the experiment, the greater is the chance of going astray. Because of a small mistake you may go thousands of miles away.

*Yama said, "I will tell you the ultimate sound of which all the Vedas have spoken, of the sound toward which all spiritual practices approach, the sound that is the reason for which seekers practice brahmacharya…"* It will be good to understand this point: that the people who indulge in sexuality too much will find it very difficult to hear the sound om. There are reasons for this. Sexual desire is not only a desire, it is also a leakage of energy. The energy which you are throwing out empties you, weakens you, brings you down and makes you dull. You become less sensitive. And one who wants to hear the sound of om should stop abusing his energy. Because when more energy starts to vibrate within you and when you have a stronger energy field, the sound om will begin to strike this energy field. But at first you will hear only this striking.

The value of celibacy is not in celibacy itself: its value is in creating a pillar of energy within you against which the sound om can strike and you can hear the striking of that sound. Without celibacy you are without this pillar, like a house without walls where whatever you may say will not come back to you, it will simply get lost in the sky. Without celibacy a man is without walls. He has no layer of energy within him against which the inner sound om can strike, return and become audible. He is just like a house without walls: if you make a sound in it, it will pass through and will be lost in the sky, in the empty space.

Celibacy is a scientific experiment whereby a new layer of energy can start accumulating with the layer which is your body. For the first time, the sound of om can resonate in this layer of energy. When you hear this resonance, it will become clear to you that there must be an origin for this resonance hidden within you. Then through this resonance you can move toward your innermost source.

This is why, in ancient times in this country, we sent our children to the *gurukul*, a mystery school, and by being celibate there the children could become acquainted with the inner sound. Once a person has come out of celibacy without having experienced the inner sound of om, then later on it will become very difficult for him to be in tune with that inner sound. It is as if your house has many holes in its walls: things will become very distorted and, by and by, it will become very difficult to fix them.

Girls and boys become sexually mature at the age of thirteen or fourteen; this is the most significant time for the sex energy. It is the time when sex energy is very strongly in their bodies. This energy is extraordinary because from this energy life will be born. It is the source of life. This energy will give birth to children. This energy belongs to existence – this is why it can create children. It is the basic energy of existence.

You have no idea how much energy every person is born with. Ten million children can be produced from the semen discharged in one act of lovemaking. According to scientific calculations, ten million sperm are released in one sex act and one sperm can give birth to one child. If all the sperm of one man were used, the whole earth could be filled with the children of one man. In a lifetime, ordinarily, one man can have sexual intercourse four thousand times, and the sperm released in one sex act can create ten million children. And the total child-producing capacity of each man is forty billion. Each man is born with so much life energy!

This life energy is extraordinary. The energy hidden within a sperm is not less powerful than the energy hidden in an atom; it is even more powerful. Before 1945 we did not know that so much energy is contained in a small atom, which cannot even be seen by the naked eye. The whole town of Hiroshima and its population of one hundred thousand human beings was turned into ashes in a single moment. We came to know for the first time that one atom can destroy one hundred thousand people in a single moment. This whole earth can be destroyed by a few atom bombs – but the energy of a sperm is more powerful than that of an atom. In ejaculation, in a single moment, one person is releasing the life energy for creating ten million people.

Sooner or later, when science becomes capable of harnessing the energy of a sperm cell, the energy of an atom bomb will look very small in comparison. The day that we can understand the energy of the sperm, we will understand the energy of the whole. We will understand the ultimate reality which is the source of all life in existence.

At the age of fourteen, if a boy can hear the sound of om before his first ejaculation happens, his whole life will be different. After that ejaculation, and after every ejaculation, it will become more and more difficult to hear the sound om. Holes will be happening in his walls so the inner sound cannot strike them; the sound will disperse and disappear into the open sky.

The motive of the people who wanted to give the lesson of celibacy to their children was very profound. And remember, such lessons should begin during the period when the sexual urge has not yet arisen in the minds of children. Once that urge is born there will be no point in giving any education on celibacy. On the contrary, it will prove dangerous or fatal because then the mind will only become perverted, sick, repressed. That will be the only result.

When children have no idea about sex and their bodies are getting ready by accumulating energy for the first sexual experience, during that period it is very easy for them to connect with the sound om. It is very easy to lead small children toward that sound, but it is very difficult for older people.

Yama said to Nachiketa, "Seekers practice celibacy and austerities to experience it. It is the essence of all the Vedas. And I tell you that this sound is om."

> *"This eternally resonating sound is the ultimate reality, is the absolute. Having experienced it, one finds what one wishes."*

This sutra is very dangerous. This is the reason why it is necessary, as a preliminary preparation, to become free from all desires. Because once you can hear the sound om, then whatsoever you desire will be fulfilled instantly. So if you experience the sound om as you are now, before dropping your desires, you will simply become suicidal.

Your situation will be like the traveler who reached heaven by mistake. He was resting under a *kalpa-vriksha,* a wish-fulfilling tree, after his tiring journey. He was not aware that he was in heaven sitting under this *kalpa-vriksha* tree; he was just there to sit in the shade of the tree. His eyes opened and he felt hungry. Just the thought came to his mind that it would be good if he could get something to eat and immediately, to his great surprise, plates full of delicious food came floating in the air and rested before him. He became a little afraid, but he was so hungry that he ate to his heart's content. After finishing his meal he started to feel that this place where he was seemed to be dangerous. He wondered, "Are there ghosts around here?" and immediately ghosts were standing all around him. He said,

"Now, I'm finished" and instantly all the ghosts jumped on his chest and started strangling him. He thought, "They will kill me" – and he was killed.

The tree was a *kalpa-vriksha*, a wish-fulfilling tree. Sitting under it, anything you desire will immediately be fulfilled. As you are, so full of desires, if you were to sit under the *kalpa-vriksha* the same thing would happen to you. Just because I have told you this story, don't think that you will do something different; it will make no difference. You will do the same thing because your desires are not under your control. If they arise you are helpless. You have a mad mind within you.

Yama is saying: *"This eternally resonating sound is the ultimate reality. Having experienced it, one finds what one wishes."* Knowing om, becoming one with om, whatsoever you desire is instantly fulfilled. That is why there is a condition that the search for om should begin only after all desires have been dropped. Otherwise, since you are filled with trivia, the great cosmic energy will be lost in trivia. You will destroy what you have attained. You have received a diamond but you will buy stones in exchange for the diamond.

This is why Yama has tested Nachiketa in so many ways, to find out if he had any desires. When Yama found that there was no desire left in him, that Nachiketa was totally desireless, only then was he ready to tell him the secrets of the soul. Because a person who is desireless and becomes absorbed in the search for om has only one longing left in him, and that is to experience godliness, to be one with the ultimate truth, to be one with the ocean and be ready to dissolve as the drop. This longing will be fulfilled with the experience of om. Any desire that remains will be immediately fulfilled as soon as the sound om begins to vibrate.

Om is just like the atomic formula of physics which became the cause of great destruction in the hands of science. A few days before his death, Einstein said that in his next life he would like to become a plumber rather than a scientist because he did not know that through his own fault, a formula with the possibility for such destructive energy was made available.

Om is a formula of great creative energy; with it we can reach to the original source of life from where the whole universe is born. The river of life begins to flow from this source, but before you reach there all desires have to disappear from their very roots.

This is why I insist on catharsis in my meditations. Before you enter meditation you should have passed through a deep catharsis, getting rid of all your psychological complexes. If any sickness remains inside and you start entering meditation, these sicknesses will be very harmful to you. It is necessary that sicknesses first be removed because meditation is a great power. If there are any diseases inside you they will receive this great energy of meditation, so let the diseases be removed first.

People come to me and ask, "What are we going to get out of jumping, crying and shouting?" They don't know what is possible through it. If some member of your family dies and you feel like crying but you don't cry, you suppress it, then you will know what can happen. What can happen by suppressing those tears is that your whole life energy will shrink, you will be filled with misery. You will become a wound which can become septic, and until you cry totally you will not be freed from the wound.

What the psychologists are saying seems to be just the opposite of our usual ideas. According to our usual understanding, more women should become insane than men. But it is a surprising finding that more men than women become insane. It should be the reverse. Though women seem to be crazier than men, they don't become insane as often. The secret is simple: they express their craziness every day so it never accumulates. Men move very cautiously so that nobody criticizes them for being stupid. A woman can weep and cry to her heart's content and nobody will comment. People will simply say, "After all, she is a woman." But if a man cries people will say, "Don't cry like a woman, be a man!" These words will stop your tears and this "manhood" will lead you into insanity. If you cling to this manhood you will end up in a madhouse.

Nature has given the same capacity for tears to men's eyes as to women's eyes. Nature has not made any distinction: it has provided the same tear glands to both men and women. If nature had wanted to make any distinction it would have given fewer tear glands to men – but nature has given an equal capacity for tears to both.

And remember, if you suppress your tears, your laughter will also become suppressed. This is a little complex – that one who cannot weep totally cannot laugh totally. He will also be afraid of laughing. In fact he will begin to control everything because he is afraid that if he is in a let-go the barriers may be broken and things may burst out from his unconscious.

More men become insane. More men commit suicide. Few women become insane and few commit suicide. Women talk much of committing suicide, but very few women actually commit suicide. Much is released in just talking about suicide, hence psychologists say that you need not worry about a person who talks a lot about committing suicide. But a person who never talks about committing suicide is dangerous – such a person *may* commit suicide. He never talks about it so it is not expressed, it goes on accumulating within him.

You need not be afraid of a man who often becomes angry about small things. He cannot create any problem. He cannot murder anybody. Great anger has to accumulate to commit a murder. That is why those who become angry about small things are very gentle and loving people. But the so-called saints and virtuous people who never become angry, who suppress their anger, are dangerous people – keep a safe distance from them. They are wicked people. Whenever they do act out their anger it will be nothing less than a murder because they have suppressed so much.

Some people ask, "What will happen by dancing and jumping, by shouting and weeping?" You have accumulated this over your whole life; that is your sickness. Because of these suppressions you are not able to be natural.

Why are children so natural and innocent? The only reason is that when there is anger, the child expresses it totally; he jumps, cries, hits, stamps his foot on the ground. Watch a child who is angry – he seems to have all the energy in the world. His face becomes red, his eyes start burning with anger and he starts thumping things. Such a small child, but a great power seems to be flowing through him. A moment later, when the anger has diffused, he is again laughing. In that laughter you will not find any trace of anger or any impact of the anger. His laughter is like a flower.

We are very surprised at this: how can one who was so angry a moment ago, be so full of joy now? The fact is that the anger has been released. Now nothing is left behind which can destroy or poison his happiness. The anger has been spent and the child is again laughing. Again, when anger arises, the child will be angry and then again he will laugh and enjoy. Whatsoever happens will happen totally, in the moment; nothing will be accumulated. The day a child starts to accumulate his childhood is over, he has begun to grow old. And you have accumulated so much! That is why you are so complex, you are no longer simple and innocent.

One who is not simple, natural and spontaneous cannot have any tuning with om. This is why I am putting so much emphasis on catharsis, on throwing out all that has been accumulated during your whole life. Don't go on suppressing it. But you are afraid that somebody may see you weeping. You have a particular image about yourself and now you are laughing like a madman? It was not expected that you would dance and jump like that.

If you stop yourself from catharsis because of the fear of what others will say, then I cannot help you. If you have no courage, if you are afraid of others' opinions, if you are being manipulated by others, then you cannot move on the path of religiousness. It is only for people who are courageous, fearless.

A friend is here in this meditation camp. He came to see me and he said to me, "My wife has also come here. If I allow the catharsis to happen, if I start jumping, dancing, shouting, then back home my wife will create trouble for me." He has an image of himself with his wife and that image will be destroyed. His wife is afraid of him because she has also come to see me. She came separately and said, "My husband is also here...!" Both are afraid of each other.

Remember, the people you are afraid of are also afraid of you. If you drop your fear of the other, then it will help the other to drop his fear of you. If one of them drops the fear and starts jumping, dancing and crying, then the other will also become free. The matter will be settled and then there will be no need to protect one's false image. By making an effort to protect your image you will only remain suppressed. You cannot hear the cosmic sound of om with such a suppressed personality because you cannot go deeper within yourself. To go deeper, a childlike innocence and simplicity are needed.

During these days, in this meditation camp, be like small children. In connection with this, add one small experiment as a morning meditation in your bed when you wake up. I have told you about a meditation that is to be done just before going to bed: exhale totally, making the sound *o...o...o* for ten minutes and then fall into sleep. Slowly move into sleep making the sound *o...o...o* with the exhalation. And in the morning, as soon as you become aware that your sleep is over, don't open your eyes. Just as cats and dogs stretch their bodies, you also stretch, strain and relax your body, so that the energy starts flowing all over the body. Stretch and relax the limbs. Stretch and relax the whole body like cats and dogs do.

This will make the energy flow all over the body. Do this for two and a half minutes. When you feel that your whole body is fresh, each cell of your body is awake and energetic, then for two and a half minutes start laughing loudly and totally. Keep your eyes closed and laugh for two and a half minutes. Leave your bed only after doing this so that the new day has a good beginning. Let the catharsis be triggered from the very beginning of the day. This will be a good preparation for the Dynamic Meditation which you will be doing here each morning.

While you are doing this laughing meditation, don't be afraid of what your neighbor will think about you – your laughter will encourage him also because he is also afraid of you! Add this experiment as your morning meditation while you are still in bed.

Yama continued, saying:

> *"It is the greatest support. It is the ultimate refuge. By experiencing this sound, the seeker will enter brahmaloka, the dimension of godliness.*
>
> *"The eternally all-knowing soul is never born and never dies. It is neither a cause nor an effect. It is ageless, unborn, permanent, eternal. Nothing can be added to it or taken away from it. Even when the body has died, the soul cannot die.*
>
> *"If a murderer believes that he can kill, and if the one to be killed believes that he can be killed, both are deluded. Neither can the soul kill nor can it be killed."*

As soon as you have had a glimpse of your being with the help and support of the sound om, death will become a fiction. Then you know that what is within you cannot be destroyed in any way because it was never born. Only that which is born will die. You are not born out of your parents; only your body has been born out of them and you have entered that body.

Scientists think that sooner or later they will be able to create human bodies in test tubes. And there doesn't seem to be much of a problem, it will happen. But scientists also think that on the day when they are able to create a child in a mechanical womb and make it grow there, on the day when there will be no need for the mother's womb and a father's sperm for a child to be born, they think that they will also have proved that there is no soul.

But those scientists are wrong. Even if they succeed it will not prove the nonexistence of the soul. It will only prove that previously the child's body had been naturally created by parents and then the soul entered it, and now the child's body is being created scientifically – but the soul still enters into it. The soul only enters the body; it is not created and it can never be created.

But even if scientists succeed in creating a child in the laboratory, they are not creating a soul. They should not be under this illusion. The scientists will only be creating a physical body mechanically instead of the body being created naturally through the parents. On the day that an artificially created human body is ready for the entry of a soul, a soul will enter it. The soul is never born and never dies. Only the body is born and only the body dies.

But this is not something to be believed or to be understood as a doctrine. It will be really understood only when you have experienced it within yourself. Hence I don't ask you to believe that the soul is immortal. I say to you, begin to search for the truth.

Today a woman came to me and told me that she is an agnostic. It is good, there is nothing wrong in it. Everybody should begin by being an agnostic. An agnostic is one who does not believe in what is not directly experienced by him. To be an agnostic is not a denial. To be an agnostic does not mean that there is no soul. If an agnostic says that there is no soul then he is going beyond agnosticism; then his declaration is not based on any experience or exploration. Then his declaration is unscientific and irrational because so far nobody has been able to say through experience that there is no soul.

All those who have known from experience have said that there is a soul. Of course, as long as you have not experienced it, you have a right to say that you don't know – this is enough.

But without having explored and without having experienced, if you declare emphatically that there is no soul, then you are not an authentic agnostic. Then you are not rational, then you are not talking as an intelligent person. Then you are a blind, superstitious believer: you have simply believed that the soul does not exist. It is not your experience. It is not wrong to be an agnostic, but it is wrong to stop at being an agnostic.

Another friend met me two days ago. He said, "I am an atheist and nothing about theism makes any sense to me."

I told him, "What is the need for it to make sense to you? Why are you worried? Be satisfied with yourself as you are."

But no, he is not satisfied with his atheism; that is why he wants to understand, he wants it to make sense. Otherwise what is the need for him to come to my meditation camp?

I told him that if atheism has given him joy and bliss, I am also ready to become an atheist.

He said, "There is no joy in being an atheist."

I told him, "I am blissful, and I invite you to move on my path for some time and find out for yourself. And if you can say with confidence that you are blissful being an atheist, then I am ready to move on your path. But I tell you with certainty that I have attained to bliss and you can verify this by walking along with me."

Atheism is impotent because you attain nothing through it. It is just a negation. It only says not this, not this, not this – but what is attained? What will one achieve through it? What can be created out of negation?

Atheism is as if a man sows stones on his farm the way seeds are sown. If I tell him that I can give him seeds he will say he does not believe in seeds, he only believes in stones. Then I would have to ask him, "Where is the crop? If you believe in stones then show me the crop because the fruit is the proof. Where are the sprouts? Where are the flowers and fruits? If your only purpose is to sow stones, it is okay. But one also has to reap the crop." Has any atheist reaped any crop up to now? If sowing stones is in itself his joy, perfectly good, he can continue to sow stones.

But man sows so that he can reap. Man sows seeds so that trees, flowers and fruits will grow, so that some fulfillment can happen, some satisfaction, so that a transformation can happen in life. Just intellectual negation never brings any kind of transformation. Nothing is solved just by saying that there is no enlightenment. You don't change, you don't become free, you don't move anywhere – no destination is reached.

But I don't say that you should believe without experiencing; I say that before you have had your own experience, neither agree nor disagree. Before knowing, you can only say that you don't know and that you are ready to seek.

The immortality of the soul as just a theory is of no use. But the experience that the soul is immortal is unique, and that essence is hidden within you. It has been there before you appeared in the form of a body and it will be there even when relatives and friends have burned your dead body in a crematorium. But to know this experience you have to move behind the body and the mind and you have to search for the innermost core beyond which there is nothing. The search for this inner center can happen through om. Om is the key for this.

> *"The soul, which resides in the inner sanctum of the heart of all living beings, is subtler than the subtle and greater than the great. The glory of the soul can only be seen by the rare, desireless and tranquil seeker through the grace of the supreme brahman, the sustainer of all."*

It is good to understand this last sutra. It is very complex and very controversial. Discussions have been going on about it for thousands of years and there are two great viewpoints opposing each other.

One doctrine says that the ultimate truth is attainable by

one's own will and effort. They say that the ultimate truth can be realized by one's own effort, perseverance and the practice of austerity, that truth cannot be attained by somebody else's grace. They say that there is no need for any grace. The question of grace does not arise.

The first viewpoint says that if truth can be attained through somebody else's grace then this whole existence is an absurd riddle; it is a nonsensical phenomenon. Then it can happen that one who searches may not receive and one who does not search at all may receive. This is why Buddha, Mahavira and all the other enlightened ones of their tradition assert that there is no question of anybody's grace; one's own effort is enough. The matter of grace is a little confusing and controversial because it has some smell of bribery.

A man may go to the temple and fall at the feet of the statue of God, rubbing his nose on the ground or hitting his head on the feet of the statue. And he may pray, "God, compassionate one, you are known as *patit-pavan,* the savior of sinners, and I am a sinner. Let your grace fall on me!" By doing all this he hopes to win God's favor. Through all this he hopes to somehow succeed in receiving the favor of God. On the other hand the other type may search and seek for his whole life, doing meditations and practicing all sorts of austerities, and never once utter the name of God. This implies that he can never receive God's favor. Hence Mahavira has said that there is no God because if there is a God then this problem of grace will always be there. He has said that man's effort is enough: the day man's effort is complete he will realize the truth. This argument has some validity in it, it has some meaning in it.

There is another doctrine, just opposite to this one, which says that nothing is in the hands of man because man is very weak, helpless, ignorant. And the efforts which an ignorant man makes will naturally come out of his ignorance. How can the efforts of an ignorant, weak, pathetic human being become a means to attaining the ultimate reality? The hands of man are so small – how can they hold the cosmic reality in their grip? The truth is so mysterious, rare, profound, and man is so weak and in such darkness, that the inner journey cannot be made without the grace of godliness; only through divine grace will man find enough strength to carry on.

This second doctrine also says that a man's effort and willpower will only enhance his ego: he will feel that he is somebody special who will find truth because of his own efforts. And the ego is the greatest obstacle; hence, don't give any space to the ego. So the second doctrine says that only divine grace, God's compassion, will make anything possible. According to them this should be emphasized so that the ego has no way of being nourished. There is also some truth in this second viewpoint.

Both viewpoints are true and both also hold some dangers. The ego is the danger for the first viewpoint and laziness and lousiness is the danger for the second.

The danger in the first is that the seeker may become an egoist. That is why a Jaina monk becomes more egoistic than the monks of any other religion. It is bound to be so. A Jaina monk never greets anyone with folded hands because when there is no God, who can be greeted? Whom should he greet? A Jaina monk can only bless, he cannot bow down or do a *namaste.* The very act of bowing down to someone creates trouble in him. That is why no monk of any other religion has such a crystallized ego as the Jaina monk. The reason for this is that he is trusting only in his own effort; there is no grace, no compassion. There is no God whose support can be expected; one has to rely only on oneself. Naturally the ego will become very strong. This is the danger on this path.

And those who believe in the grace of God don't do anything. They say that whenever God's grace descends, it will happen. They don't even move their hands and feet, they wait for the grace of God to do it for them. These people become utterly lazy. They are certainly humble, but very lethargic.

Their effort has an earnestness – but it also has great ego.

There is a humbleness in those who believe in grace. The humbleness of a devotee can never be found in a monk who lives an austere life. But a devotee becomes lazy because he thinks that it will happen when God wants it to happen. And who is he to do anything? What can happen through his own doing? These are the dangers.

I want to tell you that a great transformation will happen in your life if you can fulfill both of these dimensions: the clear understanding that you will make all the efforts needed, but that the happening will always be by divine grace. Then you will only have to make efforts that can prepare you to receive divine grace. But in the last moment the happening is always by its grace. This does not mean that if somebody does not remember God then the phenomenon will not happen. Remembrance is not the cause of grace. If you forget all about God and continue with your effort, then too a moment will come when you will receive the divine grace. There is no God sitting up there somewhere and watching who is remembering him so that he can shower his grace on him. This is about an intrinsic principle of life.

For example, whenever somebody heats water up to one hundred degrees it will evaporate, whether you believe in or worship the god of fire or not. In the same way, whenever your efforts reach to one hundred degrees, grace will be received whether or not you believe in God. But the ultimate thing will happen through grace. This has to be so because man is only a small part of the cosmic reality. To experience the cosmic reality effort is needed – but your effort alone is not enough. Something more than your own effort is needed, and that is the support of the cosmos. But one thing is certain: the experience of godliness will happen only to those who make effort.

Yama is saying that only a rare *sadhaka*, a rare seeker, attains to the ultimate truth by divine grace. Take note of the word *sadhaka*: it means one who has made a total effort.

Never forget the significance of grace and never forget your effort either. You will not receive grace because of your prayers, you will receive grace because of your efforts.

Prayers are childish, prayers are a deception. People are just standing with folded hands, asking for this and that, asking for ultimate freedom, asking for everything, but they are not worthy of receiving it. You are asking for the ocean but you have no capacity to hold even a handful of water. It is good that the ocean does not listen to your prayers, otherwise you would be drowned! Then your safety would be impossible. But the day that your worthiness is total the ocean will arrive by itself.

Kabir has said. "At first I felt that the drop had fallen into the ocean, but later on I realized that the ocean had fallen into the drop. At first I was thinking that it would be very difficult to find the drop that was once lost in the ocean again. But later on the difficulty was much greater because there was no way to find the drop – the ocean itself had fallen into the drop." This is absolute dissolution.

In the first step effort and in the last step grace: if these two things are there, there will be no delay in the showering of the ultimate bliss, the consciousness, the magnificence, the splendor. If these two opposites are fulfilled together, if these two wheels are moving together, then the chariot of your life will certainly reach to the door of ultimate freedom, of moksha.

Enough for today…

[*Osho then adds for the Western listeners:*]

For those who cannot understand Hindi, there is to be one special technique for the morning which you should start from tomorrow morning.

At night, as I have told you, you should do a method with deep exhalation, and while exhaling make the sound *o…o…o* for ten minutes. Then, by and by, relax and fall into sleep.

The next thing is that in the morning, whenever you feel that now sleep has left you, don't open your eyes. Let your eyes remain closed and for two and half minutes stretch and strain your body, tense and relax your body like a cat. All your limbs, every cell of your body, should become alive. For two and a half minutes stretch the body, make every part – legs, hands – tense, and then relax them. Make them tense and then relax them. Tense the whole body and then relax the body. Stretch like a cat. Remember when you have seen a cat stretching – just like that, be a cat. And don't open your eyes so that you can feel the inner energy flow, the wholeness of the body, the one flow of body energy.

After this, for two and half minutes, laugh as madly as possible, as loudly as possible. Go completely mad! And don't open the eyes so that you can feel the laughter going through every cell of the body and making it alive. Only then should you open your eyes and get out of bed.

And remember a few things for the night meditation, the Tratak Meditation.

One, when you are doing it your hands should be raised toward the sky to receive the grace.

You must know about the principle of gravitation, that the earth is pulling you down. Science will have to concede some day that this is only half the truth because energies must balance. If the earth is pulling you down and there is something like gravitation, then there must be something like grace which is pulling you up.

Grace is the principle which pulls you up and gravitation is the principle which pulls you down.

With your hands raised you are receptive and welcoming for the grace to descend upon you. Your eyes have to be fixed on me, staring without blinking. Even if you feel a certain strain don't be bothered by it, go on staring at me because a deep communion is going to happen. If you go on staring at me then your eyes will become a bridge and I can enter you and you can enter me. A link, a deep link is possible, so don't blink the eyes.

Thirdly, you have to constantly jump so that the energy

becomes a movement within you. The energy should not become static, it must become dynamic. So go on jumping. And I will not be speaking so I will give you indications with my hands. When I move my hands, bring your energy more and more to your jumping and to your mantra *hoo*. Bring your total energy to it. Don't withhold anything. If you are withholding anything you will miss the whole point. Bring your totality to it.

And one thing more: sometimes, when I feel that your energies are jumping and have become a dynamic force and you have become open to grace, whenever I feel that moment of tuning I will turn my palms downward. Whenever you see that my palms are turned downward, feel as if godliness, the cosmic, is descending upon you. And in that moment go completely mad with the mantra *hoo* jumping with your hands raised. Forget that you are there, just become a flow of energy.

Whenever you see that my palms are turned downward, be receptive and go completely mad. In that mad dance the cosmic can be touched. Not only will you touch it, the cosmic can touch you. It can penetrate you and that penetration will become a pregnancy, and the cosmic will become a child within you and it will grow.

And unless the cosmic, the divine grows within you – and it will grow! – but unless the cosmic, the divine, grows within you, you can never feel the absolute bliss which the mind hanker after, the body cries out for, and the whole being is thirsty for.

But remember, again I say to you: bring your total energy to the method. Only then is something possible. When you are totally in it only then the point of evaporation is reached, never before.

# 6

# Bridging the Opposites

*"Existence reaches far and wide even as it remains in one place. It moves everywhere even as it sleeps. Who better than I can know this divinity which does not swell with pride at its own opulence?*

*"By knowing the great, the omnipresent divine, which is bodiless and unchanging within the ever-changing body, the intelligent one becomes free from all sorrow and grief.*

*"Godliness is not known through speaking, through intellect or through listening to lengthy discourses. Godliness can be known only by one who it has already chosen. For this person, it reveals its true nature.*

*"Although refined of intellect, one who has not become free of unconscious conduct, or who is not serene, or whose mind and senses are undisciplined, or whose mind is not peaceful, cannot know godliness.*

*"No one knows where and how it is. All living beings, at the time of pralaya, the dissolution of the universe, will become food for it; and even death, the destroyer of all, will become no more than a garnish for it.*

*"In the human body, which is the fruit of conscious deeds,*

*there is an entity which lives in the sky of the heart, the true abode of godliness, and which savors the truth that is hidden in the miraculous recesses of the intellect. There is also the entity which suffers the inescapable impact of past actions. These two are not the same. Like sunlight and shadow, the two are different from each other – so say the great wise ones, those who know the supreme reality. The grihasthas, the householders, who have thrice chosen the Naachiket Fire and who are endowed with panchagni, the five fires, also say this.*

*"May all beings be worthy of knowing and attaining the Naachiket Fire, the bridge which can take those who perform the yagnas, the fire rituals, beyond this ocean of suffering to ineffable supreme being. This supreme being is the abode of fearlessness for those who long to cross the ocean of this world of illusion.*

*"Nachiketa, understand the embodied soul to be the rider in the chariot, the body to be the chariot, intelligence to be the charioteer and mind to be the reins.*

*"In this metaphor of the chariot, the sages say that the senses are the horses, the objects being sensed are the roads which the chariot is traveling on, and the embodied soul living in identification with the body, the senses, and the mind is the bhokta, the experiencer.*

*"For one who lives unconsciously and who has a restless mind, his senses are uncontrollable, like the untamed horses of a careless charioteer."*

First, it will be good to understand a few things about existence. Existence is a synthesis of all opposites. Everything in this world exists along with its opposite, this is the way nature exists. Nature cannot exist without opposites. If there is no night there will be no day; if there is no woman there will be no man; if there is no death there will be no birth; if there is no unhappiness there will be no happiness. The whole of life is manifested in the interrelatedness of opposites.

This is why life is a duality, a friction. Here, anything that happens will happen only with the support of the opposite. Here, when you make a friend you have begun to make an enemy. Here, you begin to love and immediately hate also begins. You cannot do anything here without simultaneously creating a balance of the opposite.

Buddha has said, "I do not make friends because I do not want to make enemies." He has said, "I do not love because I do not want to hate."

Life is both matter and consciousness. Consciousness is the opposite of matter. Eastern philosophers have always accepted this duality, hence they have supported the duality of this world. In the West, new scientific research also accepts this duality: now their concept is also that whether we know it or not, the opposite always exists.

Science has made a unique discovery, the discovery of anti-matter. They say that if there is matter there must also be anti-matter. Up to now anti-matter has not yet been identified, but since everything exists along with its opposite, there must also be anti-matter.

Because there is time, something like anti-time must also exist. Time moves forward, so anti-time will move backward. Here a child is born, then he becomes young and then becomes old. If there is something like anti-time, then first there will be an old man, then a youth and then a child – the reverse journey. And this is not said by any philosopher but by modern physicists. There has to be a flow of anti-time alongside the flow of time because time cannot exist without its opposite. Nothing can exist without its opposite.

You see a stone which is solid matter. Science says that just as a stone is solid matter occupying space, there must be holes in space which are the opposite of matter. So far it has not been possible to prove the existence of these holes, but a thesis based on this principle has been awarded a Nobel Prize. There must be holes in space. It is difficult to imagine what the purpose of these holes could be. Space is a fullness, a filling, but parallel to this there should also be empty holes, a void.

Mahavira made similar statements two thousand five hundred years ago. He said, "There is the world, and opposite to it there is also the non-world." The manifest world is matter and opposite to it is the unmanifest world, anti-matter. This is the arrangement for the visible world.

Existence is invisible, there is no polarity in it. All polar opposites are harmonized into oneness in it, all opposites lose their opposition in it.

Existence is one. If there were something like an anti-existence, then existence also would become nothing but a part of this world. But existence is greater than the world: it encompasses within itself the world and the non-world, matter and anti-matter, time and anti-time, life and death. Existence is one, where all dualities merge.

This is the first thing to be understood about existence – that it is the totality of the whole. Within it there is birth as well as death. Hence it is the creator and the destroyer, it is the friend and the enemy, it creates and it destroys.

When we use words such as *him* for existence, a difficulty arises: it seems as if God is some individual. This is a mistake of language, but language has no other way of expressing it. It is not a person, it is just an infinite expanse of energy. In that infinite expanse of energy all dualities are included. Whatsoever appears to us as opposites are both included in it, the day *and* the night. Day belongs to it and night also belongs to it. This fact will have to be accepted by science, sooner or later.

Science has accepted the fact of duality. It will also have to accept that wherever there is duality, there has to be a third force to bridge that duality; otherwise there will be no relationship between the two. A sort of harmonious movement, an accord, a music runs between the two, so certainly there can be a third force which can include both, which will encompass both.

Existence, God, means the totality, where all dualities are simultaneously present. This is difficult for the mind to understand because logic always divides; it does not know the art of uniting, just as scissors can cut but have no way of joining. If you try to join something by using scissors you will be in difficulty. The more you try to join the more it will be cut apart. Logic is like scissors. This is why we have shown Ganesh, the god of logic, riding on a rat. A rat is like scissors: it can chew up but it cannot join; hence a rat is chosen to be Ganesh's vehicle. It is symbolic.

You may be surprised to know the reason why so-called religious rituals begin with first honoring Ganesh. You may not know this, and the reason for it is very strange. Ganesh is thought to be very dangerous, a mischief maker and a destroyer who rides on logic.

The mythical story says that in ancient times Ganesh was creating many problems for people. People were so afraid of him that they thought it better to pay their respect to him before beginning any new venture, so that he would not create any problems. Hence the popular mantra, *Shree Ganeshayanamah*. The whole purpose was to placate Ganesh because everyone was afraid of him. But slowly, slowly people forgot that he is a destroyer and now he is thought to be a bringer of luck. Over long periods of time changes are bound to occur. But originally he was known as a big troublemaker. By and by this was forgotten and he became a symbol of good luck. Now people believe that he contributes to the success of things. But the reason that he was originally thought to be a troublemaker was because of his devotion to logic, to the art of dividing.

Science is based on logic. It is an extension of logic, so it analyzes. Its method is analysis. You can give anything to science and it will divide it in pieces. That is how science has reached the atom, by dividing matter more and more.

Religion goes beyond logic. Religion says that through analysis you can never know the whole. By breaking things into pieces the pieces can be understood, but in this way how can you know the whole? You may know what an atom is but how can you know the whole?

These are two extremes: if you go on analyzing you will reach the atom and if you go on synthesizing you will reach the whole. The whole means the absolute unity of all beyond which nothing can be added. And an atom is the last division beyond which no more division is possible. Hence the end result of a scientific search is the micro and the end result of the religious search is the macro. These are the two extremes. Science begins from duality and ends in multiplicity; religion also begins from duality but ends in oneness.

The religious process is a synthesis, a joining of more and more until nothing is left to join. When everything is united, that unity is called existence, God. God is not an individual – it is the name for the ultimate unity of all existence. In that unity all separate differences dissolve into oneness.

In science, all separate differences will become clearer because it is a process of analyzing. That is why science not only divides things into parts, it also divides itself. Five hundred years ago the word *science* was meaningful; now there is nothing like science. Now there is physics, chemistry, biology, but nothing like science. If you ask what a scientist is it will be difficult to say. Now there is a physicist, a chemist or a biologist but there is no "scientist." Just as it has divided everything else, science has also divided itself. It has divided itself into many small branches and among these branches there is no uniting factor.

At present the greatest difficulty of man is that between all the various branches of knowledge there is no harmony, no relationship. The physicist does not know what the chemist is doing because physics itself has expanded so much that even if a man lives for a thousand years he will not be able to know all of it. In the same way, chemistry itself has developed so much that nobody will be able to know it completely.

In ancient days one doctor would treat all diseases; this is no longer the case. Now if there is a problem with your eyes there is a specialist, for your ears another specialist, or if your foot is injured or if your stomach is upset, there are different specialists.

In the West, there is a joke that in the twenty-first century a man goes to an eye specialist. The doctor asked him, "Which eye needs to be treated, the right or the left eye? Because I am a specialist only for the right eye!" Such a thing is possible because things are being divided more and more.

Science, which divides everything, also becomes more and more divided itself. This is why there is no communication between scientists. There is so much specialization that one scientist cannot understand another scientist. Science is now afraid of the future possibility that one branch of science will be just a stranger to another branch. It will create many difficulties.

This happened during the last world war when the atom bomb was being tested: physicists said that there was no danger because they did not know biology, and biologists were not consulted. When the atom bombs were to be dropped on Hiroshima and Nagasaki, the physicists were consulted because they had made the bombs, but the biologists were not consulted about the effects that the explosion would have on life. Later on they realized that the effects were fatal and long lasting. The embryos of the women who were pregnant and survived were affected by radioactivity. Now, for thousands of years, their children and even their children's children will be diseased and crippled.

Where the atom bomb was dropped, all human beings died, but the fallout that was generated by the explosion was full of radioactivity and spread everywhere. It mixed with the water in the sea and poisoned the fish. Now there was no way of treating those fish, and the radioactivity entered the bones and blood of anyone who ate the fish. The fertilizers that were made from those fish affected the trees and they also became poisonous. A whole chain reaction began, and now scientists say that there is no way to check it. The connectedness of life is so vast that radioactivity has affected every type of life. The physicists thought that the effects would be limited only to one region, but the whole world is so interconnected that you cannot imagine how the effects will go on spreading. It affected cows' milk – and the children who drank that milk. Even the small calves of cows were poisoned by the radioactivity. It was realized too late that the biologists should have been consulted about what would be the effects on life.

This is why there is a new ecological movement spreading in the West. They say that whatever has to be done should be done only after consulting with all branches of knowledge because life is so interconnected. Science has been divided into many branches, but life is still undivided. Life is one unity. Here, even small things will create problems.

For example, now man has reached the moon. Prior to that, the scientist preparing the astronauts consulted with the space travel scientists – but life is so vast that no science can cover it all. After all the arrangements were made one thing came to their notice only later on: when rockets travel to the moon they make big holes in the ozone layer. This ozone layer surrounds the earth's atmosphere, which is about two hundred miles in depth all around the earth. Because of this atmospheric protection not only do we breathe safely, but there are many poisonous rays beyond the ozone layer which cannot penetrate the earth's atmosphere. We are alive because of this ozone layer. This layer prevents all the poisonous rays from coming to the earth from the sun and the moon and the stars and from space beyond the earth's atmosphere. If all the rays were to penetrate we would all be dead instantly.

When the rockets penetrated this ozone layer they made big holes through which many poisonous rays could reach the earth. Only afterward did they realize that the rays had entered. Some scientists feel that the increase in cases of cancer is because of those holes, but now there is no way of stopping these rays. Now plans are being proposed for daily space travel and all these facts are being kept secret from the common man.

All the oceans are being poisoned because our factories and mills are releasing poisons into them. But life is interrelated and the ocean is not the kind of place where once poisons are put into it, we are free of them. There are plants in the ocean which generate oxygen in the water; we take in that oxygen when we drink water. By and by these plants are dying and the amount of oxygen in the air is becoming less and less. Scientists say that in the last three hundred years the oxygen in the air has become so much less that it is amazing how human beings are still alive. So we are living almost half dead; there is no health to be seen anywhere.

Life is an organic unity. Everything is interconnected. It is like the web of a spider: if you touch one thread of the web the whole web will vibrate. In the same way, with whatsoever you do, will affect the web of the whole of life. That indivisible web of life is the supreme reality, the ultimate truth.

Science divides and in turn it becomes more and more divided. Religion unites and itself becomes more and more united. On the day that humanity is mature, only one religion will remain on the earth. And the more science develops the more it will multiply into different sciences.

The second thing to be understood about existence is that it is not a principle, it is an experience – just as love is an experience. Anyone who has not loved at all may read hundreds of books about love and gather information about love, but he will never know what love is. One who has loved may not have read any scriptures about love but he will know what love is from his own experience.

Existence is not a principle. Mathematics consists of principles: it is not required that you experience it, experience has nothing to do with it. Experience belongs to religion, not to principles; it has nothing to do with principles. Hence those who are in search of principles will unnecessarily go astray. But those who transform themselves and try to enter new dimensions through experience will certainly reach truth.

The third thing to be understood is that your intellect is not your totality. You are much more than your intellect – just as your hand is only your hand and you are much more than your hand; your foot is only your foot but you are much more than your foot. And just as they are your instruments, the intellect is also your instrument. Hence, anyone who searches only through the intellect cannot realize the ultimate truth.

If one wants to attain to the whole, one has to be whole himself. Intellect is useful, but it has taken complete mastery over you and because of it you have started feeling as if you exist within your brain. If somebody asks where you exist you will immediately point to your head. This is a great calamity. When a child is in the mother's womb there is not much of a brain, but still the child is complete. Even without much brain the child's body continues to grow.

Life happens prior to the brain and the life process creates the brain. When a child is born the development of its brain is only ten percent; the remaining ninety percent will develop later on. On the first day, when the egg and sperm meet in the mother's womb, there is no brain, but the life which is there still goes on growing. Just as hands and feet grow, the brain also grows. It is only a branch of a living body, so don't think that the branch is the root. If anyone tries to live thinking that the branch is all he will become crippled.

That is why people who live by intellect alone become crippled. It is like living only through a hand and keeping the remainder of the body frozen. What will be the quality of life for such a person? He will have to see through his hands, hear through his hands, walk on his hands and make the hand do everything.

But this is exactly your situation: you have made the intellect supreme and you have kept everything else tightly closed. This imprisoned, closed person can never realize the ultimate truth. This is why it is necessary to go deeper than the intellect and reach to the level of life which was there before the intellect developed and which will remain even when the head is burning on the funeral pyre.

Life is the manifestation of a vast energy and the intellect is just a small aspect of that great life energy.

One of the sutras that Shiva gave to his consort Parvati was to live as if headless, live as if you have no head. If you can remember only one thing while either sitting or just standing – that you have no head, that you have only a headless body – if you can practice it for three months you will be surprised: you will find great changes occurring in your life. Because you have no head you will start moving toward the heart and the heart will become the center of your life. With no head, how will you become uneasy, impatient, angry, anxious? By renouncing the head all problems are renounced. If you practice this for three months you will find that all your anxieties are finished, that all the storms and winds in your mind have disappeared. You have become more balanced and more peaceful. You have moved to the heart.

Below the heart there is an even deeper level, your navel – because the first experience of life begins at the navel. There are methods for reaching to that level. Whosoever comes to this navel center has reached his own center, and only from that center is a communion with existence possible.

Let us now enter the sutras:

> *"Existence reaches far and wide even as it remains in one place. It moves everywhere even as it sleeps. Who better than I can know this divinity which does not swell with pride at its own opulence?"*

This sutra is a hint of non-duality in poetic language: *"Existence reaches far and wide even as it remains in one place."* This is a very contradictory statement. How can something reach to faraway distances while remaining in one place? One has to travel to get to faraway places. But this is a poetic language that is trying to synthesize the opposites.

Yama says: *"Existence reaches far and wide even as it remains in one place. It moves everywhere even as it sleeps. Who better than I can know this divinity which does not swell with pride at its own opulence?"*

One of the names for existence is *ishwar. Ishwar* means one who is full of opulence. But people who have even a little bit of wealth become egoistic. Even a little money gives you energy and you walk with a new bounce in your step. Money is an intoxicant. When a rich man goes bankrupt all his intoxication vanishes, and afterward he walks like a person suffering from a hangover. He is no longer drunk but still he moves like a drunkard. "Once I was drunk" – only this memory lingers, but the memory brings unhappiness, an emptiness inside.

*Ishwar* is the ultimate opulence. But the indication of its transcendental nature is in the phrase "*...which does not swell with pride at its own opulence."* There is no intoxication there. The opulence is total but there is no unconsciousness at all, no ego at all.

If existence were egoistic it would be understandable, but for us to be egoistic is absolutely absurd. We are helpless, weak, but still the ego declares, "I am." It would be understandable if, full of ego, existence were to declare, "I am" – but existence would never make such a declaration. But we, as powerless and ignorant as we are, dare to declare "I am." This is why no matter how much you may shout and ask, "Where is the divine? I want to meet it!" there is no response. Your shouting and your logic can never provoke it to become manifest and to say, "Here I am." Existence, godliness, has no "I." If there were an "I," the atheists would have already been able to provoke it into revealing itself.

In Europe, Burke, who is a great atheist thinker, challenged a priest. Burke argued by removing his wristwatch and holding it in front of the priest, and he asked, "If your God is omnipotent let him stop my watch just at this moment, eight o'clock. If your God can stop my watch I will believe in his omnipotence!"

But the watch continued to work. God could not even do that much; omnipotent, and yet he could not show even that much power. Even a child could do it by smashing the watch on the ground.

Burke concluded, "It is obvious that there is no God."

But what was Burke doing? He was simply trying to hit God's ego. He was saying that if God were there he should perform the miracle. But Burke did not understand a very important fact: God has no ego, so how can it be provoked? Only those who have egos can be provoked.

Actually, only the small and petty can be provoked. There is no way to provoke the whole. Storms can only be created in the small cup of your ego, but your talk cannot affect this vast existence. Existence cannot be hit so it makes no difference whether you challenge it or not.

This sutra is saying that existence is opulent but there is no hint of any intoxication, any ego, in that opulence. This is a bridging of the opposites. Even a little opulence creates ego, so mathematically, if the opulence is great it should create a huge ego. But religion is beyond the language of mathematics – when opulence is absolute there is no ego.

It will be easier to understand it with the language of psychology. In the West, Adler, a great psychotherapist, based his whole psychology on the concept of the inferiority complex. He said that all the activities of man arise from his feelings of inferiority. When someone feels himself to be inferior he longs to reach a high post. To avoid the feeling of inferiority, he tries to occupy a high position.

Nobody suffers from inferiority complex more than politicians. Adler said that whether a Hitler, a Lenin or a Lincoln, all of them suffered from some kind of inferiority complex. To compensate, they rushed to politics. Lenin's legs were very short and the upper part of his body was much longer. Whenever he would sit on a chair his feet would not touch the ground. He suffered very much because of it. By sitting on the high throne of the great Czar, he showed that even though his feet might be not be touching the ground, they had reached the throne! Adler said that Lenin's inferiority complex always haunted him. It is probably true that Hitler was impotent, so his impotence became a hunger for power. It became so strong that he wanted to hold the world in his fist and challenge others' potency.

An inferiority complex creates a desire to move in the opposite direction. If somebody is ugly he tries to compensate in some way to cover the ugliness. If somebody is blind the whole energy of his eyes becomes available to his ears. This is why the blind man can hear much better than anyone with eyes can hear. Blind people quickly become musical experts because the energy of their eyes rushes to their ears; their ears begin to do the work of eyes. Wherever something is lacking, we cover it by doing something else in another direction.

Adler has also said that man's ego is created because of an inferiority complex. If love is lacking in your life, you fulfill it by madly accumulating money. Those who did not receive the gift of love will begin to collect gold.

It is very interesting that someone who is full of love cannot be a miser. And a miser cannot be a lover because actually, a miser is fulfilling his longing for love through money. Someone whose life is full of love feels secure – he knows that he will not die of hunger; he knows that even when he gets old somebody will look after him.

But someone whose life is loveless will be afraid and insecure. He knows that when he becomes old nobody is going to look after him. That fear will make him accumulate money because money is his only security. One whose life is missing the security of love will get a feeling of security by hoarding money. You are simply hiding, covering up, compensating. If you look deeply into your whole behavior, Adler seems to be right.

Because all is available to existence, it has no inferiority complex. Hence the nearer a person comes to reality the less egoistic he is. The more a person has the less egoistic he becomes; the less a person has the more egoistic he becomes. Ego is poor, it is a beggar.

Egolessness is the indication that you have become an emperor. Naturally, one who has the whole existence available to him will have no need for any "I."

These sutras are attempts to bridge the opposites in a poetic way. Yama is saying another interesting thing: *"Who better than I can know this divinity which does not swell with pride at its own opulence?"* Only death can know godliness. Why? Because unless you die, disappear, dissolve, you cannot become one with existence. As long as your ego is not burned to ashes you cannot become one with the quality of egolessness. If you want to be one with it you will have to be the same as it; only the same can meet the same.

Now you are just the opposite when you ask, "Where is God?" It is as if you have your back to the sun and you ask, "Where is the sun?" If you continue to stand with your back toward the sun, there is no way to know. The sun is there but your back has blocked it. You can say, "As long as it is not proved that there is a sun, why should I turn around? First prove that there is a sun, then I will turn around." All the logicians are saying this.

A real religious person says, "If you turn around you will find the sun. First transform yourself – give up your ego." This statement of Yama's is very valuable: except for him, who else can be as capable of knowing godliness? Hence Yama is for those who are ready to die and become nobodies. Jesus has said: Those who lose themselves will be saved, and those who try to save themselves will not be saved by any means.

It is just a dissolving, like when a drop falls into the sea and disappears. When a person is ready to fall and be dissolved like that, his ego will disappear immediately – and with the disappearance of the ego the inferiority that is hidden in it will also disappear.

As long as you are full of ego you will continue to feel inferior inside. You are not trying to be free of inferiority, you are simply trying to hide it. It is like covering a wound with a beautiful bandage of silk or velvet. Howsoever beautiful and attractive to others those bandages may appear, your wound will not heal because of them. The danger is that the wound may fester into an ulcer by being covered in that way. If it had remained open there would have been a possibility of healing through the sunrays, the fresh air; nature would have helped the healing to happen.

You are trying to hide or suppress your inferiority with money, position, knowledge, renunciation. By any means, you want to declare: "I am somebody." You try to create a feeling of being somebody while inside your real situation is that you are nobody.

A religious person has to pass through a death. It means that he has to give up the idea of being somebody – which is unnecessarily imposed from outside – and become ready to be a nobody. The mystery of this sutra is that whosoever is ready to be a nobody will become one with the whole, whereas one who is trying to become somebody will just shrink more and more. He will never become one with existence.

Let go of the pain of being a nobody and accept the feeling of nobodiness with ease – this is the state of a devotee. That is why Yama says, "Who can know better than I?"

> *"By knowing the great, the omnipresent divine, which is bodiless and unchanging within the ever-changing body, the intelligent one becomes free from all sorrow and grief."*

*"...which is bodiless and unchanging within the ever-changing body..."* The body is subject to change, but within this ever-changing body the unchanging is hidden. Here there is a continuous effort to bridge the opposites so that the indivisible can be

perceived. Amidst all the changes the unchangeable is hidden; within the mortal the immortal is hidden; amidst all motion is hidden the unmoving. One who knows this eternal, deathless one within knows that no grief and no unhappiness can ever affect him.

The whole suffering of man is because he is identified with the changeable. The very meaning of the word *changeable* is that it will change – and we don't want it to change. A young person wants his body not to become old, but the body is bound to become old. The old person doesn't want to die, but the body will die.

You are identified and want things to be permanent, but they cannot remain the same. It is as if a person is standing on the bank of a river wanting the river not to flow, and if it flows he will become miserable because his demand has not been fulfilled. Everything is flowing, transitory, but you hold on to transitory things and want to make them permanent. This ends in misery because the transitory cannot be eternal.

A young man is in love with a young woman and he tells her that he will love her forever; the young woman also thinks that this love will be everlasting. But the one who is speaking – and the body, heart and mind of the one who is speaking – is transitory. Anything said by the body can never be everlasting. Tomorrow the love will change leaving only ashes behind. The flame will be extinguished and only the extinguished lamp will remain. Then you will be in misery. Then you will feel that you have been deceived, that the man has said that he would love you forever and the love did not last even a few days. This will make you miserable, but the reason for your misery is not that somebody has deceived you. Nobody has deceived! Whosoever expects the changeable to be permanent will be in misery. The young man also felt, in that moment, that he would love forever. He did not intend to deceive, but later on when he sees that love has vanished what can he do?

There is a Christian sect called the Quakers. It is one of the few sects on this earth who are really trying to be religious. They do not promise anything, they do not give any consolation. They ask, "How can a transitory mind make any promises? It is not certain that we will even be here tomorrow – how can we give guarantees?" Quakers don't take oaths in court, hence many Quakers have been convicted for not taking the oath. They ask, "Who will take the oath? Tomorrow is not certain; we can change even after one moment. An oath can only be taken by someone who is certain that he will never change." When the court asks them to take an oath to speak the truth by placing a hand on the Bible, a Quaker will say, "I can take an oath now – it makes no difference – but what should I do if I change my mind afterward?" This is why they do not make promises or give anyone guarantees. Quakers say that tomorrow is not certain: "There is no certainty that we will even be here."

Everything is changing, everything is flowing like a river. Anyone who tries to remain static in a flowing river will suffer. Flowing is not static by its very nature. Only a person who can grasp the changeless hidden within him will transcend sorrow: for him there is no change, and hence, no misery. That inner essence never becomes old, never dies and never changes. It is always the same.

> *"Godliness is not known through speaking, through intellect or through listening to lengthy discourses. Godliness can be known only by one who it has already chosen. For this person, it reveals its true nature."*

This sutra is a little difficult, but it is essential to understand it because much depends on it.

You may study many scriptures, listen to discourses or try to understand intellectually, but in these ways godliness cannot be realized. There will be only empty words in your hand. Scholarship can be gained, intellect can become sharp and memory can be strengthened. You can receive answers to every question but there will be no fulfillment. The soul will remain unsatisfied.

It is as if you explain to a thirsty person that water is made from oxygen and hydrogen, $H_2O$, two atoms of hydrogen and one atom of oxygen; that water as such is not an element; the real elements are hydrogen and oxygen – he may understand that water is $H_2O$ but he will still ask, "What about my thirst?"

Remember, thirst is not quenched by knowing what $H_2O$ is or by repeatedly writing it down on paper. Many people go on writing the name Rama or Krishna...

A mad person once met me: he had made a big library of books in which on page after page "Rama, Rama" had been written by his devotees. They would keep sending him such notebooks and he would collect them in his library.

But neither can a thirst be quenched by writing $H_2O$, nor can Rama be realized by writing "Rama, Rama." It is all a waste of time. These are just signs of stupidity. But there is no lack of stupid people, you can find them everywhere. That person must be wasting one or two hours every day and he thinks that he is doing great work. What can happen through writing "Rama, Rama"? Any printing press can do this job. For this you don't have to use your intelligence at all. The printing press that can do this job will not realize truth, and you also will not realize the truth in this way.

*"Godliness is not known through speaking, through intellect or through listening to lengthy discourses."* These are not the methods for realization. Yama is saying an amazing thing: that there is only one way to realization and that only when the divine has accepted you can you realize it. This is very problematic. It means that only when you have become worthy, only when you have transformed yourself, will it accept you and will you be able to realize it. Your self-transformation, your worthiness and your readiness to be accepted will have to be so complete that the divine will not be able to reject you; it will have to accept you. Your purity, innocence and simplicity, the fragrance of your behavior, your individuality and your way of living should

become so full of meditation that the divine will have to accept you; it will be helpless to do otherwise. Unless you are in this state of being you will not realize godliness.

It is easy to read scriptures but it is very difficult to transform your life. People are always looking for shortcuts, but there are no shortcuts in life. In life one has to go on the right road and experience the inconveniences, the pains and the sufferings of the road. One has to wander, and may lose his way on this journey; but all these efforts are necessary for your transformation. You will become new. The journey is not just a journey but also a transformation.

Yama says: *"Godliness can be known only by one who it has already chosen. For this person, it reveals its true nature."* If you have not realized godliness it is because there is some obstacle within you which is preventing you from knowing. Perhaps you are standing with your eyes closed so you cannot see the sun. And to a blind man, howsoever much you may explain about the sun, it will make no difference – first the eyes and the heart have to be opened.

All meditation techniques are for opening your heart. Discourses and scriptures are all intellectual, but meditation is a heart phenomenon. Meditation will transform you. Meditation means that you are making some efforts.

A friend came to me and said, "Your discourses are very good, very pleasing." I said, "Howsoever good or pleasing they may be, they will not be helpful. They are just entertainment. You like them, good! Some people like to see films, some like to listen to the radio, some like to listen to my discourses – but what will happen in you through it? As long as you don't do anything, nothing will happen. Unless you pass through a transformation, nothing will happen. My discourses can do only one thing: they can inspire you to transform yourself – but they can do no more than that."

The buddhas can awaken a thirst in you but they cannot give you truth. But if you are satisfied with only the arising of a thirst, the thirst will become an obstacle. If only a thirst is awakened in you, what can happen? No, you will have to travel to the ocean. But sometimes a problem can be created: while the thirst is arising you can get into trouble because your thirst becomes your enjoyment – listening to me and reading my books starts satisfying your intellect. Then when will you move toward the source of water? When will you search for the ocean?

Yama rightly says:

> *"Although refined of intellect, one who has not become free of unconscious conduct…"*

One who has not become free of unconscious behavior will not be able to realize godliness – even though he may have a sharp intellect or be a profound thinker or a great logician.

> *"…or who is not serene, or whose mind and senses are undisciplined, or whose mind is not peaceful, cannot know godliness."*

Behavior is either conscious or unconscious. You are doing wrong things because you are unconscious. If you were conscious you could not do wrong, it is not possible. Wrong action happens because of your unconsciousness. When a person drinks alcohol and begins to abuse or hit others, there is no use telling him to stop abusing and hitting: he is drunk so he cannot hear or understand. He may even abuse or hit the person who is advising him. If you want to advise him you can only tell him not to drink, because you know that when he is not drunk he is not unconscious. When he is sober he neither abuses nor misbehaves. The real question is not of correcting his behavior but of increasing his consciousness or reducing his unconsciousness.

Yama is saying that no matter how much you may think or talk about understanding things, as long as your behavior is not transformed it only proves that you are still unconscious within.

As long as this unconsciousness is not broken you cannot realize godliness. Restlessness and indulgence are because of unconsciousness. While your senses are not disciplined, while your mind is not restful and you are not centered within yourself, you will not know godliness.

Yama says:

> *"No one knows where and how it is. All living beings, at the time of pralaya, the dissolution of the universe, will become food for it; and even death, the destroyer of all, will become no more than a garnish for it."*

This has to be understood: godliness can be known, but never completely. To know it completely will mean that the knower is bigger than it. Only what is smaller than you and which you can surround from all sides and understand from all angles can be completely known by you.

Nobody can know godliness completely: it is a mystery and it will remain a mystery. You may be able to jump into it and say that you have known it, recognized it or become one with it, but you will never be able to say that you have really known it. In your knowing there will always be something lacking because existence is infinite. You may become one with it but you cannot fully know it.

You can understand it in this way. For example, if you jump into the sea, it is one thing to jump into the sea, to dive into it and say afterward that you have bathed in it and known it. But the sea is vast and you have returned after knowing only a part of one shore and a small area of the sea. Even if you were to stay in the sea you would only know a part of it. In one sense it is true that you have known the sea. If you taste even one drop of the sea you will know the essence of sea because all that is hidden in the sea is also hidden in a single drop. But you can never say that you have known the whole sea in its entirety.

Try to understand that the whole emphasis of science is that it can know everything in its totality, whereas the emphasis of religion is that everything can be known but nothing can be known completely; the mystery will always remain.

This is why religion is mystery and science is an enemy of mystery. Demystification is the way of science. Wherever there is mystery, science wants to clarify, disclose and make clear whatsoever appears to be misty. Science will be totally successful only when there is no longer any mystery in this world, when whatsoever you ask science will have the answer. But religion says that this can never happen. And those who have gone very deeply into science – like Einstein, Planck or Oppenheimer – have also said the same thing.

A science teacher in a school, college or university is not a scientist. They are scholars of science, they know questions and answers. A man like Einstein who is a sage of science, who has gone very deeply into science, said at the time of his death that the mystery will never end. The more you investigate the more mysterious it becomes. It never becomes less mysterious because new questions will arise from whatever you have already investigated.

The religious experience is that the world is an infinite mystery. That is why Yama says, "Who can fully know it? – no one is bigger than it." The knower has to be bigger than the known; only then can he know something totally. But here, the knower is smaller than the known. Here, one is like the wings of a butterfly and the reality is the infinite sky. How can the wings of a butterfly span the infinite sky? This does not mean that you should feel despair. A butterfly can fly in the sky and can totally enjoy its flight in the sky. What is the need to know the whole sky? As far as its wings can take it, it is enough, more than enough.

Knowing is an infinite journey that never ends. This is the meaning of infinite truth, the beginningless truth which has no beginning or end.

> *"In the human body, which is the fruit of conscious deeds, there is an entity which lives in the sky of the heart, the true*

> *abode of godliness, and which savors the truth that is hidden in the miraculous recesses of the intellect. There is also the entity which suffers the inescapable impact of past actions. These two are not the same. Like sunlight and shadow, the two are different from each other – so it is said by the great wise ones, those who know the supreme reality."*

The Upanishads say that there are two currents living in every human being. And this is true: the one that resides within you is the witness, and the other is the doer. The Upanishads say it is like two birds sitting on a tree, with one bird sitting on a higher branch and the other on a lower branch. The bird sitting on the lower branch is hopping and jumping, tasting the fruits of the tree, dancing, loving, calling its beloved and doing many other things, whereas the bird sitting on the higher branch is just watching what the other bird is doing. It does not do anything, it is just witnessing.

The Upanishads say there are two currents in every human being. One current is just a witness, watching everything, doing nothing. And the other is the one who does everything: it runs the shop, fights, makes friends, loves, raises a family and takes sannyas – it is the doer. Behind the doer there is the other current that only witnesses everything – attraction and repulsion, right and wrong, religiousness and irreligiousness, good deeds and bad deeds.

You are not the doer. The doer is the accumulation of all your actions from endless past lives. As long as this doer does not totally dissolve there can be no ultimate freedom. You can call it "the mind"; Buddhists call it *sanghaat* and Jainas call it "impurity of past action." You can also call it "the doer element" as the Upanishads do. But there is another, deeper reality, and that is the witness.

Try to understand it this way: if a thief is going to steal, while he is on his way there is someone within him that knows that he is going to steal – this is the witness within him. When you are running a shop there is someone within you that knows that you are running a shop. You are young but someone within you knows that you are gradually becoming old. You are sick and someone inside knows that you are sick. But this knower is not very clear to you, and that is your problem. You always forget this knower and become identified with the doer. When you are losing your youth and becoming old you say, "*I* am getting old" – but this is a mistake. When you are angry you say, "*I* am angry." When you are running a shop you say, "*I* am running a shop."

Buddha has said, "Before enlightenment, hunger was there, and it is also there now. In earlier days I used to feel that *I* am hungry, but now I know that my body is hungry and I am witnessing the hunger – there is that much distance. It is a small distance but it is vast; it is subtle but endless."

When you are sick you feel, "I am sick," but that is a mistake. If you can just remember that you are the one who knows that your body is sick, you will notice that there are two separate streams: one is on the level of doing and the other is the witness.

The more this witness becomes clear to you, the nearer you will be to godliness. The more you forget this witness, the stronger your doer will become and you will be more and more deeply involved in this world. If you are identified with your actions you become part of the world. If your identification with actions is dissolved you become one with existence.

> *"May all beings be worthy of knowing and attaining to the Naachiket Fire, the bridge which can take those who perform the yagnas, the fire rituals, beyond this ocean of suffering to ineffable supreme being. This supreme being is the abode of fearlessness for those who long to cross the ocean of this world of illusion.*
>
> *"Nachiketa, understand the embodied soul to be the owner, the rider in the chariot, the body to be the chariot,*

*intelligence to be the charioteer and mind to be the reins.*

*"In this metaphor of the chariot, the sages say that the senses are the horses, the objects being sensed are the roads which the chariot is traveling on, and the embodied soul living in identification with the body, the senses, and the mind is the bhokta, the experiencer.*

*"For one who lives unconsciously and who has a restless mind, his senses are uncontrollable, like the untamed horses of a careless charioteer."*

This is a very old Indian symbolism: man is like a chariot in which the owner sits, and the owner is the witness. The senses are the horses, the reins which are controlling the horses are the mind, the road on which the horses run are desires. The charioteer who is controlling the reins is the intelligence of the mind. Behind all of these, sitting in the chariot, is the witness, the being, which is the ultimate reality. For one who begins to recognize that witness, the whole journey of his chariot becomes harmonious, disciplined.

But ordinarily you don't recognize the witness because you have settled down near the horses or you are too involved with the horses. Moreover, many horses are tied to the chariot and all the horses are galloping in different directions – one horse is galloping in one direction and another in another direction. That is why life is a great struggle, a conflict. One part of mind says "do this" and another part says "do that" and a third voice says "do another thing." There is so much confusion that you are not able to understand what to do and what not to do. You are reading the Gita and one voice tells you to go and see a movie and another says, "What a waste of time! You can read this when you are old. What is your hurry to read it right now?" All this is going on inside. All the horses are pulling in different directions and the chariot is dragged by all these horses.

If a person becomes a little more conscious he will move away from the horses and center himself with the intelligence of the mind – which is the charioteer. If a person becomes still more conscious he will move behind the mind, which is not the owner but the servant. He will understand that it is dangerous to be led by the servant.

So by looking within, a person will reach to the very center of the chariot where the witness, the watcher, dwells. Being one with the owner, you become the master of your own life. For the first time you become your own master. After this all wrongdoing will automatically cease. After this all unconscious acts will drop.

There is only one journey and that is to move away from the horses, the doer, to the witness. One who is settled in the witness is free from misery, pain and anguish in his life.

Now get ready for meditation… Get ready for our morning meditation.

7

# The Flowering of Godliness

*"The senses of one who lives consciously and with a disciplined mind, are under control, like the tame horses of a vigilant charioteer.*

*"One who lives unconsciously, whose mind is undisciplined and impure, will not attain parampada, the ultimate state. He will continue to be bound in sansara, the wheel of life and death.*

*"One who lives consciously, whose mind is disciplined and pure, will attain the ultimate state from where there will be no return through another birth.*

*"One whose consciousness is his charioteer and who keeps his mind, the reins of the horses, disciplined, will go beyond the world and the path and will attain the ultimate.*

*"Sense objects are more powerful than the senses, the mind is more powerful than sense objects, intelligence is more powerful than the mind, and the soul is greater and more powerful than intelligence.*

*"Maya, the creative energy of godliness, is more powerful than the soul; existence itself is more powerful than its creative energy. It is transcendental. There is nothing beyond*

*it. It is the ultimate. It is the final abode of all.*

*"Man is discontented, in continuous mental conflict. And this tension, this worry, this anxiety and insanity are all born out of one thing – and that is that there are many layers in his personality. He is not one, he is many layers."*

The first layer is the body: the body is a layer which has its own desires, its own passions. The body has its own attractions, attachments, greeds and lusts. Then there is another layer, the mind within the body: the mind has its own desires and aspirations. But within the mind there is a layer of wakeful intelligence, of *vivek*. The desires of this intelligence are very different, and so there is a continuous conflict between the desires of these three layers. The body wants to do one thing, the mind wants to do another thing and wakeful intelligence proposes a third thing. This creates an inner struggle within man. It is only because of this that man is disturbed, in a chaos.

If man were only a body there would be no discontentment. If man were only a mind, even then there would be no discontentment. Even if man were only a soul, still there would be no discontentment. Animals are less discontented than man because they have only bodies. There is a small glimpse of mind in animals, and their discontent is in proportion to that. Plants are even more contented, trees are even more at peace. There is no tension and no anxiety because there is not even a small glimpse of mind. In man also, the more intellectual a man is the more discontented he will be; the less intellectual a man is the less discontented he will be.

This is why as education becomes more prevalent, as the capacity for thinking grows and as the intellect becomes sharper, simultaneously discontent will also increase. America has the highest number of mad people. Don't feel happy about this; don't think that because of this you are more fortunate. It just means that today America is the most developed in the intellectual field.

In affluent families there will always be more tension and anxiety. Actually, it should be otherwise. There is not much tension in poor, village families. Affluent families are more tense because along with more money, there comes more intellect also. As the intellect grows, affluence will also grow. The poorer a person is, the less will be his intellectual development; otherwise he would also have become rich. A poor man may be unhappy, but he is not restless. It means that the more layers are active within, the more is the struggle and the tension.

If a person could live only in his body he would have no reason to be tense. But you cannot live only in the body, the mind is standing behind you. The body says one thing and the mind says another. You are eating a meal and the body says, "My stomach is full," but the mind says, "The food is very tasty, you can eat a little more." Then intelligence warns, "You are being stupid because it will make you ill." These three layers are creating the tension within you.

The body does not understand any moral rules, it is like an animal. But the mind is always in great conflict: the mind has the desires of an animal as well as the conditionings of a man, the knowledge given by the society and also the conscience. If you are hungry the body will say, "Steal! There is no harm in it" because at the body level there is no problem at all – but the mind will experience uneasiness.

The ego will say, "If you are caught stealing you will be disgraced," and the mind will say, "If you have to steal, do it in such a way that you are not caught." And the intelligence that is a deeper layer will say, "Whether you are caught or not, stealing is a wrong act." Your intelligence will go on feeling the pinch even if you are never caught.

Man's restlessness is because he is divided into many layers. If you understand this clearly then the next thing will be easy to understand.

The next point is that it is not possible to quiet a disturbance on one layer through the power of that same layer. That disturbance can be quieted only through the power of a higher layer. If there is disturbance on a body level it is not possible for the body to solve it, but the mind can do it. If there is a problem on the level of mind, mind itself cannot solve it, but intelligence can do it. If there is any problem on the level of intelligence, intelligence cannot solve it; for that one will have to move to the level of the soul. If there is any problem on the soul level, unless one reaches to the level of the universal self, there can be no solution. It means that wherever the problem is, the solution should be searched for at a higher level.

But you always seek solutions on the same level and that only increases your difficulties. Try to understand it: when sexual desire arises in your body the eyes start looking for beauty. There are a few stories of saints who gouged out their eyes because their eyes were attracted to beautiful women. The body is looking for beauty, but to remove your eyes is to look for the solution on the same level; it is not rising to a higher level. The body is attracted and you are harming the body itself. You will find no solution by removing your eyes. Even without his eyes a blind man will still be in the grip of his desires. Perhaps if he had eyes he would not have become as obsessed, but without eyes the difficulties will only multiply.

Many religious traditions have advised people in the past to cut off any limb which creates trouble. You will be surprised to know that in Russia there was a Christian sect which used to cut off their genital organs. Only after the revolution in 1917, when it was made illegal, could the sect be prevented from cutting off their genitals. There were millions of people in Russia who had cut off their genital organs only because they believed that by doing it they would become free from sexual desire.

But by cutting off the genitals one cannot become free from sex because sexual desire is not limited to the genital organs; it is deep within the brain. The genital organs are an extension of the brain, so the joy that you feel in sex is not at the level of the genitals, but rather it is first experienced in the brain.

Those who love food go on a fast, but it is only on the same level. First they were forcibly filling the body and now they are forcibly starving themselves – but the level has not changed. And unless the level changes there can be no transformation in life. Only the higher level can become the master of the lower level, this is the second thing.

The third thing to remember is that if you try to control on the same level, it will become suppression and your whole life will be poisoned. But if you are awakening the higher level then there is no suppression. When the energy of the higher level becomes available, the lower level will simply surrender.

Mind is the whole problem. People come to me and ask, "How can we be free from the mind?" – but the methods that they use to become free from the mind are done by the mind! To become free from the mind people go to a temple, but the temple is also a game created by the mind. To get rid of the mind people read religious books, but these books are also created by the mind. To become free from the mind people begin to repeat a mantra, but that is also within the jurisdiction of the mind. They use rosaries, take oaths and make vows, but all of it is done by the mind.

A friend came to me: he had taken a vow of celibacy. But if it were so simple to become a celibate there would have been no problem. Is it possible to become celibate just by making a vow? He said to me, "I am in great difficulty. I have made this vow, but celibacy is not happening – my mind is more sexual than before. My sexual desire is even stronger than before I made the vow. After I made the vow there has been nothing on my mind but sex. Before it was also possible to think about other things, but now sex has become my only preoccupation."

Only foolish people make vows. A man of understanding does not make vows, he becomes aware. Making vows is making an effort on the same level. It is like a primary school class where small children are fighting among each other and creating a great noise, and suddenly a teacher enters the class and immediately there is silence. The children all sit in their places and open their books as if nothing was happening before – a power of a higher level has entered the room and its presence has brought about the transformation.

As soon as you awaken the power of a higher level, immediately the struggle and conflict at the lower level will calm down. This needs to be understood clearly: whenever there is a conflict in your life don't fight with it directly, try to invoke the power of a higher level.

To those who ask me how to quiet the mind, I tell them not to bother about it, not to do anything with the mind. Just awaken your intelligence, become conscious. Don't struggle with the mind because it will also be the mind which fights. Even the one who advises you to be silent is also the mind. So if the mind fights with itself by dividing itself in two parts, the fight will be like my right hand fighting with my left hand. No one will win and no one will be defeated. It is within my own control. Sometimes I can make the right hand appear to be winning and at another time I can let the left hand win – but both are my hands and both are using my energy; there is no question of winning or losing. I may be identified with my right hand but at another time I may be identified with my left hand.

Thus, sometimes you become identified with the part of the mind which is full of desire and at another time you become identified with the part of the mind which makes oaths and thinks about repentance. The mind goes on swinging like a pendulum, at one moment in this direction and the next moment in another.

When there is a conflict on one level, it is necessary to search for a higher and deeper level which can be awakened. The essence of intelligence is *vivek*, wakeful intelligence. *Vivek* means awareness in thought and in action, a sort of vigilance, a constant remembrance.

You are walking on a road – this walking is mechanical. You know how to walk, the body walks mechanically. There is no need to remain aware of the fact that you are walking or that you are lifting your leg. You are breathing and it continues mechanically; you don't have to do anything to breathe, awareness is not needed at all. But you can also breathe with awareness.

Buddha's basic method and his total discipline was of breathing with awareness. Buddha used to tell his disciples that if they could breathe consciously, everything else would fall into place. Such a simple thing to do and everything becomes okay? But however simple it may appear to be on the outside, it is very difficult to do inside. It looks as simple as when you push a switch and thousands of bulbs light up. Someone may ask you how only one small switch can make thousands of bulbs light up at the same time. That one switch is visible, but the whole network of wiring that is hidden behind is not visible. In the same way awareness seems to be very easy, but it is very difficult.

Buddha has said, "Just inhale and exhale consciously, that's enough." What is going to happen just by doing this? This can do everything because with this method your inner consciousness will begin to awaken. This can also be accomplished through other methods, but whatsoever you do, if you do it consciously your wakeful intelligence will start to grow sharper and because of this your mind will start becoming more silent. When the master appears, the servant will sit quietly and wait for his orders.

Awareness is the essence of all religiousness and unconsciousness is the basis of all that is irreligious. Whatsoever we do, if it is done consciously it is right, if it is done unconsciously it is wrong. No action in itself is either right or wrong: it all depends on what is the state of your consciousness at the time of the action.

Once Buddha was passing through a village. He had not yet become a buddha at that time; he was still in search, he was a seeker, he had not yet become enlightened. He was talking with a friend and a fly sat on his forehead. Buddha continued to talk;

he just went on walking and waved the fly away just as you would do.

Suddenly he stopped and consciously raised his hand to remove the fly from his forehead – and it was no longer there. His friend asked, "Are you mad? What are you trying to remove now?"

Buddha said, "I am consciously removing the fly, as I should have done in the first place. I was busy talking with you and I removed the fly unconsciously, my hand did it mechanically. I was not aware, so now I have done it with total awareness. Now I am fully aware in the movement of my hand and I have moved with my hand to remove the fly. My mind is totally present in the action and is not anywhere else." He said, "I again removed the fly, but consciously. The first time I made a mistake so a wrong thing happened."

The fly was not hurt even the first time, so there was no reason for Buddha to call it wrong. But Buddha said, "Because I was unconscious the first time it was wrong. If I can remove a fly unconsciously, I can do anything else unconsciously. I can even kill somebody because how can an unconscious man be relied upon?"

We cannot expect anything from a person who does things unconsciously: he can commit any wrong. Buddha again went through the act of removing the fly as he should have done it the first time.

Buddha used to say to his disciples, "Whatever you do – standing, sitting or walking – do it with the flame of awareness burning continuously within you. If you took a step unconsciously, go back, repeat it again in total consciousness." As a person becomes conscious of all his actions, eating, breathing or closing his eyes… Try to experiment a little and you will be surprised to see how silent you become. Nothing needs to be done with the mind directly. You do not have to undergo any treatment for your mind. Just by remaining conscious in all your actions you will find that your mind has become quiet. The mind is disturbed because of unconsciousness. There is a sort of drunkenness spread over you. It is necessary to come out of this drunkenness and these sutras are about this.

> *"The senses of one who lives consciously and with a disciplined mind, are under control, like the tame horses of a vigilant charioteer."*

Try to understand this. Ordinarily, you begin by trying to control the horses. You begin to fight with your senses and you think that if you control your senses one by one, eventually you will win. Nobody has ever won like this; on the contrary, he has utterly failed. And things become so perverted that life loses all meaning, life makes you feel suicidal.

But there are many so-called intelligent people who go on fighting with their senses. Somebody is fighting with food and somebody else is fighting with sexual desire and somebody else with some other thing – but the fight with the senses continues.

Fighting with your senses is like fighting with your own servants. The servants need to be commanded, not fought with. Fighting with them means that you have treated them as your equals; that is your mistake. The one who treats the servant as an equal will not win, the servant will win. Once a servant comes to know that his master treats him as an equal and is ready to fight with him, he will also be ready to fight. And if a fight happens the servant can also win; he will try his best to win.

The senses do not deserve to be fought with. Fighting itself is a mistake. It is certain that if you fight you will be defeated because you are not aware that you are the master. If you are defeated by your senses you will be discouraged forever.

I was once a guest in a house in Calcutta. One very rich, old man of great understanding told me that he had taken a vow of celibacy four times!

There was another friend with me who was very impressed by this. I told him, "Don't be so impressed. First, understand what it means to make a vow of celibacy four times. Only once should be enough." I told him, "One who has taken a vow four times, ask him why he has not taken it for the fifth time."

That old man was really honest: he said, "You have raised a right question." He said, "I did not take the vow for the fifth time because after being unsuccessful four times, I have lost all hope of ever being successful."

If you fight with your senses it is certain that the only outcome will be that you will be defeated, because as soon as you have decided to fight you have already given up your mastery. Whosoever is not aware of his mastery is *bound* to be defeated.

There is no need to fight. You have only to become aware and your senses will stand aside and take orders. But once you are defeated you will be discouraged – you will feel that your senses are more powerful than you are and that you can never win. And once this desperation settles in your mind, your life will remain always in darkness.

You are all discouraged. You have lost hope, and your so-called monks and saints are responsible for this situation. They are teaching you to fight but they never teach you to become aware. They have put you in an impossible situation.

Friends come to me and they say that they have been fighting to give up smoking for twenty years! If you want to fight, fight with something big. You don't value your being at all. You are fighting for twenty years and cannot succeed over a cigarette? Then how can you trust that godliness is within you? You are bound to feel discouraged. What fool has asked you to fight with a cigarette? If you want to smoke, smoke! At least you will be your own master. If you want to give it up, give it up – but remain the master. Why have you created a problem by fighting? And fighting for twenty years! And the cigarette is winning and you are being defeated.

Never fight with small things, even by mistake. Fighting with small things means that you have lost contact with the higher. Don't fight with the trivial, search for the higher. With the presence of the higher the trivial is defeated automatically. Bring in the higher, never try to destroy the lower.

You may have heard the story of Akbar: he drew a line on a wall and asked his courtiers to make that line smaller without touching it.

It was a problem! Those courtiers must have been like your so-called saints. "Without touching or cutting the line, how can it be made smaller?"

Birbal stood up and drew a longer line next to it and the first line became smaller automatically, without his touching it. The previous line was neither cut nor erased.

This is an art of life: to awaken a higher state alongside the lower one.

Your fighting with small things will make you small. Remember, any friend will do, but choose an enemy only with great care. Whosoever chooses a small enemy will become small himself. People do not learn as much from their friends as they learn from their enemies. Because there is conflict for twenty-four hours with enemies, slowly enemies become alike.

If for a lifetime two people go on fighting as enemies, by the time of death they will have become like twin brothers. This continuous conflict for a lifetime is good companionship, learning each other's ways and subtleties of fighting. Because if they have to fight they have to study each other's tactics closely. Slowly they go on becoming more and more similar. Friends can continue to be different from each other but enemies become similar. Understand this rightly: never develop any enmity against smaller things.

Psychiatrists are saying something very valuable that will help you to understand this: they say that a father should never ask anything of his son that he will not be able to get his son to do because once the father is defeated he will never be able to regain respect in the eyes of his son.

For example, your small child is crying in front of you and you tell him to stop crying. Is it within your power to stop him from crying? He will go on crying and you will go on shouting at him to stop crying. At the most you can beat him, but that will only make him cry more. It is very difficult to *make* him stop crying. Once the child realizes that you keep shouting at him to stop crying but still he continues to cry and you cannot do anything to him – and that all your energy is exhausted – your power will then be lost for him. In the mind of this child you will not be a very powerful person.

Freud says that children are badly spoiled because parents are trying to make children do things which they cannot enforce – they fail. Freud said only to tell the child to do things which you can make him do. If you tell him, "Get out of my room!" at least you can drive him out of the room. The child will know that his father can make him do what he says he wants him to do.

In this same context, it is worth remembering that you should only ask your senses to do what you can make them do. Otherwise, don't order, wait for a while. Once your senses realize that all your talk has no value and that it is all nonsense, that you make decisions which are meaningless – that your vows and decisions are of no value, that you are not your own master and that all your decisions can be shattered – then your senses, like horses, will never stay under your control. But everybody has done this, and very sensible people are busy asking themselves to take vows.

Only take the kind of vows which can be fulfilled. But people don't take those kinds of vows. Try to understand this: you always do what you can do, so why do you need to make a vow about it? You make vows only when you know that something is difficult to carry out. You use the help of a vow and decide to show that you will see to it that it is carried out. But who are you going to show? If you are not able to do it, you will simply fall in your own eyes – and there is not a more pitiable person than one who has fallen in his own eyes.

This is why I say to you that if you want to drink alcohol, drink it; if you want to smoke cigarettes, do it, but remain your own master. Don't create a conflict that will destroy your mastery. This does not mean that I am saying to go on drinking and smoking. I am telling you that within you there is a power which does not come from struggle but from awareness. That is *vivek*, wakeful intelligence.

Awaken your wakeful intelligence. Try to do things consciously. Don't fight with small things because such fights are meaningless. It is a waste of time and energy. Even if you somehow give up smoking you will begin to take snuff through your nose, or you will begin to eat betel leaves or chew tobacco. Your vices will simply take new forms because the senses don't want to give up their mastery easily.

This sutra is stating the same thing put in a reverse way. *"The senses of one who lives consciously and with a disciplined mind are under control, like the tame horses of a vigilant charioteer."* The real thing is to live consciously. If consciousness is there, the mind is under control. If the mind is under control the senses are under control. Hence the real search is for awareness, for consciousness.

> *"One who lives unconsciously, whose mind is undisciplined and impure, cannot attain parampada, the ultimate state. He will continue to be bound in sansara, the wheel of life and death."*

All your wandering is because of your unconsciousness. From your very birth you go on living as if you are drunk. If a person lives for sixty years, he will sleep for twenty of those years. One third of a life is no small amount of time. During the remaining forty years there are only a very few moments when he is not dreaming. He is nearly always dreaming.

You are sitting in a chair at home and the dreaming continues: you imagine that you have become the president of your country; or suddenly there is money showering on your house. And this is not the end of your dreaming. You then begin to dream about how you will use that money, what sort of palace you will build and what you will do and what you will not do – but this dreaming continues.

The stories of Sheikh Chilly are not only in children's books, they are in everyone's minds also. Every man goes on building castles in the air. He does this not just once in a while, he goes on doing it every day. When for a moment he becomes aware, he laughs at himself and wonders, "What nonsense am I doing?" But after a short time the dreaming starts again. Twenty years asleep and forty years dreaming!

Gurdjieff used to say that if the small moments in which we are conscious were added up, it would not even amount to more than five minutes during a life span of sixty years. These glimpses of awareness come and are lost again. With only that much awareness, you cannot attain truth. Even those few moments of awareness come only at times when there is great danger or a life crisis.

You are driving your car or you are riding on your bicycle and inside the dream continues. Mechanically, like a robot, your hands control the steering, but the mind goes on dreaming and the inner chatter continues. You have already reached wherever you are going in your imagination – or you have not even left from where you started.

Suddenly, while you are driving, a situation occurs which may cause an accident: a truck is coming at great speed from the opposite direction. For a second you become aware, your mind stops. Your thinking is interrupted and your dreams are broken.

Have you ever noticed that at those moments you instantly feel a hit at the navel center? The navel is the root of life. When you feel the hit, a glimpse of light spreads from your navel center over your whole mind. For a second you become totally conscious and you control the steering with awareness. But then the truck passes by, your fast heartbeat slows down, your fast breathing also becomes regular, the dreaming begins and you are once again lost in your own world.

So during these moments of crisis a little awareness arises.

The wife has died or the husband has died or your child has died: there is a sudden impact of grief for a moment; the navel center gets a hit and a light shines within. Suddenly you become aware of death, that your life is not forever and that the people that you have loved are going to be separated from you. These houses of love are just houses of cards; you have built a castle of sand. But this awareness is only for a second, and that second is so small that sometimes you don't even notice that the second has happened. Again you beat your chest, cry and feel miserable, think of the past and the future – and that moment is lost forever.

Gurdjieff used to say that during a life span of sixty years a man becomes aware, at the most, for five minutes – and that too is not all together, at one time. These moments happen in small bits. Sometimes the sun is rising and its beauty enchants you. Sometimes a row of white swans flies across the sky or against black clouds like a flash of lightning, and your mind stops. Sometimes a bird is singing a song and its vibration touches your inner music – and your mind stops. These moments, although very few, are moments of bliss.

Moments of awareness are the only moments of bliss. Moments of sleep are all the moments of misery. And this awareness can be awakened if you begin to become conscious within.

You can try a small experiment in your house – and it will be more valuable than all your so-called worship and prayers. In the morning, when you are fresh, hold your wristwatch in front of you and start looking at the second hand. Decide to keep your eyes and your attention on that second hand for a full minute until it completes one full circle, without losing your awareness for even one second. Decide that you will not lose awareness and that you will go on watching as it moves, second after second. You will be surprised to find that after three or four seconds the mind has run away somewhere else and the second hand has been forgotten. After just three or four seconds!

But you cannot keep your mind on the second hand for sixty full seconds; you will remember so many other things. You will begin to think about where the watch was made: "Is it a Swiss watch? How many jewels does it have?" That small second hand will remind you of a hundred and one things. You can try it. If you try, it will take you three months to keep your awareness on the second hand for one full minute. And this will be a great achievement! To remain aware for a full circle of the second hand, it will need three months.

To be conscious is a very difficult thing. But if you can manage to remain conscious for one minute you will become a totally different person. That old personality of yours will look like a stranger to you. You will feel that the story of your life belongs to somebody else, that the old person has died and a new life has descended into you. Because the way of life of this new person will be new, now mind will no longer be his master. For the one who can remain aware for one minute, the mind will become his servant. No desire can trap a person who has been conscious for even one minute because he will also become conscious of his desires.

It is interesting that your desires can drag you down only because you are unconscious, because you are asleep. Anger *cannot* arise in you if you have learned the art of becoming conscious when anything even begins to take hold of you. One who can become aware for a full minute can also become aware at any moment. Even when sexual desire possesses him he will immediately straighten his backbone and be conscious in that moment. And suddenly a very unique experience will happen:

as soon as you become aware the sexual desire will disappear as if it had not been there at all.

Buddha has said that thieves do not enter a house where a lamp is burning; only if the lamp is not burning will the thieves enter. Buddha has also said that thieves do not even look at a house where there is a watchman sitting at the door. A house where the watchman is sleeping becomes an invitation for thieves. Your senses are like thieves. If your watchman is awake and if your inner light is burning, desires will not even try to peep in. If you are sleeping and snoring, desires will surround you. Desires are powerful only in unconsciousness, when you are sleeping, when there is darkness.

*"One who lives unconsciously, whose mind is undisciplined and impure, will not attain parampada, the ultimate state. He will continue to be bound in sansara, the wheel of life and death."* It is your unconsciousness that repeatedly leads you astray. You do not understand why this repetitive circle of life and death continues. You have no idea and no remembrance of its past repetitions, hence you are not able to get out of the circle.

Try to understand it in this way: how often have you become angry and how often have you repented, deciding never to do it again? But again you become angry. How often have you been possessed by sexual desire and become mad and unconscious? And how often have you repented, experienced misery and sadness and decided not to repeat it again? This has happened repeatedly. Again and again you are moving like the spokes of a wheel – the same spoke that is now going down will go up after a moment. The spoke of anger is now up and then it appears to go down – and then you repent. Soon the spoke will come up again and you will get angry and when it goes down you will repent. Your life is moving round and round in circles like the spokes of a wheel, hence it is not difficult to understand that this circle does not begin with this birth and it will not end with this death.

Now psychologists say that a child has a separate personality even while he is in the mother's womb. After birth, of course, the separate personality will be very clear, but in the womb too the separate personality is there. In the womb some children kick their mother's belly aggressively. They are aggressive, violent. Some children are so sad that the mother also becomes sad because of them. Some children are very cheerful in the womb and the mother also becomes cheerful because she is responding to the cheerful vibration of the child. The child and the mother are in union. That is why the personality of the woman usually changes during pregnancy. A new being and a new soul is uniting with her, influencing her. A quiet woman may become restless and a restless woman may become quiet. After the birth of the child she will return back to her own nature, but for nine months a different energy is flowing within her.

Psychologists say that a child has a personality from the very first moment. From where does he bring that personality? There must be a long story behind it. No child is just being born today: there is a long journey of infinite births and the child is born with that.

When a child is in the mother's womb, she has different dreams with each different child. That is why Jainas and Buddhists have developed a whole science of dreams:, what sort of dreams will come to the mother when a tirthankara is to be born. From those dreams it can be known that the child who is coming is going to be a tirthankara or a buddha. The dreams experienced by the mothers of many tirthankaras and buddhas were collected and sorted out, and a whole science was created. Whenever these kinds of dreams happened to a pregnant woman it was understood that some higher soul had entered her womb; under the influence of that soul she was dreaming those dreams.

This personality in the womb is not created by any society or culture: it is brought with the person himself. Your mind is very ancient and it has accumulated infinite experiences, minutely, in seed form. That accumulation of experiences is not moving like a wheel only in this birth; it has been moving for ages. Hence we have called the world "the wheel."

This sutra says:

> *"One who lives unconsciously, whose mind is undisciplined and impure, will not attain parampada, the ultimate state. He will continue to be bound in sansara, the wheel of life and death."*

> *"One who lives consciously, whose mind is disciplined and pure, will attain the ultimate state from where there will be no return through another birth."*

*Parampada,* the ultimate state, is a very ancient Indian concept. How to get out of the wheel and become liberated is a desire that is very unique to the Indian mind. This concept of moksha, liberation, is the essence of the teachings of millions of buddhas. Its concern is how to get out of the wheel. As long as you are bound by the wheel there will be no escape from misery. Anyone who appears to have escaped will return because you are totally bound. You are slaves. There is only one thread in your bindings which can lead to freedom, and that is the thread of awareness.

A man is sleeping in a prison. Can a sleepy person ever come out of a prison? The first thing is that a sleeping person does not even know that he is in prison! Even if a sleeping person dreams that he is in prison, what can he do to get out? His eyes are closed, he is sleeping, unconscious. Even if he tries to do something in his dream it will be useless because it is a dream; it can have no relationship with reality.

The first condition for getting out of a prison is that the prisoner must wake up. If he is awake something can be done.

In this century, Gurdjieff made profound experiments in the West, just as profound as those done by Mahavira or Buddha. Gurdjieff used to say that man is so asleep that he cannot be trusted to wake up on his own. That is why he said that "school work" is needed: a single man cannot make it on his own, a group is needed.

You can understand it in this way: it is a dark night, you are afraid of thieves and wild animals, and you are a group of ten people in the jungle. You cannot rely on one man to stay awake and guard. So you decide to guard in two hour shifts: each person remains on guard for two hours and wakes up the next person to take over the shift. One other person should also stay awake to watch that the guard does not fall asleep. If he falls asleep he can be awakened by this second person. A third man may even have to watch these other two because they both can fall asleep. This type of arrangement was described by Gurdjieff as "school work."

Gurdjieff created several small schools in the West where he tried with groups of a few people who would try to keep each other awake, so that nobody could sleep. After several years of effort a situation arises where people learn to stay awake. A man sleeping in a prison can never even think of getting out of prison because to be awake is the first condition.

There are only two ways to awaken a sleeping person. One is that he may be awakened by one who is already awake. An awakened one means a master. A sleeping man is sleeping. He himself does not even know that he is sleeping; only another person who is awake can know that he is sleeping. Actually, you will come to know that you had been sleeping only when you wake up in the morning. Only then you will know whether you have had a good sleep or not. The awake person will know whether he has slept well or not, but not the sleeping person. A sleeping person does not even know that he is sleeping. If you go to sleep tonight and don't wake up for twenty years you will not know that the morning has happened long ago.

I have been to see a woman who had been sleeping for nine months. She had gone into a coma during her sleep. The doctors say she might never wake up at all, that she could sleep for three years. If she wakes up she will never know that the morning happened nine months ago. She is still sleeping.

Will she ever discover that she is sleeping? If she had gone to sleep on a Friday night and she wakes up today, she will ask if it is Saturday. She will become aware of the morning and will say that she had a deep sleep, but she will never be aware of the nine months that have passed. That can only be known to one who has been awake during those nine months.

A master is an awakened person who can wake up the ones who are still sleeping. But it is very dangerous because to wake up a sleeping person is to annoy him. You are disturbing his sleep. He is enjoying his dreams, he is resting, and you are unnecessarily harassing him.

Kant, a well-known German philosopher, engaged a servant only for waking him up at four o'clock in the morning. He was fanatical about getting up in the early dawn. But he was a type that would become angry and might even beat the person who tried to wake him up. So he had a servant to do this job. Nobody in his family was ready to wake him because he would abuse and even beat the person who woke him up. But he had that obsession of getting up at four o'clock in the morning, so he kept a servant whose only job was to wake him even if it ended in a beating. It was his order that even if the servant were beaten by him, or even if the servant had to give Kant a beating, he would still wake him at four o'clock.

A master's work is really arduous. That is why people become angry with masters. Jesus was crucified by angry people whose sleep was disturbed. Ouspensky has dedicated one of his books to Gurdjieff where he has written: "Dedicated to Gurdjieff, who disturbed my sleep." But when your sleep is broken it is a matter of great agony; it is a great disturbance.

There is a struggle between the master and the disciple because the disciple wants to sleep. Actually, the disciple has really come to the master to learn some tricks to have a better sleep. He has not come to wake up, he asks for methods to sleep more peacefully.

The intentions of the master and of the disciple are very different. The disciple wants to somehow have a deeper and more peaceful sleep; that is his intention. People come in search of peace, hardly anyone comes in search of truth. No one comes to me to ask how to know the truth. The ones that come ask, "How can I have peace?" You are in search of better sleep. You are searching for some tranquilizer or for someone who can hypnotize you so that you can sleep more soundly.

But the master has a different motive. In one sense he is an enemy of the disciple. The disciple comes in search of peace and the master may give him consolation: "Come, you will sleep and you will be peaceful." But in fact, the master will awaken him. And before someone becomes awake the more his discontent will grow. Peace will come only after a long time. But meanwhile, his misery will become greater because he will become aware of all the inner turmoil which could not be known when he was totally asleep.

As someone begins to meditate he will become more unhappy, because he will see things which he was not able to see before. It is not that your unhappiness increases: you were simply not conscious of the misery which was already there. Now wherever there are thorns they will pierce you. They were always piercing you, but in your unconsciousness you did not feel the piercing. Now all those troubles will be known to you.

In the beginning the life of a seeker will pass through a great turmoil. That is the spiritual purification, and only one who can pass through it will attain peace. But the master is not trying to help you to become peaceful; his effort is to bring you to truth, the ultimate truth. And peace is but a shadow of truth, one who attains to truth will be peaceful. But the master key in the whole journey is awareness. Whosoever achieves awareness will reach to that ultimate state from where there is no return.

> *"One whose consciousness is his charioteer and who keeps his mind, the reins of the horses, disciplined, will go beyond the*

*world and the path, and will attain the ultimate."*

This has to be understood because people have a great misunderstanding about it. Ordinarily people understand God to be some person that they will meet face-to-face. This is a false notion. God is not a person that you will meet and you will interview. God is a state. As you approach nearer to that state you will go on becoming more and more godly. The day you become totally absorbed by that state you will be God. There is no one else there to meet, you yourself will become godly.

To see God means to become godly because it is a state. It is the ultimate peak of consciousness. It is the ultimate flowering of the seed that is hidden within you. It is the manifestation of the one that was hidden.

Godliness is a state. This is why it is a better word than *God* because godliness is a state, not a person. It is divine. Instead of calling the ultimate state God or *bhagwan* or the *brahman*, call it godliness or divinity. But man has a great difficulty: his languages change everything into symbols or analogies, and he does that with everything.

When we were fighting for independence in India a photo of "Mother India" was hanging in every house. There is no Mother India, but the photographs showed Mother India bound in chains with an Indian flag in her hand. Shouting "Long live Mother India!" most people forgot that there was no such thing as Mother India, it was just a symbol. The symbol is poetic and sweet but it is not a fact. God is also a symbol: there is no one sitting somewhere as God. Hence the real search for God is the search to become godly. As long as you do not become godly your search will continue because that is the ultimate search and the ultimate thirst.

It is like a seed in the earth struggling to sprout, waiting for the rain. If there are pebbles and stones in its way, that delicate seed will move them away or will try to find its way around them to the light, to come out of the earth and rise upward. And as long as the flowering does not happen, its journey will continue.

Man is a seed. You can say that he is a seed of existence or of divinity, of godliness, and as long as he does not blossom into a flower of godliness, his restlessness will continue. This restlessness is creative. Without it you will go astray. That is why those who are full of spiritual discontent are fortunate and those who are not discontented at all and are saying, "We don't need anything," are the most unfortunate.

Many people come to me and ask, "What is the need for meditation? What is the point of searching for truth? What do we have to do with religiousness?" On this earth there are no people more unfortunate than these. These are seeds who are saying, "What is the point of breaking open? What will we gain by sprouting? What is the advantage of rising into the sky? What is the benefit of a journey toward the sun?" These seeds will remain only seeds lying on the ground like pebbles and stones. They will be miserable. They *are* miserable but they are unable to experience their misery.

In my vision there is only one misery in life, and that is if you cannot realize the potential you were born to realize. You will be miserable. And there is only one bliss in life – to flower into that for which you were born. Then destiny is fulfilled, what was hidden has become manifest. There will be no end to the misery and agony in your life unless you become that which you are destined to become. And that destiny is to attain godliness.

It is fortunate that there is no end to your misery because if there were an end to your misery you would remain where you are. Only the pain goes on pushing you. That agony pushes you to go further. That disturbance and pain are the rudders that will guide your boat to the other shore.

> *"Sense objects are more powerful than the senses, the mind is more powerful than sense objects, intelligence is more*

*powerful than the mind and the soul is greater and more powerful than intelligence."*

This is why you must always remember to awaken the higher dimension that is hidden behind the level that you want to master. Catch hold of the more powerful, never fight with the powerless. This is a positive approach in the search.

There are two types of people: some are of a negative mind who waste their time in fighting, and others are of a positive mind who, instead of fighting, search for the higher. There are some people who waste their energy in conquering the wrong, the evil, and there are others who bring all their energies to giving birth to what is good, what is right. There are some who will go on fighting with darkness and there are others who will try to light a lamp.

It is interesting that the one who fights with darkness will never be able to dispel the darkness, but one who lights a lamp will be victorious over the darkness. Hence, become the one who lights the lamp. Don't fight with darkness. If negativity enters into your spiritual search your whole search will become sick. Be positive, try to attain something rather than renounce something.

This is why I say to forget the word *renunciation*. Don't ever bother to renounce anything. Instead, try to attain and achieve something. As you attain something much will drop away by itself. As you put your foot on the higher rung of the ladder the foot on the lower rung will move upward automatically. Don't bother to leave the lower rung, just try to put your foot on the higher rung. As you go on moving forward you will be free from that which is left behind. The more a person enters into godliness and starts merging with it, the more the world of the senses will be left behind.

As I see it, the enlightened ones have not renounced anything. Only ignorant people renounce. This may look a little puzzling because you say that Mahavira was a great renunciate and Buddha was a great renunciate. But according to me, this is not true. Mahavira did not renounce anything: he attained something, and attained it so much that the rubbish was dropped automatically. Will someone who receives diamonds in his hands keep holding on to pebbles? He will have to empty his hands to hold the diamonds. Unconscious people renounce and suffer, and they suffer from indulgence as well as from renunciation. I have known both types of ignorant people – while they indulge they suffer because they cannot totally enjoy the indulgence, when they renounce they suffer because of the renunciation.

A monk came to me and said that he had renounced everything forty years ago but that he has not attained anything. I told him, "You are mad! Why did you renounce? If you had renounced after attaining something, at least that suffering for forty years could have been avoided." He gave up everything for forty years and did not attain anything in return… Actually, if you give up before you receive, it creates a sort of emptiness within you which is very painful and distressing.

According to me, these so-called monks suffer more than the worldly people. A worldly man at least has the comfort of having his family life. The monk has nothing to console him: he has renounced the worldly life and there is no trace of godliness. Liberation has not been realized and worldly life has been renounced. What was in his hands was given up and nothing has been attained, his hands are empty. But he keeps his fists closed so that no one can know that his hands are empty. That is why he talks about the self and the "supreme self" – but his talk is meant for others, he is just deceiving himself. He goes on talking to others only to persuade himself that he has received something.

Don't renounce until you have received. Until then, even pebbles have some value. At least if you keep your fist closed it will give you a feeling of having something. And what is the hurry to give up pebbles and stones? When the diamonds are found the pebbles will drop by themselves, you won't have to renounce them. You will not even remember that the moment when you dropped the pebbles your fists were holding diamonds.

It is always better to have a positive approach. This is what Yama is trying to say in this sutra: whatsoever is highest and most powerful within you should be awakened.

> *"Maya, the creative energy of godliness, is more powerful than the soul; godliness itself is more powerful than its creative energy. It is transcendental. There is nothing beyond it. It is the ultimate. It is the final abode of all."*

This is why the final step of the whole search is surrender to godliness. This does not mean that there is some God living in the sky at whose feet you have to drop your head. To surrender to godliness means to surrender to the highest, the most ultimate power within you. If this surrender is total, in a moment all searching and disciplines are over.

The old scriptures say: surrender to the master. It only means that you are able to see, in the transparency of the master, one in whom godliness has manifested. Otherwise you don't know godliness within you, you have not found it within yourself. You are not able to get even a glimpse of it within you because there are thick layers of darkness inside you, there are huge walls.

Those who could see godliness in Mahavira, Buddha, Nanak, Jesus, Mohammed, sparkling in all its luminosity, surrendered. At first the surrender was to Mohammed or Mahavira – but that luminous inner radiance is the same in all. The radiance in Mohammed and in you are not different. Surrendering to that radiance, you begin to glimpse the same radiance within yourself. It is like lighting your lamp with the help of another's lamp: the presence of the other works as a catalytic agent.

The master is a catalytic agent. Until your own inner master is awake, the outer master is of great help.

To surrender to godliness means to surrender to your own highest potential, to your own ultimate destiny.

A friend came to me today and asked, "Up to *atma*, the

soul, it feels all right, but is there any *paramatma*, a supreme soul, a God?" He is a Jaina, so he has some difficulty because Jainas don't believe in a God, in a supreme soul. But do you even know the existence of your own soul? You have only read or heard about it. It simply shows in which tradition you were raised. If you have really known your soul your meeting with the supreme soul will happen simultaneously.

Mahavira has said, "The soul is the supreme soul." Mahavira's analysis is very clear. As analyzed by him the soul is in three different states: the first state is *bahiratma*, the soul when it is looking outward; the second state is *antaratma*, the soul when it is looking inward; and the third is *paramatma*, the soul when it is neither looking outward nor inward, not looking anywhere, just centered in itself. So Mahavira describes the supreme soul as one of the states of the soul.

Yama is saying the same thing. He is also saying that God is not someone on the outside. He also says that the creative energy of godliness is more powerful than the soul and that godliness itself is more powerful than its creative energy. *"It is transcendental. There is nothing beyond it. It is the ultimate. It is the final abode of all."* Everyone has to reach to that. That is the ocean into which all the rivers will fall. That ocean is not far away, although it may appear to be far away. And howsoever long it may take for you to reach the ocean, it is never too late. The Ganges is falling into the ocean each moment. Right from her source of origin, Gangotri, her attention is focused on the ocean. And she goes on falling into the ocean, her ultimate destiny. When she falls into the ocean the Ganges and the ocean are no longer separate – the Ganges has become the ocean.

Each individual's ultimate state is divine. It is godliness, the ocean into which all rivers fall.

Now get ready for meditation.

8

# The Purification of Intelligence

*"Godliness, which is hidden within all living beings as the self, is invisible. It can be seen only by one with the sharpest and highest intelligence, by one whose sight has become subtle.*

*"The intelligent seeker must first dissolve speech and all the other senses into mind, then dissolve mind into wakeful intelligence, then dissolve wakeful intelligence into the great soul, then dissolve the great soul into godliness, the universal soul which is the very abode of silence.*

*"Arise, wake up! Seeking the great self-realized ones and being with them, you will know the ultimate reality through them. The wise ones describe the way to self-realization as a path that is as difficult to walk upon as the sharp edge of a knife.*

*"One will be forever freed from the clutches of death by knowing the ultimate reality which is beyond sound, touch, form, taste and smell; which is indestructible and timeless, beginningless and endless, supreme, greater than the soul – the eternal truth."*

*The intelligent one attains to the glory of brahmaloka, the realm of the ultimate reality, by sharing or listening to this ancient discourse given by Yamaraja, the Lord of Death, to Nachiketa.*

*After becoming pure in all ways, one who shares this most mysterious knowledge in a brahma sansad, an assembly of the brahmins, or who shares it with those assembled on the occasion of a shradh, a death ceremony, will know the fruits of deathlessness. He will gain the capacity to become one with the infinite.*

There is a famous book, *Appearance and Reality*, by the English philosopher Bradley. Appearance and reality – or one might say, illusion and truth. Whatever is visible is just an appearance; that which is hidden behind the visible and remains invisible is the truth. So existence has two aspects: one as it appears to be and the other as it is.

When I look at you I see your form, your shape, your body. But *you* are not seen – you are hidden behind all of these. All these forms, all that is visible, is only the outer, the periphery; it is not the innermost center. Hence, if just by seeing you someone thinks that he has known you, it would be a great mistake. Whatsoever he has seen is only the periphery.

Just as when you see the outer walls of some house and you return saying that you have seen the house, in the same way, if someone sees your body, which is visible, and thinks that he has known you, he is under an illusion. You are hidden deep inside where the eyes cannot see, the hands cannot touch and the ears cannot hear. That is why you can be known only in moments of deep love – because only love can reach there, where the senses cannot reach.

The whole world is like that. And it is natural because everything has a circumference as well as a center. What can be seen from the outside is one aspect, and the other aspect is what can be known only by entering deeply into the heart. That is the reality which is at the center.

The circumference goes on changing continuously. When you were in your mother's womb you were a small cell. If that cell were put before you, you would not be able to recognize that you were once that small cell. But even then, at the inner center you were the same as you are today. Only your circumference has changed. Once you were a child, then you were a youth, now you have become older; your outer form has kept on changing. If you see your own photographs from childhood to old age, you will not be able to recognize that all these photographs are of the same person; everything has kept on changing.

Biologists say that the body is changing every moment and the whole body changes every seven years. If you live for seventy years you will have a new body ten times.

Every moment, something of the body dies. You go on creating your new body from the food you eat. All the dead cells are being thrown out through perspiration, excreta, hair and nails. That is why there is no pain when your hair is cut – it is a dead part of the body that is being thrown out. There is no pain when you cut your nails; they also are a dead part. You will be surprised to know that the hair and nails of a dead body continue to grow. If the dead body is preserved the nails and hair will continue to grow for some time because life has no relationship with them. These are dead parts of the body which the dead body continues to throw out.

So every seven years all the cells of your body will change and become new. This is your periphery which goes on flowing like the stream of a river. It was born on one day and it will end on some other day – but the inner center is the reality. This inner center is like a small cell that is invisible to the naked eye; that would need a microscope to see it. Once you were a child, then a youth and finally an old person who will return to dust, but this is all happening at the body level. The center remains untouched. That center is the reality and everything else on the periphery is just the appearance. It is called an illusion because so many people believe it to be the only reality that it creates the impression that it is the truth.

And this is not true only about human beings, it is true about all forms of life. The trees which you see all around have leaves and branches, but these leaves and branches are neither the origin of the tree nor the center of the tree nor the soul of the tree. These are just parts of the body of the tree. Within this body of the tree is hidden the soul – just as it is hidden in you. Wise people in India have been saying this for a very long time: that you also were once a tree. Your present human form is only a change in the circumference.

What is a tree today will become a human being at some other time. And all the trees that you see here are not at the same level of growth. In their individuality there are also differences: some of them are dull and foolish trees and others are intelligent trees. The intelligent trees are moving quickly toward going beyond being trees; they are more ready to enter the higher dimensions of life.

With human beings also, all are not the same. There are many idiots who are stuck where they are: they are clinging to the periphery believing it to be the only reality. There are also wise people who are trying to enter the higher dimensions of life and who are leaving behind the boundaries of the periphery.

If we take not only the individual forms but the whole existence into consideration, then the periphery is called *maya*, illusion, or *sansara,* appearance. The name given to the periphery is "the world." But hidden at the deepest core of *sansara* is the center, the *brahman*, the ultimate reality.

We go on living in a delusion, hypnotized by many forms and shapes. The Upanishads call a person a brahmin, the highest Hindu caste, when he has entered the search for the formless that is hidden in all forms. No one is a brahmin just by birth. If someone thinks that he is a brahmin by virtue of his being born in a brahmin family, he is mad. To become a brahmin is the achievement of a constant spiritual discipline. Everybody is a sudra by birth, which is the lowest Hindu caste.

From all these sudras only a very few transform themselves into brahmins; the rest remain sudras.

The one who leaves the circumference in search of the center, breaking through the many layers of illusion, the one who is in search of the *brahman*, the ultimate reality, becomes a brahmin. Then he is not interested in the visible. He is interested in the invisible reality which the eyes cannot see, which can only be seen with the eyes of awareness, with insight.

Now let us enter the sutras. They are, in many ways, very valuable.

> *"Godliness, which is hidden within all living beings as the self, is invisible. It can be seen only by one with the sharpest and highest intelligence, by one whose sight has become subtle."*

It is easy to misunderstand the meaning of "sharp and subtle intelligence." By this the Upanishads do not mean an ordinary sharp intellect as you normally understand it. Ordinarily, you call an intelligence "sharp and subtle when it is skilled in logic and mathematics, skilled in argument and in analysis of the smallest details.

But the Upanishads call an intelligence subtle when it is pure, innocent, silent. Thus these two are totally contradictory concepts. The Upanishads call it "subtle intelligence" when it is so pure that no impurity is left in it, because impurity makes the intelligence gross. Pure intelligence *is* subtle intelligence, which a simple, innocent man can also have; he may not necessarily be a mathematician or a philosopher. The intelligence of a mathematician or a philosopher is not subtle. If understood rightly, then you can say that they are very skillful, they have the capacity to think – but they don't have the purity of silence, of no-mind.

This is the difference between a philosopher and a sage. A philosopher tries to understand something by analyzing its parts, whereas a sage tries to understand by purifying himself; not by analyzing but by entering through the way of purity. Hence many times it happens that illiterate people can be sages and highly educated people cannot be.

Jesus was the son of a carpenter, not educated at all; anyone could have defeated him in a debate. Ramakrishna studied only up to the second standard, anyone could have defeated him in debate. Ramakrishna would have stood nowhere in what you ordinarily understand to be sharp intelligence and what the Western psychologists measure as IQ. But a Ramakrishna, a Kabir, a Nanak, a Jesus have a different type of subtlety, which is of purity – like a fresh flower blooming in the morning. It is not sharp like a thorn and it does not pierce anyone. A flower has an innocence and a purity. That innocence has a subtlety, and it is only this subtlety that can know the ultimate reality.

A person that you think of as having a sharp intelligence will become a scientist: he will analyze matter and discover its mysteries but he will not know himself, whereas a man of sharp intelligence – in the sense that the Upanishads are saying it – will enter the mystery without analyzing anything. And certainly, if you have to analyze a thing before you can know it, your intelligence cannot be considered to be very subtle or sharp because you are not able to know without first analyzing and creating a space for yourself. The subtlety of intelligence in a person who can know without analyzing is the highest. Let this difference be understood rightly because without this understanding many problems have arisen.

The scholars of Kashi, a holy city on the banks of the river Ganges, were asking Kabir how he could be self-realized without having ever studied the Sanskrit language, the scriptures and their principles. It was certain that any ordinary scholar in Kashi knew more about the scriptures than Kabir did. But compared to Kabir these scholars were just extinguished lamps, however much they had studied the scriptures. Compared to them Kabir might not have known anything, but his being was crystallized, integrated. The scholars might have had a big memory system but Kabir had the soul.

That luminous quality of the soul is described by the Upanishads as "subtle intelligence." Small children have it, true saints and innocent people have it. And only through this subtle intelligence can anyone go beyond the layers of illusion. An intellectual person becomes entangled in only understanding about the layers of illusion. This ordinary intellect becomes involved only with the outer appearance of things.

But as I have said, with love and prayerfulness comes the ability to see through and reach to the invisible and leave the visible aside. Whenever someone is really in love he is oblivious of the body – he jumps into that which is beyond the body. When you love the whole existence in that way, it is called prayerfulness.

Meditation is the process of making the intelligence more and more subtle. By and by, the impurities of intelligence drop and a moment comes when the intelligence is absolutely pure. No incompatible elements are left in it; even thoughts are not there. The intelligence becomes so pure that it doesn't even think. Only a flame is there, without any smoke. Just pure light remains. Only in that pure light can an individual become capable of knowing godliness which is hidden behind all the layers of illusion.

> *"The intelligent seeker must first dissolve speech and all the other senses into mind, then dissolve mind into wakeful intelligence, then dissolve wakeful intelligence into the great soul, then dissolve the great soul into godliness, the universal soul which is the very abode of silence."*

This is the process of purification and the sublimation of intelligence.

You must begin from where you are – with words and thoughts. Your intelligence is distorted because there is such a burden of thoughts; there are thoughts and only thoughts. It is like a sky so full of clouds that it is not possible to see the sun through them. It is like that with your intelligence: it is covered with thoughts. It is so clouded by thoughts that the luminosity of your intelligence is lost; it is hidden behind those clouds of thoughts. And even if just one cloud disperses you can see a glimpse of the clear sky behind it. If gaps appear in the thick clouds the light will begin to penetrate them and the sun will again become visible.

In the same way, intelligence is covered by so many thoughts. It is not just a single layer of thoughts – thousands of layers are there. It is like the layers of an onion: as you peel one layer another appears underneath, and as soon as you peel the second a third layer is found. Thoughts are like an onion: remove one layer of thoughts and the second will confront you, remove the second and the third will appear.

These layers and layers of thoughts have been accumulated over innumerable past lives. This is the dust that has gathered on your mind during your long journey of many lives. It is like the dust which gathers on the body of a pilgrim who has been traveling continuously but who has never bathed: so much dust will have covered his body that it becomes impossible to recognize him.

Meditation is a bath for the mind. One who is not able to meditate, his mind will be naturally loaded with rubbish. At every moment, new impressions are coming in. Scientists say that in one day nearly one million impressions are received by the mind. You cannot imagine how, from where, one million impressions are being received. Everything leaves an impression.

While I am speaking many impressions are received by you. When a bird sings, when a car sounds a horn, when the breeze rustles through the trees, when an ant bites, when there is a slight headache or when anything happens around you, impressions go on making their impact. All these thousands of impressions go on being accumulated over a period of twenty-four hours. These impressions are the dust.

You have accumulated impressions over many lives: that is why there are so many layers. Even when you are asleep the mind continues to receive impressions. When there is some noise during your sleep it will leave an impression. If it is hot during your sleep it will leave an impression. When mosquitoes buzz or bite, when you turn over, when it is cold or hot – any change while you are asleep and the mind goes on accumulating impressions. The mind has an immense capacity.

Scientists say that an infinite number of impressions can be accumulated by the brain. There are seventy million cells in such a small brain. Each cell can accumulate millions of impressions; there is no end to it. All the knowledge of the world can be stored in the brain of just one person. You are totally covered by these accumulated impressions and these coverings have to be destroyed.

To begin this: *"The intelligent seeker must first dissolve speech and all other senses into mind..."* This is why silence is so valuable. Silence means not speaking, inside or outside. To speak is the very deep-rooted nature of the mind. The mind accumulates much through speaking because whatsoever you say, not only are you saying it but you are also hearing it. Talking deepens the impressions.

When you say the same thing again and again, you don't realize that you are also hearing it again and again; the impressions are becoming deeper. And mostly, you are speaking only rubbish. You have read the newspaper in the morning and for the whole day you go on repeating that news to many people. It may be some meaningless news that has no value and no one will be benefited by it, but you go on talking about it. If you analyze what you say in a whole day you will find that ninety-nine percent of your talk was just rubbish. If you had not spoken at all nobody would have missed anything.

Remember, all your talking has not benefited anyone – but it has certainly caused some harm because you have thrown some rubbish into someone else's mind, which is a violent act.

But not only was it of no value to the one who was listening: when you spoke you have also heard it again and it has gone deeper in you and created deeper impressions, more conditioning in your mind.

If you repeat a lie again and again, you yourself will forget that it is a lie. Such a deep impression will be made on your mind that you also will start believing that it is true. Hitler has said that if you want to convert a lie into a truth there is only one trick: go on repeating the lie. Not only will others believe it, you also will start believing it. If you look into your life you will find many lies which you have taken to be true only because you have repeated them so many times that you yourself have forgotten that the first time you said them, they were lies. Repetition makes the impressions go very deep because a track is created. Hence the first thing that a seeker should do is to discipline his speaking. He should say only what is unavoidable, what is absolutely necessary.

This world would become very silent if people would say only what cannot be avoided and stop all their mechanical talking. People create unnecessary problems with their useless talk because when you speak, it is not only that you speak, others will answer. Just consider: if you had remained silent how many problems you would have saved yourself! By talking you are getting caught in so many troubles, and to come out of them you have to talk even more. Then this chain continues like a vicious circle which has no end.

This is why the true seeker is silent, he says only what cannot be avoided. He says only as much as is beneficial to somebody, otherwise he just keeps silent.

But even when you stop talking it does not mean that inside you have become silent. You may not talk to someone else but you go on talking to yourself. You are sitting still and you continuously go on talking to yourself. This talk also creates impressions because when you are talking to yourself your mind is listening; you are digging the track of impressions deeper. You also need to stop talking to yourself.

Talking is a great disturbance. It should not necessarily be a disturbance, but you have made it so. Slowly, slowly stop talking inside also. Try to be silent, allow silence to spread. As silence spreads the mind will begin to dissolve. As silence deepens the clouds of thoughts will disperse. Holes will start to appear in many places and a light will penetrate you from within.

The fundamental teaching of all the religions is silence. Mahavira remained silent for twelve years. Buddha also did not talk for many days. Jesus went into silence before he began to speak. The Koran descended upon Mohammed when he was in a state of total silence. In fact, truth has descended into this world only when someone has become totally silent within. In those moments of silence one becomes attuned to the ultimate. That silence only takes you beyond all appearances and unites you with truth.

That is why we have called a sage a *muni*. *Muni* means one who has become silent within. And only one who has become silent within has a right to speak, because his talk will have some value: he has known something which he wants to share. One who is not silent inside has no right to speak, one who goes on talking and chattering within has no right to speak. If you go on talking inside your talk on the outside is simply a disease.

When you are talking with others you are actually not talking with others – you are just emptying yourself. This is why if you cannot find anyone to listen to you, you become very uneasy. You need somebody to listen to your chatter. But the other also is only listening to your chatter so that as soon as you stop, he can begin to chatter; there is no other reason.

I have heard that a political leader was delivering a speech at a meeting, but people slowly began to leave. By the time the speech had come to an end there was only one person left. The leader thanked him and said, "In this town people seem to be very foolish, except for you."

The man said to the leader, "Oh, no – I am sitting here because I am scheduled to speak after you. I did not stay because I want to listen to you."

Nobody is listening to anybody. Nobody is interested in listening to others. You have to listen only because you want to speak: listening is just a bribe. Whenever you are listening to someone, look within yourself and you will find that you are waiting for the other person to stop so that you can start talking. If somebody goes on talking you will call him a bore. But he is a bore only because he did not give you an opportunity to bore him – he goes on talking only about himself without giving you a chance to do it. They are the so-called cultured people who allow you to bore them after they have bored you. They speak and then they let you speak. That makes good company, you don't become restless and the exchange can continue. But this is a disease.

If talking is your compulsion and if talking gives you a relief and you feel unburdened, then understand that all you are saying is just rubbish. It is not going to help anyone. You are throwing your rubbish on others, others are throwing their rubbish on you and instead of being reduced, the rubbish increases. This is why if sometimes meditators had to escape to a forest, it was more because of the rubbish you throw on them. The meditator will find it easier to be silent in a forest.

But there is no need to escape to the forests. If you understand rightly, slowly, slowly you can become silent wherever you are. Remember only one thing: not to talk unnecessarily. Unless you feel that your talking will benefit somebody, do not talk. Unless you feel that it is absolutely essential to talk, do not talk. And within you also, slowly stop the monologue. When your mind begins to chatter don't cooperate at all. You can just step aside from the mind and refuse to cooperate. Be a witness to your inner chatter, don't take any interest in it. Be indifferent, neutral.

Buddha has said that this inner indifference is essential for a seeker. It means that if the mind continues to chatter, you don't participate or take any interest; you simply let the mind do whatsoever it wants.

Remember, the mind will continue as long as you take an interest in it. This interest is of two kinds: either for or against. If some thought is going on in your mind with which you are in agreement, you become identified with it and you flow with it. You are giving energy to that thought. As it is, a thought has no life of its own – your cooperation gives it life. Or if you are its enemy, then also you give it life. This is a little more difficult to understand because when you are against a certain thought you begin to fight with it. You have started a struggle and struggle means that you are taking an interest in it – of course, as an enemy, but you are taking an interest.

Be indifferent, neither a friend nor an enemy. You have no interest in whether the thought continues or stops. You stand at a distance. And whosoever is able to remain aloof and indifferent to the mind will be able to become silent.

*"...dissolve speech and all the other senses into mind..."* When you are a witness to thoughts, your speaking will become merged with mind. Words will no longer be formed, the mind will become empty. But speech is not the only sense, although it is a dominant sense: the other senses are also doing the same thing. You not only speak with your tongue, you also speak with your eyes. You can say things with your eyes: your eyes can show your lust, your indifference, your friendship, your enmity. So don't speak with your eyes either.

You hear not only through your ears, you also hear through your eyes; they also bring impressions to your mind. Psychiatrists say that people go on communicating just by how they sit or stand, even without speaking. A man talks through his body: he expresses himself in his way of sitting, standing and walking.

In the West, much research has been done about body language. If you love somebody, when you stand you lean a little toward him. If a woman wants to protect herself from you she will lean a little backward as she talks to you. If she does not want to protect herself she will lean forward as she speaks. She is speaking through her body.

If you understand body language a little, you will be able to know whether a woman is in love with you or not; her body posture itself will tell you without her speaking. If a woman wants to make love she will sit with her legs apart; if she wants to protect herself from you she will sit cross-legged, saying that her doors are closed.

While you are traveling on a train you will be surprised to find that the bodies of people sitting around you are broadcasting many things. Every moment they are saying something. You not only speak through your mouth or hear through your ears, but you also hear through your body and speak through your body. If you observe your own body you will begin to understand that your body is also continuously transmitting signals.

This is why Buddha has put such a great emphasis on body postures: it is a body language. If you see the way Buddha is sitting – perhaps you may never have thought about it – his posture is saying that he is sufficient unto himself, that he has no desire or need to move out of himself. He has no interest in anything on the outside. He is enclosed within his own circle, totally silent. His way of sitting shows that he has no interest, no desire and no yearning for the other.

Whether you are sitting, standing or sleeping, in everything you do your body and mind go on indicating and hinting. When you take someone's hand in your hand, your body heat, your warmth and the flow of life energy within your hands give many signals. When you hold someone's hand with love, the warmth of your hand is different: then your life energy is flowing into the other hand, welcoming the touch. When you hold somebody's hand formally, without any feelings, there is no warmth in your hand; your energy appears to reverse its flow, withdrawing – the hand is cold. There is no acceptance or feeling of welcome in your hand. Every moment we are speaking and hearing through all our senses.

The nose of an egoistic person will show the depth of his ego. His eyes will say how inferior or how useless he thinks you are. His manner of standing and sitting will tell you that you are nothing. Have you ever realized how different you are with your servant and with your boss? – your whole body language changes. When you walk past your servant you pass by as if he is nothing. His presence has no meaning for you, as if he is just a thing, not a human being. And when your boss walks past you he passes by as if you are nothing, as if only he is something. All these things are not said but they are understood. There is no need for you to say these things.

When a husband enters his house he immediately knows from his wife's movements whether or not there will be trouble. Her way of standing or sitting, her face, the look in her eyes, her way of using the kitchen utensils noisily or silently, every gesture will show her mood. Psychologists say that when a wife is unhappy, miserable or worried, the noise in the house is six times more! Pots fall out of her hands, she does things with such hustle and bustle. She may not be aware of it but her body language is exposing many things. She is saying in her own language that today has been a bad day, that everything has been upside down, chaotic. And when your wife is in love there is no noise in the house, she does everything so silently and so lovingly. Her love or hate toward her husband is expressed even in household things. The changes, the vibrations from her body, tell her whole mood. The husband can feel when he enters the house that the atmosphere is different, the "temperature" is not right – and it need not be said.

The sage of this Upanishad, through Yama, is saying that all the senses should first stop communicating anything through their own languages. No sense should be allowed to say anything; no sense should say anything by its movement. All the senses should be allowed to dissolve into the mind. Then this silent mind can merge more deeply within, into the wakeful intelligence.

Just as there is a mind behind the senses, there is a wakeful intelligence behind the mind. Just to remain silent is not enough; it is needed that you also become awake to, aware of, this silence. This awareness will lead you to your wakeful intelligence.

First you need to be silent so that no energy is wasted loitering in the outer. When that energy has accumulated then it is necessary to become conscious, aware of it. It is necessary to awaken your consciousness so that it can witness whatsoever happens: "I should be a witness of it, not a victim of it. If anger comes I will watch how it has come, how it spreads all over me and then begins to subside" – because nothing remains permanently.

Buddha has said that moods come, linger around for a time and then disappear. But you are in so much hurry that you jump in and become involved in the mood. Just wait a little and go on witnessing. If anger arises it is not going to stay with you forever: be a little patient and allow it to rise. Close your eyes and watch that the anger has spread like smoke over your whole body, every cell of your body is affected. Watch, don't be in a hurry, and within a few moments the anger which has come like smoke will also disappear like smoke. Your body heat will return to its normal level and your heartbeat will again become normal. All the clouds have dispersed, you just need to wait and go on witnessing – anger will come and go and you will remain untouched.

If a person becomes capable of watching a desire even once, he will become free from all desires because now he has the key. Only because of your impatience do you try to rush things and then get entangled.

When Gurdjieff's father died, he asked Gurdjieff to promise him that whenever he became angry he would wait for twenty-four hours before answering. "If someone abuses you, answer only after twenty-four hours."

Gurdjieff said, "This is very strange, but if you say so I will do it." His father was on his deathbed, so he agreed to it.

Afterward, Gurdjieff said that by making that promise to his father, it changed the whole course of his life – because after twenty-four hours there was no longer any meaning in answering. If somebody had abused him he would tell that person to wait twenty-four hours for an answer because he had promised his father that he would do this. Many times after twenty-four hours he had cooled down so much that he would feel that he deserved the abuse and that he should go and thank the person who abused him and tell him that he was right. But sometimes he would feel that what the abuser had said was because of his own inner disease and Gurdjieff had nothing to do with it; he just became an excuse for the other to throw out his disease.

Gurdjieff has said that there was not a single occasion when he felt to react after twenty-four hours. Twenty-four hours is a long time: even if you can wait for twenty-four seconds, your life will begin to be transformed.

Allow silence to become the awakening and allow the mind to dissolve into a wakeful intelligence. "*...then dissolve that wakeful intelligence into the great soul...*" This awakening, this awareness is not yet the end because one still has to make an effort to remain aware. What happens through your effort is not your nature. If effort is needed for any achievement it is superficial and the effort needs to be continued. To keep saying to yourself, "Be aware, be conscious," is also a kind of struggle.

This Upanishad says to let this struggle, this effort, also dissolve into the soul. The soul means being and effort means doing – whatsoever you are doing. The soul means that which already is, that which cannot be achieved through any effort. To merge awareness into the soul means that awareness should become your very nature, so that you need not make an effort to remain aware. Whatever has to be practiced with effort remains superficial: if you give up the effort just a little your attainment will be lost.

Once a Sufi saint was brought to me. He was able to see God everywhere, continuously, for nearly thirty years. He had his devotees who said, "He is a unique person. He is able to see God in everything; it may be a tree or a stone or a mountain."

I asked that Sufi, "Are you still making an effort to see God?"

He asked me, "What do you mean?"

I asked him to observe himself and then tell me if he was making any effort to see God. I told him, "Don't *try* to see God for three days. If then God is still visible to you, then know that something has really happened in you. Otherwise, if you see him only through your effort, then nothing has happened."

After three days that Sufi was very angry with me and he said, "You have destroyed my efforts of thirty years! Now I am seeing a tree only as a tree."

I told him, "Nothing is wrong in it: whatever was not there has disappeared. You were seeing only because you were making a continuous effort and in thirty years it has become a habit. It was not your experience."

There is a great difference between a habit and an experience. A habit is an arrangement imposed from the outside, an experience is a flow that comes from within. This is why awareness that comes through effort is not the end. In the beginning, effort has to be made, but soon it has to merge with the effortless soul. Even this effort has to be forgotten, it should become natural. It has to be remembered that awareness should become so natural that it is there without any effort.

If all the energy of the mind comes together, that energy will become wakeful intelligence. And when the intelligence is totally awakened it is easy for it to be spontaneous.

It is like learning to swim. When you are learning swimming you have to make an effort, but once you have learned it, it is your nature, not a habit. This is the difference: if swimming has been a habit, after a gap of say thirty years you would not be able to swim, you would have to learn to swim again. The habit would be lost after thirty years. But even after three hundred lives because it is your experience and you had once known it, there will be no need to learn it again – you will just go into the water and begin to swim. Nobody can forget swimming. Once you have known it becomes your nature. There is no way to forget it, there will be no need to learn it again.

Habits disappear. Create a habit and then don't practice it for some days and it will disappear – but nature cannot disappear.

When consciousness is totally awakened then slowly, slowly go on dropping the effort for it. Relax into effortless awareness. Awareness should remain without making any effort. All effort has to disappear. With the dropping of all effort, an effortless awareness will remain and that is the merging into the soul. But the soul also is not the end.

*"...then dissolve the great soul into godliness, the universal soul which is the very abode of silence."* Now, what is left to be dissolved? At first there was language, words, the senses; you have merged with them. Then what remains is the silent mind. When you have merged with the silent mind, awareness remains. When you have merged with awareness, pure being, the soul, remains. Now into what can the soul merge? Now what is left? If what is left is the soul, it means that I still know: "I am." It is a subtle, pure ego that remains. This "I am" also has to merge with "I am not." It is called "merging into the universal soul." "Am-ness" will remain, but there will be no "I am." That pure existence, where there is no feeling of "I," is the universal soul. That center is within you. There is no ego there, no feeling of "I am" – and that is the ultimate attainment.

Yama continues:

> *"Arise, wake up! Seeking the great self-realized ones and being with them, you will know the ultimate reality through them. The wise ones describe the way to self-realization as a path that is as difficult to walk upon as the sharp edge of a knife."*

Naturally, as you go deeper within, the path will become more arduous and more subtle. One small mistake and you will go astray. The deeper you go within, the more mysterious the path becomes and you go on becoming more and more alone.

On this inner journey, if you can find the help of someone who is himself totally centered within – one who has passed through this inner journey, one who has known the obstacles, the impediments and the problems of the path, and who also knows the wrong turns on the path that can lead you astray – he can help you.

It is like when you go on some journey into the mountains, you will have two options for guidance. One is to take a map that tells you all the information about the roads, all the turns, all the valleys and all the problems that you are likely to face. This is the method used by those who are following scriptures, which are nothing but maps. But remember, all maps are lifeless and can never be a substitute for a living guide.

The other alternative is to find a local man who is living in the mountains. He may be illiterate, he may not even know how to read a map and he may not know any scriptures, but he will be a better guide than thousands of maps because the whole area is familiar to him. He does not have to read maps because he has grown up there since his childhood. He is familiar with each nook and corner of that land. Those mountains are his friends so there is no question of getting lost. The Vedas will not be of help, but even an illiterate guide like Kabir is enough because he is aware of all the pitfalls. He was born there and has grown up there and has entered the path and reached to the ultimate goal.

If you can find a living master, then dead scriptures will have no value. With the scriptures there is one big problem and that is that you will give your own meaning to them. If there is a map in your hand you will interpret it and you will give it a meaning which will be according to your capacity. But your meaning is not going to be bigger than you. That is why there are as many meanings for the Gita as there are readers; the meaning can never be Krishna's. With your meanings where will you reach? If the meanings were those of Krishna perhaps you would have reached somewhere by now.

That is why scriptures are not useful. There are so many scriptures, so many maps. There are nearly three hundred religions on the earth, which means three hundred maps for reaching God. But no map is helping. Everybody has a map and everybody is clinging to his map and he himself has to give meaning to his map. And the language of the map… The map is just symbolic, it is not the real thing.

To have a map in your hand is of no use. Many times the map itself becomes the cause for going astray. Perhaps without a map you may reach because then you will use your intelligence in the search. But when your eyes are focused on the map you don't see the path on which you are traveling at all.

These maps are also thousands of years old and many people have added or deleted many things. The original maps are no longer available. They could not be saved because whosoever has used them has deleted or added according to their ideas, has filled in colors to make the map look more beautiful, worthy of being worshipped – but it will be of no use for a journey.

All scriptures have become useful only for being worshipped. You can keep them in a temple and worship them, that is enough, but you cannot use them for your journey. Many times a mind that is full of scriptures cannot see even the simple facts directly because its knowledge comes in the way.

This is why Yama has said – and all the masters have also said – to find a master who is a living scripture. Your journey can become easy with his support because you need not interpret, you can always ask him. Slowly, slowly he will turn you toward yourself.

Buddha or Mahavira, Krishna or Christ were living masters, but later on their words also became dead scriptures. Then people seek out those dead statements and simply carry the burden of them. An intelligent seeker will first look for a living master who can become a guide. On this earth there is never a time when living masters are not available to guide you. This never happens.

*"Arise, wake up! Seeking the great self-realized ones and being with them, you will know the ultimate reality through them. The wise ones describe the way to self-realization as a path that is as difficult to walk upon as the sharp edge of a knife."* When you are alone there can be many problems. Alone, it is very difficult to decide about where you are going and what you are doing, whether what is happening is right or not. And it is dangerous to play with the inner energy because there can be many complications. If your energy awakens and it takes a wrong route, you can go mad. Many seekers have gone mad, and the only reason for going mad is that no one was available to give direction and inner discipline. There are many complicated traps on the inner journey.

One young man was brought to me. He was doing the *shirshasan*, the headstand posture, on his own and he was interpreting what was happening to him. When he felt that through this posture he was feeling fresh and healthy and was feeling a sort of well-being all day, he went on increasing the time that he remained in this posture. After a certain period it began to affect his health: he began to feel that his head was heavy like a stone and that all the happiness he had found in it was lost. Then he became very confused.

The energies within the body are very subtle. Only a certain amount of blood can be allowed to flow into the brain. If more blood is allowed to flow into the brain the delicate, tiny capillaries will burst and the bursting of these capillaries will cause much brain damage.

Actually, the human being has been able to develop his brain so much because he has stopped walking on four legs and has learned to stand erect, on two legs. The brains of animals could not develop because blood rushes into the head at great speed and the delicate tissues are destroyed. It is like when the strong current of a river destroys many small things in its path.

When you stand on your head the blood rushes downward because of gravitation. When you stand on your legs only a minimum quantity of blood reaches to your head. This is why your brain could develop: the delicate capillaries were not destroyed by excess blood.

When animals walk on four legs their heads as well as their whole bodies are under the same gravitational pull. This is why it is not easy to sleep standing up. When you lie down on the ground you are again in the position of an animal and you can sleep more easily. It is necessary to lie down to sleep or to rest. Actually, you will feel more restful in any animal posture because it helps to release the tensions.

That young man's delicate brain tissues burst and his brain was in a condition of madness. *Shirshasan* can be of help only under the guidance of a living master because he can decide the time when it should be done and for how long it should be done. It cannot be done at all times of the day because the results will be different according to the timing. The results will be different in the morning or night, or during sunrise or after sunset. If it is a dark night the effect will be different. If it is done on a full-moon night it will have a different result because life is not a small phenomenon, it is a vast network.

Did you know that more people go mad on a full-moon night and more crimes are committed on a full-moon night? More murders and more suicides are committed on a full-moon night because the full moon affects people's minds just as it pulls the waves of the ocean. Hence the word *lunatic* that is used for a madman comes from *luna*, the moon.

The moon somehow makes people go mad. That is why lovers are very happy on a full-moon night because then they have permission to be mad! Poets write poems on full-moon nights because they are also a little eccentric; the full moon pulls them more. On a full-moon night a poem descends more easily than on a moonless night. A night of no moon is very peaceful; fewer crimes happen on earth on those nights. This looks paradoxical: we think that on a moonless night more crimes are supposed to happen. But people sleep more restfully because there is no pull from the moon and when people are at rest fewer quarrels and fights happen.

The moon has a great effect, it affects your every nerve. Your body is seventy-five percent water and the quality of this water is the same as that of sea water. Hence the moon pulls seventy-five percent of your physiology and disturbs it.

On a full-moon night *shirshasan* can be very dangerous; it is not as dangerous on a moonless night. But this can all be guided by a living master. This is not written in any scriptures. Many subtle things cannot be written because every individual is different. If a person is very intelligent he will be helped by only a little *shirshasan* and a dullard will be helped by doing *shirshasan* for a longer time. It depends on what type of capillaries, delicate or thick, a person has in his brain; thick capillaries can withstand *shirshasan* for a longer period.

You will be surprised to know that no person who has been doing *shirshasan* has ever won a Nobel Prize, nor has such a person proved to have any high intelligence – and there are reasons for it. *Shirshasan* is a very intricate experiment: if there is not a living master there to guide you it can do more harm than good.

It is as if you would rush into an allopathic chemist's shop where there are many poisons, prepare a mixture on your own, drink it and tell the doctor, "How would you know about my sickness? I know my disease better than you do!" Or you might pick up a copy of the *Materia Medica* and begin to experiment with medicines: your disease will not be gone, but you will be! But you never try such mad experiments with your own body. You willingly go to a doctor and whatsoever he prescribes you follow it in complete trust. The mind is more subtle than the body; hence it is better to approach a master for a prescription – but for your mind you want to write your own prescriptions.

Many people are doing one thing or the other: someone is doing meditation in this way, another does it in another way. People invent different things on their own. But your created maps and your interpretations are dangerous – beware of yourself!

But why is it so? What is the problem with going to a living master? The ego is the only difficulty: the ego feels much pain to approach a master. It is like the pain a camel feels when it approaches a mountain because there, for the first time, the camel will feel that he is nothing. Camels avoid mountains – and people also avoid going to a master. Even if they go to one, they try to protect themselves so that the master cannot do anything. They are so afraid that he may change something in them or that he may change the whole direction of their lives – and the ego is the cause of this fear.

Only those who are ready to let go of and disappear as an ego can approach a living master.

> *"One will be forever freed from the clutches of death by knowing the ultimate reality which is beyond sound, touch, form, taste and smell; which is indestructible and timeless, beginningless and endless, supreme, greater than the soul – the eternal truth."*

> *The intelligent one attains to the glory of brahmaloka, the realm of the ultimate reality, by sharing or listening to this ancient discourse given by Yamaraja, the Lord of Death, to Nachiketa.*

> *After becoming pure in all ways, the one who shares this most mysterious knowledge in a brahma sansad, an assembly of brahmins, or who shares it with those assembled on the occasion of a shradh, a death ceremony, will know the fruits of deathlessness. He will gain the capacity to become one with the infinite.*

This last sutra should be deeply understood because it has been interpreted in a very wrong way.

First, an assembly of brahmins does not mean an assembly of those who have been born into the brahmin caste: it is a gathering of those who are in search of *brahman*, of the ultimate reality.

These words cannot be said to just anybody. These statements will be useless to those who have no inner thirst. It is simply foolish to explain these statements to people who have no inner thirst. Just as only a sick person needs medicine, only those who are thirsty are in need of these statements. They are not meant for everyone.

Religion is never meaningful for everyone. Religion becomes meaningful only after a certain stage of inner growth. Before that, even if you listen to these statements, they will be meaningless. It is as useless and meaningless as someone reading Vatsyayana's sutras on sex to a seven-year-old child. For a seven-year-old child, fairy tales, Tarzan, ghost stories, are meaningful. Unless the sexual urge has awakened, what is the point of *Kamasutra*? The child will only be puzzled by what you are saying: "What are you talking about?" It is totally meaningless. But as soon as this child becomes fourteen years old and he is full of sexual energy, he will find the *Kamasutra* himself even though you may try to hide it from him. He may read the *Kamasutra* hidden inside a copy of the Bhagavadgita because now it has become meaningful to him. Only when sexual desire arises does the *Kamasutra* become meaningful. Sexual desire is in the hands of nature; nature fills everyone with a sexual urge at the age of fourteen years. But the spiritual quest is not in the hands of nature: sometimes it takes many lifetimes to feel this thirst. It is in your own hands.

Spirituality is your choice, hence it is your freedom. The sexual urge is a compulsion and is not in your hands.

Nature will make you sexually mature because nature has a purpose behind it. Nature needs your sexual desire, not you: you may die but your offspring should continue, life should continue.

This is why nature uses any means so that life should continue uninterrupted. Just think for a moment: what would happen if the sexual urge were to vanish from the world for twenty-four hours? In just twenty-four hours the whole world would be ruined! So nature has arranged that the sexual urge be accompanied by strong passions and howsoever you may fight and try to control it the sexual desire will possess you. The sexual urge is hidden in your glands, your hormones and in every cell of your body and at certain moments it will possess you.

But spirituality is not a natural phenomenon. Spirituality is the art of transcending nature. One day you will become mature through your own experience, contemplation, reflection and search. Nothing can be done before that.

This is why Yama says, "...in the assembly of brahmins" – in the assembly of those who are in search of the *brahman*, who desire to know the ultimate truth.

*After becoming pure in all ways, one who shares this most mysterious knowledge in a brahma sansad, an assembly of brahmins, or who shares it with those assembled on the occasion of a shradh, a death ceremony, will know the fruits of deathlessness. He will gain the capacity to become one with the infinite.* A second thing also needs to be understood. The *shradh*, the death ceremony, has become a tradition. During this death ceremony people arrange to have a brahmin recite some scriptures – an Upanishad, or the Kathopanishad. These traditions naturally become rigid and by repetition their meanings are lost – but the meaning can be found again.

Yama is saying: "...on the occasion of a person's *shradh*..." This whole Upanishad is concerned with death and how to go beyond it. When a close relative or a dear friend dies, for the first time death becomes very significant for you. Whenever someone close to you dies, something inside you also dies; some part of you is shattered.

You love a woman, your wife – or your son, husband or your mother – and when the wife dies whatever space she had occupied within you, all those places in your heart where she had entered, all that will be shattered immediately. Not only does the wife die, part of the husband will also die on that day. A wound will be left. Then death will become very meaningful to you.

One thing is certain: that at the moment of your own death you will not be conscious, so to hear the Kathopanishad at that moment will not help because the listener will be unconscious. But when your loved one dies, although you also partially die, you are still conscious and the Kathopanishad can be meaningful for *you*. Those are moments of great sensitivity: you are receptive. At such a moment you want to understand what death is. At such a time you also want to know if there is anything beyond death – if your beloved, your friend, your son, your mother or your father have really, completely died, or has something remained behind? At such a time your whole consciousness moves around death. During the days of the death ceremony these thoughts will be meaningful and helpful to you. And only when you have become sensitive to death can the search for the deathless begin.

There are some moments in life which are very significant. The day you were born, when you left the womb of your mother, is a very significant moment in your life. Psychologists say that there is no other moment as significant as this: for the first time you breathe independently. There was a mother's body from which you were suddenly thrown out with a push and you entered the world. The impact of that moment is traumatic.

Wilhelm Reich, a great psychologist, has said that as long as we cannot transform that moment of birth, we cannot transform humanity. At that moment the child is full of agony and that is why many children are born crying and screaming. It is a moment of deep pain because the whole comfort of the womb has been snatched away. The peace and the natural bliss of the womb has been lost, and the world of anxiety and disturbance has begun.

The child hears outside noises for the first time. For nine months the child was in absolute silence, soundlessness. For nine months there was no anxiety, no responsibility. There was no need to search for food or to do any work. Even breathing was not needed; there was nothing to be done. The child was just existing and his existence was enough and complete in itself. To come suddenly out of such bliss into this world is painful.

Reich has said that unless we transform that moment of birth into a moment of bliss, man will remain miserable. And there is truth in his statement.

There is another very significant moment in life: when you fall in love. Just as the moment of birth is significant because you are becoming separate from somebody, the moment of love is significant because again you are uniting with somebody. You again merge yourself, your heart, with someone. It is again a new birth. In this moment too, you are totally open.

The third most significant moment is the death of a loved one. At such a time you are shattered. And the fourth is the moment of your own death. These four moments are the most valuable. To participate in these moments, to gather the experiences of these moments in the right way, is part of the art of life. But you almost always miss all four of these moments.

Biologists have developed a new theory about the moment a child is born. They say that the surrounding atmosphere and the events that happen at the moment of birth leave a deep impact on the child. The impact of the surroundings is so deep that it is very difficult for the child to come out of it.

One scientist was experimenting with hens. When a chicken comes out of the egg, the first exposure it has is to the mother hen. She has been sitting very carefully and lovingly on the egg. When the chick comes out it begins to run after the mother. Then the scientist placed a rubber balloon over the egg and removed the hen. As soon as the chicken came out of the egg it saw the rubber balloon – and instead of the hen that rubber balloon became the mother. The chicken began to run after the balloon wherever it moved, it did not worry about the mother at all. Even if the mother hen went near the baby chicken it would not bother about it. That balloon became a problem for the whole life of that chicken. That chicken could never love any rooster, a rubber balloon became its love.

Many similar experiments have been done which have made it clear that the moment of birth is very important. Whatever impressions are received at that moment will remain with us for the rest of our lives.

That is why psychologists say that every son is in search of a woman who is like his mother. He may or may not be aware of this, but it is true. And it is very difficult to find a woman just like your mother! Hence every woman creates unhappiness for you. The problem will continue because the one for whom you are searching will never be found – and no woman is marrying you to adopt you as her son. She is looking for her father; you are looking for your mother. It is a complicated business! There is not going to be any happiness in this. Hence marriage is a hell because so many unconscious impressions from within you are functioning and creating the struggle.

All the impressions that happen during this first moment will remain with you for your whole life. The impressions at the time of your falling in love will also leave their impact on your whole life. Also, the impact at the time of the death of your loved one will remain with you for the rest of your life.

And the impressions that gather at the time of your own death will remain with you into your next life.

This Upanishad is about death. This is why it is worth reading and understanding at the time of a death ceremony. At the moment when the impact of death is deep on you, when the shadow of death is hovering around you and when life appears meaningless to you, if someone who knows the mysteries of this Upanishad reveals its secrets to you, then the impact will be profound. It can be the alchemy that will transform your whole life.

Now get ready for meditation.

# 9

# This, Is That

*"Existence, self-illumined and self-manifesting, has made the doors of the senses to be outer-directed; hence, through the senses, one can perceive only outer objects, not the inner being. It is the blessed one, the intelligent one alone, in his longing to attain to the divine state, who turns his eyes and all his other senses inward from outer objects; thus he realizes his inner being.*

*"In his pursuit of outer pleasures the one with an immature intellect will fall into the trap of death, which is everywhere. The intelligent one who realizes the deathless state through his awareness will abandon all desire for the transitory pleasures of the world.*

*"There is the One by whose grace man experiences sound, touch, form, taste, smell and sexual pleasure. By this One's grace will man also know that in all this there is really nothing.*
*"This, is that.*

*"The intelligent one does not grieve because he has known the all-pervading soul through which he perceives all experiences, both in the dream state and in the waking state.*

*"The one who knows the divine to be so near to himself – the*

*divine which gives the fruits of actions, which gives life to all, which is the ruler of the past, present and future – will, by this knowing, never condemn any man.*
*"This, is that.*

*"The one who sees the never-born One – the One who was before the five elements; the supreme One that arises out of purity; the One who, once having entered the inner sanctum of the heart of all living beings, remains there – this one truly sees.*
*"This, is that.*

*"The one who sees the goddess Aditi – she who is the life within life, she who is born in all living beings, and who, once having entered the inner sanctum of the heart, never leaves there – this one truly sees.*
*"This, is that.*

*"The Fire God is well protected. It is hidden and alive inside aranis, the fire-creating wood, just as the womb of the pregnant woman is protected and nurtured; the Fire God is worthy of daily obeisance by one who has what is needed for obeisance.*
*"This, is that.*

*"From where the Sun God is born and into where the Sun God disappears, all gods are surrendered to this; none can transcend this godliness.*
*"This, is that.*

*"The same godliness that is here is also there; the same godliness that is there is also here. But one who sees it to be many goes on traveling from death to death."*

Man's senses are directed outward, and they can only be directed outward. There is no point in their being directed inward. It is the same as when a scientist makes a telescope for exploring the faraway stars: he can see the far, far distant stars through it, but the one who is standing right behind the telescope cannot be seen through it. The telescope magnifies the stars that are located billions of miles away, but it does not magnify the scientist that is standing with his eyes pressed to it. The telescope is made for seeing faraway objects, but to see the one who is seeing through it, no telescope is needed.

The senses are meant for perceiving material objects; no senses are needed to perceive your own self. Your own self can be seen without any senses. This is because the sense organs travel outward, not inward. But this creates a great problem: constantly observing the faraway stars, slowly, slowly the scientist can forget his own existence. The stars may become everything. Constantly being with the telescope and continuously observing what is out there and far away, the observer can be forgotten completely. The one that is hidden within and is not seen can remain unnoticed – and this is what has happened.

All our senses extend to the outside world. With my hands I can touch you. With my hands I can even touch my own body because that too is outside; it is also "the other." But with my hands I cannot touch the self which is hidden in the body. With my hands I cannot touch the one who is actually touching.

When I extend my hand toward you, I am not extending only my hand; hidden within the hand I also am reaching out to you. It is I who wants to reach out, wants to touch you; that is why my hand is extended. My hand follows me like a shadow: I want to touch you so the hand follows me and obeys me. But when I am touching you two things are happening simultaneously: one is the "you " that I have touched and the "I" who has touched; the other is the hand through which I have touched and your body through which you are being touched.

The eye sees outside, they are able to see everything – only the "I" which is hidden within cannot be seen by them. The ears hear the external. Taste, touch and smell are all related to the external. The senses are created so that we can relate with the outside world; it is an arrangement for relating with others. But the one who is hidden inside is forgotten and remains uninvolved in this relating. Your being goes on becoming more and more covered. In the constant process of knowing things, you forget the knower completely. This is the first point of these sutras.

> *"Existence, self-illumined and self-manifesting, has made the doors of the senses to be outer-directed; hence, through the senses, one can perceive only outer objects, not the inner being. It is the blessed one, the intelligent one alone, in his longing to attain to the divine state, who turns his eyes and all his other senses inward from outer objects; thus he realizes his inner being."*

Here, one thing needs to be understood, because there is much misunderstanding about it in the world of seekers. What is the meaning of turning one's eyes inward? Can the eyes be turned inward? No, the eyes cannot be turned inward. The eyes can only see the outer, there is no way for them to see inward. There is no way for the eyes to see the seer which is behind them.

But the mystics have always said, "Turn back your eyes, reverse the flow." All that is meant by *reverse* is that you don't go outward; you don't allow your energy to move out through your eyes. If the exit door is closed then the observer who used to move out, finding no way out, will turn back to itself. Within there will be no eyes, but of course no eyes are needed for seeing one's own self. Seeing one's own self happens without eyes; it is a seeing without eyes.

In order to listen to yourself there is no need to turn your ears inward: all that is needed is that the ears stop hearing the outer. Once the contact with the network of sound waves is broken, once the ears are indifferent to the outer and the energy that was moving out stops, then the same energy will be able to hear the sound of the inner on its own. To hear this sound ears are not needed at all. All that is meant by reversing the senses is that the senses do not move outward, their energy does not move outward.

It is as if the passage of a flowing waterfall in the mountains is blocked: finding nowhere to go, it will reverse and a lake will be formed. In the same way, your consciousness is flowing outward through your five senses. If consciousness stops going outward a lake of consciousness will be formed within you. This lake is endowed with self-awareness – it has the ability to see itself, to hear itself, to touch itself. But all these experiences are beyond the senses, they have nothing to do with the senses.

Bayazid, a Sufi mystic, used to tell a story that his master gave a pigeon each to three young men and asked them to go and kill it at a place where no one could see it. One of the youths came back within five minutes after killing the pigeon. He had just walked to a nearby street which was empty, with nobody around, strangled it by its neck and come back.

The second youth came back after three days. He had made a deeper search for a place where nobody could see him killing the pigeon. So he found a deep cave, went in and closed the entrance behind him with a rock. Now there was no way for anybody to walk in, even accidentally. There was a deep darkness inside the cave; even if somebody happened to enter he wouldn't be able to see anything. There he strangled the pigeon by its neck.

The third youth returned after three months with a live pigeon.

The master asked him, "Couldn't you find any place even in three months where there was nobody?"

The youth replied, "It is not possible to find such a place even in three lifetimes. For three months I tried hard. I went into the deepest caves, it was dark – but even there I was present, the pigeon was present, and we two would be witnessing the killing. Even if I closed the eyes of the pigeon, I, the murderer, would be seeing it no matter how dark the place was."

Bayazid said, "Out of the three, only you will be able to discover yourself. The other two do not have any thirst for the inner search yet."

He sent the two young men back and said to the third one, "You have at least this much awareness – that when even your senses are unable to see, when there is no light at all, even then, you are a witness. And to perceive the inner witness the senses are not needed."

No matter how dark a room may be, where you are unable to see anything at all, even there you are conscious of your own presence. You may not be able to see the walls of the room or the objects in the room or the other people in the room, but no darkness can erase the experience of your own presence. Under all circumstances you will be there and you will know it, that you are there. Your own presence is self-evident, it is not proved through any medium. This is why all the enlightened ones have said that all the experiences of the world are indirect; only the experience of your own self, of self-realization, is direct.

This looks very paradoxical. We normally think that everything is direct, a firsthand experience. The trees are visible, people are visible, everything is in front of your eyes. But the awakened ones say that all the experiences of the world, of the outer, are indirect because our eyes are working as a medium, they are in between. You are hidden behind the eyes, the object to be known is outside and in the middle are the eyes, like a broker.

The eyes can deceive. This knowledge is not direct, not immediate: there is a medium between the knowledge and the knower. So if somebody is suffering from jaundice he will see yellow where in fact there is no yellow. If somebody has some defect in his eyes – say, they are colorblind – then that man cannot distinguish between colors at all. How reliable are your eyes? What is the guarantee that your eyes are reporting rightly?

But one simply trusts the eyes. Now this is a very amazing fact: that people ask for proof of everything but they never ask their own senses for any proof of what they are reporting. What is the evidence that your eyes are seeing correctly? The *charvakas* and other atheists have accepted only one evidence: that which is manifest, visible; they say they will believe only what is in front of their eyes. But those *charvakas* never ask themselves on what basis they are they trusting their eyes so much. Does the eye always see rightly? No, because it also sees dreams in the night: they are visible, manifest, but not real. Sometimes they see a rope lying on the path as a snake, and when they see the snake in the rope the snake looks very real. But when light is brought in you don't find any snake there. You can also see a mirage in the desert.

When a three-dimensional movie was made for the first time, the people who went to watch it became afraid. In the first film of this kind which was shown in London, a horseman threw a spear and all the people in the movie hall ducked to one side because in a three-dimensional film the spear looked so real. For a moment it seemed as if the spear was really coming. All the viewers leaned sideways and there was nothing on the screen – no real spear, nothing to approach you or pass by you. There was nothing but a play of light and shadow, but the eyes were deceived. Eyes are not so trustworthy. Our senses are not so trustworthy.

The enlightened ones say that only self-realization is direct, immediate; all other knowledge is indirect because in between there is some medium. And the mediums cannot be totally relied upon. Whatever has been seen directly is the only thing that has been truly seen. Anything that is seen through some medium is not worth trusting. If you come in and tell me that it is light outside, I will just have to believe you. You may be telling the truth, you may be telling a lie, or you yourself may be under some illusion. How can the statement be trusted unless I go out and see it for myself?

But all material knowledge is bound to be indirect. Only the knowledge of the self can be direct because there is nobody in between. Only I am there, I alone; no other entity is in between to deceive or distort. Hence what is direct in your common experience is an indirect experience as far as an enlightened one is concerned, and what you never perceive in your common experience is immediate and direct for an enlightened one.

The soul is self-illumined: to see it no light from the senses is needed. A blind man is as capable of seeing it as a man with eyes. A deaf person is as capable of hearing it as a man with ears. A paralyzed person is as capable of experiencing it as a man who has the ability to climb Everest. The ability or inability of the body make no difference at all.

The body is not used at all for knowing the soul. One's body may be strong or weak, healthy or unhealthy, beautiful or ugly, black or white, it makes no difference. The body is of no use in self-realization. The body is useful for knowing others; that is its utility. Your eyes should be healthy, your ears should be healthy, your body should be strong; only then can you relate with the other. But as far as one's own self is concerned the connection is already there, there is nothing to be established.

This is why the sutra says that the divine is self-manifesting. The senses are not needed to know it, it manifests on its own. In fact, it is already manifest. But the world does not manifest on its own; in order to know the world, senses are needed. This is why the more numerous are the senses the more the world can be known.

In this world there are many varieties of sentient, living beings. Man has five senses. Then there is the amoeba, a tiny, living cell, which has only the one sense, its body. It experiences only touch, it has no other sense organ. The amoeba is one of the least developed living beings in the world – not from the point of view of a soul, but from the point of view of knowing the world. All its information is based only on touch; that is the entire range of its knowledge. Then there are living beings with two senses, three senses and four senses. As the number of senses increases, in the same proportion, knowledge about the world increases.

It won't be surprising at all if on some other planet, in some other solar systems, there are living beings that have more than five senses. Man's knowledge will pale in comparison with their knowledge. There can be ten senses without any problem; there seems to be no reason why it cannot be so. We can't even imagine what the sixth sense could be for because our knowledge is of five senses. Our imagination too is only in these five dimensions. The creatures which have only four senses cannot even imagine what the fifth sense could be about. They have only four senses and their area of knowledge is limited to those four.

Leaving other creatures aside – even a blind man cannot conceive what light is. He cannot even imagine what an eye that sees the light will look like because he neither has any experience of the eye nor of the light. He has only four senses; his knowledge becomes limited to only those four.

You may be amazed to know that eighty percent of your knowledge comes to you through your eyes; the remaining four senses contribute only twenty percent. That is why you feel more pity for a blind person. You don't feel that much pity for the crippled, for the dumb or the deaf. The reason is that a blind man's life is eighty percent in darkness. He is missing out on eighty percent of his life, and with no possibility of knowing about it. His condition is more pitiable.

But the knowledge that these five senses provide is only of the outer. No senses are needed for knowing the inner. There you can enter only after you have left all the senses outside. To disengage from one's senses is the only way to enter.

*"Existence, self-illumined and self-manifesting, has made the doors of the senses to be outer-directed; hence, through the senses, one can perceive only outer objects, not the inner being. It is the blessed one, the intelligent one alone, in his longing to attain to the divine state, who turns his eyes and all his other senses inward*

*from outer objects; thus he realizes his inner being."* All kinds of meditation experiments and techniques accept one thing fundamentally: that all your senses have to come to a standstill. There are differences in methods as to how this should happen, but there is no controversy about the happening itself. It is a state where all the senses have calmed down and you remain alone within yourself. Where the world has remained outside, you have remained inside and there exists no bridge, no connection between the two – in that moment, your inner self becomes manifest.

In the experiment that we are doing here, all your senses are used in the first three steps. You have to use them as intensely as you can. You have to tire them so that even if out of tiredness the senses become silent, you may still have a glimpse of the inner.

The Sufis have a dance – the Dervish dance – which is very valuable. As you begin to gather more courage we will soon be doing this Dervish dance too. But this dance goes on for a very long time, for some five hours. Slowly, slowly you will be able to do it. The Sufi goes on whirling for five hours and everything in him becomes tired. He goes on whirling until the body falls down on its own. He does not stop it on his part; on his part he does not do anything. One has to go on dancing, go on dancing until the last iota of energy is spent. Insincerity will not do, that one thinks, "Now I am too tired, now I will sit down." No, as long as you are feeling that you can sit down, you still have energy at least for sitting down. You have to use even this energy for whirling until you see the body falling down on its own.

It is a very unique experience to feel that all your energies are exhausted and your body is falling down, that you cannot do anything either to stop the dance or continue the dance or to prevent the body from falling; you just see it falling. In that moment, the witness suddenly arises. And when the body is completely tired, no senses can remain active: all doors close, all bridges collapse and the Sufi enters his center.

The Kirtan Meditation that we are doing here is part of Sufi dancing. Many people come and tell me that this kind of *kirtan* does not happen in India. Yes, it is true, it does not have any direct link with the Indian *kirtan*: it is not some kind of worship or chanting ritual. It has nothing to do with any Krishna or Gopala. All those words are just excuses; they are just like a peg on the wall. They are all excuses used in the effort to exhaust you. So anybody who tries to withhold something will miss the whole point of it. You have to tire yourself, you have to use the energy so totally and intensely that you become completely exhausted. Your body becomes almost like a corpse, as if all life has gone out of it. That is the moment when the senses cease and a glimpse of the innermost self happens.

And once you have had a glimpse, then there is no difficulty. Once the way has been cleared then it is not necessary that you tire yourself out: then you can move inside just by closing your eyes. Once the way is cleared and the path is recognized – it is like a flash of lightning that for a moment, on a dark night, illumines the entire pathway. And once the path has been seen clearly, even if for one moment, then if the lightning disappears it doesn't matter; you can go on walking even in the darkness. Now you know that the path exists. It is there, you have seen it, and now you can retrace it.

All these meditation experiments are basically techniques to tire you out so that the senses relax out of sheer tiredness. One way is to force them to quieten down. I am not in favor of that because senses cannot be forced to quieten down. It creates the same situation as when you ask a small child to sit quietly: he may sit down but he will be using his whole energy to somehow manage to remain seated. He will be tense, every limb will move this way and that. He cannot relax, he cannot be at rest; he is full of tension. But if you ask that child to run, to take a couple of dozen rounds around the block, then you will not have to ask him to sit down quietly – after that much running he will sit down quietly on his own. And that quietness will be of an entirely different nature. There will be no tension, no restlessness in that quietness. There will be a kind of joy, a great relief, a glimpse of relaxation in that quietness.

Tire your senses out so much that if they can enter relaxation even for a moment, for that moment you will be able to turn within.

> *"In his pursuit of outer pleasures the one with an immature intellect will fall into the trap of death, which is everywhere. The intelligent one who realizes the deathless state through his awareness will abandon all desire for the transitory pleasures of the world."*

The meaning of intelligence is only this: that the meaningless should be seen as meaningless and the significant should be seen as significant. No matter what you desire in the world, the first thing is that if it is not achieved it brings misery; and secondly, even if it is achieved it does not bring happiness. A man wants wealth: he is unhappy and miserable as long as he does not have it, but as soon as he has acquired it he discovers that he has attained nothing. He has accumulated much wealth, but now what?

Whatsoever you have desired in the past, you were feeling unhappy as long as the desire was not fulfilled. But what happiness have you truly found when your desires have been fulfilled? No, only as long as the desire has not been fulfilled does it appear to bring you happiness.

In this world, unhappiness is real; happiness is only a hope – it is only found in the desires that have not yet been fulfilled. As soon as you have something it loses all the promise of happiness it may have had. Hence, nobody anywhere is happy.

I have a friend. When he was a member in the state assembly, he would say to me, "Give me your blessings. I don't desire anything else; just bless me so I will at least become deputy minister in the cabinet."

I said to him, "You will become one because the kind of

madness that you have about it won't allow you to relax unless you do. But if you think that this will bring some great happiness in your life, you are mistaken."

Then he did become a deputy minister, and he again came to me and said, "Now I have only one desire: to become a minister."

I asked him, "Have you found the happiness that for years you were thinking would happen when you became a deputy minister?"

He said, "There is nothing in being a deputy minister. If anything is possible, it will be only by becoming a minister." Then he also became a minister, but now he talks of becoming the chief minister.

I asked him, "Where will you stop? Learn something from your past experiences!"

Man is unhappy, wherever he is. It is difficult to find a happy man. Have you come across a happy man? The only happy man is a man who is happy in his present situation. Any man who thinks his happiness is somewhere or in something other than where he is and in what he is, is doomed to remain miserable. The man who is happy, wherever he is, is the seeker. The man who is unhappy, wherever he is, is the worldly man: he is always living in the future, his happiness is always tomorrow. For him, paradise is tomorrow, today is always empty. Such a man will sacrifice his today for tomorrow. He will waste his today in the service of tomorrow. He will sacrifice his today for tomorrow so that he can attain to some future paradise. And tomorrow never comes – whenever it comes it will be today. And this today he will again sacrifice for that tomorrow. In this way he goes on sacrificing his todays, and one day only death comes into his hands.

This Upanishad is saying: "*...the one with an immature intellect...* "The people with immature, undeveloped intellects spend their lives pursuing outer things and pleasures. The intelligent, the aware person is one who, through his own experience, through his own experiments with life, comes to understand the mystery, comes to know the truth that no bliss has ever been attained on the outside – nor will it ever be attained. He drops the very desire for all temporary, outer pleasures.

*"...abandon all desire for the transitory pleasures of the world."* Some fools are busy renouncing outer things, outer possessions. But to renounce the very desire for outer things is one thing: to let go of outer things is not the same. Not only is it different, but it is diametrically opposite. A man who before has been interested in accumulating outer things will now be interested in renouncing them. First he was busy accumulating, now he is busy renouncing – but his focus still remains on outer things. There are some people who are mad after money and there are some people who are afraid to even touch money.

I know a so-called saint; he is famous and has many followers. He never touches money. If you bring money into contact with his body he goes mad! He becomes so furious that it is unbelievable. He takes a bath if even accidentally he has any contact with money. People respect him for this very reason, that this is renunciation!

This is madness, this is insanity. The disease is old, not new. Before, he must have had an obsessive interest in money. You can see it from the fact that now he has such an intense problem to touch money. What a burning interest for money he must have had in the past – this is the criterion. And even now that interest has not changed, it has only reversed itself. The interest is still there, only the opposite feeling toward money has developed. He has not become free of the attachment to money, he is still tied to it. Yesterday he was tied to it like a friend, now he is tied to it like an enemy – but one has to be attentive to a friend and one has to be even more attentive to the enemy. Wherever he sits, first he takes a good look all around to make sure that there is no money, no coins of any kind lying around. This is going on around the clock, as if he is doing *prabhu-smaran*, remembrance of the divine.

And there are many people like this in this country, whose

desires and attitudes only go into a headstand. Intrinsically they remain the same, unchanged. The same man was previously standing on his feet, is now standing on his head – but the man himself is the same, nothing has changed in him at all. No revolution, no transformation has taken place in the man. But this behavior looks like a revolution, which is a fallacy.

Outer things are not worth holding on to, nor are they worth renouncing. Outer things are outside you: you can neither hold them nor renounce them. Who are you? You held on, that was your illusion; you are renouncing, this is also an illusion. Both your holding on and your renouncing make no difference to the outer things.

Yesterday you were saying, "This is my house." The house has never said that you are its owner, its master. And if the house had even an iota of consciousness it would laugh at you: "What a strange master you are! Before you somebody else was saying the same thing, and even before that somebody else was saying the same. And I know that there will be people after you who will be saying the same – that they are my owners." Then one day you say, "I have renounced this house." The house was never yours, so how can you renounce it? To talk about renouncing it is as insane as declaring ownership of it.

Only an owner can renounce. A self-realized one knows this truth: that when he is not an owner of something in the first place, how can he renounce or not renounce?

The renunciation of desire is a profound realization within you that in this world, neither can things be held nor can they be renounced. To hold on and to renounce are both misunderstandings. In this world, neither is there anything worth holding onto nor is there anything worth renouncing. A man who settles in this kind of neutrality is a man of awareness. His desires disappear. He drops all ambition in the outer world.

> *"There is the One by whose grace man experiences sound, touch, form, taste, smell and sexual pleasure. By this*

> *One's grace will man also know that in all of this there is really nothing.*
> *"This, is that."*

Yama is describing the divine to Nachiketa, the divine about which he has asked. The first thing Yama is saying is that whatsoever we are enjoying in this world – taste, beauty, pleasures – is of the divine. The divine is behind it all, and none of it can happen without the divine. You can taste because you are there, inside yourself. If you were to disappear from within yourself, your body would not be able to taste anything. You are able to smell because you are present inside yourself. If you were not present, you would not experience smell. On what base are all your experiences of this world happening? – on the base of the consciousness that is hidden within you.

Your attention moves to a flower when there is a fragrance emanating from it, but your attention does not move to the one who is experiencing the fragrance. There are three things in this: one, the flower has blossomed, two, the fragrance has spread, and three, you are sitting or standing or passing by and you experience the fragrance. Three things: the flower is there, you are there and there is the fragrance floating between the two. One is the object of knowing, one is the knower and one is the knowing. This *triveni,* this trinity, is everywhere.

But your attention always goes to the object, the object of knowing, the thing that is known. Your eyes reach out to the flower. You say, "What a beautiful flower!" You never say, "What a beautiful self that can experience this fragrance." It never comes to your attention that you are a beautiful consciousness. You simply fail to remember that which is hidden within you.

But both the fragrance and the flower are not as precious as the one who has made it possible to experience them. In all the experiences that are happening in your life, behind them all is your consciousness.

Yama is saying: The consciousness that is hidden behind the one who experiences all the pleasures – the experiencer who also experiences that there is nothing here; who is also able to experience that everything here is futile, meaningless; who also experiences that there is nothing here worth experiencing, worth attaining; that nothing, in fact, can be attained here – is this. This is the divine that Nachiketa has asked about.

Yama is giving his first definition of the divine: that the consciousness hidden within you – this capacity to perceive, this source of your life – is the godliness about which Nachiketa has asked.

So the first definition of the divine, of godliness is the inner watcher.

> *"The intelligent one does not grieve because he has known the all-pervading soul through which he perceives all experiences, both in the dream state and in the waking state."*

It is a precious sutra, worth understanding deeply. Yama is saying, *"...through which he perceives all experiences, both in the dream state and in the waking state."* This is a very interesting thing. Perhaps you may not have observed it, you may have missed it. But it is worth not missing because many new dimensions can open up in life on the basis of this. You have dreams during the night and when you are dreaming, your dreams look real to you. It is impossible to know that a dream is unreal while you are dreaming it. As long as the dream lasts it is completely real to you. Even the most illogical dream is real when you are dreaming. You may be a beggar by the side of the road, but if you become an emperor in a dream you don't doubt at all: "How can I be an emperor? I am just a beggar!" No, even when a beggar becomes an emperor in a dream he completely believes in it.

Everybody is a believer in dreams. So far, I have not come across a single person who is an atheist, a non-believer in dreams, who suspects them, who doubts them. One *has* to believe that the dream is real. And it is not only that the beggar believes that he is an emperor: even an emperor dreaming that he is a beggar believes it. Any rational or irrational thing can happen in a dream and no doubt arises in you. No matter what happens, no matter how weird it is, one's mind is full of trust in it.

All dreams are real while you are dreaming them. When you come out of the dream, after you are awake, only then do they become unreal. The moment you wake up and find that you are lying in your bed or sitting under a tree, the idea of being a beggar or being an emperor – all those cobwebs of the dream shatter immediately. You will say it was all false.

But there is another interesting thing: when you go into a dream in the night, then all that you had seen during your waking state becomes false to you, even more false than the dream-reality because the dream, to a certain extent, remains in the memory even after you wake up, but experiences from your waking state are completely forgotten in your dream. When you wake up in the morning you can remember some bits of your dream, but when you fall asleep at night do any experiences from the waking state enter there? No, not at all.

Hence, Indian mystics who understand something of psychology have said that the dreaming state is an even deeper experience than the waking state. The waking state is not able to completely wipe out your dream experiences; some of them linger in your memory when you wake up in the morning. But the dreaming state totally erases your waking state. Nothing of it can be remembered, not a bit. Certainly the current of the dream state must be stronger.

The waking state becomes false during the dream state and the dream state becomes false during the waking state. Then what is the reality?

There is a very famous anecdote from Chuang Tzu's life.

One night he had a dream and in the morning as he woke up, sitting in his bed, he was very sad. His disciples asked him, "You, and sad? What has happened?"

Chuang Tzu said, "In the night I dreamed that I had become a butterfly."

The disciples said, "Come on! You don't need to be sad because of a dream? Now you are awake!"

Chuang Tzu said, "No, no! A very strange problem has arisen for me. Now I am at a loss. If in a dream Chuang Tzu can become a butterfly, who knows? – maybe now the butterfly has gone to sleep and is dreaming that it has become Chuang Tzu? What am I supposed to do now? Because if Chuang Tzu can dream of becoming a butterfly, what prevents a butterfly from dreaming of becoming Chuang Tzu? Who am I now? – an awake Chuang Tzu or a sleeping butterfly? Right now am I a butterfly's dream or am I as real as I am visible?

Dreams make the waking state unreal and the waking state makes the dreams unreal – so then, what is real? Neither of the two are real. Only the observer, which neither state can falsify, is real. In the night, one thing is also present there: the watcher who watches the dreams. And in the day the same thing is also present: the watcher who watches all the experiences of the waking state. The dreams change, the waking state changes, but the observer constantly remains present, unchanged.

That watcher alone is the reality, the truth. All that is seen becomes unreal, only the seer remains real.

Remember, even to see the false a real seer is needed. Even for watching a false dream a real watcher is needed. If there is no seer within, the false also cannot be seen.

So the next thing that Yama is saying is: *"The intelligent one does not grieve because he has known the all-pervading soul through which he perceives all experiences, both in the dream state and in the waking state."*

One who has known the seer will never grieve again.

There is a very popular story in China about an emperor

whose only son had fallen sick and was about to die. The emperor was awake the whole night taking care of his dying son. At about four o'clock in the morning he fell asleep. He had thought to stay awake the whole night because his son was dying. As a father he wanted to be near his son in the last moments of his life, but he dozed off.

In his sleep the emperor dreamed that he was the emperor of the whole world. He had twelve sons and each had his own golden palace because the empire had limitless wealth. As he was seeing this dream, his son died. His wife screamed loudly in grief and the emperor woke up.

As he woke up, instead of crying over the tragedy, the emperor started laughing. The wife asked, "Have you gone mad in your grief? Why are you laughing?"

The emperor said, "I am laughing over my inability to decide for whom I should weep. Just a moment ago I had twelve sons, as handsome as I have ever seen. I had a vast empire, inexhaustible treasures, and it has all disappeared now. When I was with those twelve sons I had completely forgotten this one son – that he even existed. What to say about his death? Now those twelve sons have disappeared, they have died, and this one son has also died. And I am in a quandary: who should I cry for? What is real?"

Neither were the twelve sons in the dream real nor was the son in this waking dream real. The only real thing is the seer. One who starts to perceive this seer has taken the first step toward being a *siddha*, a fulfilled one. Then no grief or misery can touch you because grief and misery come from your clinging to the outer objects. The one who is rooted in the inner seer, the inner watcher, will have no cause to suffer any longer. Bliss will become his natural state.

> *"The one who knows the divine to be so near to himself – the divine which gives the fruits of actions, which gives life to all, which is the ruler of the past, present and future – will, by*

*this knowing, never condemn any man.*
*"This, is that."*

If you start to experience the seer, if your attention moves away from the seeing and the seen and even a slight harmony with the seer starts to happen, you will find that there is nothing closer to you than godliness. As you are now, nothing is further away from you than godliness. As you are now godliness is nothing but an empty word for you. Whenever you think of God you imagine it to be someone sitting on a high throne far away in the sky, and it feels like such a long, long journey to reach to him! But he is sitting right here, right behind your breath.

Mohammed has said that the vein in your neck is so close to you that if you were to cut it, it would kill you immediately – but godliness is even closer to you than that vein. It is the closest of all because you are that. But this understanding will come to you only if your attention starts to shift to the seer. Then godliness is the closest. And remember, the one who starts feeling godliness so near within himself will also start feeling it within everybody else.

This is an essential law of life: what you see within yourself, you start seeing the same within others. If you are a thief you will start seeing a thief in everybody and you will feel as if everyone is conspiring against you. If you are dishonest then nobody will look honest to you. It will seem as if everybody is dishonest and that they are hiding it behind masks and at any moment they can deceive you.

I have heard that two youths who were friends were walking down a street. They both were pickpockets and were traveling together. The first youth would grope for something in his pocket again and again and the second one would keep taking out his pocket watch and looking at the time.

The first youth asked, "Why are you looking at your watch so many times?"

The second one asked, "And what are you looking for in your pocket so often? I'm a pickpocket, and I have to look at my pocket-watch so often to make sure that it is still there, that it is not gone. But what are you searching for in your pockets?"

The other one said, "I am also a pickpocket and I have some money in my pocket. I have to look for it every now and then to make sure that it is still there!"

The opinions that we have about others are, deep down, opinions about our own selves. If you are extra alert against thieves, understand well that the thief is hidden within you; otherwise you wouldn't be so alert against them. What is the idea behind the need to stay so alert? Your idea about others is what is within you. That is why an evil person can never believe that there can be any good in people. The evil man believes that the good man just appears to be good. He may be pretending but he cannot be truly good.

That is why an evil person is always trying to prove only one thing: if you say to him that such and such a person is a good person, he will shake his head in disbelief; he will say, "Just wait! You will find out the reality some day. Nothing can remain hidden for very long. The truth will come to light." And he will try his best to prove that the man must be evil. He has complete faith as far as that man being evil is concerned; being good can, at the most, be a cover-up, a pretension.

Only a good man believes that any other can be good. A good man finds it difficult to believe that someone could be evil. Why would he be? And remember, if you immediately believe in the idea of someone being evil, then don't be in the illusion that you are a good man. This is the criterion. For a good man it becomes very difficult to accept the idea that another person is evil, even if the other person is truly evil. Exactly in the same way, it becomes difficult for an evil person to believe that the other is a good man, even if the other is truly good.

You simply cannot think beyond yourself. Hence if you start

experiencing the watcher in yourself, you will also start experiencing the watcher in everybody else. The watcher does not focus on the body, it starts seeing the interiority. It feels godliness all around, so any condemnation becomes impossible for it.

Condemnation will become impossible only when you can see godliness in others. Then only praise will be possible because no reason will remain for any condemnation. What you see all around you is the Devil, hence your condemnation of others can continue. A devil will see a devil, godliness will see the divine. What you are is also your experience of the world around you; it is just a projection of the same experience. Only on the day when you have ceased to see any bad should you understand that goodness has arisen within you.

Rabiya was a Sufi woman, a mystic. There is a statement in the Koran that says to hate the Devil, so she crossed out this statement from her copy of the Koran. It is considered to be very arrogant, unaesthetic, very uncultured to change these things; nothing can be changed in the Koran, in the Vedas or in the Gita.

Another mystic, Hassan, was a guest at Rabiya's house. In the early morning he picked up Rabiya's Koran and started reading it. Then he noticed that a line had been crossed out in it, a correction had been made. Hassan shouted, "Who is the fool who has committed this sin? How can anybody make corrections in the Koran?"

Rabiya said, "It is nobody but me, I myself have deleted that line."

Hassan asked in amazement, "Rabiya, you have committed such an act of blasphemy, of infidelity?"

Rabiya said, "I am in great difficulty. Since I have started experiencing the divine, I don't see any Devil anywhere – so who am I supposed to hate? This statement is no longer relevant for me. It has no validity for me anymore. Where is this Devil? Now even if the Devil stood in front of me I would see only godliness in him. So there is no way for me to hate. That is why I crossed that line out. Any line which has no relevance or validity for me cannot remain in my copy of the Koran."

This sutra is saying that as soon as a person experiences that the divine is near, actually the closest, then he can no longer condemn anyone. Praise and lovingness become natural to him because he starts seeing godliness in everybody. It is the same light in all the lamps: *"This, is that."*

> *"The one who sees the never-born One – the One who was before the five elements; the supreme One that arises out of purity; the One who, once having entered the inner sanctum of the heart of all living beings, remains there – this one truly sees. "This, is that."*

Who truly sees? Who has right vision? And if the seeing is not right, then it is impossible to see godliness. So who sees rightly, truly? – only one who has recognized the never born, the eternal One that is hidden in the inner sanctum of the heart.

The heart has been born, it has come into being and will one day disappear. The body is created and will disintegrate: it is born and it will die. But there is the unborn in the innermost cave of the heart, who has never been born and who will never die: he who sees this One, truly sees. Only he has eyes, all others are blind; from the point of view of the inner vision, all others are blind. No matter how skillful one is in seeing on the outside, if one fails to see oneself, his having or not having eyes makes no difference.

This Upanishad is saying that only one who realizes the unborn, the eternal in the cave of the heart, truly sees – and that it is the godliness that Nachiketa is seeking.

> *"The one who sees the goddess Aditi – she who is the life within life, she who is born in all living beings, and who, once having entered the inner sanctum of the heart, never*

*leaves there – this one truly sees.*
*"This, is that."*

The symbol for the vital energy is Aditi. The symbol for life energy is Aditi: the one who has recognized the current of life which flows within. You recognize the body, but the body is not the river or the current; it is just the bank of the river. The river of life is flowing between the two banks of the body. We see the banks but we do not see the river. The river is like the river Saraswati, invisible. Only the banks are seen: its dry bed can be seen but not the river itself.

The body is only a riverbank. Something else which is invisible is flowing with the support of the body. Each moment energy is flowing in your every fiber, but the energy is not visible.

These electric bulbs here are lit: the bulbs are visible but the energy flowing through the wires is not visible. Up to now nobody has seen electricity: only its effects are seen, only its manifestations in usage are seen. So far no energy has been visible to the eyes, only the expressions of its effects have been seen. Electricity is there: the bulb is lit, this fan is running, but these are only the effects. What is the actual electricity itself? So far no one has seen it, and no one will ever see it.

Energy cannot be seen. Energy is formless, shapeless. You walk, you rise, you sit, you talk – all this is visible. But who really walks, who really rises or sits, who really talks, who really keeps quiet? That One is not visible at all. The name of that life energy is Aditi. The one who has known Aditi within himself has truly seen.

> *"The Fire God is well protected. It is hidden and alive inside the aranis, the fire-creating wood, just as the womb of the pregnant woman is protected and nurtured; the Fire God is worthy of daily obeisance by one who has what is needed for obeisance.*
> *"This, is that."*

In ancient times, when there were no other means for creating fire, it was done by rubbing two sticks of wood against each other. This wood was called *arani.* The hidden fire would manifest because of the friction, but the fire already existed, hidden in the wood. Have you seen a flint stone? – the fire is hidden in the flint: when some friction is applied to it the fire is sparked. Nothing is created by the friction, it only becomes manifest. What was dormant becomes manifest.

The divine is hidden in you. It is only a matter of some rubbing – some efforts, some self-purification, some meditation – and the dormant will become manifest; it will start burning like a blaze. But if a man just sits over two sticks – the night is cold, it is snowing, he is trembling in cold and just sits over the two pieces of wood – then nothing will happen. No heat and no light can arise from a dormant fire. And the fire is dormant and lying there, right in front of you. It is only a matter of rubbing the two pieces of wood together and the fire will manifest, the darkness will be gone, the cold will be destroyed. The Fire God can become manifest.

The worship of fire is very ancient. This was the original reason behind fire worship: that even as fire is hidden in matter and has to be made manifest, the divine too is hidden and has to be made manifest.

There is one other reason why fire has always been venerated. One characteristic of fire is that it always moves upward, its journey is always upward. Even if you turn a burning lamp upside down, its flame will still rise upward. You can turn the lamp upside down but you cannot turn the flame upside down.

Water flows downward, fire moves upward. Even water starts moving upward with the support of fire: it becomes hot, boils and then becomes steam. The direction of its flow is reversed and the very nature of the water is changed. That which used to flow downward starts rising upward, skyward.

In the very ancient times of the world, man came to experience that except for fire, no other thing has the capacity to move upward. Fire is anti-gravitational. earth pulls down, but it is unable to pull fire down: fire believes in levitation. Fire moves upward and the earth cannot do anything about it.

Fire became a symbol for the consciousness moving upward. And godliness, the universal self, is the name for the consciousness that is always moving upward. This fire is dormant within everybody. All the components are within you, it is just a matter of some rubbing. That rubbing is called sadhana, spiritual discipline. One has to shake a little, one has to create some friction between the *aranis* which are dormant within you. All these meditation experiments that I have been giving you are actually nothing but techniques for creating friction between the *aranis*.

People come and ask me, "Is there anything wrong if I do the Dynamic Meditation just sitting down?" In essence what they are asking is, "Can't the fire be created if I keep the *aranis* lying quietly?" No, it won't be created – you will have to rub the two pieces of wood together. The energy within you will have to pass through some friction. If it were something that could happen without any effort it would have happened long ago. But it has not happened. Some effort is essential to kindle that fire.

> *"From where the Sun God is born and into where the Sun God disappears, all gods are surrendered to this..."*

From where the sun is born and into where the sun will die, from where life arises and into where life will disappear – to that original source, to that final destination, the gods are surrendered...

> *"...none can transcend this godliness."*

Godliness is the original source of all and the final abode of all. There is no way to go beyond it. There can be no transcendence of godliness because what you attain after having transcended everything else *is* godliness. There is no way to go beyond it, it is the ultimate. It is the ultimate limit of existence.

*"This, is that.*

*"The godliness that is here..."*

Try to understand this sutra...

*"The same godliness that is here is also there; the same godliness that is there is also here. But one who sees it to be many goes on traveling from death to death."*

If somebody says that godliness is not here but only in the next world, then that person is simply ignorant. If somebody says that it is not in the next world but only here, he is also deluded because the ultimate reality is everywhere. That which is hidden in the *isness* of all is here, is there, is on this shore, is on the other shore. As far as existence goes, it is *isness*, it is only the *isness*. It is not that the ultimate is on the other shore, in the other world; it is also in this world. All that is needed is an eye that can see. And one who has the eye to see will be able to see it right here.

And remember, one who is unable to see it here will not be able to see it there either. It depends on the eye that can see. When that eye is born the divine becomes manifest everywhere; if that eye is asleep the divine does not become manifest anywhere.

But people go on deceiving themselves. They say, "It is not becoming manifest because it is not here, it is only in the other world." In this way the blind people protect themselves. Then they don't even remember that the reason they cannot see it is because they are blind.

The blind have created a paradise, a heaven, "the other world" and whatnot. All this is nothing but their effort to say, "If we cannot see it, it is not because there is something wrong with us. We cannot see it because it does not exist here, it exists only in the next world – so when we reach to the next world we will see it." This gives comfort to the blind, a consolation.

But remember, this sutra is saying something else. It is saying that it is as much here as it is there. If you cannot see it, the reason is not because it is not here. You cannot see it because you have no eye. An effort will be needed to give birth to the eye.

There is a famous statement by Rinzai, a Zen master. This statement has been discussed over the centuries. The statement looks very paradoxical. Rinzai has said, "The world and nirvana are one and the same." Now this is a very contradictory statement. You say, "Renounce the world, drop everything," and this Rinzai is saying, "The world and nirvana are one and the same, and one who makes even a small distinction between them is ignorant."

Had Rinzai read this sutra of this Upanishad, he would have danced with joy! He would have said, "Right! That which is there is also here. The world and nirvana are one." The only difference is because of the blind people: they don't see it here, yet this does not make them realize that they have no eyes. Instead they think, "It is not here so there is no need to search for it. When we go to the next world..."

This is why as a man starts growing older and the next world feels as if it is coming closer, he starts becoming religious. In the temples, in the mosques, in the gurdwaras, you will find many old people; you won't see many young people there. And if sometimes you do see a young man there you can be sure that for one reason or other he must have become old. Something has gone wrong with him. Even the old people will look at a young man in amazement: "Why is he here?" They tell their sons, "Religion is not for you yet. There is a right age for it. When you become old, then..."

In fact, when the phenomenon of death starts coming closer, when you begin to realize that soon now you may have to go to the next world, then you start becoming religious because the ultimate reality, the divine, is not in this world.

But this situation is deceptive: one who is not already religious here will not become religious just because of death. To one who is unable to see the ultimate reality here, death does not give him the eyes to be able to see it in the next world.

As you are, if you are suddenly brought into the middle of any other dimension, you will see the world there too. You will quickly begin to make some arrangements there also: you will start setting up a shop, you will start creating a marriage and a family, one thing or the other. Whatever your world was here, you will start arranging the same there.

But an intelligent person sees only freedom, only liberation already in this world. There is no way for him to see otherwise. *"The same godliness that is here is also there; the same godliness that is there is also here. But one who sees it to be many goes on traveling from death to death."* Not as one… This too needs to be clearly understood. We see this world as the many: the trees are separate, the rocks are separate, you are separate, I am separate, the neighbor is separate. Everything is separate, divided, not united. Your situation is the same as when the moon rises in the night and there are thousands of ponds and lakes and reservoirs of water on the earth and the moon is reflected in all of them. The moon in the sky is one, but all these reflections that are formed are in the millions. You go on counting each and every reflection separately and think this must be the number of moons and you do not raise your eyes to the one moon that is being reflected in all these others.

All existence in this world, all the forms, they are all reflections of the one divine. Within you, in the lake of your consciousness, is the reflection of that one reality.

The sutra is saying that someone who sees reality here as many will wander aimlessly into birth and death. Someone who sees the reality as one, here, will become free this very moment.

To recognize the One is the ultimate knowledge and to go on seeing the many is ignorance.

Now get ready for the meditation.

# 10

# One Reality

*"Ultimate reality can be known only by the pure mind. In this world, there is only the ultimate reality. Hence, one who sees the many in this world will wander from death to death; he will be caught in the endless cycle of birth and death.*

*"The soul, which is the size of the tip of the thumb, resides in the sky of the heart in the middle of the body. It is the ruler of the past, present and future. Knowing it, one can no longer condemn.*
*"This, is that.*

*"The soul, which is the size of the tip of the thumb, is like a smokeless flame. It is this soul, the ruler of past, present and future, which is today and which is tomorrow. This soul is the eternal.*
*"This, is that.*

*"Even as rainwater falling on a high peak will flow to many different places on the mountain, the man who worships gods and demons which are endowed with diverse natures, thinking them to be other than divine, will continue to pursue them. He will wander lost in their good or evil realms and in the higher and lower species.*

*"Nachiketa, of the lineage of the sage Gautama! Even as the*

*pure rainwater remains the same when mixed with other pure waters, when the self of the sage has known the Supreme Self, it becomes the Supreme Self.*

*"Ultimate reality can be known only by the pure mind. In this world, there is only the ultimate reality. Hence, one who sees the many in this world will wander from death to death; he will be caught in the endless cycle of birth and death."*

It will be good to understand what is meant here by "pure mind." What you normally understand to be a pure mind is not pure. People think that a pure mind is a mind that is full of good thoughts, a mind full of moral thoughts; a moral mind. People think that a pure mind is free of all that you consider to be bad or immoral – but in the Upanishads even this so-called moral mind is thought to be impure.

According to the Upanishads, a pure mind is a mind which has neither bad thoughts nor good thoughts, which is neither moral nor immoral, neither *shubh*, good, nor *ashubh*, evil – where all the ripples of thought have disappeared. As long as there are thoughts in the mind, mind is impure. The minds of the so-called saint or of the so-called sinner are equally impure, but the impurity in the sinner's mind is bad thoughts and the impurity in the saint's mind is good thoughts.

The sage is one who is pure of mind; there are neither good thoughts nor bad thoughts. This seems to be a little complex because you think that good thoughts indicate the presence of purity. But good thoughts are also a foreign element: a good thought also creates ripples in the mind, a good thought also creates a disturbance in the mind, a good thought also creates a limit to the mind. A mind is pure only when there is no foreign element in it.

For example, a thief is standing in front of a mirror: the mirror is impure because the thief is being reflected in it. But in fact the mirror is also impure when a saint is standing in front of it and is reflected in it. The mirror is pure only when there is nothing in front of it. In this same way, the sage is neither a saint nor a sinner; the sage is totally different from both.

The Upanishadic concept of the sage is very profound. This concept of purity is very subtle: that the mind is impure as long as there is even a single ripple of thought arising in it. When the mind is without any ripples and has become empty, the mirror is without any reflection. When the desire to do good or bad disappears, no desire is left. Sin or virtue do not fill the mind, selfishness or unselfishness do not fill the mind – and when nothing occupies the mind then mind becomes unlimited, limitless. Then the capacity of the mind is there in its pure state. Then nothing remains to ponder over, to think about; then it is just an empty mirror.

The Upanishads say that when the mind becomes just a mirror and when there is no reflection, no image, no picture, no shadow in it, then with this mind one can know the ultimate reality.

This is the difference between religion and morality: according to morality the good mind is pure, and according to religion the empty mind is the pure mind.

To be a moralist, it is not necessary to be religious. Even an atheist can be very moral – and very often he is more of a moralist than the theist. Compared to India, the Soviet Union is much more moralistic, and the Soviet Union is an atheist country. There is not as much stealing and corruption, there is not as much adultery. An atheist can be very moralistic, and the fact of the matter is that for an atheist there is no other alternative than to be moralistic, because he cannot be religious. For an atheist the ultimate state is to renounce evil and to hold on to being virtuous.

But for a religious person this is not enough. His journey is very long. He says, "I have given up evil and now I am clinging to virtue, but my clinging remains. Until yesterday I had been holding on to the bad and now I am holding on to the good.

Until yesterday the chains were made of iron and now they are made of gold – but the chains are still there." He wants that nothing should bind him, that he should hold on to nothing. There should be no clinging; the mind should become free of any holding or clinging, totally empty.

Of course, religiousness goes beyond immorality – but it also goes beyond morality. In fact, a religious man is neither moral nor immoral. This is why it is difficult to understand the behavior of a religious man. We can understand the behavior of a moralist: we know what is good and what is bad. We understand the person who does good and we also understand the person who does bad.

But the sage goes beyond both good and bad. His behavior becomes spontaneous. He does whatsoever is natural to him, he is not considering about what is good or bad. So many times a sage may not do what others think to be good. Sometimes a sage may do what the society considers to be bad. People like Jesus, Kabir, Buddha and Mahavira are beyond the concepts of society. Mahavira lived naked, and according to the concepts of society it is immoral and indecent to live naked. Society cannot tolerate naked people.

There is a reason for this: society has not only covered the body, with it, it has also covered sex. There is so much fear of sex that it has to be kept hidden. A naked man's genitals are exposed – that is why the society does not like nudity and considers it to be something immoral.

Mahavira went naked; this was very objectionable! He was beaten up and stoned and thrown out of every village and town. Stones were hurled at him, he was condemned everywhere.

He was also in silence; he was naked *and* silent. He did not speak, he did not explain why he was naked, what the purpose was of his standing there naked. He became a mystery, it was difficult for people to understand him. Mahavira's nakedness was not immoral, but at the same time it is difficult to say that Mahavira's nakedness was moral. Mahavira's nakedness was spontaneous, as innocent as a child's. It was neither moral nor immoral. Mahavira had become so innocent and simple that there was nothing to hide.

If someone has to hide or cover something up, then he is a complicated person. Anyone who wants to hide something still has some complexity within him. Mahavira had become innocent and his innocence went so far as giving up the use of clothes. But ordinary society will think Mahavira's nudity is immoral; it is very difficult to understand that Mahavira is a sage.

When Jesus was passing through a village, a prostitute threw herself at his feet. Tears started flowing from her eyes, so she washed his feet with her tears.

The moralists of that village said that it was not proper that Jesus should be touched by a prostitute.

Jesus said, "Nobody has ever before touched my feet with as much reverence as this woman. People have washed my feet with water, but this woman has washed them with her own soul's tears."

This was one of the many charges against Jesus for which he was crucified. This was against the general concept of morality of his society.

A woman was brought before Jesus because she was an adulteress, and according to the Jewish law a woman who commits adultery should be stoned to death. Jesus was staying outside of the village so people went there and told him, "It is proved beyond a doubt that this woman is an adulteress, and she has also confessed to it. The ancient scriptures say that it is proper and legal to stone her to death. What do you say?"

Jesus said, "The scriptures are right – but only those people have the right to stone her who have never committed adultery or have never even thought of doing it. Now you can pick up the stones!"

But there was not one person there who had not committed

adultery or had not even thought about it. All the leaders, scholars and heads of the society who had gathered there quietly stepped behind the crowd. The people who had brought stones with them just dropped them and returned to the village. But this also was a charge against Jesus: that he had saved an adulteress.

Jesus' behavior was spontaneous; it cannot be limited to the ordinary concept of morality. He was doing whatsoever was spontaneously arising in his consciousness; he did not worry about whether or not his behavior was according to the social norms. It is the moralist who has to think in this way.

A religious, a spiritual person is a unique phenomenon. It does not mean that a religious person will inevitably become immoral. His behavior is free of both morality and immorality. Sometimes it is in accord with morality and sometimes it is not in accord with morality, but he is not concerned about it. As long as you think that your behavior should be in accord with some concept, then it is false and hypocritical. It is not coming from within you. It is not the expression of your inner consciousness; it is being judged by outer criteria and is in the service of society.

A moralist follows the society. That is why the people you call saints are usually moralists – but they are not religious. Whenever a person becomes religious a difficulty arises for you because you simply cannot fit his behavior into any of your norms. He is much bigger than your norms or your notions; all your ideas just fall apart.

The Upanishad calls the mind "pure" when it has no ripples of morality or immorality, when it has no foreign element in it, when it has become totally empty – and thought is a foreign element.

When someone mixes water with milk we say that the milk is not pure. But what is interesting is that if pure water is mixed with milk, then what? Is the milk then pure or not? – no, it is impure. Even if pure milk and pure water are mixed, then too the milk will become impure. Impurity is not related to the purity or impurity of the mixed elements: it is related with the mixing of a *foreign* element. When water is mixed with milk the water may be pure but it is a foreign element and the entry of a foreign element is the impurity.

Whatsoever enters into the mind from the outside will cause impurity. It does not make any difference whether it is a pure thought or an impure thought – whatsoever comes into the mind from the outside causes impurity. When nothing enters the mind from the outside and the mind is alone, by itself, only then it is pure. This state of purity needs to be clearly understood.

This is why when the Upanishads were translated in the West for the first time and commentaries were written on them, Western thinkers said that the Upanishads seem to be immoral. In his famous translation, Dewson has expressed his doubt about there being any moral teaching in the Upanishads. Unlike the Bible, there are no clear-cut instructions in the Upanishads: do not steal, do not cheat, do not commit adultery. Dewson's doubt is right, but his understanding is totally wrong. However he is right in saying that in the Upanishads there is nothing like the Ten Commandments of the Bible: "Do this and don't do that!"

Actually, the Upanishad says nothing about "doing." It says, "Be this." Doing is secondary, action is secondary – being is the primary thing. It does not say, "Do good, don't do evil." It says, "Merge with existence. Then good will happen through you, but that will not be your concern. Then no evil will happen through you, but you will not have to do anything to prevent it."

The concept of the Upanishads is that as long as you have to make an effort to stop any bad action, the bad is still in you. As long as you have to make some effort to do good, the good is not natural to you. It is not your real treasure; it is just false, hypocritical, shallow. As long as you have to make an effort, no light is lit within you.

The Upanishads say that if your being, your very soul, is transformed, then your behavior will automatically change. You don't have to worry about it. It is just like a shadow that follows a man and he does not have to turn around to see if it is following or not; he does not have to take care of the shadow, it just follows. In the same way, behavior follows – your behavior will be in accord with your being.

So what should be changed, your behavior or your being?

Ordinary scriptures say to change your behavior. The extraordinary scriptures say that your being should be transformed. Ordinary scriptures are written with the understanding of the ordinary man in mind; the extraordinary scripture is written with the view of the man's ultimate potential.

The Upanishads are extraordinary scriptures. They are the final statements: nothing more can be said or added to them.

> *"Ultimate reality can be known only by the pure mind. In this world, there is only the ultimate reality."*

As the mind becomes more pure, the world will be seen more and more as one reality. Because of the impure mind the world seems to consist of many diverse realities. The impurities of the mind divide reality into many fragments and the mind itself becomes fragmented because of its impurity.

Try to understand it in this way: there is a mirror and you break it into fifty pieces, so instead of one reflection now there will be fifty reflections. The mirror which had been reflecting only one will now reflect fifty. If you break the mirror into five hundred pieces then there will be five hundred reflections because every piece has become a mirror. You may have seen a hall where the walls are studded with many small pieces of mirror. If you stand in the middle of the hall then you will see thousands of reflections. If there had been one mirror then there would be only one reflection, but if there are thousands of mirrors then there will be thousands of reflections.

Mind becomes fragmented into many pieces depending on its impurity. The impure mind is fragmented, and to a fragmented mind the world appears fragmentary. When the mind becomes pure and only one mirror remains, then the world will be seen as just one existence.

That there is one reality is not just an idea: the one reality is the experience of a mind which has become one, undivided. So the question is not at all of searching for the truth – the people who are searching for the truth are on a wrong journey. The real question is to become an integrated mind.

People ask, "Where is truth?" This is a stupid question, it should not be asked. Instead of asking this, one should ask, "How can my fragmented mind become one, integrated?" – because whenever the mind becomes integrated and one, glimpses of the one reality will begin to happen. Existence will appear to be one or fragmented according to the state of your mind, whether it is disintegrated and in pieces or an integrated whole.

The mind is like a mirror in which we see existence. If this world appears to consist of many diverse realities, then know well that your mind is not integrated. And as long as this mind is not integrated, for you the world will remain fragmented. So the real search is not for truth but for the pure and integrated mind.

*"Ultimate reality can be known only by the pure mind. In this world, there is only the ultimate reality."* There is only one reality – and this experience of one reality is not only of religion, but also of science. This is also the ultimate understanding of science. If we look at the progress of science during the last five thousand years, then five thousand years ago scientists said that there are five elements; this was the discovery of the scientists of five thousand years ago. This old concept of five elements has entered our language in India. We still say that this body is made of five elements and this world is made of five elements. But this scientific discovery of five elements is five thousand years old. As the scientific methods became more sharp and subtle, more and more elements have been discovered. What we had called elements are no longer considered elements by the science of today.

Water is not an element because water is made up of oxygen and hydrogen. It is a compound; oxygen and hydrogen are elements. So by constant research science discovered ninety-two elements, but none of the five original elements are included in these. Earth, water, air, and fire are not elements, they are compounds. But five thousand years ago we had no way to test it, so water was considered an element because we did not have the method to analyze it to see whether it was a compound or an element. An element is something which exists independently, which is not a by-product of some mixture. So water proved to be a compound and not an element. Then the number of elements became ninety-eight and by and by, the number increased to one hundred and eleven and it has become apparent that the number of elements discovered seems to be growing more and more.

But during the last twenty years, the one hundred and eleven elements has disappeared and only one has remained because more research was done on each element. First water was analyzed and oxygen and hydrogen were found. By analyzing oxygen the atom was found and by analyzing hydrogen again the atom was found. Then all the elements were analyzed and in the end electricity was found. Now science says that the whole world is a network of electricity; everything is a play and a manifestation of electricity.

Science has reached the one reality through matter and religion has reached the one reality through consciousness – so science has called it electricity and religion has called it consciousness. Both are different dimensions, but the conclusions are very similar. But on one point they both agree, and that is that there is an expansion of only one reality.

But there will be no transformation in your life through the experiments of science. It will not transform you or make any difference to you whether the elements are one hundred and eleven or five or only one. If there are one hundred and eleven you will still remain as you are and if there are five you will still remain as you are. If there is one, even then you will remain the same. But in the religious process, to know the one reality will completely transform you.

To know that one reality you will have to transform your mind. A scientist does not have to transform himself at all: he just goes on experimenting with different means and he himself remains untouched. A religious person becomes his own laboratory: he does not have to transform anything except himself. As he goes on transforming himself he moves nearer to the one reality. When he becomes absolutely pure then what is left is the manifestation of that one reality.

That is why a scientist does not know any bliss. The greatest scientist is as miserable and unhappy as an ordinary, simple villager. The villager may be even less miserable because a little intelligence is needed to be miserable. The scientist does not undergo any transformation within himself and a religious person cannot experience the one reality unless he first transforms himself. Science is an effort with matter and religion is an effort with oneself.

As soon as the mind is purified:

> *"...there is only the ultimate reality. Hence, one who sees the many in this world will wander from death to death; he will be caught in the endless cycle of birth and death."*

The cause of your being born and dying again and again is that you have not realized the great ocean that you are. You see yourself as a small spring which goes on appearing and disappearing, but the ocean is eternally there.

Whatsoever you believe to be your self will be your culmination. If you believe that you are a small spring, then when the summer comes you will dry up and evaporate. Then again the rains will come, it will shower again and you will again become a spring; your spring will again start flowing but in the summer you will dry up again. You will just go on existing and not existing – this is the meaning of passing through "*...the endless cycle of birth and death.*" But if you know yourself to be the great ocean, it is eternal; it never ceases to be and never comes into existence anew. It does not become big or small; it neither floods nor dries up. It always remains as it is. And our oceans are very small; the ocean of consciousness is infinite, it can never be less or more.

That is why the Upanishads have said: If you remove the whole from the whole, even then, what remains is the whole. From the whole we can take out as much as we like and even then it will not become less. We can add the whole to it and even then nothing will have been added because the infinite means that whatsoever you add or take away makes no difference: nothing can be added and nothing can be taken away. One who has seen himself as that great ocean...

So there are two steps: the first step is purification of the mind. As soon as the mind is pure the ultimate reality becomes visible. But be aware, the presence of the other is still there: the first is the one who is seeing and the other is that which is seen – but the observer and the observed are still two.

The second step is that the purified mind dissolves because it too is not needed. The mirror is not only broken, it is completely destroyed. The mirror which had been creating the separation between the two is no longer there. Now only the one remains. But that one will not be known as one. That is why in India we have called this one "the non-dual" because to call it "one" is not right. Only this much has been said: that it is not two. Because if we call it "one," a question can arise that there may be another one. As soon as we say "one" the two enters. "One" means that the counting of numbers has begun, but "non-dual" means that we are ignoring numbers completely. We are saying that it cannot be counted: it is not two, this much is clear. We are not saying what it is, we are just saying what it is not.

This needs to be understood: any positive statement about the ultimate reality cannot be true. Only negative statements like *neti, neti* – not this, not that – can be true. We can only say what it is not, we cannot say what it is. It is so vast that no words will be adequate to describe it. But we can certainly say what it is not. What it is not can be said, so we say, "It is not two"; we say, "It is not unhappiness."

When somebody asked Buddha, "Will there be bliss in your *mahaparinirvana*?" Buddha said, "This I don't know. I can only say that there is no misery." We can negate. We cannot say that it is light, we can only say that there is no darkness.

This way of negation, this *via negativa* is very original and very basic. Whenever the ultimate reality has to be described you cannot say, "This is it," because if you indicate toward the reality in this way it will become limited. If I point my finger and say, "This is the ultimate reality," then this becomes a limitation. Whatever can be indicated by a finger cannot be limitless.

The ultimate reality can only be indicated by a closed fist. No other gesture will do. All gestures are only a small support for you to understand. They are like the crutches of a lame man who walks with their help: the crutches are not his feet. The lame man is only waiting for his feet to be healed and then he will throw away the crutches.

All the words that can be said about reality are just crutches, not the truth. As soon as you have the experience you will throw away these words just like a lame person who has been healed will throw away his crutches. Then they are not needed and to go on carrying them would be simply stupid.

> *"The soul, which is the size of the tip of the thumb, resides in the sky of the heart in the middle of the body. It is the ruler of the past, present and future. Knowing it, one can no longer condemn.*
> *"This, is that."*

This doctrine is a little controversial. It is a very old controversy about the form of the soul and its location in the body.

The Upanishads believe its form is the size of the tip of the thumb and that it is situated in the middle of the body, in the space of the heart. The Jainas say that this is very strange: "The soul, the size of a thumb?" The Jaina's concept is that the soul is the same size as the body, that it occupies the whole body. But this theory also creates much controversy because after its death an ant can be reborn as an elephant. When after death an ant can be reborn as an elephant, then the question is how it is possible for the soul, which is the size of an ant in an ant's body, to become the size of an elephant in an elephant's body.

So the Jainas had to create another concept: that the soul is flexible and can expand and shrink. It will expand according to the size of the body it is in. When it is in the body of an elephant it expands and becomes the size of an elephant and when it is in the body of an ant it shrinks to the size of an ant.

But the Upanishads ask, "Is the soul some object which can expand and shrink? Is it something material?" But the Jaina philosophers then ask, "If there is no possibility of expanding and shrinking, then why do you say that it is the size of the tip of the thumb? Is it some object which can be the size of the tip of the thumb? Then what about ants? How can a soul the size of a thumb enter the body of an ant?" It would be very difficult – the ant would be inside the soul but the soul wouldn't be in the ant! This controversy has been going on for thousands of years and there cannot be any end to it because the very basis of it is wrong.

It will be easier to understand it in the language of science. An earthen lamp is lit and its flame is very small but the light fills the whole room. Howsoever big or small the room may be, the walls will bring a limit to the light. A small lamp is lit but the limit of the light is decided by the walls of the room. This concept of the Upanishads that the soul is the size of a thumb is actually based on the concept of the flame of a lamp. It is like the flame of a lamp which is the size of a thumb: the light of this small flame fills the whole body: it makes no difference whether the body is big or small. The flame of the lamp can either be big or small.

When it is said that the soul is the size of a thumb, it means the soul of man, the lamp. The body of an ant is small, so its flame is also small; the body of an elephant – the lamp – is big, so its flame is also big, but the quality of the light is the same. The flame may be big or small – it may be a big sun but it makes no difference to the quality of the light. Whatever the boundaries of a body – the size of the room – the flame will fill it with light.

The concept that the soul is the size of the tip of the thumb is based on this idea of the flame of the earthen lamp. The soul fills your whole body with light. It is not the soul itself, but the light of the soul which reaches to your fingers. That much light is enough to keep your body alive; you are alive because of that much energy. The light of a dying man goes on becoming dimmer and dimmer and the body becomes weaker because the flame of his lamp is getting ready to leave that house.

Secondly, it is not right to take the words of the Upanishads literally when they say that the soul is the size of the tip of the thumb and that it is located in the sky of the heart. It is not fair to hold on to these words because they are only indications. The real meaning is not that the soul is the size of the tip of the thumb; this is only an indication, only a hint.

In this body, in the center of the heart, there is a contact point to the soul. The concept of the Upanishads is that the soul is omnipresent; it is the ultimate reality which surrounds everything and prevails everywhere – but the contact place within you is in the middle of the heart. From there you are plugged into the ultimate reality.

You have fixed an electric light bulb to a very small socket, but it has a large flow of electricity behind it. If you have put in a five-watt bulb you will get the light of five watts; if the bulb is a fifty-watt bulb you will get the light of fifty watts and if you put in a two-hundred-watt bulb you will get the light of two hundred watts. The flow of electricity is unlimited but the bulb will use the electricity according to its own capacity.

Our souls are the same because we are all connected with the ultimate source. The contact point to that reality in us is called the soul. Then, according to our capacity – according to the capacity of our "candle" – we take light from that source. Some have the capacity of five candles – but a person like Buddha has the capacity of five thousand candles so he can spread the light of five thousand candles around him. But we are all plugged into the great source. The ant has a very small candle, man has a little bigger candle, a Buddha has much more – but the infinite source is just the same.

The Upanishads are talking about the contact point with the great source that is within you, where you are connected with the ultimate reality which is of the size of the tip of a thumb. You will receive energy from this great source according to your purity; it all depends on your purity. If you become absolutely pure then the great source will manifest through you.

Those whom we call avatars, tirthankaras, buddhas, are the people who have purified themselves so totally that they have disappeared and the great source has manifested through them. Then it does not fit to call them just human beings: we feel to remember them by the name of the great source with which they have become merged.

> *"The soul, which is the size of the tip of the thumb, resides in the sky of the heart in the middle of the body. It is the ruler of the past, present and future. Knowing it, one can no longer condemn.*
> *"This, is that.*
>
> *"The soul, which is the size of the tip of the thumb, is like a smokeless flame. It is this soul, the ruler of past, present and future, which is today and which is tomorrow. This soul is the eternal.*
> *"This, is that."*

A smokeless flame: this has to be understood. Whenever you light a fire there is smoke. Why is there smoke from a fire? What is the reason for the smoke? Is the fire responsible for the smoke? Is it the nature of fire to create smoke? No, the fuel is the cause of the smoke. Smoke has no connection with the nature of fire. When you burn a piece of wet wood there is so much smoke that you can hardly see the fire. If you burn a dry piece of wood there will be much less smoke and the flames will be more easily visible. If you burn a totally dry piece of wood then there will be almost no smoke. This makes one thing clear: smoke is related with the fuel, not with the fire. This also means that a flame can only be completely smokeless when there is no fuel. Otherwise whatever the type of fuel, some kind of smoke will be present. If you burn the purest fuel, such as spirit, it will create some smoke which may not even be visible to the eye, because when something is burned there are two things involved: the burning material and the fire. The burning material will create smoke.

Smoke is carbon, and whenever something burns carbon is created. If we could discover a fire which would be smokeless… It is very interesting that in the last three hundred years all the great scientific institutions like the Royal Society, the French Academy of Science, the American Association for the Advancement of Science, the Science Academy of Russia – they have all received letters from thousands of people each year who claim that they have discovered a fire which will burn without fuel. But all these claims have proved to be untrue. This is an ancient search. And now countries like France and England have asked people to stop making these claims because it unnecessarily wastes a lot of time. Hundreds of people in this world have applied for patents claiming to have found a source of energy that needs no fuel, but all these claims are false.

On the day that we are able to find an energy that needs no fuel, we will have found a great energy source. All other types of fuel will become obsolete. If we go on burning oil at the rate that we are doing now, scientists say that in five thousand years not even a drop will be left. And everything seems to be dependent on oil, but there is a limit to the supply.

We have destroyed the forests by burning the wood and now we are paying for it because there is no rain. There is soil erosion and the land is barren. In Pakistan, five thousand children are born every hour, and every hour one acre of land is being destroyed. Children don't bring even an inch of land with them and every hour one acre is lost through soil erosion because the forests have been cut down. The trees were holding the soil with their roots: when there are no trees there is no hold on the soil and it starts disintegrating. If you cut down all the forests all the land will disintegrate and turn to dust because the roots of the trees are holding the soil together.

It is not only the trees which are taking food from the land, the land is also taking support from the trees. The trees are constantly drawing nourishment from the sky and passing it on to the land. When the trees are removed the land will become just barren.

So a great search is going on for such a fuel because forests have been cut down and there is a shortage of wood. We are taking coal out from the mines and it is being depleted; we are exhausting the oil. One day, when all the fuel is finished, man will simply die. Now you cannot conceive what it will be like when there is no longer any oil. What will be the condition of the world then? Airplanes will not be able to fly and cars will not run. It is not so difficult in India, but people in America and Europe just cannot imagine a life without a car; it is impossible. Life seems just impossible without oil.

This is why there are so many eccentric people who make false claims that they have found a smokeless fuel. So after much consideration. many governments have now decided that they will not accept these applications for a patent because it is not possible to create a smokeless fuel.

But the Upanishads say that the energy source within man

is a smokeless fuel. The ultimate reality is a fire without any fuel; hence, it is smokeless, no smoke comes from it.

You might think that this is a little difficult to understand, and if you ask medical science they too will not agree with this. They will say, "You are alive because you are fueled by the food you eat. If you stop eating food then your life will end. With the breath you are ingesting fuel, oxygen is going in. If oxygen did not go in then you would die. In many ways you are taking in fuel so why do you call the inner soul a 'smokeless flame'?"

Much research is needed to be done on this. There are a few examples in this century. In past centuries there were many examples of people living without food but it is difficult to find examples of this today. But still, there are some people who live in this way.

There was a woman in Europe called Thérèse Newman, who lived without food for thirty years and she did not lose a single gram of weight. Medical science was puzzled by her case. There was a woman in Bengal who died in 1950: she lived without food for forty years. She was absolutely healthy, healthier than an ordinary healthy person. She was never sick, she was as energetic as a young person until the day she died. She never lost any weight. It all happened by coincidence: her husband died, and because of her love for her husband she became so unhappy that she stopped eating. But she did not die from this lack of food; on the contrary, she became more and more healthy. She used to get sick often when she first gave up food, but after she stopped eating all her diseases disappeared. It was a miracle that happened because she lived without food for forty years!

Now, in the West, a new theory is developing which says that eating is just a habit of man's, it is not a need; and he does not get fuel from food – it is only a habit, an addiction. Just as we say that smoking or drinking are addictions, in the same way, some researchers say that food is also an addiction. It is not man's need, man can live without food.

In Jaina scriptures it is said that before the days of their first tirthankara, Rishabhadev, people used to live without food. This story could be true. It was Rishabhadev who for the first time began to eat food, so he might be the first person to create our habit of eating food. Perhaps people had started forgetting the art of living without food and so eating food was discovered.

To live without food depends on a certain art of breathing. But still, one thing remains: those two women were breathing, and breathing can give you nourishment. A tree is taking in food just by breathing, so there is no reason why a man also cannot take in food just by breathing.

You will be surprised to know that the wood and leaves of a tree and its fruits do not come from the earth. Rather, they are created from what they absorb from the sky. During the last century botanists did many experiments, and they were surprised because it was always thought that the trees are drawing their nourishment from the earth. But one scientist planted a root in a pot and he measured the soil in it. The plant started growing and it became quite big. Then he took it out and weighed it and it was much heavier, but the soil in the pot was exactly the same old weight; there was no difference in it. The question is: from where did the plant gain the weight? The weight was taken from the air, not from the earth. Otherwise there are so many trees on the earth that the earth would have been totally eaten by now. There would be empty pits everywhere! But no, the earth has remained the same.

If the plants are taking their nourishment from the sky, if they are taking all the substances they need from the rays of the sun and from the air, then why can't man live without food? And of course, man lives through the plants: he eats their fruits and grains and the plants draw from the sky and create fruits. So it is possible that man can live directly, without the plant being the medium.

Mahavira must have known this art of living without food because in eleven years he ate only on three hundred and sixty-five days. Sometimes for three months, sometimes for four or five months, he would not eat. Seeing statues of him, it does not look as if he is starving – his body looks very strong. He had a very strong body. When Jaina monks fast for four months they become just bones; they don't know the art that Mahavira must have known. He certainly must have known some method for getting his fuel directly through breathing.

Those two women certainly prove that man can live without food – but without breathing? But there are also proofs of people who can live without breathing. Recently there have been very surprising proofs.

In Egypt, in 1880, a Sufi fakir went into deep meditation and he gave instructions to keep his body in a grave which should be opened after forty years, in 1920. The people who had put him in the grave had all died. Actually, people had almost forgotten about him. Forty years! By chance, in 1920, one man came across a forty-year-old newspaper where it was written that a man is being buried today while he is in samadhi and that after forty years he should be dug out. That reader contacted the government and they dug the fakir out of the grave where he had been buried for forty years. He came out alive! He had lived for forty years without breathing and he lived for one more year after he was dug out.

In India, yogis have done this for from three weeks to three months. But an experiment of three weeks does not prove much because the pit in which the yogi is buried contains enough oxygen to last for three weeks. But it is impossible to have enough oxygen in a small pit which can last for forty years.

There are animals that can live without breathing, like the polar bears from Siberia. There it is daylight for six months and night for another six months. When it is night for six months and it snows everywhere the polar bear goes into hibernation and almost stops breathing. For six months it goes to sleep and hardly breathes at all. When the sun comes out again after six months and it becomes daytime and it starts getting warmer and the snow starts melting, the polar bear starts to breathe again. If a bear can live for six months almost without breathing, then why can't man live without breathing?

In India also, when the summer approaches, the frogs go to sleep underground: they stop breathing, they stop all activity, but they don't die. When the rains come, again the frogs wake up. This long sleep is happening without breathing.

Within man – in fact within all life – there is an element that can function without fuel. This flame without fuel is called by the Upanishads "the smokeless flame."

*"The soul, which is the size of the tip of the thumb, is like a smokeless flame. It is this soul, the ruler of past, present and future, which is today and which is tomorrow. This soul is the eternal."* There is no way that it can be destroyed because when its life is causeless, there cannot be any cause for its death. Anything that does not need food for fuel is enough unto itself; it cannot be destroyed. There is no way for it to perish. If you are dependent on anything then you will die because there will be no possibility for your survival if the thing on which you are dependent should perish.

The ultimate reality is *swayambhu*, self-created, self-contained. It is a power in itself; it is not dependent on anything. This is why the universe goes on, existence goes on flowing. It never dies and it is never born.

> *"This, is that.*
>
> *"Even as rainwater falling on a high peak will flow to many different places on the mountain, the man who worships gods and demons which are endowed with diverse natures, thinking them to be other than divine, will continue to pursue them. He will wander lost in their good or evil realms and in the higher and lower species.*
>
> *"Nachiketa, of the lineage of the sage Gautama! Even as the*

*pure rainwater remains the same when mixed with other pure waters, when the self of the sage has known the Supreme Self, it becomes the Supreme Self."*

There are two ways of looking at the world: one is to see it as one reality and the other is to see it as consisting of many diverse realities. He who sees it as many is blind, he has the vision of a blind man. He who sees reality as one, his eyes are open and he is really seeing. He does not see the insignificant boundaries, he sees the divine reality that is present in all.

Yama says, "Nachiketa, the person who knows the One is just like the rainwater that goes on flowing downward, is merged with the ocean and becomes the ocean. The person who sees the One goes on flowing: he is merged in the ocean of the ultimate reality, he becomes one with it."

Your misery is that you have stopped flowing. You have become frozen, rigid, just like a river that has become frozen and cannot flow and reach to the ocean. Heat is needed for it to melt, sun is needed for it to melt; melting is needed for it to flow toward the ocean. You are all frozen in your bodies, you have become like ice. And the way to melt is through methods of purification, spiritual discipline, right efforts.

My whole effort with the experiments that we are doing here is so that you can melt at least a little bit, so that you can flow again. The ocean is not far away, but if you remain frozen then you are like an iceberg in the ocean that cannot melt into the ocean.

Try to melt, try to become a flow. But the ego is as hard as stone: it stops you from melting. It says, "What are you doing? You are going to disappear! Hold onto yourself!" – but the one who holds on to himself will remain rigid and frozen. Melt yourself in these meditation experiments. This is why I insist that you dance, jump, become flowing again like a small child. Put your ego aside and let the body melt. Let the energy of the body flow; it should not remain frozen. Become hot. Breathe deeply so that the oxygen can hit hard, shout loudly so that the kundalini receives a shock; become fire within. The fire will be kindled by a spark from *aranis* and the small flame that is hidden within you will become an intense fire.

When this fire is lit, as long as you remain as an ego, there will be some smoke because *you* are the fuel. As soon as you disappear the smoke will also disappear – the smokeless flame.

And for one who has experienced the smokeless flame, there is nothing more for him to experience.

Now get ready for meditation.

# 11

# One Space and One Soul

*"The human body is a pur, a city. It is a city of godliness with eleven gates. Godliness is simple. It is never born, it is pure consciousness. It is because of the existence of the body that man can accomplish spiritual disciplines, such as meditation; he will thereby transcend grief and become a jivanmukta, one who is liberated while living in the body. He will be eternally bodiless after death.*
*"This, is that.*

*"The self-illumined One lives in the pure and ultimate abode: it is the god Vasu of the sky; it is the guest in every house; it is the sacred fire that receives the offerings at the yagnas, the fire rituals, and it is also the blessed offerer; it is the dweller in all human beings; it is the dweller in all the gods beyond man; it is the dweller within the truth; it is the dweller of the sky; it is the One who lives within the myriad life forms of the water; it is the One who appears in the myriad life forms of the earth; it is the One who is manifested in deeds of goodness; it is the One who lives in the many life forms of the mountains. This omnipresent One is the ultimate reality.*

*"All gods honor this One. It lives in the middle of the body; it raises the prana upward and pushes the apana downward.*

*"When the embodied soul leaves the body on its journey to a new body, what is left behind?*
*"This, is that.*

*"No mortal, living being lives either through the prana vayu, the upward current of life energy, or through the apana vayu, the downward current: they both live through something else which sustains the two.*

*"Nachiketa, of the lineage of the sage Gautama, I will tell you what the mysterious and eternal brahman is; I will tell you once again what happens to the embodied soul after death.*

*"According to their actions, according to the inclinations developed from all they have heard and learned, many disembodied souls find other wombs; many others enter the realm of the inanimate – trees, creepers, mountains…*

*"The One – which is the creator of all situations that living beings will experience according to their past actions, which remains awake when all else has gone to sleep in pralaya, the end of creation – is the purest essence; it is the brahman. It is immortal and all the worlds dwell in it. None can transcend it.*
*"This, is that."*

In the minds of the sages of the Upanishads, there is no condemnation of the human body. They have a great reverence, a feeling of trust for the human body because it is actually a temple. How can the body be condemned when it is the dwelling place of the supreme self? The body becomes sacred simply because of the fact that the supreme reality dwells within it.

According to the Upanishads, this body is not impure. The so-called religious people are full of a deep condemnation for the body – as if the body is evil, something to be hated; as if the body is the cause of all the unhappiness, the misery, the bondage in life. For them it is as if the body is the gate to hell. But this so-called religious concept has no foundation: only the sick-minded think like this.

The body is not binding you, it is not holding you. How can it hold you? It is you who are holding the body. You have chosen this body: it is the manifested form of all your desires and longings. So the first thing to be understood is that whatever body you have, whether it is human or animal, bird or tree or stone, whether it is of a woman or a man, beautiful or ugly, healthy or sick – whatever body you have – it is the manifestation of your desires, your passions, your longings. You have exactly what you have desired. But you cannot see this because there is a great distance of time between the desire and its fulfillment.

A man sows a seed and after many years it sprouts. In the meantime, he has totally forgotten that he had sown the seed. You will be surprised to know that there were many tribes around the world, and even today there are some African tribes, that don't know that a child is born out of sexual intercourse because months have passed since the intercourse took place and here, now the child is born. So many tribes could not understand this connection. And each sexual intercourse does not create a child. Out of hundreds, one results in the birth of a child and that too takes nine months.

Sometimes it takes a very long time to see the fulfillment of your desires, longings and wishes: you yourself have forgotten that you had desired it. Psychologists say that you invite many diseases: at some time you have desired them and that desire has remained suppressed in your unconscious mind. Then gradually the body creates that disease. It will be a little difficult to understand it because nobody likes sickness. Then why would someone desire to be sick? Why would someone sow the seeds of illness? There are profound reasons for this in the life of a person and it is a very complex network.

Whenever a small child becomes ill, people give him a lot of attention and they care for him. When he is well nobody pays any attention to him. So in his unconscious mind it becomes clear that it is to his advantage to be ill because only then people will pay attention to him.

Everyone wants attention. It is a deep longing that people should pay attention to you because attention is food. Whenever someone looks at you, you feel nourished, and you become sad when nobody looks at you. Slowly, slowly a small child experiences that whenever he is ill something important happens – his father gives him more love and his mother sits near him. He has always wanted his father to be more loving toward him, for his mother to sit with him and everyone to care about him, but nobody ever bothered about him. But all his wishes are fulfilled when he is ill. Then his longing for attention becomes connected with illness. Later on, after many years, whenever this person feels neglected by others, his unconscious desire to be ill will become very strong. This desire will not be conscious, it will be deep in his unconscious mind.

Most women's illnesses are because of the lack of attention given to them. Whenever a man is in love with a woman she remains healthy, but as soon as the love affair is over she starts becoming sick – her sickness is saying that nobody is paying attention to her. Fifty percent of women's diseases arise out of the desire for attention. A wife gets sick as soon as her husband comes home: she was okay when he was out of the house. And it is also not true that she is pretending, no. But seeing the husband, she gets sick. Seeing him, the desire arises in her for her husband to pay attention to her, to care for her and worry about her. This desire goes deep down into her unconscious and she creates the situation in which her husband will be attentive to her, will care for her and serve her.

Now psychologists say that the mind is very complex, but the sages of the East have always said that whatsoever we are and whatsoever we have become is the condensed form of our old desires. Whatever we have wished for is fulfilled now, in this birth. So there is no reason to hate the body: you have asked for this body and you have got it.

The second thing to remember is that this body is not holding you; in fact, you are holding it. How can the body hold you? The day you are able to let go of the body, the body will let go of you. If you can let go of the body totally, even for a moment, the body will start to die.

This is why mystics are able to decide when to die. The secret of this art is that they know how to separate themselves from the body. They hold on to a few desires which function as a connecting link with the body so that the body can fulfill its purpose. But on the day that they see it is time to depart, they disconnect the last link and their boat leaves this shore.

This is why mystics can announce their death beforehand, that they will die on a certain day. People think that it is because the mystic can see the future. No, it is not because of that: a mystic does not know the future, he can simply free himself from the body whenever he wants to. This is his freedom: he can give up the body whenever he wants to. He has understood the secret: this body is not holding him, it is he who is holding on to the body. So he can hold on to his body as long as he wants and he can drop the body whenever he wants. You have forgotten this. You think that the body is holding on to you – and this misunderstanding has created so much nonsense.

The so-called saints of a certain Christian sect used to whip themselves day and night just to torture the body because they felt it to be an enemy. And the one who whipped himself more was thought to be a greater saint. Nowadays, we call these people masochists – they are sick people who enjoy torturing themselves. Now we put them in a madhouse as sick people, but in the Middle Ages, the whole of Europe was full of these types of so-called saints. Actually, they were just mentally ill people, not saints.

There were some Christian saints who used to wear shoes with nails inside, who used belts which had spikes in them so that the body was in pain all the time. And people would give them much respect. We also give respect to people who are torturing their bodies. Somebody is torturing the body by fasting, somebody else is torturing the body by standing in the sun, somebody is torturing the body just by continuously standing and not sitting down at all, someone is torturing the body by lying down on thorns. If you go to Varanasi you will see many such exhibitions; the Kumbha Mela is full of these insane exhibitions.

But it is surprising that you also feel respect for these people who are torturing their bodies, as if they are doing something great! Nothing great is being done – it simply means that you don't even know that it is not the body that is holding you, it is you who are holding the body. It is just as if you beat up your car because it is taking you to the wrong place. How can a car take you anywhere? You are putting the gas into it, you are decorating it, you are steering it and it goes wherever you want it to go. Although you are sitting in the car, the car is following you, you are not following the car.

This Upanishad says that the body is like a chariot, a car that you are sitting inside and driving. So if you are going toward sin don't think that the body is taking you there; this is utter stupidity. If you want to sin the body supports you: if you drive your car toward the red-light district the car will go there. The car is not concerned about where you are going, it just goes wherever you take it. If you want to take it to a temple it will stop at the entrance to the temple. But when it stops at the door of a brothel and then you start kicking the car, you are just being stupid.

It is not only you, but people that are widely respected have behaved like this. Some saints have destroyed their eyes because they say the eyes have created lust in them. They have cut off their hands because their hands have done some evil act. How can the hands do any evil? How can the eyes create lust? You are hidden behind the eyes, the eyes go wherever you take them. You are the driving force behind your eyes. You yourself are the culprit – who are you punishing by destroying your eyes?

Some saints have cut out their tongues, have cut off their sex organs – this is sheer insanity! You don't understand that the body is only a mechanism; it has no consciousness. *You* are the consciousness. You are responsible for your good and bad deeds. It is you who create your hell and it is you who create your heaven. One who blames the body is totally unintelligent.

Now that you have understood this concept of the Upanishads, let us enter this sutra.

> *"The human body is a pur, a city. It is a city of godliness with eleven gates. Godliness is simple. It is never born, it is pure consciousness."*

The body is the *pur,* the city. This is why we have called man *purush,* which means: the godliness that lives in that *pur*, the godliness that is hidden in that city. *Purush* is a very meaningful word. *Pur* means city, and the body is a city. It cannot be called a house because a house is a very small thing. Your body is really a city and its population is not small: billions of cells are living there. It is a huge city! If each cell were measured and enlarged to your height, your body would be as big as the city of London. There are roads the same as in London; a river flows and a network of telegraph and telephone lines are there just like in London. Just as in London there are roads, traffic, a vast network of telephone and other communication cables, a river flowing in the middle of the city, the police, the military, the citizens, the masters, the servants, the rich and the poor, so it is the same arrangement with these billions of residents in the body. There are even police constables in them – if you ask medical science, you will be amazed.

The body is a very unique phenomenon. If you are even a little injured, you will find that within moments a white liquid will accumulate there. You may never have thought about why this white liquid film is formed immediately when you are injured. It is not simply pus: these are the white cells of your blood which do the work of policemen in your body all the time. Whenever and wherever there is trouble, an accident, danger, they immediately rush and reach to that place and cover it because after that place is covered no infection can enter. If that place had remained uncovered, any bacteria or germs carrying diseases could enter immediately. So these are the white cells of your blood which immediately rush to the injured place, surrounding and covering it. You may have thought it is only pus, but it is not: it is a safety measure of the body. It is a very amazing phenomenon.

It was not easy for medical science to finally understand how these white cells come to know whether the injury is on the hand or on the head or on the foot. They rush with the blood from all over the body to the exact place of the injury and cover it immediately. If the quantity of white cells in your body decreases then you will get sick very often because your security force has become weak. That is why your body needs a certain quantity, a certain number of white cells. Without that specific quantity your resistance and your power to fight against diseases will be less. These cells go on fighting the infection and they don't know anything about you.

The most surprising thing is that this city of billions of cells has no knowledge of your existence; it cannot have. They have never met you. They go on doing their work: some are making blood, some are digesting the food. You eat food and these cells are breaking it down, digesting it and turning it into nutrients, blood and flesh are created. All this work is going on and it is all properly assigned.

In ancient times Hindus conceived the idea of four castes, and there are also four types of cells in the body. The sudra cells go on doing service, the vaishya cells are doing the business of converting things, transforming things. They transform one thing into another: they turn one chemical into a hormone and another into something else – all the time they are busy with their business. There are kshatriya cells which are guarding and defending all the time and there are brahmin cells which go on thinking all the time. Your brain cells are the brahmin cells. The Hindus have described the sudras as the feet and the brahmins as the head – these symbols are very significant.

The whole body is divided and there is every possibility that *yogins,* mystics, have organized the society according to how they experienced the inner arrangement of the body. This may be the model for the origins of the caste system; the possibility is there. Otherwise how did this idea of four castes arise? And it has happened only in India; outside India nobody has created these four castes. Actually, outside India, nobody has ever made an effort to enter the city of the body. Mystics must have thought of it only after they saw the workings of the inner system of the body; they must have applied the same system that they found in the body to the society.

Whether the world thinks in terms of four castes or not, the fact is that there are always four castes. Whether it is in Russia or in America, the sudra always exists. In Russia the sudra is known as "the proletariat." The change in name does not make any difference; there is someone who is continuously doing the work of a sudra. Even if the society or the administration of the state or the economic situation changes, there will always be someone doing the work of the sudra. Whether it is a democracy, a dictatorship or any other kind of system, there will be someone who will be dominating it like the kshatriya. And no matter what the system, it is impossible to bring the brahmins down from their heads!

Today, in Russia, the status of professors, doctors, engineers and scientists is very high – these are the brahmins, they deal in knowledge. In America a fear is growing that in the coming hundred years scientists can become so powerful that they may overpower the government because all the keys are in their hands. Today the politician seems to be very powerful on the surface, but behind him it is the scientist who is more powerful because he has the key to the atom. Sooner or later he is going to be on the top. Even now politicians seek their advice. As soon as Kennedy became the President of America, he immediately called the best minds from all over America as his advisors. Kennedy gathered great professors, great writers, great poets and great scientists around him because the kshatriya himself is not so intelligent; he has always been taking advice from the brahmin. The kshatriya is up in the front but it is the brahmin who directs him from behind.

There is a big city within the body and the work of this city is so organized that no other city can compare to it. The work is very systematic and it happens so silently; it is totally automatic. Whether you are asleep or awake the work goes on; whether you are working or resting this work goes on. And you are not disturbed by it, it goes on automatically. You don't know when your food is digested, when it becomes blood, when it becomes bones or when the dead cells are thrown out. This whole city is automatic.

You are at the center of this city; it is worthy of respect. This city has given you an opportunity to reach to heaven or to hell through it; or if you wish, you can be free of heaven and hell and attain to moksha, liberation – and the body is only the means.

This sutra says: *"The human body is a pur, a city. It is a city of godliness with eleven gates. Godliness is simple. It is never born, it is pure consciousness."* There are five senses, five organs of action and one mind: these are the eleven gates.

> *"It is because of the existence of the body that man can accomplish spiritual disciplines, such as meditation; he will thereby transcend grief and become a jivanmukta – one who is liberated while living in the body. He will be eternally bodiless after death.*
> *"This, is that."*

Then this body, this city, is not needed at all. Then one is free of this mechanism of the body.

This machine-like body can be used in two ways: one is for self-forgetfulness, which is what desires and passions are; the other is for self-remembrance, which is what meditation is. You can use this body in the search for the trivial pleasures of life.

And what is this pleasure? Wherever you can forget yourself for a while, you think that is pleasure. Pleasure is simply forgetting yourself. Somebody forgets himself by drinking alcohol, somebody forgets himself by listening to music, somebody forgets himself in sex, somebody forgets himself in eating food, somebody forgets himself sitting on a throne – and they think that all these things are giving them pleasure.

What is your definition of pleasure? Wherever you forget yourself you feel pleasure and wherever you remember yourself you feel misery. Actually, whenever you start remembering yourself, your pain starts becoming more intense because then you ask, "What am I doing? Where am I? What is this all about?" Then you become worried, anxious; then you want to forget yourself. Someone is trying to forget himself by reading the newspaper and someone else by reading the Bhagavadgita. There are many ways of forgetting yourself, but the effort to forget continues.

Lust and desire are self-forgetfulness, a way to forget yourself. And how can one who is busy forgetting himself reach to his soul? How can he attain consciousness? Godliness will be very far away from him. The more you forget yourself the further away you will be from godliness.

This is why all the religions are against alcohol. Actually, they are not against alcohol; it is an innocent thing, why should they oppose it? The opposition is only because it helps you to forget yourself. If you could remain aware after drinking alcohol then there would be no objection.

Only the *tantrikas* have made this effort of being conscious even after drinking alcohol. Slowly, slowly they increase the quantity of alcohol and try to remain conscious; they increase only as much as allows them to remain conscious. They go on increasing, and finally the *tantrikas* can drink poison without losing consciousness. When alcohol and poison cannot affect their consciousness, then they tame a snake and make the snake bite their tongue. When that also has no effect they can say that now they are really awake; now nothing can make them unconscious. So in a way, the *tantrikas* are also opposed to alcohol.

In fact all the traditions are opposed to unconsciousness. The spiritual search is a search for consciousness, but the ways can be different. Jaina and Buddhist monks cannot even conceive that alcohol or poison can be used as a means to become aware. A *tantrika* says, "Drink, but don't lose awareness – remain conscious." And both are saying the same thing. One says, "Do not drink because you cannot remain aware," and the *tantrika* says, "Drink to see if you can remain aware. Your awareness should go on growing more and more."

And I believe that the awareness of the *tantrika* is truer than that of any monks, because the *tantrika* tries to remain conscious even in difficult situations. The depth and the height of his awareness is great. If all the monks in the world were gathered together and made to drink alcohol, only the *tantrikas* would stay conscious; the rest of them would be in trouble. Even if poison is given to them the *tantrikas* do not become unconscious.

So the path of Tantra is very arduous. Ordinarily man can deceive himself by thinking that he is drinking alcohol because he is a *tantrika*. And Tantra has not condemned the so-called evils: it says awareness can be there in so-called evil. That is why it is not against sex. If you can remain aware during sexual intercourse, then sexual intercourse has become a meditation. But one thing is clear: religions may or may not be against each other, but all of them are against unconsciousness and are for consciousness.

One who uses the body to remain conscious will become free of the body even while living in the body. As awareness goes on increasing one can see that the body is separate: "I am separate." The distance between the two, the body and the self, goes on growing. Then whatsoever happens to the body it does not seem to be happening to *you*, it feels as if it is happening only to the body.

If you are driving a car and it starts making some noise you know that something is wrong with the engine, you don't feel that something is wrong with you. You simply stop the car and check the engine. In the same way, if you are aware and something happens to your body, you don't feel that it is happening to you. You know that something is wrong with the body so you see a doctor, but you will not suffer and get upset about it. When you feel hungry you will know that the body is hungry, just as when a car needs petrol. When the petrol is finished then you put some more petrol in but you are not putting the petrol in *you*.

As awareness grows, all activities are experienced as belonging to the body. Only one thing belongs to you and that is witnessing, meditation. Only meditation is spiritual, everything else is physical. So anyone who is not meditating is only living in the body, he cannot enter his being. There is only one thread leading to your being, and that is meditation.

The sutra says that the person who practices spiritual disciplines, meditation, will never grieve because for him the presence of the body is no reason for unhappiness. Unhappiness comes because of your deep conviction that you are the body, your identification with the body. But as soon as you experience that you are not the body, all misery will disappear and you will be liberated while living in your body.

The *jivanmukta,* the one liberated while living in the body, is the person who has known that he is not the body. He can still remain in the body for some time more. Just as you are living in the body, the liberated one also lives in the body for some time after his enlightenment. Mahavira stayed in his body for forty years after he was enlightened. When Buddha became enlightened, he also stayed in his body for forty years. Why did they stay? You live in a body, a Mahavira and a Buddha also lived in a body – but you live in a body to fulfill your own desires and lusts, and Buddha and Mahavira lived in the body because of their compassion for others. They wanted to share all that they had received in enlightenment.

After many, many lives Buddha attained enlightenment. He could have left his body at that time if he had wanted to. Actually, Buddha wanted to leave his body immediately. When he became enlightened he remained silent for seven days afterward.

There is a very sweet story that the gods bowed at his feet and asked him to speak, to help people understand, because only after many centuries does somebody attain to the state of buddhahood: "Do not remain silent! Do not dissolve and disappear! Stay on this shore for some time more." So Buddha stayed on this shore for forty years. His staying here was not to attain anything for himself, it was to share something. You are holding on to the body to get something, but a buddha holds on to the body to give something.

A *jivanmukta* can still remain in his body. But as soon as one becomes a *jivanmukta* one thing becomes certain – that after leaving this body there will be no return to another body, it is not possible. After leaving this house there will be no other house.

After his enlightenment the first words that Buddha uttered were, "O, God of Desires, now you will not need to make another house for me. You have made my last house and now it is not needed. Now you don't have to create new bodies for me. God of Desires, you have created so many different bodies for me in so many, many lives – now you are free, now your services are no longer needed."

A person who has realized that he is not the body while still living in this body will enter the bodiless state as soon as he dies and leaves this body. He will exist but he will have no form. Then he lives without a house. He is one with this vast universe – just as a drop lives in the ocean but not as a drop, it has become the ocean; just as the flame of an earthen lamp is lost in the sky but actually is not lost because no energy is ever lost, it becomes part of the great sun, it becomes part of the great light.

But this is so only for the one who experiences that he is not the body while still in this body.

Some people think that they can realize this state in the last moments of their lives. Some people stretch this logic to such an extent that when they are almost dead, when they are not even able to hear anymore, then they have others recite mantras, the Gita or the Namokar Mantra, into their ears. And they did not have the intelligence to listen to all these scriptures while they were alive! Other people also make them drink the water of the holy Ganges hoping that then they will be delivered from bondage. When they were alive they never even went near the Ganges and now when they are dying bottled Ganges water is given to them. While still alive they never searched for truth, now the words from dead scriptures are recited to them, and that too is done by hired people who repeat the words for the money they will get. They themselves don't know what they are repeating; they will themselves need hired people to recite the scriptures to them when they are about to die.

Man has not only deceived himself in this life, he has made arrangements to try to deceive in the afterlife. You are so cunning that you think that somehow you can even deceive existence. So you have invented stories like the one where a sinner, who named his son Narayan, which means God, was dying. As he was dying he called out to his son, "Narayan!" and the Lord Narayan in heaven thought that the man was calling him. And so the dying man, who had never thought about God in his whole life, went straight to heaven!

Such a story must have been invented by some sinner. Now this sinner must have been calling out to his son Narayan to pass on some secret of his trade. He had cheated, stolen and picked pockets for his whole life so he must have been wanting to pass the secrets of his trade on to his son. But Lord Narayan was deceived. It proves that this Lord Narayan in the sky must have been a perfect idiot! But sinners invent these stories just to console themselves.

There is no way to deceive existence. There is no way to deceive the divine. It is not a government office where files can be tampered with, misinterpreted, misplaced. The truth of your life is your only connection with existence. There we are absolutely naked, there we are as we really are; there is no way or means to hide. So don't console yourself with these kinds of stories thinking: "No problem, I will also name my son Narayan."

Perhaps that's why people name their sons Rama, Krishna, Narayan and so on: they think that they will also be able to play the same trick which that sinner, whose name was Ajamil, played; that it may be useful sometime; or that a hired priest will repeat the name of God in their ears. But can a hired person pronounce God's name for you? Can anyone else pray on your behalf? Can somebody else worship for you? It means that you don't understand the meaning and the significance of worship, of prayerfulness.

It's as if you are in love with someone and you appoint a servant to make love on your behalf because you have no time. No, you would not do such a thing where your love is concerned. But people have been doing this with prayer for centuries. Prayerfulness is the greatest love that can exist, but the rich build temples in their houses and hire priests who will worship on their behalf.

The Tibetans are cleverer: they have invented a wheel which they call a prayer wheel. It is a small, round wheel on which a mantra has been written. They go on doing their other work and at the same time turning the wheel; the mantra is repeated each time as the wheel makes a full round.

One Tibetan lama came to me with his prayer wheel in hand. I asked him, "What are you doing? Get it connected to electricity – then it will go on turning automatically without disturbing your work at all. As it is you have to keep revolving it again and again and it is hindering your work. This work of turning the wheel can be done by electricity."

But can prayer be done this way? Because man is so dishonest, his dishonesty spreads in all dimensions. His dishonesty is also spread in the dimension of the divine.

> *"It is because of the existence of the body that man can accomplish spiritual disciplines, such as meditation; he will thereby transcend grief and become a jivanmukta, one who is liberated while living in the body. He will be eternally bodiless after death.*
> *"This, is that.*
>
> *"The self-illumined One lives in the pure and ultimate abode: it is the god Vasu of the sky; it is the guest in every house; it is the sacred fire that receives the offerings at the yagnas, the fire rituals, and it is also the blessed offerer; it is the dweller in all human beings; it is the dweller in all the gods beyond man; it is the dweller within the truth; it is the dweller of the sky; it is the One who lives within the myriad life forms of the water; it is the One who appears in the myriad life forms of the earth; it is the One who is manifested in deeds of goodness; it is the One who lives in the many life forms of the mountains. This omnipresent One, is the ultimate reality."*

Everywhere, here and there, above and below, without and within, godliness is manifest. But you will realize this One only when your meditation has gone so deep that you can see that you are separate from your body. As long as you are identified with your body you will see the many because there are many bodies all around you.

It is as if you put one thousand pitchers here; in all the places where you are sitting we put a pitcher next to you. The same space would be there in each of the pitchers, but anyone who was to count the pitchers would say, "There are one thousand separate spaces in these one thousand pitchers. Each pitcher encloses its own separate space inside it. How can the enclosed space of one pitcher be the same as the enclosed space of another pitcher? Each pitcher has its own separate space." If seen in this way then there are one thousand separate pitchers with one thousand separate spaces.

Then someone comes along and strikes each pitcher with a stick and breaks them all: then there will be only one space left.

Your body is nothing but a pitcher. When death demolishes your pitcher, and if you have not been identified with your pitcher during your life, only then will you be able to say, "It is okay, take this pitcher. The space cannot be taken, only this pitcher will be gone. In any case this pitcher has become old." At the moment of death, if you can realize that the pitcher is breaking and that the inner space is untouched, then you will not need to find another pitcher – then you will not enter another body.

But you believe your body to be your existence. And there are so many bodies in this world; naturally, then so many personalities and so many differences. Each body then becomes a wall and that encircles and separates the one space.

In existence there is only one space and one soul. But nothing will happen if you go on repeating this all your life as a theory: you will have to experience it. You will have to know it by separating the pitcher from your self; only then will all the pitchers disappear and only one space will be left. The name of that one space is the *brahman,* godliness. It is godliness that is outside and inside, below and above, that is everywhere; in the small and in the vast, in the lower and in the higher, in mountains and in rivers, in earth and in sky – it is everywhere.

> *"All gods honor this One. It lives in the middle of the body; it raises the prana upward and pushes the apana downward."*

There is a very profound research of Indian Yoga hidden in this sutra. Even today Western medical science is almost ignorant about it. This research is about prana and *apana.* The

Indian medical science, ayurveda, Yoga and Tantra all say that there are two directions of energy currents in the body. The current of energy which goes upward is known as prana and the current of energy which goes downward is *apana*. There are two qualities of energy in the body and also two kinds of flow. *Apana* causes the movement of urine and stool; the current of energy that goes downward causes the stool and the urine to move out. And all that goes upward in the body is caused by prana. This is why the more proficient one is in pranayama, the more one will rise upward because pranayama is nothing but expanding, extending and enlarging the prana, the current of energy that flows upward.

These are the two currents of energy in the body. Exactly at the center of these two dwells godliness, the soul, consciousness, or whatsoever name you want to give it. The soul, which is the size and shape of the tip of the thumb, is situated just at the center of these two currents: it pushes the energy downward and it pushes the energy upward. The current of energy that moves upward is prana and the current of energy that moves downward is *apana*.

Up to now Western medical science has not been able to recognize this double current of energy. They think that there is only one kind of energy. Because of their awareness of these two directions of energy, what allopathic medicine cannot do, ayurveda can do. A person who understands these two currents of energy can revolutionize his life.

You may have noticed that when a little baby breathes, his belly moves up and down, but his chest is not affected and it does not move up and down. When a baby is lying down and breathing his belly moves up and down and his breathing is very deep. When you breathe only your chest moves: your breath is very shallow, it is not deep. Psychiatrists are puzzled over this fact: "Why does this happen, why does the breath become shallow as people grow older and why is the breath of a child so deep?" An animal's breathing is also deep, the aboriginals also breathe deeply. The more civilized a man, the shallower his breath will be. It is a little difficult to understand what relationship civilization can have with breathing. What happens in the moment when a child stops breathing deeply?

Yoga knows this secret. It is becoming a little bit clearer now to psychology also, because psychologists say that the child's breathing becomes shallow as soon as he learns to be afraid of sex, when his parents have warned him against sex. When breathing goes deep it hits the sex center; it becomes *apana* and awakens the sexual urge. The deeper the breathing the stronger will be the urge for sex.

Children are made to feel guilty and afraid: they are told that sex is evil, that sex is sin. They become frightened and start supporting the shallow breathing, they don't allow it to go deep. Slowly, slowly their breathing will start to reach only the upper part of the body so a distance is created between their being and their sex center. Their sexual energy becomes perverted: they cannot enjoy any sexual pleasures because for that, deep breathing is needed. When the breathing is deep the whole body vibrates. In this vibration of the whole body, when the whole body is immersed in this energy, some semblance of joy happens. But even that much semblance of joy becomes impossible when the breathing is not deep.

Many diseases are created by this, because your *apana* has become weak. The people whose breathing is shallow are constipated because the *apana*, the current of energy which goes downward and throws out the excrement, is not moving downward. But the fear is the same because semen is also a type of excrement, and to throw it out the energy has to move down, it has to become *apana*. A person who is afraid of sex will also be constipated because it is the same energy that pushes these two.

Brahmacharya, celibacy, cannot be attained by blocking the *apana*: it can be attained only by increasing the prana. It will be good to understand this difference very clearly. Many people, in the name of brahmacharya, have made the mistake of blocking the *apana*. Because of this they have become morbid, sick. The grace and health of their personality is destroyed. The body becomes full of many poisons because the *apana* which was throwing all the poisons out of the body cannot throw them out. You are afraid: this is a negative process of celibacy.

There is a positive process: you don't interfere with the *apana* but you increase the prana. The prana should increase so much that in comparison to it, the *apana* becomes weaker. You just draw a bigger line – the apana should remain but the prana should become vast. Then your energy will start flowing upward.

This is why pranayama is so important in yoga – because it pushes the energy upward. The sex energy which becomes sex through the apana becomes kundalini through the prana and begins to flow upward. It finally reaches to the head where its lotus blooms. With the push of the apana the sex energy causes the birth of a baby, and with the push of the prana the same sex energy causes your own rebirth – but only when it has reached to the head. The prana is what takes the energy upward.

The sutra says that godliness is hidden between the prana and the apana. It takes the apana downward, thus it is the base for the manifest world; and it takes the prana upward, thus it is the base for the realm of godliness. It is up to you to decide into which current you want to enter. If you want to enter the current that goes downward then you will have to increase the apana.

All animals have a very strong apana, but their prana is very weak. Only yogins have a strong prana. Their apana is healthy but their prana is so strong that even the healthy apana cannot overpower their prana; the apana is under the control of the prana. The ordinary man's prana is already weak and he also makes his apana weak because of his fear.

A fearful person does not breathe deeply, only a fearless person will breathe deeply. A person who is afraid for any reason will not breathe deeply. Your breathing will stop immediately if someone puts a dagger to your chest. Whenever you feel terrified your breathing will stop. Whenever you feel nervous – for example, you are going to meet a big official and you are nervous – immediately your breathing will become shallow. You will breathe normally again only when you have come out of his office. People have frightened each other so much that their whole breathing system has become unhealthy. Existence is hidden between these two, the prana and the *apana*, but it is the master of both.

There is no need to be afraid of the *apana* because the total health of the body depends on it. It causes excretion, and if excretion does not happen properly many poisons and toxins will accumulate in the body. They have already accumulated in the body: there is poison flowing in everyone's blood. If a person does exercises such as walking, running or swimming then his *apana* will become stronger. This is why the body becomes fresher and healthier after exercise. You can just breathe deeply – but pranayama is not only breathing deeply, pranayama is breathing deeply with awareness.

Try to understand this difference. Many people do pranayama without any understanding or awareness; they just go on breathing deeply. If you just breathe deeply the *apana* will become healthier. That is also good but there will be no upward journey. The upward journey is possible only when awareness is joined together with deep breathing.

Buddha has said that when you breathe you should remain aware of the breath touching your nose. You should be conscious of the breath touching your nose as it goes in, and when the breath goes down into the throat you should be aware that it is touching the throat, and when the breath reaches to the lungs and goes down into the belly you should continue to witness it. Your awareness should follow it. Then the breath will stop for a moment, there will be a gap – and that gap is very valuable. When you take a deep breath in, for a moment there will be no breath, in or out, everything will stop. The breath will go out; after resting for a few seconds it goes out. Then your awareness should also go out with it, rise with it, come to the throat with it, come to the nose with it. When it goes out you just go on following it. Again, after it has gone out, everything will stop for a second; then a new breath will start, again in and again out. Buddha has said that you should make a string of beads with the breath and in this way you can awaken your remembrance with each breath.

If there is awareness with deep breathing, the prana will expand and the life energy will start to rise upward. Awareness is the key for rising upward and unconsciousness is the key for falling downward.

If a person can come to awareness through breathing then he needs no other practice, this is enough – but it is very difficult. For twenty-four hours a day, whenever you remember, be aware of your breath. Nobody will know, it can happen quietly; nobody will ever know what you are doing. Jesus has said that your right hand should not know what your left hand is doing. This also is something that no one else will know about. Silently, along with your breathing, your remembrance will gradually grow. As the breathing becomes deeper and the remembrance becomes more profound, it will hit and raise your energy upward through the spine.

This is not imaginary: you will certainly feel the electric current rising in your spine. The electric waves moving in your spine will be hot. If you want to, you can even feel this when you touch your spine with your hand: it will be hot where the waves are vibrating. With the rising energy your spine will become hot: you will be able to feel the point up to where the energy has risen. Again it will fall down and again it will rise.

By constant practice, one day this energy will reach to your *sahasrar*, the crown chakra. But meanwhile it will pass through other chakras and on each chakra there are different experiences; on each chakra your life will be filled with a new light. And as your energy passes through each chakra, new fragrances, new meanings, a new significance will start to happen in your life; new flowers will bloom in your life.

After experimenting many thousands of times, the science of Yoga discovered what exactly happens on each chakra. I will give one or two examples so that you can understand, because the chakras have also been named according to the experiences connected with them.

For example, Yoga has named the chakra between the two eyes the *agya chakra*, the command chakra. It has been called the *agya chakra* because the day on which your energy passes through that chakra, your body and your senses will start obeying you. Whatsoever you desire will immediately happen. You will have command over your personality, you will become the master. Before your energy reaches to this chakra you are a slave. You will become the master only on the day your energy enters into this chakra. From that day onward your body will obey you. Now you are obeying your body because you are empty in the place from where the body can be mastered. The energy is not in the place from where you can command it. This is why this chakra is called "the command chakra." All the chakras are named in this way. These names are meaningful because there is a particular state connected with each chakra.

The seventh, the last chakra, is *sahasrar*. *Sahasrar* means the lotus with a thousand petals. And on the day when the energy reaches there your whole head will feel as if transformed into a lotus with a thousand petals. Now your lotus has blossomed and all the petals have opened and are facing the sky. For the first time in life there is an experience of bliss, a unique shower of fragrance and total light.

We have chosen the name of the lotus rightly, and there are many reasons for this. We have called it *sahasrar* or *sahasradal kamaal*. The unique quality of the lotus is that it is born out of mud – and there is nothing more beautiful and more pure than the lotus. It is born out of the dirty mud, a stem comes out of the mud, grows and rises above the water: this stem is your spine and the dirty mud is your sexual desire. One day a flower blossoms out of the stem of your spine and when this lotus that has been born out of water and mud blossoms, the water cannot touch it. Even if the water were to fall on it, it would remain untouched. Nothing can touch it, it remains untouched and unaffected.

The lotus flower is the ultimate expression of sannyas – nothing can touch it. Anything can fall on it but it remains untouched. Born out of mud and yet beyond mud – this possibility for the lotus to attain to such purity is also the potential of each human being. That is why we have called the last chakra *sahasradal kamaal*. These two, the prana and the *apana* are the energy currents, and godliness dwells just exactly in the middle, between these two.

> *"When the embodied soul leaves the body on its journey to a new body, what is left behind?*
> *"This, is that.*
>
> *"No mortal, living being lives either through the prana vayu, the upward current of life energy, or through the apana vayu, the downward current: they both live through something else which also sustains the two.*
>
> *"Nachiketa, of the lineage of the sage Gautama, I will tell you what the mysterious and eternal brahman is; I will tell you once again what happens to the embodied soul after death."*

There are some truths which must be told again and again. It is not that the person telling them gains anything by repeating them, but that you are so deaf that perhaps you may not have heard the first time so it has to be repeated.

Buddha had the habit of saying everything three times. Now the people who are translating Buddha's words leave out two parts because they say it is a repetition: "What is the need for this repetition?" They think they are more intelligent than Buddha himself. Repetition was needed because the people to whom Buddha was talking were incapable of hearing the first time. By repeating three times Buddha was trying his best to hammer it in somehow.

Yama also says to Nachiketa, "Nachiketa, now I will tell you again…"

> *"According to their actions, according to the inclinations developed from all they have heard and learned, many disembodied souls find other wombs; many others enter the realm of the inanimate – trees, creepers, mountains…*
>
> *"The One which is the creator of all situations that living beings will experience according to their past actions, which remains awake when all else has gone to sleep in pralaya, the end of creation, is the purest essence; it is the brahman. It is immortal and all the worlds dwell in it. None can transcend it. "This, is that."*

In this sutra one thing needs to be understood: *"It remains awake when all else has gone to sleep in pralaya…"* This is the very divine about which Nachiketa has asked. When everything is annihilated in *pralaya*, or when all goes to sleep and all of nature's working stops, even then, what remains awake?

How to understand this? You don't have any experience of *pralaya*, the end of creation. It will be easy to understand it by looking at your sleep.

The body goes to sleep; "the body," meaning the manifestation of godliness, goes to sleep. But have you ever realized that something remains awake in you?

When a mother is sleeping with her little baby, nothing disturbs her. There may be a storm outside, there may be thunder and rain, there may be lightning, but nothing disturbs her sleep, she sleeps soundly. But if her baby cries just a little she will wake up immediately. It is amazing that outside there was thunder and lightning and her sleep was not broken and then she wakes up with just the small sound of her baby. There is something in her which keeps remembering the baby. If there are a thousand people sleeping here, in deep sleep, and I call out the name Rama, nobody but the person named Rama will wake up and ask who is disturbing his sleep. Certainly, some part of him which knows that his name is Rama must be awake.

When you get up in the morning and say that last night you slept soundly, who knows it? If you were absolutely asleep then who is it that knows that he had a sound sleep? Who is the knower of sleep? If your sleep were sound then there would be no one: all parts of you would have been asleep. But there was something that remained awake; some part was watching if the sleep was sound or not, if there were dreams or not. Some part inside remembers the dreams that you see at night. If you were totally asleep then who has this memory? Who remembers the dreams after waking up? No, you were not absolutely asleep.

Hypnosis causes the deepest sleep. Many experiments in hypnosis are happening in the West. It has become a legitimate science now; it is no longer considered to be magic. Hypnosis is now even being used in hospitals. They are using it not only for minor things but also for major surgical operations. You cannot undergo surgery in ordinary sleep; the patient will wake up even if he is pricked with a needle. But a major surgery can be performed in a hypnotized state: an appendix can be removed or the stomach can be operated on. The surgery may take many hours but the patient will remain asleep. So hypnotism is the deepest sleep. But there is one very interesting thing about hypnosis and that is that the patient will keep on sleeping even when his stomach is being cut open, but if you want him to do something which is against his morality, against his beliefs, then he will immediately wake up.

For example, if a Hindu woman, who in accord with the Hindu tradition has not loved anyone except her husband, is hypnotized – if she has loved another man then that would be a different thing – and told to kiss the man who is sitting next to her, she will immediately come out of the hypnosis no matter how deep it had been. She will get up and say, "What did you say? This is impossible!" But you can cut her stomach open and it won't break a hypnotic sleep. Inside, some part remains awake.

And if the woman agrees to give the kiss, then psychiatrists will say that it is because she wanted to do it but it was suppressed in her unconscious because of her moral code. Now in a hypnotic trance she has the opportunity and she will not be held responsible for her action. She can say that she was unconscious: "I can't take any responsibility for what I did" – so she can give the kiss.

A person will wake up from deep hypnosis if something goes against his moral values. He will do only what he wants to do. Ultimately the choice is his.

Even in the deepest sleep, within you there is something that is awake. This sutra says that the One that is awake while the body is asleep, that very essence remains awake when all of nature has gone to sleep in *pralaya*, the end of creation.

Western scientists and mathematicians have now begun to respect the insights which have been prevalent in India. In the West, the Christian theory is that God created this world just four thousand years ago. Now this idea has been proved to be wrong. This has harmed Christianity because they keep on insisting that it is written in their holy book, so it must be true. But their own scientists have discovered that this earth has existed for four billion years and the Christians say that it is only four thousand years old. On this earth there are fossils which prove to be millions of years old, so this Christian theory has been proved wrong.

The Hindu calculation goes back billions of years, and they say that billions of years are like one day to existence. They say that the beginning of creation and the end of creation are the same as one day to the *brahman*; billions of our years are as one day to existence.

Then comes night and the whole of nature goes to sleep;

finally, nature also becomes tired. It is not only that you get tired in a day: the trees, plants, these mountains, this earth, this moon and these stars also get tired. This understanding of the phenomenon of tiredness is very clear to the Indian sages. If you can become tired, then one day everything will become tired. It does not matter how long it takes – the day on which all of creation tires and goes to rest, then this will be *pralaya*. When everything returns to sleep then it is the beginning of the night of the *brahman*. But even then, the one that will remain awake is existence.

The relationship between your body and you is the same as the relationship between physical nature and existence. It can be said that this whole universe is the body of existence. You are but a miniature existence, a miniature universe. You and your body, it is the same as the physical universe and existence. And when all else has gone to sleep, even then, existence will remain awake. This is why in the Gita, Krishna has said that a *yogin* remains awake also when the worldly person has gone to sleep. He is wakeful even when he sleeps at night. His body sleeps but inside he remains continuously awake, aware.

As your awareness grows you will find that you can be awake even in your sleep. The day that you feel that even in sleep you are awake and sleep has become your direct experience, on that day, understand that now your anchors in the shore of the body have started loosening and your boat has begun to move toward the shore of the soul.

Now get ready for meditation.

# 12

# The Nature of Consciousness

*"Although godliness, the innermost soul of all living beings, is one, in the bodies of different creatures it is reflected in their forms, just as the one fire in all the world takes myriad forms. The godliness that dwells within also dwells without.*

*"Although the innermost soul of all living beings is one, in the bodies of different creatures it is reflected in their forms, just as the one air that permeates the world takes myriad forms. The godliness that dwells within also dwells without.*

*"Even as the sun, the illuminator of the world, does not become identified with the flaws in man's vision, godliness, which is the innermost soul of all living beings, does not become identified with man's misery. Though it is within all, it is separate from all.*

*"Only the wise ones, no others, who see the godliness that is living within them in each moment – the godliness which is the knower of all inner thoughts and feelings; which is the non-dual; which is the mover of all – will know the unchanging, eternal bliss.*

*"Only the wise ones who see the godliness that is living within them in each moment – the godliness which is the stillness in the unmoving, which is the witness within all*

*consciousness and which alone ordains the fruits of the actions of all living beings – will know the unchanging, eternal peace."*

*As he heard of the majesty, the bliss and peace that comes of knowing godliness, Nachiketa thought, "How can I truly know this indescribable supreme bliss which the wise ones call godliness? Does it reveal itself, or is it experienced?"*

*Listening to Nachiketa's inner thoughts, Yama, the Lord of Death, said, "The sun does not shine there, nor do the moon or the stars; nor does lightning or electrical phenomena cast any light there. Where then does the fire of this world stand? All the suns and the moons and the stars are illumined by its light... the whole existence is illumined by its light."*

In India, there are three points of view about the ultimate mystery of existence. The first is of the Hindu Upanishads, the Vedas and the Gita. According to their view, ultimate reality is one; all else are expressions of this one. There are no individual souls, there is only a universal soul. There are no separate individuals, there is only one universal existence.

The second viewpoint is of the Jainas. According to them ultimate reality is not just one, it is split into many: there is no universal soul, there are only individual souls. There is not one single totality; instead, there are many separate beings.

The third vision is of the Buddhists. For them there is neither a universal soul nor an individual soul, neither the whole nor the individual. For them there is nothingness, *shunyata*, the ultimate void.

These three viewpoints are very contradictory. And for thousands of years arguments have been going on over them but there has never been any conclusion. The propounders of these three views are the enlightened ones who have experienced and known the truth, so it is very difficult to understand why there are these great differences. One can understand the arguments and debates of the scholars because they don't have any inner experience. They just use complicated words and they try to propound principles and explain theories according to their own logic, but they don't have any inner experience of their own.

But Mahavira, Buddha and Shankara are not scholars. Whatsoever they are saying is not from their thinking. It is not philosophy, they are telling of their own experiences. They are simply talking about that which they have known. There is no mistake, no flaw in their knowing. Then why is there so much controversy? Because of this controversy, in India there are three different attitudes toward life. Hinduism, Jainism and Buddhism are the three main streams of thinking which dominate the Indian mind. And because there is no end to the controversy, the Indian mind is also full of confusion. It will be good to understand this more deeply.

I see absolutely no difference in these three views. The statements are absolutely different but there is no difference in the essence. And these statements are not only different, they are diametrically opposite – but their meaning and purpose are the same. And one who cannot see this one purpose will never be able to see the oneness in all the religions. Yet there are reasons why these three insights have been presented in three different ways.

The Vedas, the Upanishads, the Brahma Sutra and the Gita say that existence is one, but the unconscious people interpreted this in a wrong way and it became disastrous. They said, "If there is only the one, then there is no point in doing anything – all forms are forms of existence: it is in sin and in virtue, in the good man as well as in the thief, in the bondage of the world and in liberation; it is here, it is there, it is everywhere. It is also in evil. Then what is the need to do anything? Nothing remains to be done."

If this whole existence is only one reality, only one essence, then there is no need to do anything in life. Then what is the difference between good and evil? What is the difference between religion and irreligion? What is the difference between maya, illusion, and *brahman*, the ultimate reality? If in reality there is only the one, then there is nothing left to be done. What is there to aspire to? What is there to renounce? The result of this unique concept of one ultimate reality has been a profound laziness. Great laziness has overpowered the Indian mind. So people would just read the Vedas and the Upanishads; they would memorize the Gita and think that there was nothing left for them to do. But in this way there was no transformation in life.

This was not the intention of the enlightened people who shared these truths, but the intention of the awakened ones and the understanding of the ignorant are never the same. The intention of those who say there is only one reality is to help you to let go of your self – and then only *it* is.

Your ego is false. You think that you are separate, but this is just your illusion. This is the obstacle in your life; this is the cause of all your misery and your bondage. You should allow yourself to dissolve and disappear into this vastness. Don't try to save yourself, to keep yourself separate. All the pain of life arises out of the belief that you are separate.

If you are separate then you have to protect yourself. If you are separate then you have to fight with everyone because nobody is with you in the difficulties of life. All are your competitors. Life becomes a quarrel and a fight, and in this fight there is only worry and anxiety. If you are separate then the fear of death grips you because you know that you will have to die.

Every day you see someone dying, but the whole never dies. People go on dying but this vast immensity lives eternally. Life is never destroyed but every day you see embodied life dying. Earthen lamps are extinguished every day but the light as such remains. This is why the fear of death possesses you: if you are separate, then you will certainly die. And if you have merged and become one with this vast existence, then there is no way to die. Then life is deathless, life is eternal.

The intention of those who wanted the concept of the one reality to prevail was so that the ego could dissolve, disappear, evaporate. But the ego did not dissolve, even though that was the intention of the awakened ones. The ignorant misinterpreted the concept of one ultimate reality so that instead of dissolving their egos, it only enhanced and supported the ego. The seers have said, "I am the ultimate reality." Their meaning was, "I am not, only the ultimate reality is." But the ignorant thought, "*I* am the ultimate reality!" Those who declared "I am the ultimate reality" meant that there is no drop, only the ocean is. But hearing this the drop thought, "*I* am the ocean." Because of this the drop could not dissolve, it became even more egoistic.

The awakened ones were thinking that on the day man realizes that there is only one reality there will no longer be any sin, because sin is against the other. When do you sin? – when you sacrifice the other for your own happiness, that is sin. But if I am in all, spread in all and there is only one reality and there is no one else, then there is no possibility of sin. For sin, the other is needed; for sin, the other must be sacrificed. For my benefit, the other's benefit has to be destroyed. But if there is only one reality and no other, there is no possibility for selfishness or sin. Then to harm the other means to harm yourself.

The intention of the seers was for you to realize that when you cease to be as an ego, when you are no more, there will be no way to sin. But the ignorant interpreted that if there is only one reality then there is no sin or virtue; whatsoever you do is okay because this one reality is omnipresent in all.

When Mahavira saw what was happening to this supreme understanding he tried to destroy it from the very roots, so he said that there is no one ultimate reality; every person is himself divine and the drop does not need to dissolve itself into the ocean. The drop simply has to go on purifying itself, it has to become absolutely pure. He said that the very idea of dissolving is wrong because the meaning that the ignorant wrongly derived from it made the whole country lethargic and lazy. Godliness became the basis for ignorance and not an inspiration for destroying ignorance.

So Mahavira did not talk about the ultimate reality. He said, "There is no universal soul, only the individual soul exists. You must become pure. Sin is sin, virtue is virtue – the same reality is not present in all. Bad is bad and good is good and the difference between the two should be kept clear. That dividing line should not be dissolved."

Mahavira has called his insight *bheda-vigyan,* the science of differentiation. The Upanishads say *abheda,* no difference. But Mahavira has called his whole technique *bheda-vigyan*, the clear awareness of difference: what wrong is and what right is, where wrong is and where right is, where good is and where evil is, from where goodness begins and from where evil begins, where worldliness ends and where liberation from it begins?

Mahavira made the understanding of this clear distinction the basis of spirituality. He said that each individual is separate, he does not have to dissolve. And when each individual is separate then the whole responsibility for his life is the person's own. If you are suffering it is your own responsibility, not the responsibility of existence. If you experience bliss then only you are responsible and it is not because of any blessing from existence.

Mahavira dropped prayer, only meditation remained. Meditation to him means that one has to purify oneself so much that one day only pure consciousness is left. Mahavira called that pure consciousness *paramatma*. *Paramatma* does not mean God, it means *param atma*, the ultimate soul, the purest soul.

Mahavira's intention was to help people to overcome their lethargy. People are sleepy and unconscious because they are living in a deception that has been created by the principles they believe in and which give them the permission to remain asleep. Mahavira wanted to destroy the whole basis of these theories so that man would become more aware, more silent, more conscious, standing on his own feet not waiting for any divine blessing or grace or support. This was a very important technique for the purification of man – but the end result of this too was exactly the same as it has always been and will always be.

Mahavira wanted man to purify himself and rise to his divinity, but the ignorant understood, "I exist, and there is no divine to dissolve myself into; my existence is the end, the only reality." Mahavira's concept of the individual soul simply enhanced the egos of the ignorant: neither did they realize the soul nor did they purify themselves and rise to their own divinity. Instead they became full of a very strong ego that believed that there is nothing divine and that only "I am."

As this ego of "I am" becomes stronger, unconsciousness also becomes stronger because then the ego is an intoxicant. This intoxication increases in the same proportion as the ego; to the same extent a man's life becomes more unconscious. When there is nothing divine there is no reason to bow down, so the people who were egoistic were supported by this. They were happy with the idea that there is no need to bow down, no need to surrender. Humbleness was no longer seen as a quality of saintliness; there was only pride and arrogance.

Mahavira said, "Be independent. Don't become lazy and dependent on prayer," and the ignorant understood, "I am all there is and I have only to trust in my own strength. I have to rely only on myself." The ego became stronger and this ego destroyed the Jaina philosophy. Just as the concept of *brahman*, the universal reality, made the Hindus lazy and lethargic, so has the concept of the individual soul made the Jainas very arrogant and egoistic.

When Buddha saw that both views – universal reality and the individual soul – caused the downfall of man, he then said that there is no universal reality and no individual soul; there is only *shunya,* vast emptiness. His expression was very unique. He said that there is no universal reality and no individual soul because it was necessary to cut the very roots of the mistake made in the Hindu's way of thinking and in the Jaina's philosophy. "You are not, there is nobody within you." Buddha says that to attain to this nothingness is the ultimate knowing.

This is why Buddha has not used the word *brahmalok,* the abode of godliness; neither did he use the word *moksha*, ultimate liberation. He used the word *nirvana*, the extinguishing of the flame of an earthen lamp. When the flame of an earthen lamp is burned out we don't ask, "Where is the flame? Where has it gone?" It simply does not exist anymore. Buddha says that it is not the earthen lamp of the awakened one that burns out but the flame of his ego that is extinguished. What remains within is the ultimate emptiness, pure silence. And to attain to that emptiness is nirvana. This was a very profound insight because with this there was no longer any space for man's laziness to continue and there was no longer support for the ego to survive.

But when the ignorant heard that there is neither a universal reality nor an individual soul, they interpreted that there is nothing worth attaining! "What is the point when there is nothing? And when emptiness is already there within, why make any effort? Why practice any spiritual discipline?" Buddha's insight seemed like atheism to the ignorant: "When there is nothing, then whatever pleasures are available in this life, we should enjoy them! When there is nothing eternal then why give up the transitory? It is better to hold on to whatever is available now because later on there will be nothing to attain; there is only the void, emptiness." And Buddha's vision also failed because of this teaching of emptiness.

It is very strange that whatsoever was the deepest insight of any vision became the cause of its failure. Unconscious people are strange: the enlightened ones are always defeated by them. To save themselves, the ignorant always find loopholes in everything. And they even argue and say that their theory is right and the other's is wrong.

Theories have no value in religion; the value is in the intention behind it. Try to understand this. Theories are of value to the scholars, who themselves are not worth much. The enlightened ones are concerned only with the intent of religion. What is Shankara's motive? What is the motive of Mahavira? What does Buddha intend? Whatsoever they are saying is not as important as their motive. Whatsoever they are saying is only a device, an indication. What are they indicating? But scholars take hold of the words and go on fighting and arguing over the words for centuries! The Jaina scholars go on proving that there is no universal reality, that only an individual soul exists, the Hindu scholars go on proving that there is no individual soul, that only one universal reality exists and the Buddhist scholars go on proving that there is neither a universal reality nor an individual soul, there is only emptiness.

But there is no question of proving anything; only the purpose and the meaning have to be understood. The indication has to be understood. The only motive of a Mahavira, a Buddha or a Shankara is that you should be transformed, that you become reborn; that the dust on your mirror should be removed, that it should become clean so that you can see that which is. Call it whatsoever you like: the *brahman*, nirvana, *shunya*, *atman* – these are only words. Any word can be used, but that which is has no name. Their only desire is that you should be able to experience it.

But you go on discussing what they say and you don't experiment with what they say. You just think about it and talk about it but you don't meditate on what they say. You just stuff your mind with their words. But by doing all of this your life will not be transformed, no revolution will happen. So, in a way, all the enlightened ones have failed.

Whenever someone becomes enlightened, he finds it very difficult to communicate because it has been said in a thousand and one ways, but you are somehow able to protect yourself from listening to their actual message. Cunning people can always find ways not to listen. Just a few simple people who are not so cunning do listen, and they are benefited by it. But all the traditions are created by cunning people. The enlightened one shares his religiousness and the cunning ones create the traditions.

According to the Upanishads, it is the simple and innocent people who have the subtle intelligence, and they are the people who transform themselves and don't create any traditions. They don't care whether what is said is the actual truth; they understand that what is said is only indicating toward truth.

All words are just indications. The only value of the indication is that it takes you forward, keeps you moving further and further, just as the arrows on the milestones on the road show the right direction. If you are going to Delhi, the arrow is pointing you toward Delhi. But you are so unconscious that when you see the milestone with the arrow and with "Delhi" written on it, you become attached to the milestone and you stop there in the belief that you have arrived in Delhi. You pay no attention to the arrow. That stone with "Delhi" written on it is not Delhi; the milestones only indicate that Delhi is some distance away. When you see a zero on the milestone then you know that you have arrived in Delhi. Then there will be no arrow on it, no word on it, only a zero will be there. But as long as there are arrows to point the way, understand that the destination is still far away.

No scripture is truth. All scriptures are like milestones that say, "Go forward." But you start worshipping the milestones, and different people keep different kinds of milestones on their heads. And then great discussions go on to prove whose Delhi is the real one. No scripture is truth, all scriptures are just indications toward the truth. And one who holds on to the scripture will only prove that the scripture is wrong, and he himself will go astray.

All the scriptures say to go on moving, go forward until you reach the zero where all words disappear and nothing more is written. And when you have reached the zero you will realize that all the words were different indications, different devices of the enlightened ones to take you to the zero, to the wordless silence.

Now we will enter this sutra.

*"Although godliness, the innermost soul of all living beings, is one, in the bodies of different creatures it is reflected in their forms, just as the one fire in all the world takes myriad forms. The godliness that dwells within also dwells without."*

Just like fire, the divine energy has taken many different forms. The forms are different but the energy, the formless within the form, is one.

*"Although the innermost soul of all living beings is one, in the bodies of different creatures it is reflected in their forms, just as the one air that permeates the world takes myriad forms. The godliness that dwells within also dwells without.*

*"Even as the sun, the illuminator of the world, does not become identified with the flaws in man's vision, godliness, which is the innermost soul of all living beings, does not become identified with man's misery. Though it is within all, it is separate from all."*

This sutra has to be deeply understood. It can be very useful for the seeker on the path.

In one of his memoirs, Rabindranath Tagore has written: One early morning I was going toward the sea. It was monsoon time. All the pits, ponds and ditches were full of water. Some puddles were clean and some were dirty. As I reached nearer the sea, the sun rose and its reflection could be seen in the dirty water of the puddles, in the clean water and also in the sea. Rabindranath has said, "This phenomenon filled me with wonder! I immediately understood that whether the reflection happens in dirty water or in clean water, it does not make any difference for the reflection. How can a reflection become dirty? How can the reflection of the sun in a dirty puddle become dirty? No dirt can make the reflection dirty. The reflection in the sea is of the same sun and the reflection in the dirty pond is of the same sun and the reflection in a small puddle is also of the same sun, and there is no difference in these reflections."

Rabindranath has said, "That day, I understood the meaning of the words of the Upanishads – that godliness is manifest in all; the forms are different but that which is manifested in all the forms is the One."

So the second thing that this sutra is saying is that your own impurity cannot make godliness impure; the impurity of the puddle cannot make the reflection impure. This is why the Upanishads say that godliness within the sinner does not become a sinner and godliness within the saint does not become a saint – because it was never a sinner in the first place, so how can it become a saint? The Upanishads say that godliness is pure consciousness. All impurities are confined to the form. This form may become dirty or impure, but godliness that is hidden within it is not touched by impurities of any kind; it simply cannot be affected by them.

This statement is very revolutionary. It is very dangerous too because the sinner will say, "Then it is okay – if I cannot become impure, then why should I stop sinning? And when I cannot become pure by being virtuous because I have never in the first place become impure, then what is the need to be virtuous?" This type of interpretation by the unconscious people has created much confusion.

The Upanishads say that godliness can never become impure. If you can understand the meaning of this then the burden of any feelings of guilt about the past will disappear in one moment. If you understand that the godliness within you has never become impure, then the burden of sin and guilt in your mind will immediately disappear.

Psychologists say that the greatest misfortune in human life is the feeling of guilt. They say that in the West, Christianity has done much harm by creating the guilt complex. But in this country, we have done as much harm to people by removing the feelings of guilt in them. Christianity has helped and benefited a few people and a few people in this country have been helped by the other insight – but it seems that those who can transform themselves will transform themselves in any case, and those who are in the habit of missing and always harming themselves will do it, no matter what the circumstances. There are people who can support life even with poison and there are people who can commit suicide even with nectar. It depends on the people, whether they want to harm themselves or help themselves. Nectar or poison alone cannot do anything; it depends on how you use them.

In the West, Christianity emphasizes that man is a sinner and that he is born in sin; the first man was born in sin. God banished Adam from heaven because he had sinned by disobeying his order, and the gates of heaven will remain closed to him until he frees himself from sin. And every human being is suffering for the sin committed by Adam, and they have to make efforts to get out of the state of sin. Christianity insists that man is a sinner, that he is born in sin. This has certainly created a deep feeling of guilt.

Those who understand things rightly try to be free of sin by changing their lives. But foolish people think that if man is born in sin then it is impossible for him to become free of sin: "If the first man, Adam, was a sinner, and if he could sin even in heaven in the presence of God, then we, who are just ordinary people and Adam's progeny, can do nothing to become free of sin. Thousands of centuries of sin lie on our shoulders. It is such a great burden that it seems impossible to ever throw it off. Our very beings have become sinful so there is no way but to accept sin."

Because of this, the West has become very materialistic. The reason for this is that the West has just accepted sin because it could see no way to be free of it – man will always be a sinner. Yes, if God is kind he will pull man out of sin. But then again if it were a question of God's kindness, he could have saved Adam from sin. There was no need to create this long chain of sins. The West has become materialistic because it thinks there is no way to get out of sin. The question becomes only of how to sin more cleverly, more efficiently, of how to do it as much as you can. There is no other way. Since every cell of our being is born in sin, we cannot do anything but sin.

In India, we have tried exactly the opposite experiment: we have said that the ultimate, the pure soul, can never be a sinner. It is ultimate purity and it can never become impure; no amount of sin can affect its purity. Those who really understood this truth gave up any idea of sinning because they realized that there is no point in it; they simply dropped out of it. Because of this understanding of the ultimate purity of reality, the concept of sin simply disappeared, the desire to sin disappeared and the question of doing evil disappeared.

But the majority of people said, "If it does not affect the purity of the ultimate reality, why not sin? When it remains always pure, then we can go on sinning." The enlightened ones explain that the soul is absolutely pure and mostly the sinners go on nodding their heads and saying, "Absolutely right!" They think, "Yes, we are absolutely pure – there is no difference between us and a Buddha, between us and a Mahavira. The difference is only superficial, within we are all the same."

But this statement is very valuable in itself: consciousness cannot be made impure. You may go on trying for lifetimes to make it impure, but consciousness cannot be made impure because the nature of consciousness is purity. You can accumulate dust on its surface but the diamond inside, the shining light inside, cannot be destroyed; you can only cover it. Those who understand this will give up the effort to change the surface and will start searching for the diamond inside which sin can never touch.

This can become clear with a little experience, because the godliness within you is not the doer: it is the witness. When you are stealing, someone inside you is aware that you are stealing. This awareness, this witnessing, cannot be affected by the sin of stealing. It is the witness that has seen you stealing. When you go to a temple to pray, even then it is the witness that knows that you are going to a temple to pray. No virtue can touch it. Whatsoever you are doing remains outside. Doing is on the periphery and awareness is within, at the very center. This awareness can never become the doing and the doing can never become awareness.

So there are two separate currents within you. One is of doing, which is born out of your body. Lately, many experiments have been done to find out where desire actually arises in man, because it is desire which makes you act. These scientific experiments are amazing because they prove that all desires are born in the body.

There are male and female hormones and these are different chemicals. If male hormones are injected into a woman then her whole behavior will change: her voice will become deep like a man's, the woman's delicacy and sweetness will disappear and she will become aggressive. The woman is not aggressive, she waits. Even in love she does not take the initiative. No woman ever tells the man in the beginning that she loves him or that she will die without him. If any woman says this then the man should run away from her because that woman is not a woman anymore.

It is always the man who says, "I love you and I will die without you." The woman will just agree, will condescend to agree. Even her yes will be silent and receptive; she is not active. It is because of her body structure and the system of her body – the woman receives the man into herself.

The man takes the initiative, man's nature is aggressive – but if male hormones are injected into the woman then she also will become aggressive. If female hormones are injected into the man then he will become receptive, he will wait for a woman to take the initiative.

One scientist was experimenting with a group of monkeys.

He chose a female monkey who was very humble and very feminine and who had no place in the hierarchy of that group of monkeys. Monkeys have a hierarchy system: just as politicians have a hierarchy, in the same way, monkeys also have a hierarchy. Some monkey is the president, someone else is the prime minister, some are cabinet members; in this way, the hierarchy goes on. Scientists say that politicians are just continuing with this habit that monkeys have; there is no difference.

A large dose of male hormones was injected into this female monkey who did not hold any position and was at the bottom of the hierarchy. After twenty-four hours this injection started affecting her. She became so aggressive that she attacked all the male monkeys that were holding the high positions. She almost came out on top like Indira Gandhi! All the other politicians, the Kamrajas and the Nijalingappas in the group, were pulled down. The scientist has written that that female monkey managed to put all the old fighters in their place. They all became sad and she dominated them so much that she did not even allow them to do any mischief – which is the nature of a monkey. And this change was just because of an injection of male hormones!

What you do is a contribution of your body; your behavior, your way of walking, talking and sitting, your desires, your wishes, your ambitions, your struggle for things – your hormones are responsible. Just a few chemicals can make the whole difference.

Scientists have said that there are just five rupees worth of chemicals in a man's body. It was cheaper in the ancient times, now they are worth about fifteen rupees. A female body is worth sixteen rupees, so remember that chemically, a woman is more costly. Only one rupee worth of chemicals makes all the difference between a man and a woman! This is why scientists say that a woman's body can be turned into a male body just by giving an injection, and a male body can be turned into a female body. By the end of this century, you will be able to decide whether you want to be a man or a woman; this will be possible. Now there is no difficulty for this experiment.

Scientists say that it is because of some chemicals in the body that one man steals and another man murders or is violent, and it is sheer stupidity to punish them. It is just like punishing a man who is suffering from TB and you say, "Why have you got TB?" What can that man do?

Scientists say that we go on punishing people who murder because until now we have not been able to discover which chemicals in the body compel them to murder. It will be better to change the hormones than to hang them or to sentence them to life imprisonment – a simple injection can put them right.

This is a very valuable discovery, but it is also very dangerous. All valuable discoveries are dangerous in the hands of ignorant people. This means that if by one injection we can turn a murderer into a non-murderer, then by one injection we can also turn a non-murderer into a murderer. If the country is at war you can inject all the soldiers and they will go on madly killing people, "the enemies." Then the other country will not be able to win if they don't know this trick of injecting people. If people are rebelling they just have to be injected: they will become totally obedient and will start praising you! So this is a dangerous discovery, but at the same time very valuable.

The Indian seers have always been saying that the godliness that is hidden within is only a witness, it is not a doer. The doer is outside. All actions are connected with the body and the mind. The inner, pure consciousness is a witness, it only watches; it has never done any act. If slowly you start becoming a witness to your actions, the witnessing consciousness within you will begin to awaken. It is sleeping because you have never used it.

So basically, all the techniques of meditation are an effort to awaken the witness within you. As the witness becomes more awake, all the wrong things in your life will drop on their own and whatsoever is right will go on growing because the body cannot act without your cooperation; your support is needed. *You* do not act, but inner cooperation is needed also by the body.

If a person has totally become the witness, then even if you give him many injections to make him aggressive and violent, he will not become aggressive. This has to be deeply understood.

All twenty-four tirthankaras of the Jainas are kshatriyas, warriors, and have been born into warrior families. If their hormones could ever be tested – it is difficult to do it now – then it might be proved that there were very aggressive hormones in their bodies because they were the sons of kings, born into kshatriya families. Their whole tradition, the lifestyle of their parents, was aggressive. Hormones are genetically inherited.

All the twenty-four Jaina tirthankaras and Gautama the Buddha, all were kshatriyas – and all of them preached nonviolence. They were born in violent families, violence was their heritage, but all of them preached nonviolence. Certainly they must have become witnesses to the extent that their aggressive hormones could not affect them at all anymore.

It is interesting to note that until now not a single brahmin has preached nonviolence. The most dangerous brahmin we know of is Parashurama, who killed all the kshatriyas on this earth several times over. And these twenty-five – Buddha and the twenty-four Jaina tirthankaras – are kshatriyas: fighting was in their blood but they became teachers of nonviolence. But the phenomenon is the same – witnessing – that was happening to Parashurama and to the people I have just mentioned. Parashurama was a witness, all his hormones were of nonviolence; but by witnessing, Parashurama could see that the kshatriyas were playing havoc all over the earth. Life everywhere was full of trouble and the kshatriyas were the cause of all that trouble, all that violence. To end the violence, Parashurama started killing all the kshatriyas! If the witness awakens, then even a brahmin can be violent.

One who becomes a witness and becomes separate from his acts is able to see what is right and what is wrong. All these twenty-five, Buddha and the twenty-four tirthankaras, inherited violence; fighting and aggressiveness was in their blood. But by witnessing they were able to see that fighting was futile, nobody would gain anything out of it. They became peaceful and silent and all the violence simply disappeared from their lives.

What I am saying is that if the witness has been awakened within you, your hormones will no longer have any effect. They will not affect a Parashurama or a Mahavira because the witnessing consciousness makes its own decisions. The body is no longer the master; the body cannot influence the witness. And the witnessing consciousness lives life in a natural way. The witnessing consciousness has its own spontaneity and that spontaneity has no limitations.

Secondly, whatsoever the witnessing consciousness does, even while doing it knows: "I am not the doer, I am only the witness." So I accept that Parashurama was not affected by any sin – could not be. Parashurama's personality is worth understanding. No sin could touch him because these killings were done when he was in a profound state of witnessing. It is this kind of killing that Krishna is suggesting to Arjuna in the Gita. He says to Arjuna, "Go to war not as a doer, but as a witness. You are just the medium." But the difficulty for Arjuna was that he was unable to fight and remain a witness; he went on feeling that he was the doer: "How can I kill my loved ones?" He was identified with the doer, with his actions. And Krishna's whole effort was to create witnessing in Arjuna even as he fought in the war.

But as soon as a person becomes full of awareness he ceases to be a doer.

The sutra says: *"Even as the sun, the illuminator of the world, does not become identified with the flaws in man's vision, godliness, which is the innermost soul of all living beings, does not become identified with man's misery. Though it is within all, it is separate from all."* That awareness that you are separate is the realization of the witness.

> *"Only the wise ones, no others, who see the godliness that is*

> *living within them in each moment – the godliness which is the knower of all inner thoughts and feelings, which is the non-dual; which is the mover of all – will know the unchanging, eternal bliss."*

Only those who are able to separate the witness from the doer experience bliss. As this experience grows deeper, the bliss also goes on growing. At the peak point, when the witness is absolutely separate and the seer is absolutely separate from the doer, one experiences the ultimate bliss.

> *"Only the wise ones, no others, who see the godliness that is living within them in each moment – the godliness which is the stillness in the unmoving, which is the witness within all consciousness and which alone ordains the fruits of the actions of all living beings – will know the unchanging, eternal peace."*

> *As he heard of the majesty, the bliss and peace that comes of knowing godliness, Nachiketa thought, "How can I truly know this indescribable supreme bliss which the wise ones call godliness? Does it reveal itself, or is it experienced?"*

A very profound question has arisen in Nachiketa's mind about godliness: does the bestower of ultimate peace and the ultimate bliss reveal itself, or is it to be experienced? This difference has to be understood.

I see you: I am not experiencing you, you are revealed to me. If it becomes dark then I will not be able to see you. Light is needed to see the other; the other can be seen only when it is revealed in the light. But light is not needed for me to see myself, the experience is enough; it can also happen in darkness.

The question arose in Nachiketa's mind: "Will godliness be revealed like an outer object, that I will see the ultimate reality standing in front of me shining in some profound light, or will I experience it within me where no outside light is needed? Will godliness manifest itself like matter as another, or will it be experienced as consciousness, as myself? Will godliness be revealed within me or outside of me? Is this divine within or without?"

To see the things that are outside, light is needed, some medium is needed to reveal them; only then do they become visible. But for the inside no medium, no light is needed. Only through experiencing does the phenomenon happen.

So the question has arisen in Nachiketa's mind: "Does godliness become revealed or is it to be experienced? Because if it is revealed, then it is away from me and I have to go in search of it. I have to search for its palace, its temple, its throne. If it is revealed then I will have to search for the light by which I will be able to see it. The process will be totally different. If it is an experience then I don't have to go anywhere. If it becomes an experience then no light is needed. Then I will know it by diving deeply into myself."

These are two different paths. Generally, people pray to the divine, and prayer means that it is outside you. Prayer will serve as a light, a focus: you can see it. You can worship the divine: worship is the light. It will become revealed in the light of worship and you can see it. One path is that of worship, prayer and devotion. The concept of worship means that the divine is outside, that it is hidden somewhere out there in the sky and it will be revealed to you only if you become worthy.

The second path is of meditation, of spiritual discipline. Then the divine, godliness, is not outside; it is present within – there is no question of worship or prayer in it. It is only a question of purifying oneself. If you go on purifying yourself, awakening yourself, then it will become your experience. For this, no outer worship or ritual is needed.

The first path is absolutely wrong but it appeals to the majority of people. The second path is totally correct but it attracts very few people. Why? – because the first path seems easy. You are more attracted to the easy than to the truth. On the first path you don't have to transform yourself. What is the difficulty in collecting all the things that are needed for worship? What is the difficulty in lighting an earthen lamp, burning incense, ringing a bell? You remain just the same.

The person who is going to the temple is the same person who was sitting in his shop; there is not even the slightest change in him. The way he will perform the rituals of worship in the temple will be the same as what he was doing working in the shop. He will come out of the temple the same person as when he went in. You will not find the slightest difference in him when he returns to the shop. He may become even more dangerous because the hour that he wasted in a temple may have to be compensated for by taking revenge on the customers in the shop! He will extort more money from his customers, he will exploit them more because of the hour that was wasted in praying.

This is why shopkeepers with so-called religious leanings are more dangerous. Beware of a shopkeeper with religious leanings, because he is devoting some time for God – which he knows is a sheer waste of time – and he would like to make up for it from somewhere. No change seems to happen in his life. In spite of his going to the temple, in his life he remains just the same.

But it is easier to go to a place of worship than to go within. This is why people choose the easy option, but this easiness has nothing to do with truth. Convenience has nothing to do with truth. This is why most people prefer to worship and to pray. Very few people meditate – but only those who meditate will finally know truth.

This question arose in Nachiketa's mind: "Should I pray or should I meditate? Should I look for the divine on the outside, through some ritual, or should I search within by awakening myself? Does it become revealed or is it to be experienced?"

> *Listening to Nachiketa's inner thoughts, Yama, the Lord of Death, said, "The sun does not shine there, nor do the moon or stars; nor does lightning or electrical phenomena cast any*

> *light there. Where then does the fire of this world stand? All the suns and the moons and the stars are illumined by its light...the whole existence is illumined by its light."*

When the sun rises, how do you come to know it?

One morning Mulla Nasruddin was telling his servant, "It is very cold. Look outside and see if the sun has risen."

The servant went out, then came back and said, "It is very dark outside!"

Nasruddin said, "So light a lamp so you can see if the sun has risen!"

But no lamp is needed to see the sun, the sun is illuminates itself. We see other things by the light of the sun, but the sun itself is not seen by any other light. And Yama is saying that even the light of the sun is there because of the divine light. This divine energy is hidden behind the sun. Godliness is the light in every fire, and all light is the light of godliness.

So in what light will you be able to see godliness? No light is needed to see it because it is the original source of all light.

Godliness is not revealed by any light, it has to be experienced.

It will be experienced only by moving to the original source. For that, one does not have to search with an earthen lamp. In fact, one does not have to go anywhere in search of godliness. You simply have to go within yourself. You have to enter your interiority to the original source of life: godliness is there, and all is illuminated by it. Your eyes can see only because of its light. The moon and the stars are illuminated only because of its light. The whole existence is its heartbeat. And no medium is needed to know it. You can know it directly, in this moment, because no medium is needed. This knowing is direct, immediate, without any medium.

Get ready for meditation.

# 13

# Transformation Is Possible

*"This manifest world is likened to an eternal pipal tree, if the tree were to have its roots above and its branches below. In the deepest roots of this tree lives the brahman; it is the deathless. All the worlds are sustained in it. None can transcend it.*
*"This, is that.*

*"The entire universe has emerged out of this ultimate reality and all life functions within this. Those who know this ultimate reality to be fearsome as a thunderbolt set to strike become the deathless ones. They become free from the cycle of birth and death.*

*"The heat of fire is because of this divine dread, the shine of the sun is because of this divine dread; Indra, Vayu and the gods of death, all five do their work because of this divine dread.*

*"If one can realize godliness while still in human form, before the body has returned to the earth, it is well; else he will wander aimlessly through many worlds and many species, for millennia.*
*"This, is that."*

A tree that stands near the bank of a lake will be reflected in the lake upside down. The branches of the tree that spread near the bank of the lake are pointing toward the sky and its roots spread down within the earth, but the reflection will be reversed. In the reflection the roots will point upward and the branches will point downward. All reflection is in reverse; reflection is never straight.

If we keep this scientific fact in mind then it will be easy to understand this sutra: when things are seen they are seen as the reverse of how they actually are, because seeing is only a reflection.

The eye is also a mirror: only reflections are made on the eye and the reflections are always in reverse. It is also true that this world is not as you see it. The laws of the world are just the opposite of what they seem to be.

Appearances are the exact opposite of reality. On the basis of this fundamental understanding, Indian seers have used a very old symbol. That symbol is mentioned in this sutra:

> *"This manifest world is likened to an eternal pipal tree, if the tree were to have its roots above and its branches below. In the roots of this tree lives the brahman; it is the deathless."*

*"This manifest world is likened to an eternal pipal tree, if the tree were to have its roots above and its branches below."* Normally, a tree has its roots at the bottom and its branches at the top. But in this sutra Yama is saying that in this other dimension, roots grow upward and branches grow downward. The truth of existence is just the opposite of what is seen by us in this manifest world. And this is the case in all different aspects of life.

Try to understand this. You think that death is an enemy of life, but the truth is just the opposite: life cannot exist without death. So death is not the enemy of life at all; on the contrary, it is a friend. There is no possibility for life to exist without death. The day death disappears, life also will disappear. But all things become upside down in the process of our seeing. We think that life and death are opposites, but actually death is the foundation of life. Life cannot exist without death.

Your experience is that love and hate are opposites, but the reality is just the contrary. Psychologists say that love and hate are two aspects of the same energy, they are both together. In this century Freud has discovered many important facts of life. One of his discoveries is that man hates the very same person that he loves. If you ponder over it a little, you also can understand this. You cannot just make someone an enemy directly. To make someone an enemy you first have to make him a friend. Enmity cannot be created directly. For enmity, first friendship is needed. Friendship is the first essential step for enmity; after that, enmity can happen.

So friendship and enmity are not opposites, they are two sides of the same coin. Whosoever you love you also hate and whosoever you hate you also love. You are very much attached to your enemies; you remember them. You would be incomplete without them. Without them something in your life would be missing in the same way as it happens when a friend dies. Friends fill you, and enemies also fill you.

Buddha has said, "I do not make friends because I do not want to create enemies." But you think that the enemy and the friend are opposites. In life, it is not so. You think that day and night are opposites, light and darkness are opposites. The fact is that darkness is another form of light and light is a way for darkness to exist – they are different processes of the same energy. The ordinary intellect assumes that if darkness totally disappears from this world then only light will remain, but science will not agree with this. Science will say that if darkness disappears totally then there will be no light, or if light disappears totally then darkness will also disappear.

If you want to get rid of hatred from the world then love also has to be totally withdrawn. Hatred will continue as long as love is there. As long as there are friends there will be enemies. If death has to be wiped away then birth also will cease, and death will continue only as long as there is birth.

You think that if you can stop wars then there will be

absolute peace in the world – but peace would disappear if war were to totally disappear. It seems a little difficult to understand, but this is the paradox of appearances and reality: peace can prevail in the world only as long as wars continue. War and peace are two sides of the same coin: if one is lost then the other is also lost.

You think that illness and health are opposites. You wish for a time when there will be no illness in the life of man, but the day this happens, there will be no health either. It is possible only if all the limbs of man are changed and replaced by plastic and stainless steel limbs, artificial limbs. Then sickness will disappear, but with it the experience of health will also disappear. The joy of health and well-being cannot be experienced with stainless steel and plastic limbs: health is connected with illness.

Now there are ways to replace the heart; parts of the brain can also be replaced. Soon it will be possible to replace all the parts of the human body which have the possibility of getting sick. Plastic cannot become sick, stainless steel will last for a long time. Instead of bones, there can be stainless steel in your hands. Nerves can be made of plastic and soon we can find a better chemical than blood. The whole body can be made like a machine, then it will not become sick – but the being which is hidden inside will never be able to experience health.

Actually, health is a sort of balance between diseases and disease is nothing but an imbalance of health. Both are together: eliminate one totally and the other will also disappear. But you don't see it like this. You think that if one is destroyed then the other will remain. This is the paradox of false appearances. So whatsoever appears to you as true, look deeply into it and think of the opposite: the greater is the possibility that the opposite will be true.

Try to understand it in this way: wherever man experiences happiness, in the end, what comes to his hands is just misery. The mind says that happiness must be where it appears to be, but searching for it, in the end only misery is experienced. Many times in life you have experienced it: wherever there was a promise of happiness, you ran toward it and have found only misery.

The sages have reversed this idea: they have said that wherever there appears to be misery, try to enter it. When what appears to be happiness leads to misery, then wherever there appears to be misery, if you go into it you will find happiness. It is this scientific process that is called *tapa*, discipline for purification. *Tapa* means a search for happiness even in misery. The people who are looking for happiness are finding only misery, so the process is reversed. The first process was leading into more illusion and misery so they have changed the direction.

We call a person a *bhogi*, an indulger, who thinks that he will find happiness if he searches for it in apparent pleasures. And we call a person a yogi, a meditator, who no longer has this illusion, who has reversed the process and is trying to enter into and understand his misery. And the person who enters into his misery will certainly find happiness because people who are searching for happiness have found nothing but misery.

Always remember this basic principle of life: the truths of life are seen upside down by us because our minds reflect them, just as the reflection of a tree near the lake looks upside down. So understand this clearly; keep this in your mind before you choose your path in life, before you choose your philosophy of life and living, before you choose your goals in life.

This is why the sages have said that the tree that you see as having its roots below and its branches above is actually just the reverse: the branches of the tree of life are not above, they are below, and the roots are not below but above. The sages have called this phenomenon "the ageless, eternal pipal tree." This is only a poetic symbolism, but the meaning of it will not become clear unless it is applied to different aspects of life.

*"This manifest world is likened to an eternal pipal tree, if the tree were to have its roots above and its branches below. In the deepest roots of this tree lives the brahman…"* But it is not visible. We see only the manifestation, the visible, but the reality is

invisible. To us godliness is invisible and matter is visible. When someone reverses this phenomenon of life then matter starts receding and godliness starts becoming apparent. The day when matter recedes totally and you see only godliness, understand that you have known the truth.

This is why in that ultimate state of consciousness the enlightened ones have said that this world is maya, illusion. They say this because for them the world is no longer there, it has become unreal – just as the unenlightened say that godliness is unreal. But unconscious people are bound to say this because the common understanding is that what cannot be seen does not exist. So the ignorant ask, "Where is the divine?" There is no way to show where the divine is because it is not a question of whether or not it exists, but of the blindness of the one who is looking. The ignorant man's way of seeing is such that he can only see matter and he cannot see godliness.

The enlightened one sees only godliness, he does not recognize any reality in the material world. Ignorant people say, "This world is the reality and godliness is an illusion." But the enlightened one says, "Godliness is the essential reality and this world is just illusory" – it is reversed. If you understand this process and start experimenting even a little bit with it in your life, you will find that you have started changing, you have started becoming new.

How to experiment with this? I have just given you the metaphysical explanation, but this can be practiced in your daily life too.

This is a very valuable sutra. When someone abuses you, you become annoyed – but this is the natural state of any unconscious person. The enlightened ones say that when someone becomes angry with you, compassion has to be your response: the process has to be reversed. When someone is angry then you should forgive, nourish the feeling of forgiveness. Your life will start becoming new. If somebody abuses you and you become angry then your life will remain the same as it was before.

Then no transformation is possible because you are not changing the base.

When someone respects you, praises you, you are pleased, you are happy. The enlightened ones say that when someone respects you then you should remain indifferent to it; you should even be sad. Ordinarily when someone shows respect you feel very happy. Why? because your ego is fulfilled, and the ego is a disease. This is why your enemies cannot harm you as much as your admirers: they are nourishing your ego. Kabir has said that you should arrange it so that people who criticize you live near your house. This is just the reverse: give shelter to people who abuse you, let them live near you so that they can go on abusing you day and night. Because people who criticize you are shattering your ego and people who praise you are enhancing your ego. And the ego is the great disease, it is the source of all misery.

Practically, this sutra means: don't go with what seems to be the natural reaction. Do just the reverse of it and then, by and by, your life will become religious.

When Jesus was being crucified he was asked if he wanted to say something. Jesus raised his face toward the sky and said, "Father, forgive these people because they know not what they are doing."

If somebody wants to crucify *you,* your mind will be full of curses for him; there is no way for blessings to shower through you. A curse is the natural reaction. Even the animal will react the same way and the stone will also do the same. To react in this way it is not necessary to be a human being: this is the principle of inanimate life.

Just as water flows downward and fire burns, in the same way, animal nature creates a double anger in reaction to anger. This is simply the natural way of animality. *Pashu,* animal, means that which is static, which is not moving forward. *Pashu* means one who is dispirited, who is stuck and whose life has no spiritual growth.

The Sanskrit word *pashu* is beautiful – all Sanskrit words are beautiful. In this sense, no other language is as scientific as Sanskrit because each word has its philosophy behind it and each word has been coined with great thought and understanding. These words are not coined just for their functional usage. *Pashu* comes from *pash,* which means something that binds, a bondage. *Pashu* means the one who is bound. *Pashu* does not mean animal; it means one who is tied, one who is caught, one who is a slave to the rules of nature, one who is not free.

If you want to rise above the spontaneous reaction of nature, then to do the reverse should be your sadhana, your spiritual discipline. When someone praises you, you should cry and when someone abuses you, you should laugh. If you follow this small practice when you go in search of godliness, the divine will come searching for you. Then there will be no need to search for it. Once you change the ordinary reactions of life into their opposite, then you have entered the world of truth. You have entered on the path of grace from where truth itself will pull you.

As you are you are standing upside down. What you think of as standing straight up is nothing but a *shirshasana,* a headstand. You are seeing everything upside down. You have to stand on your feet. As you are you have to be in the reverse position.

The only effort of all the sages is that the blind reactions in your life should become full of awareness. Wherever you behave like a robot, like a machine, there you should become aware. And one becomes aware only when one transcends nature. When someone abuses you then no awareness is needed to become angry. Anger is unconsciousness, awareness is not needed for it. But to forgive someone who has abused you one has to be conscious, very alert.

Consciousness has to be raised to a higher level and the inner light needs to be intensified. Even then there will be the possibility of the old habit of anger possessing you and pulling you down again. But it is a very rewarding process. If someone starts reversing his automatic reactions in life, he will experience great joy. Then life will become a laboratory. Then even others will be surprised – and others are surprised only when they find that you are no longer blind. Others are surprised and in trouble only when you don't behave according to their normal expectations. If someone abuses Buddha, he just listens.

Someone spat on Buddha and he quietly wiped it with his cloth and asked the person who had spat on him, "Have you anything more to say?"

His disciple, Ananda, became very angry and said, "What are you asking this man? He is mad! He has spat on you! Just allow me to put him right."

Buddha said, "I forgive this man because he is unconscious. But you, who have lived with me for so many years, are behaving totally unconsciously. This man wants to say something which he cannot express in words so he is saying it by spitting."

Spitting is also a language. Many times the feeling is very deep, you cannot express it so you embrace someone – that is also a language. Something is so deep in the heart that words cannot express it, so you just embrace the other.

Buddha said, "There is some emotion so deep in this man's mind that he cannot express it in words, so he is saying it by spitting. He is filled with such a deep anger that it cannot be expressed in words. That is why I am asking him, 'Do you want to say something more? I have understood what you have said, but do you have something more to say? Do you want to add something to what you have already said?'"

The man became very restless and nervous because when someone spits on you he is expecting some reaction from you. But here, a philosophical discussion was happening about spitting – that spitting is also a language, and this man has said something through it – so the man felt very uneasy. He must have also felt guilty that he had spat on the wrong person.

He went away, but the next morning he came back and

placed his head at Buddha's feet, started crying, tears flowing from his eyes. He said, "Forgive me! I spat on you yesterday, but I have made a great mistake. Afterward I repented and I could not sleep the whole night."

Buddha said, "You are really silly! So much time has passed since you spat on me! Since then much water has flowed down the Ganges. Why do you still hold on to it? And although you spat I did not accept it, so don't repent unnecessarily. You spat at me but I was not hurt by it, so don't repent."

Then Buddha told Ananda, "Ananda, look! This man again wants to say something, but he is unable to express it in words because it is so profound – so he has washed my feet with his tears."

As a person starts rising above the ordinary reactions of life, a very beautiful process begins, a very sweet, delightful journey which becomes sweeter every day, which becomes more and more full of fragrance every day. Within you, bliss starts flowing. And it is at the culmination of this journey that the nectar showers.

But as you are, wherever you are, you are just upside down. You are doing that which should not be done, you are living in a way which should not be lived. You are planting thorn bushes and putting rocks in your way with your own hands. And this will make the journey impossible. You are your own enemy.

If in theory and in practice you understand this sutra – that your mind is seeing things upside down – then you have the key in your hand to transform your life.

> *"...it is the deathless. All the worlds are sustained in it. No one can transcend it.*
> *"This, is that."*

Nobody can transcend godliness. There is no way to go beyond it because godliness means that which is the ultimate, that which cannot be transcended. There is nothing beyond it. And if something still remains beyond it then where you are is not the divine.

Try to understand it in this way: as long as you have any desire in your mind to achieve anything, you are not godly. The moment you have no desire left to achieve anything, which means that nothing remains to be achieved, you become godly.

So the enlightened ones have defined godliness as desireless consciousness. Because desire always wants to move forward; and it takes many forms, it is never satisfied anywhere. In this very moment, if you can become satisfied with yourself as you are and feel that you don't need anything more... Just saying won't do: it should be your deep inner state, not only saying it but feeling it deeply. Then all darkness disappears – and you are godly.

Godliness means absolute contentment in this very moment, beyond which nothing remains. But man is always creating trouble for himself: he gives up trouble on one side only when he has created trouble on the other side.

A friend who is old came to see me. He was very emotional. He was crying and saying that his kundalini had not yet awakened. He said that he had been wandering for the last twenty years going to many ashrams and many gurus and had tried many methods, but his kundalini had not awakened.

His efforts are sincere, his feelings are genuine, his search is authentic – but his basic understanding is wrong. He is searching for kundalini just as people search for money. They cry when they don't get it, they feel miserable, upset, they suffer when they don't get it. Kundalini has become this man's greed.

And note this well: the main difficulty on the inner journey is that nobody can enter it with greed. The entry happens only through your inner contentment. So don't be worried about what you haven't got: be grateful for that which you have and you will move deeper and deeper.

But this man is in anguish with this anxiety that the kundalini is not going to awaken. In fact it is delayed because of this anxiety. It is not that it has not happened although he has searched for twenty years: on the contrary, it has been delayed because of this twenty-year search that was full of the tension to "get it." Everything has become contracted inside him.

When there is tension to achieve something, you are in this world. This rushing to achieve *is* the world. To be accepting of, to relax with non-attainment, is to start moving out of the world. Somebody is running after fame or money and somebody is running after power or position; someone else is running after moksha, liberation – what is the difference? There is no difference.

Rushing and running is not the way for liberation. On the contrary, one who stops running attains liberation. One has to run after money because money cannot be acquired by just standing and doing nothing. When even the person who is running after money cannot get it, then how can one who is just standing still get it? Fame, position, money, all of them are races. Liberation is not a race: liberation means that you have utterly stopped.

One woman seeker told me just today that she has not experienced anything yet. What is there to experience? Is it going to help you if you see light or colors? What will you gain if you start experiencing fragrance in you, or ashes start falling from your palm or charms start appearing from your palm? What will you gain within you if sick people are healed by your touch? These are all games of the mind and of the world.

The search for experience is sheer greed. Drop this search for experiences. Experiences are not needed; rather, the experiencer is needed. Become acquainted with the one who is experiencing. All experiences are alien, they are outside of your being.

Spirituality is not an experience. Spirituality is to be one with the experiencer in whose presence the experiences of light appear, the experiences of fragrance come; in whose presence there is a play of colors as if a rainbow has appeared; in whose presence music is heard. But all these experiences are happening on the outside. Although these experiences are happening with closed eyes, still they are outside of you. The experiencer, the one who knows all this, is beyond. The knower is always beyond what he is knowing. Until you become one with the knower you cannot have any glimpse of spirituality.

Some are searching for excitement on the outside: they go to the movies or they listen to the radio or go to see some dancer. Some are searching on the outside for beauty and some are searching within themselves for lights and colors. They try to awaken their kundalini or they try to see some inner light or attain to some inner bliss – but the search is the same. The search is for sensation or for excitement, and neither of these two are spirituality.

Spirituality is the search for consciousness, for that witnessing consciousness where all experiences have ended and only the experiencer remains; where all visions disappear and only the seer remains; where everything belonging to the realm of the knowable has disappeared and only the knower has remained. The search for that state of absolute aloneness, *kaivalya,* is spirituality.

*"All the worlds are sustained in it. None can transcend it. This, is that."* So the moment you reach to that state where there is nothing left to transcend, understand that you have arrived home. Understand that the temple you were searching for has been found. This can happen in this very moment because godliness has nothing to do with time – that it will take a year or two years, two lifetimes or fifty lifetimes to realize it. It all depends on you: it can take many lifetimes, or just one moment is enough.

When this understanding becomes clear – that there is nothing to transcend, nowhere to go, nothing to achieve, that: "Whatsoever I am, I am totally content in it," and the flame of contentment burns bright – that very moment you have entered that which cannot be transcended. The one who is trying to transcend will go on wandering in this world.

All of you are trying to transcend, to go further, to do more and more. Whatsoever it is – it may be kundalini or it may be money, but mind is craving for more and more. Whatsoever you have, the desire to get more never ends. This struggle for more continues inside, and this desire for more is the world.

To be content with what is – a total acceptance of everything, the feeling of suchness, a feeling of total gratitude, with no wish to transcend and have more…

The desire to go further and further is called ambition. Someone has ten rupees, and ambition says, "How can I make do without a hundred rupees?" If someone has one hundred rupees then the ambition, the desire, is for one thousand rupees. This desire never ends.

When Andrew Carnegie died he had ten billion dollars. Two days before he died he said, "I am dying dissatisfied because I intended to collect one hundred billion dollars. Only ten billion!" It is the same as a beggar saying, "Only ten cents!" He had wanted to collect one hundred billion! And don't assume that one hundred billion would have made any difference. When ten billion dollars did not make any difference, then how can one hundred billion make any difference?

Once you have amassed one hundred billion dollars, ambition will desire one thousand billion. Ambition is always ahead of you. Just as the shadow walks behind, in the same way, ambition goes ahead. Wherever you reach, ambition is always ahead of you.

Bayazid, the Sufi master, has said that ambition is like the horizon: you may travel as far as you can, but the distance between you and the horizon remains the same because the horizon is not there; it only appears to be there. From a distance it seems as if the sky is touching the earth, but the sky is not touching the earth anywhere. As you move toward the horizon, it feels as if soon you will reach the place where the sky is touching the earth, but the horizon goes on moving ahead at the same rate as you move. The horizon is always at the same distance. You can keep on going forward, you can go around the whole earth and come back to your place, but the distance will remain the same.

The sky never touches the earth, it only seems to be touching. There is no way to shorten the distance between you and the horizon. You may think that if you go by car or by plane you will reach the horizon. No, there is no way because the horizon is not a reality; otherwise there could be a way. It is an illusion. It appears to be there but in reality it is not there.

Ambition is like the horizon. It seems that the limit to reach is ten billion, but when you reach there you find that the limit has shifted farther away and the distance is just the same. This is an amazing phenomenon. Looked at from this angle you can understand a very basic thing about money. There may be a quantitative difference of money between the rich and the poor, but there is no difference in their poverty. A person has ten cents and he desires one hundred cents, so he is poor by ninety cents; another person has ten dollars and he desires a hundred dollars, so he is poor by ninety dollars – the number ninety will always be there. If someone has ten billion and he desires one hundred billion, the figure ninety still remains. It is the same as the distance between the man and the horizon, it is always ninety times. It does not matter what you have and how much you have, you will remain ninety times poor.

The beggar and the king are equally poor. Their bank accounts and their account books show different figures but the desire, the very human desire of both, is the same. Whatsoever one has, ambition is always at a certain distance away. Do you think that the distance to the horizon will be different for the king and for the beggar? The distance to the horizon is the same for both. And even if they travel – the king with all his wealth and the beggar with his poverty – wherever they stand, the distance from the horizon will be the same as before for both of them. The distance to the horizon will never become more or less for either of them.

There are two kinds of poor people in this world: first, those who have money and second, those who don't have money. But there is no difference in their poverty, both are poor.

Then who is rich? Only the person whose horizon is exactly under his feet, not far away and distant, is rich. This means absolute contentment: one whose horizon line is under his feet, who sees the horizon where his feet are standing, who says that, "Wherever I step, *here* the sky is touching the earth, nowhere else." When a person is filled with this feeling, this state of feeling is called sannyas: one is free from all desire, in a state of total contentment, or whatsoever name you want to give it. This person is free from the rushing, he has stopped running. He is free from the madness of going farther and farther. And he enters existence which cannot be transcended.

> *"The entire universe has emerged out of this ultimate reality, and all life functions within this. Those who know this ultimate reality to be fearsome as a thunderbolt set to strike, become the deathless ones. They become free from the cycle of birth and death."*

A very important word has been used here; it should be understood very deeply. With seekers of truth there are two different schools of thought. One says that the nature of God, godliness, the ultimate reality, is love; and the second says that its nature is frightening, it is to be feared. And the two are very much in opposition.

Tulsidas has said, "One cannot love without fear; you cannot love the divine if you don't fear it."

But the other school believes that it is love – as Jesus has said, "God is love." They say that love cannot exist if there is fear. How can you love anyone that you fear? You can hate him but how can you love him? Where there is fear you may bow down because of the fear, but you cannot trust the person. Out of fear you may put your head at the person's feet but you cannot surrender, you cannot be devoted. There is no possibility for love where fear exists.

But there are those who believe that it is frightening and

because of this fear the moon and the stars move; because of fear nature functions; because of fear everything is in order. They believe that the whole order will break down if there is no fear, that because of fear there is discipline. And this concept also needs to be understood. Both concepts need to be understood because they can both lead to godliness.

It is very easy to understand that God is love. It should be so – it is the ultimate love, the abode of love. Love flows from it toward us. It is not difficult to understand this view because your idea of the divine is the same as how you feel toward your parents. This is why you have called God "father," "great father," or "mother." There is a reason for it.

Psychotherapists like Freud say that the concept of God is the expansion of the concept of the father; it is a projection of the same concept. The children who grow up in the love of their father and who are full of love and respect for their father will become religious later on; and the children who are rebellious and against their fathers will become atheists later on. The relationship between the individual and God depends on the type of relationship he had as a child with his father. There is truth in this concept of Freud's. But if we deeply understand the relationship between father and child, we will find both currents present there: the father is loving toward the child but at the same time the child is also afraid of the father. The father is not only love, fear is also included. And the biggest fear is that, if he wants to, the father can withdraw his love.

What is a child's greatest fear? – that the mother or the father can reject, can deny him their love. They can give love but they can also withhold it. And for the child this is the most terrifying situation because the child is helpless: if he is denied love from his father and mother he will be finished. It is like death to the child. You cannot conceive the pain and suffering of a child when his mother rejects him, says that she has nothing to do with him, becomes indifferent.

Like a shadow, there is a hidden fear about the person you

love – the fear is of losing the love. Love can be withdrawn, that possibility is there. Obstacles can always appear between lovers.

So the child not only loves the father, the child is frightened also; these two feelings are mixed together. And the greatest art is that the father should create a balance between these two, otherwise in every situation he will prove to be an unworthy father.

And it is very difficult to be worthy of being a father. It is very easy to produce children – what could be easier than this? – but it is very difficult to be a real mother. The difficulty is to create a balance between love and fear. If a father creates so much fear in the child that the child loses trust in love, then his whole life will be ruined. He will never be able to love anyone in his life.

The child who is not loved in his childhood will live the rest of his life without love. He may talk much about love, he may write poems of love, he may write books on love, but his own life will be without love. The first loving touch which could have created the seed of love never sprouted in his life. If parents could not give love to the child, the child will never be able to love anyone. And later on that angry child will be the cause of destruction in every way.

These days there is chaos in all the universities of the world. This fire of rebellion is spreading very fast, especially in Western countries. Now it is also spreading in the Eastern countries because the Eastern educational institutions are no longer Eastern; they are imitative, just copies of the Western system. So whatever diseases are born in the West take three to four years to reach the East – even in that we lag behind! If some new medicine is out on the market there, that also takes three years to reach our hospitals here. Even if a disease is born there, it takes time to reach here. In every sphere we lag behind.

The younger generation in the West is strongly rebelling against the older generation, against education, against culture and against society. Now psychologists say that the basic reason for this is that these children never got their parents' love, this generation has grown up without love. And in the West love has become rare because mostly the parents are divorced before the children have grown up. Out of a hundred marriages fifty end in divorce, so families are broken; fathers are changed, mothers are changed and the children have to grow up with a stepmother or a stepfather. The flow of love in life is hindered from everywhere. The children born during the increase in divorce cases in the last thirty years did not get enough love – and they are taking their revenge. These children cannot love; they are full of destructive energy. Love is creative. And when a person does not get love he starts being destructive.

Those who have studied the life of Hitler say that Hitler did not get love from his parents, so he wanted to destroy everything; the result was the Second World War. He was not interested in creating; he wanted to destroy in every way because when there is no love there is no interest in creating anything. The day love enters in your life creativity happens simultaneously. As soon as a man falls in love with a woman he immediately starts thinking of creating his home. A creative process immediately starts about how to earn more and how to decorate his home. Where there is no love then a desire for destruction possesses you.

The rebellion of young people around the whole world is because of this lack of love. Young people are becoming atheists the whole world over. It is bound to be so because those who have not received any love from their father and mother, how can they imagine that this existence is a father or mother? Or even if there is a father, he deserves to be shot, not admired.

It is a great art to be a father or a mother. Parents who are very particular about enforcing discipline are afraid that the child may become spoiled because of their love, so they stop giving their love in every possible way. They make the child afraid and try to control the child through a fear of punishment. Finally, this type of improvement and discipline makes the child emotionally crippled.

But on the other hand there is also a pitfall: Western psychologists have created a fear in parents that the child will rebel if they enforce any discipline on him, or frighten him, or impose anything on him. They should only love him. But love alone can also become poisonous because love alone can become licentiousness. Then children think that it is their right to be loved, that there is no question of earning love. The son thinks he has nothing to do to earn love because it is his right to get love – he feels no responsibility to do anything.

If parents give him only love and there is a complete absence of fear, then the child will be spoiled. Then he will start demanding love from the whole world – but the world is not his father and mother. The world is not there just to give him love. When you go into the world there is competition, struggle, fight; no one is ready to give you love.

The child becomes very fragile if his parents have given him only love. He becomes so fragile that he cannot stand any conflict, he is easily shattered. He expects love from everyone and he goes on begging for love from others. But he does not know that the world will give him love only when he has earned it. He has to do something in life; he cannot get love for free, he has to earn it. He can get love from his parents without earning it but later on, in the outside world, he won't get it for free. He even has to earn the love of his wife; that too he will not get for free.

So this person will go on looking, searching for his parents. He may become a believer sitting in a temple with his hands raised toward the sky, calling, "Oh, father! Oh, almighty father!" but his life will be barren because the maturity and strength which comes from facing the struggles of life will not have happened in him.

So now psychologists say that the art of parenthood is to bring a balance between fear and love. Fear only to the extent that the child does not become a constant fighter, and love to the extent that the child does not get into the habit of asking for love without earning it. This is a very complex matter. It is like tightrope walking: the rope is tied between two hills and the person walking on the rope has to maintain his balance all the time – when he feels himself leaning a little more to the left side, then immediately he moves his balance to the right side so he doesn't fall off on the left side; and when he leans to the right side and feels out of balance, he immediately shifts his balance to the left side.

When there is even a little fear of fear in the child – then, love. And when there is even a little fear of unearned love – then, fear. One who balances between these two like a tightrope walker can become a skilled father or a skilled mother.

Christianity believes that God is love – and this was the conflict between Christianity and Judaism, which believes that God is to be feared. The Jewish scriptures would agree with Yama's statement that the divine is fearsome, like a thunderbolt ready to strike. All the time God is holding a weapon in his hand and at the slightest provocation he will destroy. Just a little annoyance and he can spread fire, just a little anger and there will be a flood.

Judaism is based on fear: they say that God is terrifying, that it is a vast, universal energy which is not loving. Try to understand this idea, that this vast energy is not loving. It is full of kindness for those who function according to it and it destroys those who go against it. You may not like to hear this, but science agrees with this view. It says that no law of nature is ever loving – but this does not mean that nature is your enemy.

For example, there is gravitation on the earth. If you don't walk properly then you are going to fall down and get a fracture. The gravitation of the earth is not going to forgive you just because you had bowed your head down on the ground many times and called her "Mother Earth." If you don't walk properly, fractures will happen and Mother Earth will have no mercy on you! If you go against the law you will be hurt; but if you are careful while you walk then the earth is not interested in breaking your bones.

Science also says that the laws of nature are not loving. But this does not mean that nature is your enemy; it only means that it is impartial. So you will achieve happiness if you go according to the laws of nature, and if you go against them then you will suffer.

The old religions like Judaism which believe that God is to be feared also say that it is not your enemy. But it is an eternal law – if you go according to it then you will reach to ultimate freedom and if you go against it you will fall into eternal hell.

Yama is describing the frightening nature of the divine to Nachiketa. There is a reason for this because Yama himself is a process of fear. Yama is the Lord of Death. How can the Lord of Death talk about love? The Lord of Death can only talk about fear.

What Yama is saying is only half true – that those who expect only love from the divine will perish because they will not make any efforts to change themselves. But also, those who are afraid of the divine will understand that their prayers are of no use if they go against the law. The divine, godliness cannot be influenced by praise and flattery, but only by one's right action.

If I change myself and my conduct is right, then I flow with the current of existence. When somebody flows with the current of the river, the river takes him to the sea. But when someone fights by going against the current of the river, the river will become fearsome. If we go against the law, then it is fierce. Existence is loving when we are in tune with it: if we are flowing with the current of the river, existence will take us. Then we don't even need to swim, the river itself will take us.

Ramakrishna used to say, "You only have to feel the direction of God's wind – then just open the sails of your boat. Then you will not even have to use the oars, his wind will take your boat to the destination. But you have to understand the direction of the wind: if you go against the wind then you will have to work hard. Even then, you will not succeed; you will only fail because nobody can succeed by fighting with God."

To call the "fearsome" only means that one should not

fight with it – just be in accord with it, be surrendered and in a let-go.

*"Those who know this ultimate reality to be fearsome as a thunderbolt set to strike, become the deathless ones. They become free from the cycle of birth and death."* If you understand it rightly, death is also the result of your wrong way of living. You identify yourself with the body: that is why death happens to you. If you don't identify yourself with the body, then death will not happen. Death happens to the body, not to you – but you are identified with your body. It is as if someone rides in a paper boat and the boat sinks: it is neither the fault of the boat nor of the sea. And you are sitting in a paper boat! It is certain that the paper boat will capsize, it is a miracle that it could sail even for a short time.

If you are identified with the body you have prepared yourself for death because the body is mortal. If you are identified with the mortal you are living against immortality; you will die again and again. Yama is saying that the person who is not identified with the mortal body and who lives in accord with his real being is free of all fear. He is free of death, he is free of the cycle of birth and death.

If you can understand this fearsome but impartial law of the divine, and if you can discipline your life in accordance with it, you will become immortal.

> *"The heat of fire is because of this divine dread; the shine of the sun is because of this divine dread; Indra, Vayu and the gods of death, all five do their work because of this divine dread.*
>
> *"If one can realize godliness while still in human form, before the body has returned to the earth, it is well; else he will wander aimlessly through many worlds and many species, for millennia."*

To be born in a human body is a rare and special privilege.

There are many species below human beings: there are animals, birds, trees and other species. There are also many species above the human – the *devas,* those who live in higher dimensions. There are species above and below human beings; to be born as a human being is exactly in the middle. But because of this situation of being in the middle, human beings have a special privilege.

Man is like a middle point, a crossroads: there is a road going above and there is a road going below – and there is also the possibility of becoming free from these two roads.

Try to understand this. The species below the human beings are in deep suffering. We can say that below the human species is hell because there is only suffering. There is so much suffering that there is no hope of ever coming out of it. The hope to become free from suffering can arise only when even a small glimpse of the possibility of happiness has happened.

Psychologists who study revolutions say that a revolution cannot happen if there is too much suffering. This looks very paradoxical. The students of politics think that a revolution can take place only when there is too much misery and suffering in the society. But this understanding is wrong. There can be no revolution if there is too much misery because people become addicted to their suffering. And if there is no hope for any happiness, why revolt?

Politicians think that it is the poor who revolt, but this is not so. The poor cannot revolt. All the revolutionaries are born into middle-class families. It may be a Lenin or a Marx, but all revolutionaries are born in middle-class families. Neither are they born in rich families nor in poor families, but in middle-class families that have experienced suffering but also have some hope for happiness. They have not reached the palace but they are not living in a hut either; they are living in the middle, in an ordinary house. If they make efforts then it can become a palace and if they don't try then soon it can become a hut. Only those who are stuck in the middle – who know suffering and are also carrying a dream of happiness – can create a revolution.

Below the human being is the world of suffering. That is why no animal tries to attain moksha, liberation. The misery and unconsciousness is so much that there is no hope. If there is no hope then one does not even try.

In the last five thousand years of Indian history the sudras, the untouchables, have never revolted. There was no hope for them so there was no reason to revolt. After the English came to India the untouchables began to have aspirations. The rulers were not Hindus, so a revolt became possible because now there was some hope. The untouchables could also become educated: they could not be educated under the reign of the Hindus. But when the English came to India, a sudra could even become educated and have a job. Thus some of the sudras became middle-class people and, naturally, those middle-class sudras started thinking of revolution.

You will be surprised to know that in India the people who fought for freedom were those who had returned to India after being educated in the West. It is very interesting that it was the people who were educated in the West who fought for freedom, whether it was Gandhi, Nehru or Aurobindo. The slavery was created by the West and the idea of freedom was also created by the West. What could be the reason for this? – those who lived only in India had no aspirations, no hope.

Subhash, an Indian freedom fighter, has written somewhere in his memoirs that when he went to Europe to be educated and an Englishman was polishing his shoes, he realized that it was not inevitable that people had to be slaves. Even Englishmen can polish shoes, so the rule of the British also was not absolute.

The children who went out of India for their education became hopeful. The result of that hope was that India began the struggle for freedom. But the children who studied only in India could not even conceive of such a hope.

The species below human beings are full of suffering. There is no hope in that state, so there can be no revolution. And the species above human beings are full of happiness. No one revolts when there is pleasure and happiness because anyone who has something to lose would not like anything to change.

This is why if you want to crush a revolutionary, give him something, some position. Howsoever revolutionary a communist may be, give him a ministry, make him a minister, and his revolution will be over. Even a Fiat car can crush a revolution! If there is something to lose then revolution will create fear. The rich, happy person does not want change. Richness always wants to maintain the status quo, for conditions to remain the same. This is why rich, happy people don't want any change.

Hence, there can be no revolution in heaven. Up until now no buddha has been born in heaven – neither were Mahavira nor Krishna born there. In heaven there are only gods, like the lustful Indra. Indra has no value from the viewpoint of wisdom, and his only job is to make the celestial nymphs dance. He has never done any meditation or *sadhana:* on the contrary, he is very interested in disturbing people who are meditating! If any seer or sage is meditating in his hut or on a mountain or under a tree, then these gods really enjoy disturbing him. They send celestial nymphs like Urvashi to harass him.

Nobody has ever attained liberation while in heaven. No one can, because no one desires to be free of pleasure and happiness. So too much happiness is also a curse. Too much misery is certainly a misfortune but too much happiness also proves to be a misfortune.

To be born as a human being is to be in the middle – you are neither in heaven nor in hell, you are just in the middle. If you make a slight mistake you can fall into hell and if you behave a little intelligently you can enter heaven. You are in the middle.

And to be born as a human being is to be in a state where transformation is possible. If a man understands rightly, he will not like to be either in heaven or in hell, because to indulge in pleasures again and again also becomes boring and brings one to misery.

If you go to heaven you will find the gods yawning everywhere – they are simply bored! If beautiful women surround you all the time you would like to run away, you will want to be alone. Too much beauty can become repulsive. Eating too many sweets, the tongue will long for the opposite. Being in too much comfort, the mind will desire some challenge. The gods that are sitting in heaven are completely bored. Boredom is the sign of heaven! Everyone in heaven is bored. This is why they have to make so many arrangements for their entertainment: drinking, singing and dancing are going on all the time.

In the Mohammedan heaven they say that there are springs of wine flowing. Bottles are not enough, so they have springs. So not only can you drink it, you can even swim and bathe in it, you can drown in it! In heaven there is only entertainment.

Try to understand it. Today, America is closer to heaven and there is great boredom there. Every convenience is available and there is no interest left in anything. Entertainment is easily available everywhere, and from morning till night people are busy entertaining themselves – but all the joy is lost. And whenever a great event happens their interest in it is finished within minutes.

The desire of man to reach the moon is very ancient. Man has been dreaming of reaching the moon ever since he has been on this earth. Little babies raise their arms to catch the moon in their small hands. For thousands of years man's ambition has been to reach the moon. Then one day the first man landed on the moon and within fifteen minutes America lost interest in it. People watched it on television for ten minutes and then finished, some other program was switched on. Psychologists say that after just fifteen minutes nobody was interested that man had landed on the moon. In fifteen minutes this great event became boring: "So someone has reached the moon, now what?" They have seen that man has landed on the moon, so what's next? There is so much boredom.

In heaven also there must be very much boredom because there are so many means of entertainment. Wherever there is boredom new entertainments have to be found and the boredom goes on growing as more entertainments are made available. There are many stories of gods who are longing to descend to earth to make love to a woman. Urvashi craves to love a strong man on the earth. Here on earth there is still some interest because life is not all a bed of roses. Here, life is a struggle; there are difficulties and inconveniences here.

The person who understands that misery is certainly misery, but happiness also becomes a misery, will want to be free of both misery and happiness. One who understands this truth will desire neither heaven nor hell: he will search for liberation, he will want to go beyond all desire.

So there are three paths that begin at the point where a human being is: one is of happiness, the second is of misery and the third is of liberation.

Liberation is neither happiness nor misery, liberation is beyond both. *"If one can realize godliness while still in human form, before the body has returned to the earth, it is well; else he will wander aimlessly through many worlds and many species, for millennia."* It is only after a long, long journey that consciousness comes to the stage of a human being. If this opportunity is missed, a vicious circle of another long journey will begin again.

For those who are in a human body and yet are not thirsty for liberation, the future is full of darkness. Nobody knows how far the journey will again be; it is difficult to say how much time it will take to reach to the crossroads again. It is very easy to miss the crossroads because there is not much time there. And to receive this opportunity again can be very difficult.

It is almost like this…

I have heard that a man was driving his car very fast. He stopped and asked a man sitting under the tree, "How far is it to Delhi?"

The man answered, "It depends! Delhi is very far from the direction you are going in because Delhi is behind you. If you are ready to turn back then Delhi is just nearby – but you have to change your direction."

Man is running fast toward death and he is leaving the place from where he can achieve liberation behind him every moment. And nobody knows when he will get such an opportunity again.

If he can simply stop and forget all about the going farther and start going within – change his direction from the outer to the inner, from the outer world to the inner reality – then he will become free from the cycle of birth and death. Then he is liberated. Then he does not enter another womb.

And Yama said to Nachiketa:

> *"This, is that."*

Now get ready for meditation.

# 14

# The Fear of Dissolving

*"The brahman is seen in the pure antahkaran, the pure inner sense, just as an object before a mirror is reflected in it.*

*"The brahman is seen in the pitrilok, the realm of the spirits of man's deceased ancestors, just like objects seen in a dream. Reflections of the brahman are seen in gandharvalok, the realm of celestial musicians, like forms reflected in water. And the true nature of the brahman and of the soul are seen clearly in brahmalok, the ultimate reality, just as one can clearly see light and shadow.*

*"The sense organs exist separately because of their separate functions. To be born and to die is their intrinsic nature. By knowing the nature of the soul to be different from these, the intelligent ones will go beyond grief.*

*"Mind is higher than the sense organs, intelligence is higher than the mind, the soul is higher than intelligence, the unmanifest energy is higher than the soul.*

*"But the ultimate reality, which is the all-pervading, the formless, is higher even than the unmanifest energy. The one who realizes this truth while living in the body, is liberated: he becomes the brahman, divine.*

*"The divine is the deathless. It is the very seat of bliss."*

First, there are a few more things about yesterday's *sutra.* Rudolf Otto, a great German thinker, has written a very important book, *The Holy.* In that book he has repeatedly used a word, *tremendum*: it means that the divine is fearsome, terrifying. Yama has also expressed this point of view to Nachiketa: that the divine is fearsome. There is a possibility of misunderstanding this viewpoint, so we will enter it more deeply.

The first thing is that in fact, it is not the divine, godliness, that is fearsome, it is your own fear – *you* are afraid. Instead of saying that the divine is fearsome, it will be better to say that you are afraid of it. And it will help you immensely to understand the reason for your fear.

It is just like when a drop is afraid before it falls into the ocean because to fall into the ocean means to dissolve, to disappear. It is natural for the drop to be afraid: to meet the ocean means its death, and death creates fear. But if the drop could know that there is also another aspect to dissolving into the ocean – the drop will disappear as a drop and it will become the ocean; it will disappear as a small drop but it will become one with the vast – if the drop could only realize that its death is also its life as the vast, as the deathless, then it would not be afraid. If the drop could see that its death is in reality the opening to eternal life, then it would experience godliness as the very embodiment of love.

Whether the divine is the embodiment of fear or of love depends on your viewpoint, on your outlook. When someone begins to seek and search for the ultimate reality, there comes a moment of disappearing. A moment comes when one has to lose oneself, and whenever the moment of losing oneself arrives the heart trembles with fear, which is natural. Why are you afraid of death? You are afraid of death because it will efface you.

But even death cannot efface you as totally as the divine existence will efface you because even after death you will remain. You will enter new bodies and you will continue on your journey into new births. In death only your body will die, not your being. But existence will efface even your being. All your forms will dissolve into the formless. Death will snatch away only your body, but existence will snatch away your separate identity, your separate existence, your ego – that is the great death.

So if you are afraid of death then it is natural for you to also be afraid of the divine. It is not the nature of existence to be fearsome, it is your own ego that is afraid. But existence is not frightening to those who are ready to disappear. For those who are ready to lose themselves, it is the embodiment of love.

Try to understand it in this way: people are unable to love because of their fear, because love also effaces the lover. His whole identity as a separate being will be dissolved. And the lover who is not ready to lose himself in love can never know love. Love means the readiness to dissolve, the readiness to disappear. Love also means the ego will dissolve. A frightened person cannot love. But for the one who is ready to lose himself, great love will arise in his life and bliss will shower on him. So fear and love depend on one thing: whether you are ready to dissolve or not.

Sooner or later, the people who go deep into meditation come to me and say, "There was a moment when we became afraid of disappearing; we became frightened and rushed back to our normal state." But that was the moment when existence was very close by! And many meditators rush back to their minds at the last moment – just as the drop which was about to take the jump and fall into the ocean turned back; it returned to the shore. But it is natural for people to do this.

Meditation is also a death because meditation is a jump into the vast. When fear grips you, then understand that the right moment has arrived and it is not the time to turn back. One who is courageous at that moment is a true seeker. But the one who becomes afraid in that moment and goes back to his mind and settles in his old pattern will miss a great opportunity. Nobody knows when this opportunity will come again. If you have missed such an opportunity, then be aware not to miss it again. Actually, you have been searching for that moment, you have been searching for that dissolution.

But the ego holds on until the very last moment. The fear of death grips the mind and with that fear you come back into your body – again you hold tightly on to the bank so that the drop will not be lost.

The death which you know is a small death: only the body dies but the mind, the ego and everything else remains. And the greater the death the greater will be the birth of life. The new life will happen in the same proportion as your readiness to die. And if you are ready to die completely, you will know eternal life.

Jesus has said: You cannot achieve godliness until you lose yourself. The one who tries to save himself will be lost and the one who effaces himself will be saved. Many times Jesus has given the example of a seed: he has said that the seed sprouts only when it is dissolved in the earth. In the same way, when you are dissolved in the ultimate reality, eternal life will be born in you. And that life has no end because you have already lost that which could be destroyed. You yourself have let go of that which could have died; now only what cannot die remains. Only that which can never be lost by any means remains.

This is why the ultimate seems to be fearsome – but that fear is your own projection. And because these words are spoken by the Lord of Death, they are bound to be incomplete. If there were a Lord of Birth, he would define the ultimate as the embodiment of love.

Try to understand this: if there were a Lord of Birth, he would say that godliness is the embodiment of love because the process of birth begins with love, the seed of birth begins with love. The beginning of life is from love; the first throbbing of life is born out of love. If there were a Lord of Love he also would know only half of the truth: he would say, "Godliness is the embodiment of love, the abode of love." If Nachiketa had asked this question of Brahma, who is known as the God of Creation, he would not have said that the ultimate is fearsome:

then the ultimate would have been defined as love – but that statement would also have been incomplete.

The Lord of Death knows death. He has not experienced the first flicker of life, he has only experienced the end of life, the extinguishing of the earthen lamp. And whenever the Lord of Death has seen anyone dying he has seen him trembling with fear, which is quite natural. The Lord of Death has witnessed the death of millions and billions of people and he has seen everyone trembling with fear as they die. So his statement is meaningful, but incomplete.

The Lord of Death knows that to dissolve into the ultimate reality is the great death. He knows that in his presence people tremble with fear; they don't want to die and they try to save themselves in every possible way. Man always wants to save himself at any cost. Even if he is a cripple, lame, blind, ill, a leper; he may be starving, lying in the street, having nothing – but still he wants to live, he is not willing to die. Nobody agrees to die even if everything has been lost and only breathing is left. In spite of pain, misery, suffering like in hell, no one is willing to die.

The experience of the Lord of Death brings him to the logical conclusion that the ultimate reality must be frightening, because all must dissolve in it. Only the void will remain, only emptiness will be left. Instead of your separate existence there will be only emptiness. The ultimate reality will dissolve you *absolutely*.

This is a statement of the Lord of Death, so naturally it is incomplete. If the Lord of Birth were to say something, that would also be incomplete. But the enlightened ones, those who have known both birth and death, will make both statements: they will say either that the ultimate reality is both, the embodiment of fear and of love, or they will say that the ultimate reality is neither of the two. It will appear to be loving or fierce according to your projection. And the second view is closer to the truth.

The ultimate reality is simply neutral. According to whatever your mental state is, you project and then you see your own projections. Your mind, your thoughts, your instincts, your psychological conditioning, your understanding, all give it a different color and form. But the ultimate is colorless and formless. It is neither the embodiment of fear nor of love. It is impartial. It seems to be fearsome because you are afraid of disappearing, but if you are ready to dissolve and disappear, then it will appear to you as the embodiment of love.

To Jesus, the ultimate was the embodiment of love, so he defined it as love. Jesus was ready to die; even on the cross he was not at all afraid of death. He was ready to die so easily on the cross that the cross became a symbol of Jesus, that death is acceptable as a natural phenomenon. And this is why to Jesus the ultimate reality appeared as love. Your "ultimate" is the projection of your mind. It is your own creation; you create your own concept.

In my vision, it is neither of the two: it is a vast, formless, empty, void: existence. We see ourselves in it, so as man grows spiritually his experience of it will also change.

Actually, it never changes – it is as it is. It is your concept about it, your view, your vision which goes on changing. Different ages have different concepts about it. Different tribes, different castes have different concepts of the ultimate. Different individuals also have different visions and different representations of it.

But it is one; just everyone sees it from different perspectives and projects their different meanings. As long as you see any meaning in it you should know that you have not realized the truth; you are seeing your own reflection. The day you cease to find any meaning in the ultimate and there are no reflections there – the mirror is empty, nothing can be seen in it and only emptiness remains – then understand that what you are realizing now is the truth, it is not the projection of your mind.

This is why Buddha calls the ultimate truth *shunya,* emptiness. Unless for you the ultimate truth becomes emptiness, know well that you are projecting yourself on it. But it is quite natural for man to do this, and it is natural for Yama also.

The ultimate reality is a neutral energy. It does not favor

anyone. It is choiceless, there is no choice there. That state is formless. So remember that whatsoever you see in it depends on you. The day when you do not see anything in it, only a vast emptiness will remain – neither Krishna nor Rama will appear, neither Buddha nor Jesus will be there, neither love nor fear. When nothing can be seen there, that is possible only when your mind becomes so silent and free of thoughts that nothing from the mind will be projected onto reality. The day you become empty within, the ultimate reality will also look to you like emptiness. I want to make it clear to you that the ultimate reality will appear to you *as you are*.

This statement of Yama's is incomplete. Even Brahma's statement would be incomplete because both are acquainted with only one aspect. One knows only birth and the other knows only death. But you, who are both birth and death, you who are born and will also die, you who are touching both ends, if you become aware you will find that the ultimate reality is neutral – it is neither the embodiment of fear nor of love.

Now we will enter the sutra.

> *"The brahman is seen in the pure antahkaran, the pure inner sense, just as an object before a mirror is reflected in it."*

Ultimate reality is seen in the pure inner being. The more pure the inner is, the clearer the perception of reality will be. If the inner is absolutely pure then the ultimate reality will be absolutely clear. But if the mirror is dirty, covered with dust, the reflection will also be dirty. If the mirror is damaged and broken, the reflection will also be affected in the same way. If the mirror is crooked, the reflection also will be crooked. For the pure realization of reality it is essential that the mirror should be totally clear; the mirror of the inner sense should be absolutely pure. But the ultimate reality can be perceived in different states because the mirror can be in many states, in many conditions. This sutra is about the different states of the mirror.

> *"The brahman is seen in the pitrilok, the realm of the spirits of man's deceased ancestors, just like objects seen in a dream."*

All of these *lokas*, these realms, are symbols for the different states of your inner sense, your inner world. The first thing is, if the inner sense is pure then right here on this very earth, the ultimate reality can be directly realized. If the inner sense is not so pure, then after leaving the body to the realm which is called *pitrilok,* the realm where bodiless souls dwell, the ultimate reality can be known there. The impurities of the mind which are caused by the body do not remain after death. After death the ultimate reality can be seen clearly, like vivid dreams.

> *"Reflections of the brahman are seen in gandharvalok, the realm of celestial musicians, like forms reflected in water."*

In heaven, in the *gandharvaloks,* where the celestial musicians dwell, there is only a faint appearance, a slight glimpse, just as when you see a reflection in water. In heaven there is only a reflection of reality.

Heaven is full of excitement, of many pleasures. You are aware that misery is a disturbance, but you don't realize that happiness is also a disturbance. It is not only misery that disturbs the mind; the mind is also disturbed and excited by happiness. Medical science says that happiness can cause even more heart attacks than misery. So those who are really in search of bliss want to be free of all excitement, whether it is happiness or misery.

You will be surprised to know that happiness is also a disturbance. Medical science says that the incidence of heart attacks is less frequent when people are miserable than when they are happy. Heart attacks don't happen as much from misery as they do from happiness. It should not be so, it should be just the opposite. Actually, a really miserable person should die of misery, but this does not happen. Instead, the happy person dies from the very shock of happiness. This is why as a country becomes richer, the rate of heart disease goes on growing. In poor countries there is almost no heart disease. Aboriginals don't know what heart disease is. Their misery is great but they don't have much heart disease. To get heart disease you need to be rich.

Medical science says that it is very strange to see that when someone is happy his heart becomes so agitated, so shaken that it simply stops beating. In misery, the heart is not so shaken – it is easier to suffer misery than it is to endure happiness. Many people come out of misery intact, but it needs great skill to go through happiness and remain intact. People are more shattered by happiness. You may know how shocking it is when some happy event suddenly happens. Right now, if someone were to bring the news that you have won a lottery of five million dollars, you would be so shocked that you might not survive to get your money! It will be too much for you. If you lose five million dollars you will also be shocked, but not as much. To win five million will disturb your heart more than to lose it.

Happiness is a great excitement. *Gandharvalok*, which is just pleasure and excitement… These *lokas* are just symbols. Some of you are living in *gandharvalok* right here, some of you are in *pitrilok* right here and some of you are in *narkalok*, in hell, and many of you are living in *brahmalok* right here and now. These are not geographical places, they are psychological states.

When you are very happy you can sometimes have just a small glimpse of the ultimate because your mirror will always be distorted by excitement. You can understand from this why it is that when they are happy people forget all about the search for truth. When you are happy you forget all about worship, prayer, meditation, temples – you forget all this. When you are in misery you might remember, but when you are happy you never remember. Man just wants to get rid of his misery so he searches for truth; but no one wants to get rid of his happiness – then there is no question of searching for truth.

There was a Sufi fakir, a mystic named Junnaid. He was always suffering from some disease or other. His disciples said, "Junnaid, how can you be so sick? If you just mention it to God that you don't want to be sick, the matter will be finished."

Junnaid said "But I go on praying to God to keep me sick in some way or other."

The disciples said, "Have you gone mad? What kind of prayer is this?"

Junnaid replied, "When I am sick, I remember God. Sickness makes me suffer and in my suffering I am more easily able to remember. Once, when I had not been sick for a long time, I forgot all about God. Since then my only prayer is, 'Please continue to give me some illness or some suffering so that I cannot forget you.'"

In misery you may remember God, but in happiness you just forget all about it. But in happiness sometimes it is possible to have some glimpse of godliness, but it is like a reflection that is seen in the water.

Someone who has become a *videha*, who has transcended the body, the state that Yama is calling *pitrilok*… And *videha* does not mean that you have left your body, it means that you are no longer identified with your body. This is why we have called King Janak a *videha*: while he was still in his body, there was no identification with the body. It does not make any difference whether the body is alive or not – the attachment with the body has been left behind. So in the state of *videha*, a glimpse of godliness is like a dream. It is like dreaming with closed eyes: there are visions, glimpses of godliness, but exactly like in a dream – these visions will disappear as soon as you open your eyes.

> *"And the true nature of the brahman and of the soul are seen clearly in brahmalok, the ultimate reality, just as one can clearly see light and shadow."*

So in the state of *videha*, a glimpse of godliness is like a dream. It is only seen as a dream, and as soon as one opens one's eyes it disappears. As soon as one sees the outer world again it becomes vague, unclear. Another state is where the mind is full of the excitement of happiness: then one just has an inkling, a small glimpse of godliness like the echo of a faraway sound, or like a reflection in water. Water is moving every moment so a reflection in the water can never be very clear.

The third is the state of *brahmalok*. It is a state when you are absolutely pure, when the inner sense is totally pure – you have become like godliness. There is no impurity, things are very clear. They are not seen as if in a dream but as clearly as when you are in the waking state, the way you see things clearly when you are awake. This realm, *brahmalok*, is the ultimate purity of the inner sense.

Try to understand the term *antahkaran,* "inner sense." What you call conscience is not the inner sense. This word *conscience* is very much misunderstood. The English word is *conscience*, but in Sanskrit the word is *antahkaran*, the inner voice. For example, you want to steal but you hear a voice within you that says, "Stealing is a sin, don't do it" and you think this is your conscience. But it is not conscience, it is pseudo-conscience. This is not *your* conscience, this has been given to you by society. There are tribes who don't consider stealing to be a sin.

There are tribes in Rajasthan where for centuries they have not considered stealing to be wrong. In the olden days, a young man of that tribe was not allowed to get married until he had committed two or three successful thefts! When he was about to be married he was asked the question, "How many thefts have you successfully committed?" That was the proof of his skill.

Stealing is a skill, not everybody can do it. Some intelligence is needed. An unintelligent person cannot do it; the intelligence needs to be very sharp. Courage is also needed: a cowardly person just cannot do it. A fearful person has no capacity because he will tremble just carrying his own money! You have to have a very strong heart to believe someone else's money is yours. It is difficult even to walk in the darkness in your own house; to walk in the darkness in someone else's house one needs to have eyes in his feet and an unwavering heart. Your heart should not tremble; a special type of concentration is needed. A thief has great concentration, his mind is single-pointed. If the mind of a thief goes on wandering then he will get into difficulty. He must have only one aim and all his energy should flow toward it.

Not all societies have considered stealing to be wrong. And in the society which does not consider stealing to be wrong, a person's conscience will not stop him from stealing.

If a Hindu marries a second time while his first wife is still alive, his conscience will tell him that he is doing wrong. But a Mohammedan can easily marry four women without any prick of conscience because the Koran allows four marriages. Mohammed himself married nine women and he had no guilt feelings. And don't think that Mohammed has done something wrong: you should remember the story of Krishna – Mohammed is nothing compared to him! But you have never condemned Krishna, and his is a story of sixteen thousand wives. To you it may look like just a story. Sixteen thousand wives? – and only one woman can create so much trouble! Krishna must certainly have been a very courageous man. But there was no rejection in his society because kings always married many women.

In this century, the Nizam of Hyderabad had five hundred wives; on the day that India became independent he had five hundred wives. If in the twentieth century someone can have five hundred wives, then sixteen thousand is only thirty-two times more. It is not such a big deal. There is no need to say it is only a story, it could be factual. There would have been no difficulty because the belief of the society was that a king should have many wives. A king's greatness was proved by how many wives he had. It was a sign of his wealth. A poor man cannot afford even one wife. To have a wife is an expensive affair; not everyone can afford a wife. So the greater the king, the more wives he would have. This was the accepted norm. This is why in those days there was no problem for an emperor or a king to marry a thousand times. Nobody objected to it, and even the conscience of the emperor would not say, "What are you doing?" or "This is wrong." It all depends on what the society teaches.

Gambling was acceptable in those days. So Yudhishthira used to gamble, but we never bring him down from his status of *dharmaraj,* a king of religion. Today, even if an ordinary man gambles people will not be happy about it, but Yudhishthira's conscience did not trouble him at all. And his gambling was not small: he gambled away everything, and finally he even staked his own wife!

Can you stake your own wife today? No, your conscience will not allow it. But Yudhishthira's conscience did not condemn him and none of the thinkers that came after Yudhishthira ever raised any question about it. Nobody ever doubted that he was a *dharmaraj*, because gambling was just a game that was acceptable to that society. The greater the player, the greater the stakes were. Yudhishthira was a great player so he had the courage to even stake his wife. It was not considered immoral; there was no trouble about it.

Draupadi had five husbands, but we have counted her as one of the five *mahakanyas*, the great virgins! The people who considered her to be one of the five *mahakanyas* must have had a totally different moral code. What will you do with a woman today who has five husbands? What will you think of her? You will certainly not think of her as one of the five virgins to be remembered and worshipped in the morning! But the people who thought of her as one of the five virgins had no hesitation about it. Then, someone could have five husbands or five wives because polygamy was acceptable. To have many wives or many husbands was acceptable so there was no guilty conscience.

This conscience depends on the society. This is not the real, the true conscience; it has been implanted in you by the society. It is imposed from the outside. Truth has nothing to do with the purification of this conscience. The conscience about which this Upanishad is speaking is an inner sense, an inner voice.

All your senses are outgoing: you know outside things through them. The inner sense is that by which you can have an inner knowing, through which your consciousness is awakened. This state of inner knowing – which is called *vivek* and *pragya,* the intelligence to discriminate and wisdom – is the inner sense.

The methods for purifying the inner sense have nothing to do with following the conscience that has been given by society. Purification cannot happen by going *against* this conscience either. There is no need for you to get into unnecessary trouble by denying the norms of the society. There is no need to do this. One needs to compromise with the society, to create an arrangement to live in the society. When so many people believe in a certain thing, then to silently go along with them will create less trouble for you and you will be able to continue on your inner journey more easily. Otherwise there will be so much fight over small things and you will become stuck in the outer.

The seekers have accepted the beliefs of the society not because those beliefs are right, but because it allows them to move into their search more peacefully. Try to understand it rightly: mystics have accepted the social arrangement, the system, not because it is totally right – no social arrangement can be totally right. Until each individual is right there will be no way for the collective society to be right. Society is certainly wrong, and it will always be wrong. It is already too much just to hope that gradually it will become less and less wrong. Society is a crowd, and only the individual can be totally right. Just as water flows downward, in the same way, a crowd comes down to the level of its lowest person.

It is not important whether the concepts of society are correct or not: the seeker accepts them so that there should not be unnecessary troubles on the outside and he can continue on his inner journey more easily.

But this conscience is not the ultimate value. The true

conscience is the conscious energy within you that enables you to look within. You close your eyes and there is darkness inside, but even in that darkness there seems to be somebody there who knows it. You close your ears and you will hear the sound of silence within you, but in that silence too, somebody seems to be listening. The one who knows, who listens and sees within you is your real conscience, your inner sense. This inner sense has to be strengthened.

In the beginning, you will have only a very faint glimpse of it because you are so accustomed to looking on the outside that your eyes have become fixed on the outside. If you suddenly close your eyes you will not be able to see anything inside. It is just like when you enter a dark room after being outside in the sunlight: at first you will not be able to see anything, but if you sit for a while, soon your eyes will change their focus and will become adjusted to the darkness in the room. Then the darkness will seem to be less. Then as you go on sitting in the room and become more in tune with the darkness in the room, soon the room will seem to be growing light. Even in the darkest room, if you can just sit and wait patiently, after some time you will be able to see a little.

But you never sit in your dark inner room. Sometimes you close your eyes for only a few moments. People come and tell me, "You tell us, 'Look inside! Look inside!' but when we close our eyes we can't see anything." For many, many lives you have been looking on the outside, so when for the first time you look within after such a long time, you are sure to see only darkness. It does not mean that it is dark there: the light that you are accustomed to seeing is not there, it is a different kind of light. And much patience is needed to see that different kind of light.

If a seeker can sit with closed eyes for at least one hour a day and go on looking within – whether he sees anything or not – within three months he will start seeing some light inside. Only for one hour a day! But this much patience is needed – that he should not do anything else in this hour. But you have no patience at all. If someone sits with closed eyes for just two minutes, he says, "It is useless, there is nothing to see. I see no self or godliness inside. I could have used my time to listen to the radio or read the newspaper again."

You have no patience. And patience is the very soul for the inner journey. Patience is the soul in *any* endeavor. You only have to sit with closed eyes for one hour every day – whether something happens or not, it does not matter – and after a few days you will find that the darkness is not as dense as it seemed to be at first and a little light has started appearing. Looking for three months patiently, you will understand what the inner sense is.

*Antahkaran* is the name for that inner sense, the sense by which you are able to look within. *Karan* means sense, and *antah* means that which leads inward. All your other senses are going out; you don't use the sense that takes you in. And remember, any sense which is not used will by and by lose its capacity to function. If you bind your feet and you don't use them for a year, you will not be able to move them. Before, they could walk, but because they were not used for a year they will lose the capacity to move. Any sense or limb which is not used will become almost frozen. Usage is part of life; things can remain alive only when they are used. You have stopped using many things and they have become dead – and you have not used your inner sense for many lifetimes. This is the reason why great patience is needed. Feet that are not used for many days will have to be massaged and exercised before they can walk again. Slowly, slowly movement will return, blood circulation will come back and life will flow again. And this is exactly the condition of your inner sense.

Yama is saying to Nachiketa, "*...the pure, inner sense...*" The moment this inner sense becomes absolutely strong and is able to see without projecting, in this purity it will be able to see things clearly. The final stage of this purity is *brahmalok*, where you become divine. Then things will become as clear as when you are awake, not like in a dream or in a reflection. In *brahmalok* the truth is realized directly.

> *"The sense organs exist separately because of their separate functions. To be born and to die is their intrinsic nature. By knowing the nature of the soul to be different from these, the intelligent ones will go beyond grief."*

As your inner sense becomes more and more pure, you will experience that all the energy of the other senses has dissolved into the inner sense. As the inner sense becomes more awake, the energy of all the senses which had been flowing outward, which had been leaking uselessly from them, the totality of this energy will become available to the inner sense. And a moment comes when all the other senses pour their whole energy into the inner sense. Ears, eyes, tongue, nose – all their energy is absorbed in the inner sense. *Absorbing* means that the inner sense attains the capacity to smell, which normally belongs to the nose; the capacity of the eyes to see becomes available to the inner sense. Now scientists also agree with this in some other way.

Did you know that a blind man can hear better than you? This is why a blind man can become a better musician than you can. What is the reason for this? The energy of his eyes has become available to his ears, it is transferred to the ears. When the eyes are not working, then eighty percent of the energy of the body which was going out through the eyes is transferred to your other senses.

You become more tired from the misuse of your eyes than from anything else. New research in America has found that watching television is causing cancer, because watching television is so tiring to the eyes, like nothing else. There is a fear in America that the whole quality of life is becoming unhealthy because of television. It is driving the small children crazy because they go on watching it the whole day; whenever they have an opportunity they are glued to the television. They are not interested in playing or in going out, their whole interest is only in watching the television.

To use the energy of your eyes in this way can cause cancer. It is difficult to find a cure because it is not actually a disease: it is the exhaustion of the whole mechanism. The whole mechanism of the body becomes so tired that it starts wishing to die, it becomes suicidal. Each cell of the body starts wanting to die, and it is very difficult to bring these cells back to life. Nothing else can exhaust you as much as your eyes can.

A blind person's energy is not flowing out through the eyes, so the energy is transferred to the ears. Helen Keller was blind, deaf and dumb, so all her energy started flowing through her hands. Her hands became very sensitive; no one else on this earth had such sensitive hands. She did every type of work with her hands: she could read books with her hands; meeting with people, she would touch their faces with her hands. Once she had touched a person's face with her hands she would remember the face, the memory would remain in her hands. She could recognize the face by touching it even after ten years. All the energy of her senses had moved to her hands; touch became everything for her.

Scientists accept the fact that energies can be transferred. Energy can be used from one place by another place; the energy of one sense can be absorbed in another sense. But there is a very old concept of Yoga that within us there is a sixth sense in which all the energies of the five senses can be absorbed. The moment the sixth sense awakens and all the energies of the five senses are absorbed in it, the experiences of the inner begin.

And there is such a fragrance within that there is no way to know it or to experience it from the outside. There is such a *nad,* a soundless sound within that even the most beautiful music in the outer world is only a faraway echo of it. And there is such a light within that Kabir has said that the light inside is as if thousands of suns have risen at once.

Aurobindo used to say, "What I understood to be life before

I became awakened now seems like death. Now that I have known the inner life, now I can compare. What I thought was happiness then now seems to be utter misery. Now the inner bliss has blossomed, so I can compare and say that the outer happiness was really misery and nothing else."

Inner experience begins the moment the energy of all the senses is dissolved into the original inner sense. And this inner beauty, this inner fragrance, this inner taste is incomparable: the outer is just a shadow of it. Then the world of the outer loses all its charm. The mystics who appear to have renounced the world have in fact found the ultimate joy to be within themselves, hence everything in the outer world has become meaningless for them.

This is why I go on repeating that only ignorant people renounce the world. The wise never renounce, they attain to the highest – and after they have known the highest, the outer becomes simply meaningless. It is as if you are playing with pebbles and somebody gives you the Kohinoor diamond: by having the most precious diamond in your hand the pebbles will drop by themselves. There will be no need to explain to you that, "These are just stones, now renounce them." There will be no need to explain this to you. Those pebbles appeared to you like diamonds only because you had not known the real diamond. As soon as you have known the real diamond, you will recognize pebbles as pebbles because now you can compare.

The experiences of the inner sense will make all the happiness and pleasures of this world pale by comparison. Outer lovemaking is but a momentary pleasure; when the inner sense receives all that sexual energy, the bliss of the inner orgasm is indefinable.

The meeting of the inner man and the inner woman is represented by the image of *ardhanarishwar.* We have created the image of Shiva – half of it is man and half of it is woman. Nowhere else in the world except in India is there such a statue. This is an outer representation of the inner experience. And within each person there are the energies of both man and woman, and these energies can unite within. A man is not only a man and a woman is not only a woman, no – every man is half man and half woman and every woman is half woman and half man.

In this regard, the discovery of Karl Gustav Jung, a great psychologist of this century, is very important. Jung has proved that every person is both man and woman because everyone is born out of the union of a man and a woman, both parents have contributed. Whatever you are, you have a part of your father and a part of your mother.

So you are not totally a man or totally a woman: your father and your mother have both contributed. The difference is only of quantity: if your mother's contribution is more, then you will become a woman; if the contribution of the father is more, then you will become a man. But this is only a difference of quantity. If sixty percent is man and forty percent is woman, then you will be a man; if sixty percent is woman and forty percent man, you will become a woman. Sometimes there are also borderline cases, when it is almost fifty-fifty; then it becomes a case of "the third sex." Sometimes there are cases of fifty-one percent and forty-nine percent: then physically the man is a man but his behavior will be womanly, effeminate. A woman is biologically a woman but in her behavior she will be very male.

We don't know what was the balance of Durgawati, Joan of Arc or Laxmibai, but most probably the percentage of the male contribution was more in their physiology. "She fought like a man" is not only a poetic expression: if research is ever done it will be proved as a scientific fact.

But the society we are living in is male-dominated. If a woman wields a sword she is praised by saying of her, "How fantastic, she is so manly!" But if a man grows his hair long and dances gracefully like a woman, we call him impotent. In this male-dominated society it seems to be a great qualification just to be a man, but to be a woman is a crime. You condemn the man who grows his hair long and lives out his femininity and you praise a woman who wields a sword in battle. It is strange!

If a manly woman is praiseworthy, then why shouldn't an effeminate man be praised? Both of them have qualities: if one is to be condemned then the other should also be condemned. But the man praises himself and condemns the woman.

Society is ruled by men and men have done so much mischief that they have even been able to influence the woman's mind; women have also learned to agree with the thinking of men. Women will also say, "How great Laxmibai is, she is so manly!" but if they see an effeminate man they condemn him.

But every person has both male and female; humanity is bisexual. So sometimes it happens that suddenly a man becomes a woman just by a small change in his hormones due to some illness or some accidental injury, or a woman becomes a man. In England there have been such cases in the court where a man was married to a woman, but later on, after a few years he became a woman, so the court had to agree to a divorce. Then scientists investigated these occurrences more deeply and now they say that by surgery any man can be changed into a woman and vice versa.

A person is both man and woman. This is why the man in you is interested in the outer woman and the woman in you is interested in the outer man – but this interest in the outer woman or man will be finished as soon as you have met your inner woman or man.

The image of *ardhanarishwar* is half man, half woman: it is the symbol of the ultimate union that happens within. When the inner man and the inner woman meet within you, for the first time you become an individual. Nothing is divided inside; your contradictions, the opposites in you meet and merge together. A circle is created. The name for that circle, for that inner intercourse, is samadhi.

When the inner sense has the energy of all the outer senses, then within you there is a showering of bliss, a flow of nectar. Kabir says, "The rain of nectar is pouring everywhere and Kabir is bathed in it! Thousands of suns have risen and the light is so tremendous and so vast that it has no limits!"

The enlightened ones have always found it difficult to speak about what they have realized because whatsoever they say, they have to use the same marketplace language. The outside world appears so colorless, so pale that it becomes meaningless to use its language. Everything of the outer seems stale. And inside there is such a fresh, vibrant flow of life that to use ordinary words feels like it is doing an injustice to the inner experience.

That is why many enlightened ones have remained silent. If they have spoken at all, then they have created symbols or they have coined their own language. Scholars call the language of a Kabir, a Dadu, a Nanak *sadhukkadi,* the language of the mystics, because they have created their own language. They started creating words of their own.

Kabir has written *ulatbasiyan,* paradoxes, which are full of such outrageous contradictions in themselves that you cannot find any meaning in them. For example, Kabir has said, "A fish has climbed a tree." Now can a fish ever climb a tree? Or, "The river is on fire" – can a river catch fire? But Kabir is helpless. If he uses the language that you use, what he wants to say is so vast that it cannot be contained in that language. So he uses a paradoxical language which may shock you or surprise you; then you may become curious about understanding what he is saying. You may start asking, "What does it mean for a river to catch fire or for a fish to climb a tree?" You will feel bewildered.

This sort of language is shock treatment, a push which can destroy your old conceptions. Your old pattern of language will be very disturbed, but only then can something be indicated.

> *"By knowing the nature of the soul to be different from these, the intelligent ones will go beyond grief."*

There is no longer any cause for him to be miserable; he is utterly filled with bliss.

*"Mind is higher than the sense organs, intelligence is higher than the mind, the soul is higher than intelligence, the unmanifest energy is higher than the soul.*

*"But the ultimate reality, which is the all-pervading, the formless, is higher even than the unmanifest energy. The one who realizes this truth while living in the body, is liberated: he becomes the brahman, divine.*

*"The divine is the deathless. It is the very seat of bliss."*

When you return from within, back to the outer world of the senses, there are stopping points along the way. These same stopping points will also be there when you go from the outer to the inner. When consciousness comes down to the level of matter, it has many stops: it comes down step by step. When it rises again it climbs the same steps. The *sankhya* philosophy has described these stopping points very clearly – which is the first stop and how it is divided into three, then how it falls lower and lower, and at how many places the consciousness takes new forms before it comes down to the level of a body.

It is like when you heat water, or when you start to heat ice: when you heat ice it starts melting and becomes water; at a certain temperature ice becomes water. Then as you continue heating the water, at a certain temperature the water starts boiling, and when it reaches one hundred degrees Celsius it becomes vapor. If you want to make ice again then you will have to reverse the process: you will have to cool down the vapor by driving the heat out and it will turn into water; if you make the water colder, at a certain temperature it will become ice. You have to pass through the same degrees in a reverse process.

This sutra is describing the degrees along the inner journey. Mind is higher than the sense organs, so when the inner journey begins first of all the senses will be dissolved into mind. Intelligence is higher than the mind, so as you go in the mind will be dissolved into intelligence. The soul is higher than the intelligence, so the intelligence will be dissolved into the soul – and the unmanifest energy is higher than the soul.

We call this unmanifest energy *ishwar.* In our common language the name for the unmanifest energy is *ishwar*: it continues to work but remains unrevealed. *Ishwar* is the name for the active aspect of godliness.

*"But the ultimate reality, which is the all-pervading, the formless, is higher even than the unmanifest energy. The one who realizes this truth while living in the body is liberated; he becomes the brahman, divine. The divine is the deathless. It is the very seat of bliss."* Beyond the soul and the unmanifest energy is the ultimate, the formless. And this is the route to be traveled that goes back to the outer senses: the ultimate reality dissolves and becomes *ishwar*, the unmanifest energy; *ishwar* dissolves and becomes the soul; the soul dissolves and becomes intelligence; intelligence dissolves and becomes mind; mind dissolves and becomes the sense organs; the sense organs are the last stopping point. We have to return by the same route – one by one each layer has to be dissolved into the hidden energy behind it.

When there is nothing left to dissolve, when even the state of *ishwar* has dissolved, there is no other state beyond it. Then there is only a state of "no state" beyond it: the realization of the ultimate reality which the Upanishads have called the *brahman*. Buddha has called it nirvana and Mahavira has called it moksha.

One has to move within, from the senses to the ultimate reality. This is possible because in the same way that you have traveled out to the senses you can also return. If you can travel out to the senses you can return to the source from the senses.

It is just as you have come from your home to this Mount Abu camp and on the same route you will go back to your home; the path will be the same and you will be the same, but the first the path brought you to Mount Abu and now the same path will take you in the opposite direction. The difference will be only of a change in the direction. When you came here you were facing Mount Abu and when you return your back will be toward Mount Abu – that will be the only difference, everything else will be the same. Home will be the same and the way will be the same; you will be the same and the energy that walks on the path will be the same. Everything will be the same except for the direction. Coming here you were facing Mount Abu; returning, your back will be to Mount Abu.

Now you are facing the senses. The moment you turn your back to them, the journey toward home will begin.

And there can be no peace in man's life until he again finds his lost home.

Get ready for meditation.

# 15

# The Art of Effortlessness

*"The true nature of God is not seen as one sees sense objects; it cannot be seen with those eyes. When brought into one's meditation through persistent contemplation, it is seen by the pure intelligence of a clear and unwavering heart. The one who knows this to be so has gone beyond death.*

*"When the five senses and mind come to a stop and the intellect is also making no effort, this is the state that the sages have called paramgati, the ultimate state.*

*"When the senses have come to a harmonious standstill, this state is Yoga, union, because in this state there is no trace of unawareness within the meditator. But the state of Yoga rises and falls, hence the meditator must continue to strive to remain rooted in the state of Yoga.*

*"The true nature of God is not seen as one sees sense objects; it cannot be seen with those eyes. When brought into one's meditation through persistent contemplation, it is seen by the pure intelligence of a clear and unwavering heart. The one who knows this to be so has gone beyond death."*

The first thing to be understood: God is not a person. But all the religions have talked about it in such a way that people get a false impression that God is a person, a personality. If you believe that God is a person then naturally you will want to see him, to know him, to recognize him; you will want to be near him. But God is not a person. The idea that God is a person is only a poetic symbol. God is an energy, not a person. This is why you will not find him anywhere; there will never be a moment when you will meet with him face-to-face. So this sutra is saying that there is no way to see God directly because it is only people or things that can be seen directly.

This also needs to be understood: that when I say God is an energy, that energy is also unique. Electricity is also an energy, gravitation is also an energy – energy is all around. It is not enough just to say that God, godliness is an energy. Godliness is a subjective energy, it is not objective. There is an energy which can be seen and there is another energy which is hidden within the seer. It is not in the seen but in the seer. One is objective energy like electricity, which can be seen. And there is a subjective energy, the energy of the inner being, which can never be seen because it is within the seer. Or it will be better to say that we ourselves are that energy and that energy is everywhere. It is also outside, but to see it on the outside first you will have to experience it within yourself.

And to the person who has experienced that energy within himself, it becomes manifest everywhere. This whole universe becomes nothing but the manifestation of this light to one who sees this light within. But the first experience of it, the first realization, will be within. It is the innermost energy.

Hence the search for godliness is not an outer search. In this search it is not necessary to go to the Himalayas or to wander in the mountains of Tibet; Kashi and Prayag will not help either, nor will Girnar or Jerusalem. No outer search has anything to do with godliness; hence you will not find it in any temple or place of pilgrimage. And because of this, a difficulty arises: if it were in some temple, in some holy place on Mount Everest or on Kailash, you could easily go there. That would be very easy because the outer journey is not difficult at all, you can travel anywhere you want.

But in the search for godliness, the difficulty is that it is not at the end of the journey – it is present within the seeker from the very beginning. It is not a goal to be reached, it is the innermost core of the traveler. If you are searching for it on the outside you will not find it, exactly because of your outside searching. You are looking in the wrong place. If you want to search for it you will have to look within. If you want to search you will have to stop wandering to holy places and look within.

To seek godliness all the doors of the senses need to be closed because the more you search on the outside the farther away you will go from it. The more you think that it is outside you the more you will forget that it is within you.

Godliness is not a person, so there is no way to see it on the outside. Godliness is an energy. But that energy also is not material: it is subjective, it is your innermost energy. This is why the first realization of it happens only when you look within yourself.

You never remember to look within yourself. You wander everywhere, you search everywhere; your eyes, your ears, your hands don't leave any place unexplored. And everyone is not searching for godliness exactly: someone is searching for bliss, someone is searching for peace, someone else is searching for liberation. You may give it different names, but all these names are for the same search, the search for godliness. One thing is certain: everyone is searching, though the names for their search are different.

And there are only two alternatives: you can either search within yourself or you can search on the outside. These are the two dimensions. And the one who searches on the outside will go on wandering because even the first small glimpses will be happening from within. First it must be known within your innermost core of being. Because how can someone who cannot realize godliness within himself see it on the outside? If your inner flame is unlit, you can go on searching everywhere, and wherever you will go you will find only darkness because you are carrying it within yourself. You will not find the light. But if your inner flame is lit, you can go into deep darkness and there will be light because you carry your light within you. The search for godliness is a search into the depths of your own interiority, your own subjectivity.

This sutra says: *"The true nature of God is not seen as one sees sense objects; it is not seen with those eyes. When brought into one's meditation through persistent contemplation, it is seen by the pure intelligence of a clear and unwavering heart. The one who knows this to be so has gone beyond death."*

This has to be understood step by step. The first point: "*...through persistent contemplation...*" You know nothing about God. You don't have his address and you don't even know his name. You are not even sure about his existence. From where to begin this unknown journey? From where to lift the curtain? If you could have a clue to help you to unfold this mystery, it would become easy for you to begin the search.

It is as if a blind man is standing in a dark room, not even knowing in which direction the door is. If he had eyes he could find it, but he cannot see. And even if he had eyes it would still be difficult because it is very dark; he is not even certain if the door exists. The room may have walls all around it, like a prison – from where can this blind man begin? The blind man will start groping in the dark, and there will be many mistakes in his groping because he will not immediately find the door. His hands will touch the walls and there is the possibility that many times he can miss the door.

Contemplation is like groping in darkness. It means that you don't know anything, you are groping. You think, you ponder, you raise questions and try to find the solution, but it is all a groping. Ninety-nine times you will collide with the wall and only once will you confront the door. And the problem is that when you have collided with the wall ninety-nine times out of a hundred, you will become so accustomed to the wall that when you find the door you may not trust that it is really the door. You will have collided with the wall so many times that you may take the door also to be a wall.

And ninety-nine times out of a hundred, contemplation will lead to godlessness; only once will it take you to godliness. This needs to be understood: whosoever begins with contemplation will first become irreligious. At first he will confront the wall because the wall is big and the door is very small. Rarely does it happen that without first groping a seeker will immediately find the door in this life – only if he has been searching and groping for many lives. Otherwise, in the beginning, the search will lead to godlessness; first the seeker will become irreligious. So the person who is afraid of being an atheist will not be able to take even the first step.

This is why I don't consider godlessness to be the opposite of godliness: I consider it to be the first step toward it. I don't condemn the atheist: I totally support him because one who has never been an atheist will have no possibility of becoming religious. If you have become religious without first being an atheist, then your religiousness is just bogus, blind, pseudo. This religiousness will have no insight because the yes of one who is not courageous enough to say no will have no strength. His yes is just impotent. If someone has not sharpened his intelligence because of his fear of becoming an atheist, his theism will be of no value.

This is why a very strange phenomenon has happened in the world: the majority of the people do not sharpen their intelligence because they are afraid to be godless. They are afraid of thinking, and a theism that is afraid of thinking is useless. A theism that does not pass through contemplation will lead nowhere.

Thinking has no strength, and anything that can be destroyed just by thinking must be very weak. Logic has no weight, it is only a game of words. A religion that is afraid of logic has no foundation. It is like a house of cards which can fall down with just a small breeze of logic. Are you afraid? Does your trust waver? Then know well that you have missed the first step – you have not contemplated rightly.

Ninety-nine people out of a hundred are just pseudo-religious. Once in a while only one in a hundred will gather courage to be godless. It needs great courage to be godless, and this is so because the whole system, the whole society is with the theist; all the values of life are supporting theism and all your selfish motives are supported by theism.

Godlessness creates insecurity in you. The godless man is an outsider, he belongs to no one. He becomes an outcast, nobody's companion, nobody's friend. He is not part of any society. There is no society of atheists, no traditions: an atheist does not belong to any temple or church, Koran or Bible or creed. He is stuck in a vacuum, in an emptiness. One person out of a hundred gathers the courage to become an atheist; ninety-nine people are just pseudo-theists. But then the person who has gathered the courage to be an atheist becomes stuck being an atheist.

Atheism is not an end, it is the first step. As it is, it is like a person raising one foot and then remaining in that position. That is why an atheist becomes very restless. Compared to the atheist, the pseudo-theist is less restless, less disturbed, because he has both feet firmly on the ground. He has not yet lifted his foot, he has not yet started the journey; he has just accepted what has been told to him by others. He has blindly said yes to whatsoever has been said to him by his parents, his teachers, his family, his society. He has never pondered over anything; otherwise it would be difficult for him to say yes.

And this is why the whole society is against thinking. If a child in your family is a thinker, all of you try to stop him from arguing because arguing is rebellious. And one who thinks will not say yes to everything; it will be rare when he says yes. Mostly, he will say no. So society is not in favor of authentic thinking. This is why you destroy the ability of children to think for themselves. You try your best to destroy your children's intelligence, and you think that perhaps in this way you will be able to stop children from becoming atheists. On the contrary, you are stopping them from becoming authentically religious – they will become just pseudo-theists.

An authentic atheist is better than a pseudo-theist. But atheism is only the first step, it is not the end of the journey. And the one who stops after taking the first step will end up in great trouble.

This is why a godless person is very restless and anxious, his mind is never at peace. He is full of tension and anguish; life is meaningless for him. It must be so because without God this existence is meaningless. This existence can have meaning only with God. If there is no God then everything seems to be meaningless. Then you are just accidental, your birth is just a coincidence. There is no purpose in your existence and you are not going anywhere – you are just wandering aimlessly. And you *cannot* reach anywhere because then there is no destination, because only God can be the destination. So the person who becomes godless is very tense; he is in a difficulty. Every situation is difficult for him because it is very difficult to live by saying no to everything. Without a yes, there is no foundation to life. No just leaves you in a vacuum. No cannot bring happiness to anyone. No beauty, no bliss, no trust is created in life by denial. No is just a negation. No is the symbol of death, yes is the symbol of life – so the atheist is in a great difficulty.

But one who contemplates rightly will first become godless. Why? – because he will begin to doubt everything that he has been taught. First of all, all his beliefs and faiths will be shattered and only emptiness will be left. When this emptiness happens, understand that you have become free from the society. Contemplation is the method to make you free from the society. Whatsoever was taught to you has been erased; you become like a clean slate, a tabula rasa. Now if there is any meaning in existence, it can reveal itself on this clean slate. Whatsoever was written by others on this slate has been wiped off; now the slate is totally clean.

Godlessness is a very valuable experiment as long as it is not the end. Everyone should go through the fire of godlessness because godlessness cleanses you, shakes off all the dust. It frees you from borrowed knowledge – and it is essential to become free of borrowed knowledge before you can experience your own truth. First you have to get rid of other's teachings which are not your experience and then the real wisdom will awaken in you. Ignorance and borrowed knowledge, both need to be shaken off. You have read the Gita, the Koran, the Bible and you have heard about Krishna, Mohammed and Jesus. You have filled your mind with all this but you have no experience of your own. It is all borrowed and stale; it is just dead.

If you ask the Christian priests they will say, "Jesus has said this" – but if you ask him what *he* has to say, then he has nothing of his own to say. He can only repeat the Bible. Is he a man or a machine? If you ask a devotee of the Gita he will say, "Krishna says so." You should ask him, "What do *you* say? For what do *you* exist? Are you Krishna's gramophone record, 'His Master's Voice'?" Then there would be no need for anyone to be born after Krishna; then existence just unnecessarily goes on creating more people.

Remember, there is no repetition in existence. Existence never creates the same person again, there are no carbon copies. Existence is not an ordinary creator – it creates each person as unique. There is no end to its art. Only those whose art reaches to a dead end will repeat the same thing.

Godliness, the energy of this vast existence, creates new waves every moment. It does not repeat a Krishna again. That is why Krishna is not born again nor is Buddha born again. Otherwise, existence would have thought, "What is the need to create you when great people like Krishna and Buddha have already been created?" Existence would have created assembly lines of Krishnas and Buddhas, just like the rows of cars produced in a factory. But existence does not like to repeat a Krishna, it likes to create *you!* Certainly it has some purpose in creating you, something is to be fulfilled through you. If you go on imitating Krishna then you are becoming an obstacle in that purpose.

Every person is unique. Nobody like you has existed before and nobody will be like you again. So if you are imitating someone, repeating someone, you are missing a great opportunity.

Pundits and scholars become just like parrots: they go on repeating, they repeat what they have memorized. And these things have no connection with their being. The Gita, the Koran or the Bible; Mohammed, Krishna or Mahavira – they are all very nice people, but they cannot be repeated. There is no need to be like them. And anyway, you cannot be like them just by repeating their words. Mahavira was born twenty-five centuries ago: in this time thousands of people have repeated his words like parrots but none of them could become a Mahavira. It is not possible.

Mahavira never repeated anyone else – that is why he could be Mahavira. Krishna never repeated anyone else's words – that is why he could be Krishna. Jesus has not quoted anything from the old scriptures: he has said what he has known; that is why he could be Jesus. And you want to become like them by repeating their words?

A person who is caught up in repeating will lose the capacity to think on his own. Intelligence is born out of the search for your own truth. One who accepts the truth of others does not search, and the one who does not search does not need to think. Why should he think? All doors inside the one who does not think or contemplate become closed. He does not even grope: only walls are left around him and he goes on sitting in his prison.

It is possible that sitting in the prison, he may start thinking that there is no prison, that all prisons are maya, illusions – but this will not give him freedom. He will still be sitting in his prison and he will not experience the breeze at all, the open sky and the light which is outside the prison. He can close his eyes and go on repeating, "The prison is my illusion and I am not in bondage." But if the prison is really an illusion and you are not in bondage, then what is the need to repeat this? Get up and walk out of it! But the walls are everywhere, and to walk out, the door first needs to be found.

This sutra says "*...through persistent contemplation...*" If you go on inquiring and contemplating you will first be rid of all your borrowed knowledge; you will become free of scriptures and gurus. You will be left with emptiness inside: you will become godless. The attitude of denial will be born: "This is not it, that is not it." If you become afraid in this phase, you will go on clinging to your borrowed God – and one who goes on clinging to a borrowed God will be in misery.

You need courage to move a little further. If God *is,* then it cannot be destroyed just by your inquiry and contemplation. If God *is,* then it can certainly be realized through contemplation. If you have not realized it then it only means that you have not yet thought so totally that you go beyond thinking. God is experienced the moment contemplation reaches to its very climax. The first ray of godliness will descend on the summit of contemplation. The reality of existence is a virgin realization that happens at the highest peaks of contemplation. It is not the consequence of blind faith but of your reaching to the very pinnacle of contemplation.

One who fearlessly goes on contemplating without any hesitation, ready for any consequences – if it shatters the tradition, let it, if it proves the scriptures wrong, so be it; no matter what is shattered, let it be shattered, he will go on contemplating. On the day he becomes free from all that is borrowed, then suddenly his eyes will become crystal clear. Whereas before this he was not able to perceive godliness, he will have the first glimpse, the first perception.

The authentic theist is a great inquirer, an intensely contemplative person. He has reached to the very climax of thinking. He has thought to such an extent that he has even gone beyond thinking. He has followed thinking to the very end where finally thinking has dropped and he has gone beyond it.

The first glimpse, the first conviction of godliness will happen through contemplation. It is not the experience, it is only a glimpse, just a conviction that godliness is. And the one who stops at this glimpse will never enter godliness; he will never experience it. This first glimpse is needed but it is not enough.

*"When brought into one's meditation through persistent contemplation, it is seen by the pure intelligence of a clear and unwavering heart."* This first glimpse has to be transformed into meditation. This first glimpse needs to be remembered and nurtured continuously. While awake or asleep, this glimpse needs to be continuously nourished just like a mother nourishes the child in her womb. She is very careful: walking or working, this remembrance continues in her that she is pregnant, a new life is growing within her which should not be harmed. The one who has had a glimpse of godliness has to take great care of it.

Kabir has said that it is just like when women in a village fetch water from the river and carry the pitchers on their heads – they go on laughing and gossiping as they walk back home, but every moment they are aware of the pitchers on their heads; they keep a balance so that the pitchers don't fall down. They go on walking, gossiping, singing, but their inner attention is unwavering, it is constantly on the pitcher. Some inner current of remembrance takes care of the pitcher. Kabir and Nanak call this remembrance *surati*. *Surati* is the changed version of Buddha's word *smriti*. Buddha has used the word *smriti* – mindfulness, remembrance – a constant awareness of one's true nature. One can forget everything else but this mindfulness should not be forgotten. Kabir, Dadu and Nanak have called this *surati*, the remembrance that is always there.

The ancient sages have told a very meaningful story:

A seeker met many saints but his quest was not satisfied anywhere. Finally, the last master told him to go and meet Emperor Janak. But the seeker said, "When I could not get anything from all these saints that I have visited, then what can I get from this materialistic king?"

The master said, "Even still, go. If you did not get anything from all the saints, then you might as well try this hedonistic king also. Perhaps..."

When he arrived at the palace, it was evening. Janak was sitting with his friends, gossiping and drinking. There was music and beautiful, young girls were dancing all around. The seeker was very disappointed and felt that he had come to the wrong place. He was about to leave when Janak stopped him and said, "Don't leave so soon. A seeker should have some patience."

The seeker felt that since he had come, it would be better to stay at least for one night. And it was not easy to go back into the jungle at night; he could leave in the morning. He felt that there was no way to ask anything: "This man cannot give me any understanding. He himself is drowning in ignorance – how can he help me to awaken?" But he stayed for the night.

After dinner the king took him to a room and told him to rest there. It was a beautifully decorated room for special guests. There were very comfortable mattresses, the atmosphere was very pleasant, the room was fragrant. But as soon as he lay down on the bed he became afraid because there was a naked sword over his bed hanging from the ceiling on a very thin thread. He became very afraid because that sword could fall down at any moment. He thought, "Is this any way to welcome a guest? Does he want to kill me? This sword can fall at any moment. Only a thin thread is holding it. A little breeze..."

He tried hard to sleep but he could not sleep the whole night. He went on tossing and turning in the bed and looking at the sword. He could not sleep the whole night!

The king came in the morning and asked him, "Did you sleep well last night?"

He said, "How could I? What kind of hospitality is this? That sword is hanging above me from the ceiling tied with a thin thread! It was impossible to sleep because all the time I was remembering that sword."

The king said, "A sword is also hanging over my head all the time. You cannot see it, but I see it. It is the sword of death. I may be drinking, I may be surrounded by dancing girls or I may be listening to music, but I never forget that sword hanging over my head. You could not sleep for one night, but I have not slept for my whole life. Since I have realized that death is a certainty it has become impossible for me to be asleep."

When there is a continuous current of awareness within, it is called meditation. There is a constant remembrance happening within. When you have a glimpse of godliness through contemplation, when you get a clear perception of the reality of existence, when a feeling of yes replaces the no, then taking care of this feeling is called meditation.

*"When brought into one's meditation through persistent contemplation, it is seen by the pure intelligence of a clear and unwavering heart."* The one who is constantly aware of godliness just as a pregnant woman is aware of her womb, will succeed in realizing godliness through his pure intelligence and his clear, unwavering heart.

This meditation will bear fruit only if you continuously take care to remember godliness. It can also be any other remembrance – the object of remembrance does not matter – but the essential thing is your constant remembrance. You can be mindful of your breath for twenty-four hours a day, the breath coming in and going out.

Buddha has given much importance to this method. He has called it Anapanasati yoga, the yoga of remembering the breath coming in and going out, coming in and going out… You have to be constantly mindful of your breathing, and he says that then it does not matter whether or not you remember godliness. If you can remember to watch your breathing then your awareness will grow – and this awareness will transform your life. As soon as your awareness grows, the grip of all desires in your life will lose their hold on you.

You can understand it by doing a small experiment. When you get angry, don't do anything with the anger: immediately close your eyes, inhale deeply and watch the breath. Breathe deeply seven times, watching the breath going in and coming out. Do this seven times. Then open your eyes and look for the anger – you will be surprised that the anger has vanished. Your remembrance and your awareness of the seven deep breaths have made the anger simply dissolve.

When sexual desire arises, breathe deeply seven times and see – you will find that the sexual urge has disappeared from your body. Such small experiments will help you to understand that as your remembrance is awakened, your desires will become weaker. As awareness goes on growing the hold of desires in the mind will shrink and your heart will become pure. If you want to get rid of anything, don't fight with it: instead, remember to watch your breathing.

In Japan they teach little children that whenever they become angry, to take a deep breath. In the whole world, Japan is the least angry country; the smile that you see on the faces of Japanese people is not seen in other countries. A Japanese is a very balanced and self-disciplined person – if you abuse a Japanese he will not get angry. But anywhere else in the world people will react with anger. Now this grace is also disappearing in Japan because of the Western influence, but there are still some of these qualities in the Japanese personality.

An American traveler has written that he went to Japan for the first time nearly thirty years ago. When he walked out of the Tokyo airport he saw two men fighting. They were not fighting physically but they were abusing each other, showing fists and making faces as if they were going to kill each other. A big crowd had gathered around to watch these two men. This went on for some time. He also stood there and watched. He simply could not understand what was going on: "When they are getting ready to fight, then why don't they start?" They would only move very close to each other and again move back.

So he asked someone what was going on: "They are making so much noise and fuss and taking so long just to get ready to fight. The whole thing could have been finished by now. And what are you people doing just standing and watching?"

The man said, "We are waiting to see who is going to be defeated first" – but defeat meant who will get angry first. "Both of them are trying to make the other one angry first, but neither of them is angry yet. The one who gets angry first will be the loser. Only then will the crowd disperse. And the one who loses control will have no prestige anymore. There is no need to physically fight; the question is of who will get angry first. Both of them are still in control and they are simply trying to provoke each other with abuses. The crowd will disperse as soon as one of them gets angry and attacks – then he is defeated. It is not a question of who wins. The question is: Who will be defeated by getting angry first?"

Japan has also done some very profound experiments with breathing. And the most important experiment is that whenever some desire passes through the mind, to start breathing deeply. Not only do you have to breathe deeply, you also have to breathe with awareness: the breath goes in, the breath goes out – and you are aware. Soon you will find that the desire has disappeared. There was no need to suppress it or fight with it, no effort was made to get rid of it; the consciousness has simply moved somewhere else. When consciousness is withdrawn from desire, the contact is broken. When the mind is diverted the support is taken away. When the attention is not given the energy which you were giving to the desire is withdrawn; as a result, the desire will vanish.

Desires remain alive because of your support. A person who masters any type of remembrance, his heart will become pure and his intelligence will become clean. His power of discrimination will become sharp and clear. Godliness is experienced only in a consciousness with a discriminating intelligence and a pure heart, a consciousness that has mastered a constant remembrance.

*"The one who knows this to be so has gone beyond death."* And once you know that God is hidden within you, you will be beyond death. Now there is no death for you. There was no death even before, but you had been thinking that you will die so you were anxious and afraid. But the experience of godliness is the experience of immortality, the experience of the deathless.

> *"When the five senses and mind come to a stop and the intellect is also making no effort, this is the state that the sages have called paramgati, the ultimate state."*

When all activity stops within you and there is no ripple of activity in the body, in the senses or in the mind; all activity has stopped, you have become drowned in stillness; nothing is happening, only you *are;* you are not doing anything, only your being is – this state of the unmoving, silent mind, this state of an unwavering flame of consciousness is called by the yogis *paramgati.* It is very interesting that when all *gati,* which also means all movements, cease, it is called *paramgati,* the ultimate state.

And the state where all movement, all activity is happening is called *durgati,* the state of misfortune and misery. Everything is active – the eyes, the ears and the mind are all active. All the senses are active and they are each functioning separately, on their own. Your state is like that of a bullock cart with the oxen going in all directions, with all the oxen pulling the cart in different directions – that bullock cart will not reach anywhere; its screws and bolts will just become loose. The stronger ox will pull the cart in one direction, but when he becomes tired another ox will pull it in another direction. In the end you will be almost in the same state as you were in the beginning, when you were born; nothing has moved.

A dying man is usually in the same state, the state of *durgati*, as when he was born – which is really a condition to be pitied. For all the sixty, seventy or eighty years of his life his senses went on pulling him in different directions. It seems as if he has traveled much but he has not reached anywhere.

This movement of the senses, this state of activity, is your restlessness. People want to become peaceful, people want to be blissful but they don't understand this subtle sutra, this secret: that inactivity is the nature of bliss and activity is the nature of misery.

So whatsoever is achieved through effort will bring misery. And whatsoever comes effortlessly will bring bliss because what you get through your doing is not your real nature. You don't need to do anything to achieve your nature. You don't need to do anything to achieve that which you already are.

Godliness is your very nature – it is not something that you have to do something to attain. You are already that: you have only to know this. You have only to uncover it: there is a curtain which has to be pulled open, there is a layer which has to be removed. There is something hidden within you which has to be brought out. It is like a spring which is hidden under a rock: as soon as the rock is removed the stream will flow. You don't have to go anywhere to get to the spring, you just have to remove the obstacle. *Sat-chit-anand* – truth, consciousness and bliss – are hidden in the very nature of man. To attain it, no activity is needed. That is why all the great yogis of the world have taught non-doing: they say that you should arrive at a state where you are not doing anything.

The meditation which I am teaching you involves tremendous activity. So the question arises, "If I have to learn non-doing, why take deep breaths? Why jump and dance? Why scream and shout? Why all this doing and effort?" In non-doing is meditation, but I am asking you to do so much because you are so full of activity that you cannot be inactive unless you are exhausted, unless you have thrown out all your activity. It is necessary to first exhaust your activity. When you are so completely exhausted that you yourself will feel that you don't want to do anything…

Just my telling you not to do any activity will not help. Even if you make your body inactive, your mind will go on being active because the energy which had been going into the body will be diverted to the mind. This is why I say to bring your activity to such a peak that your every cell will start shouting, "Stop!" Your body will ask you to stop and even your mind will be so exhausted that it will ask for rest. And when your whole being asks for a rest, only then will meditation happen.

So the first three stages are not the stages of meditation, they are the preparations for meditation. The fourth stage is meditation – when I say, "Stop!" and you become absolutely inactive.

I have done all kinds of experiments with many, many types of people, and I have observed that if I asked people to stop and be still from the very beginning, they were not able to stop. When I asked them to relax right from the very beginning, hardly any of them could relax; at the most, five to seven percent of people could relax. I tried to understand why people could not relax; they understood what I was saying but they could not do it.

The reason is that there is a certain momentum in the body, just as when someone is cycling and he pedals to get moving. The cycle cannot run without pedaling. And if a person has been pedaling for ten miles and he suddenly stops pedaling, then the cycle will go on for another half mile because of the momentum. Pedaling for ten miles, the wheels of the cycle have accumulated momentum because of the speed, so the cycle can go on for half a mile more without any pedaling. But if it is on a downward slope then it becomes even more difficult to stop – and most people are on a downward slope.

Nobody is going uphill, all are going downhill. They have gathered so much momentum through so many lives that even if they stop outwardly it will not make any difference, the movement will go on automatically – the cycle will keep on running. If they suddenly brake with force, instead of coming to a halt, more is the possibility that the cycle may overturn because of the momentum. You cannot put a brake to a cycle that is moving very fast. If you do then certainly you will be thrown over. That much movement cannot be stopped all at once.

So I felt that when people are full of so much movement and activity, it is necessary for them to throw it out and go through some catharsis. When I was teaching people to do silent meditation, only five to seven percent of the people could enter it. Now I try first to create a tension in you, I put you into activity. Now I find that instead of seven percent, seventy percent are able to relax. For the thirty percent that cannot relax, it is because of the fact that they are not participating totally in the activity; they are doing it halfheartedly. If they can get into the movement totally, then when I say "stop" their whole energy will be longing to stop. They will stop completely. And if everything stops completely even for a moment – all the senses, the body and the mind – then in that moment your tuning can happen; the window can open and you can have a glimpse. It is like a flash of lightning in the darkness.

When you switch on the radio some tuning is needed. If the dial on the radio is not set, if it is loose or unsteady, several stations will come through at the same time. Many people's minds are catching many stations at the same time so they cannot feel what is going on inside them. Is it the news from a newspaper, or is it some music or some drama that is happening? If an amplifier can be attached to your head and what is going on in your head could be heard on the outside…

Scientists say that very soon this will be possible because this research is almost complete. Some scientists who have done research on the brain have started making graphs of it. Just like the graph of a cardiogram showing the heartbeat, the blood circulation and the electricity of the body, in the same way, graphs of the brain are also made. Electrodes are fixed on the head and they go on making a graph on a paper that shows the movement of electricity in your brain, whether it is going fast or slow.

From that movement it can be understood how much disturbance is in the brain, how much silence, how much restlessness, what is going on in the brain. When you are sleeping at night a graph can be made of your brain activity during the whole night that shows when you were dreaming and when you were not dreaming, because when you are dreaming the needle moves very fast and when you don't dream the graph indicates space.

Scientists say that sooner or later it will be possible to amplify the brain: whatsoever is going on inside your head can be heard on the outside. You will feel that everybody has gone mad! Many stations are switched on at the same time and you will be shocked to hear what is going on in you. But you have become habituated to it. This madness goes on boiling in you and it can reach to a hundred degrees at any moment.

So there is not much qualitative difference between an insane person and a sane person; the difference is only of degrees. You are at ninety-nine degrees, someone else is at ninety-eight degrees, someone else is at a hundred degrees and some courageous person has reached a hundred and one degrees and he is in the madhouse. The difference is very little: just a little push and you will also land there. You may go bankrupt or your wife may die, or any shock of this sort: one degree more and you will land in the madhouse. The distance between the inside and the outside of a madhouse is not more than one inch.

This state of turmoil in the mind, this activity which is going on with great intensity within you and is making each and every nerve and cell of your brain very tense, stretched in tension – when all this turmoil stops, the yogis say it is called *paramgati*, the ultimate state. That is the moment of samadhi, enlightenment, when everything stops and you have arrived home.

To get anything in the outside world one has to walk, and the one who runs will get it sooner. People who walk slowly will lose in the competition of the world. But the person who goes fast, who can push others aside and use their heads as a stepladder, will achieve something. In the outer world one reaches to a goal by running, but in the inner world you can arrive only by stopping. Only the one who knows the art of stopping, and has actually stopped, will arrive.

"When the five senses and the mind come to a stop and the intellect also makes no effort..." When intellect does not make any effort, when there is no effort within you...

Try to understand the meaning of the word *effort*. What is effort? Whenever you want to get something you make an effort to get it, whatsoever you may want to achieve. It may be samadhi, enlightenment, or it may be moksha, liberation; it may be money or position or it may be anything, but if you want to achieve anything you will have to make an effort.

All the yogis of the world are saying that to know godliness, no effort has to be made. One has simply to relax into a state of effortlessness. It is like swimming in the river: if the river is big and turbulent and the struggle is hard, then even the one who knows how to swim will drown. He will get tired and drown. Actually, the more he tries to swim the sooner he will become tired and drown. It is an interesting thing that the one who swims, the one who struggles, the one who makes all the effort drowns, but as soon as he dies his body floats to the surface of the river. The living person drowns, goes under the water, and the dead person comes up.

A river is very strange, the rules of a river are very strange – it drowns the alive person and allows the dead man to float. The dead man who cannot swim starts to float and the alive person drowns. Certainly the dead must know some art which the living don't know. The dead must know some secret – the secret of being effortless. The dead man does not make any effort.

It will be good to understand this: you drown in a river not because of the river but because of your effort. If you can relax like a corpse then no river can drown you. But you cannot be like a corpse because you are alive, and you will do something or other. You are afraid that if you relax like a corpse the river will drown you. You become afraid so you do something or other. And you know that no river ever drowns a corpse, the corpse floats on the river. So why do you drown? –

you drown because of your struggle and effort.

There are whirlpools in rivers and people get caught in the whirlpools. And the art of getting out of a whirlpool is that one should never try to get out of the whirlpool. Those who know the art of swimming say that if you get caught in a whirlpool the only way to be saved is to become one with the whirlpool. If it pulls you down, go down with it because the whirlpool is big on the surface, but as it goes deeper its circles become smaller and smaller. Deep down it becomes so small that it cannot hold you. But if you try to fight then you will get exhausted at the very beginning and you will be dead by the time you have gone deeper.

The technique of swimming says that if you get caught in a whirlpool, never try to get out of it. Just relax and go down with it and you will be thrown out of it. So the one who tries to save himself from the whirlpool drowns and one who goes with it is saved. A corpse floats on the river and an alive person drowns.

Those who want to know godliness have to learn the art of effortlessness. No effort is needed here. One has to remain in a state of non-doing. But you will not let go of doing as long as you want to achieve something, as long as you want to become something. This is why I say that the basic principle of religiousness is that religion is desirelessness; it is not an object of desire. If you turn to religion with some desire, you are not going toward religion. You are still wandering in the world. You have changed the name of your world and have put a new label on your destination, but still your expectation continues. And one who goes on asking may get everything but he will not know godliness.

Yama is telling Nachiketa, "Be effortless, where your intellect makes no effort." And effort will disappear only when desire has ceased.

But people's minds are so strange that I am surprised. People come to me and ask me, "How can I become silent?" I tell them, "If you give up desire you will become silent." They come back again and ask, "How can we become desireless?"

They have made desirelessness their object of desire; now they are asking for some method to become desireless. They want to become desireless because desire creates misery and desirelessness is bliss, so they desire to be desireless. They could not understand, they have missed the whole point.

Desirelessness means that you don't desire anything – you don't even desire to be desireless. Even desirelessness is not your demand anymore, that now you don't desire anything. When a person is in such a state of desirelessness, he is in tune with existence. One moment of desirelessness, and bliss showers. The needle on the radio dial is tuned to the right station so the other stations disappear. When the needle on the dial is tuned into desirelessness, you become tuned into godliness, you are connected with existence, you are on the same wavelength as existence. If this can happen even for a moment, the path will become clear. But don't think that because it has happened once then that is the end. The next sutra will clarify this point.

> *"When the senses have come to a harmonious standstill, this state is Yoga, union, because in this state there is no trace of unawareness within the meditator."*

When your consciousness is in tune with existence, you are dissolved. Your ego disappears and godliness fills you. All at once the ocean falls into the drop. The drop is completely merged with the ocean and disappears; it is not to be found anymore.

> *"But the state of Yoga rises and falls, hence the meditator must strive to remain rooted in the state of Yoga."*

One should not think that if the phenomenon has happened once, if a glimpse has happened once, then what is the need to do anything more? The tuning will be disturbed many times even though the first glimpse has happened. That first glimpse is only the beginning.

In Japan, the Zen masters call this first glimpse satori. Satori is not samadhi, enlightenment; it is the first glimpse of samadhi. Life will become blissful. The old in you will disappear and the new will be born. You will be a new person – but this is not the end. This tuning, this glimpse brings so much bliss, but as long as the needle of intellect is there it will keep on wavering. There will always be situations that will upset this tuning; many times you will miss the right tuning. Hence, to be continuously in tune, one has to continue to be in the state of non-doing, effortlessly going into meditation again and again.

Then a moment will come when the needle itself will dissolve. It will no longer be there to waver; the mind has disappeared. Kabir has called it the state of no-mind. And when mind has disappeared there is no longer need for any discipline to be practiced.

Kabir continued to weave cloth even after his enlightenment. He would go to the market to sell the cloth and his disciples would tell him, "Why are you doing this? You have attained the ultimate state of wisdom. Now you should spend all your time in spiritual practice." Kabir said, "Now there is no one left inside to practice anything. The one who had practiced is no more." So Kabir has said, *"Sahaj samadhi bhali"*: natural samadhi is right. "Now the moment has come when my samadhi continues whether or not I do anything. I may stand, or sit, or work, or not work – samadhi is undisturbed. Samadhi has become my natural state of being."

Until samadhi becomes his natural state of being, the seeker will have to continuously practice non-doing and effortless merging in meditation.

*"When the senses have come to a harmonious standstill, this state is Yoga, union. because in this state there is no trace of unawareness within the meditator. But the state of Yoga rises and falls, hence the meditator must continue to strive to remain rooted in the state of Yoga."* Many people start meditating many times and give up again and again, but this giving up so often is a

waste of time and energy. If you have started meditating, then it has to be continued. It has to be hammered continuously. This continuous hammering will one day completely break the rock which is between you and the ultimate truth.

And before this happens you will have many glimpses – but don't be satisfied with glimpses. Many people are satisfied only with glimpses, but the path to the whole vast experience will become closed to one who is satisfied with glimpses. Don't be so easily satisfied! Don't be satisfied until your meditation becomes natural and spontaneous, like breathing. Your meditation should continue even when you are asleep. You might be doing things but your meditation should continue, nothing should disturb your meditation. Until this state has happened, the search will need to be continued without a break.

But many times people give up and then start their search all over again. The result is as futile as what Jalaluddin Rumi has observed…

One day Jalaluddin took his disciples to a field and told them, "Look at the art of this farmer." There were eight big pits in the field, and a ninth one was being dug – the whole field was ruined.

Even the disciples could not understand what was going on, so they asked the farmer and he said, "A well is being dug."

They said, "But this whole field is becoming a well and not a single pit has any water in it."

The farmer said, "We dug down to eight feet with one, but there was no water so we gave up. Then we started to dig another well, and we dug down to ten feet but we gave up because there was no water. Some time later we tried a third place, but still no water. So we went on digging pits one after the other and now the ninth pit is being dug."

Rumi said to his disciples, "Understand this man, because he is the perfect representative of people on this earth: they dig a little and think there is no water, so they give up. After a few years they dig again at another place, and again at a third place. If this man had continued digging in one place then he would have been sure to find water at deeper levels. But the way he is digging, his whole field will be ruined and he will never find any water."

So once you have started digging, go on digging. Leaving it again and again and then digging at different places will bring disastrous results. Continue to meditate: water is definitely inside. If water has come in the well of Buddha and in the well of Krishna, then it will also come in your well. You are born with all the potentialities that Buddha and Krishna were born with – the only difference is that you have not dug your well rightly, or if you have dug it, you have dug it in many different places.

The source of water is within you, but continuous digging will be needed. Go on digging. First you will come across stones, then it will be dry earth, and then, slowly, slowly, the wet earth will appear. When you start feeling silence in your meditation, know that you have reached to the wet earth. Now don't stop, because silence is the first fragrance of bliss. The earth is wet so the water must be nearby.

A silent mind is an indication that the source of bliss is not very far away. A little more effort, a little more devotion and a little more patience and waiting are needed, and the source of water will certainly burst forth.

Now get ready for meditation.

# 16

# A Trusting Heart

*"The ultimate reality cannot be known through speech, through mind or through the eyes. Who but the one who says, 'it is' can know it?*

*"One must first be rooted in the trust that it is. Then one must allow this reality to become ever more refined. To the meditator who embraces this trust in the reality of godliness, the true nature of godliness will be effortlessly revealed in the purity of his heart.*

*"When all desires in the heart of the seeker are dissolved at the root, the seeker will become immortal. He will know godliness, the ultimate reality, to be here.*

*"When all the knots in the heart are completely untied, the seeker will become immortal in his present body. This is the eternal teaching."*

This sutra is about God, godliness, the ultimate reality. It is very subtle and very profound. It must be so because the ultimate reality is itself the ultimate depth, there is nothing deeper than it. There is nothing before it, there is nothing after it and there is nothing beyond it. Nothing can transcend it. So naturally, whatsoever can be said about it will have to be as deep and as infinite as the ultimate reality itself.

There was a wonderful Christian sage named Tertullian. Before we enter this sutra, one of his statements is worth understanding. He has said, "I trust in the existence of God because it cannot be proved by logic." It is a very contradictory statement. Usually you believe in the existence of something which can be proved by some logic. But Tertullian says that he believes in the reality of God because it is beyond logic, it cannot be proved by any argument.

The fact is that there is nothing more unbelievable than godliness because even to imagine it, even to conceive of it, is almost impossible. All efforts to figure it out prove to be futile. In this search, finally, along the way, the seeker himself will dissolve. It is an effort to enter the impossible.

Tertullian says, "I believe in God because God is absurd. It is illogical and beyond imagining. God cannot be proved in any way – that is why I believe in him." Then what is the basis for his belief? If the basis is not logic or thinking or contemplation, then the basis of belief can only be the heart.

It is like when you fall in love with someone – there is no logic or reason for it. If someone wants to argue with you, you will not be able to give any logical reasons for it and whatever reasons you may give will be meaningless. For example, you may say that the person you love is very beautiful – but that person does not look beautiful to others, only to you. The reality is quite the opposite: you don't love the person because he or she is beautiful, the person looks beautiful because you love them. It is your love which makes the person beautiful. Beauty is not an objective phenomenon, it is the feeling of your heart. You don't love the beautiful, whoever you love becomes beautiful. Love gives beauty to everything.

The one who is surrounded by love becomes beautiful. This is why the beloved looks beautiful only to the lover and to anyone else she may not look beautiful. No argument will prove the reason for your love. And whatever reasons you may give are only invented by you later on. First love happens, then you think, you try to rationalize and give reasons for it. But has anyone ever fallen in love with mathematical calculations, that first he thinks about everything, settles all the pros and cons, gives reasons and thinks about the end result? A person first falls in love and then later on finds reasons, so the reasons which are found later on cannot be the real reasons or they would also have been there from the beginning.

The phenomenon of love is not the result of logic, it is a happening of the heart. "Happening of the heart" means that you can experience it but you cannot explain it. Your whole being says, "Yes, it is," but you cannot make anyone else understand it. No answer can be given for it, but still you will be ready to die for it. The happening of the heart means that you are ready to die for something that you cannot explain. If you are ready to lose your life for something, then that something is certainly more valuable to you than your life. Love possesses you, but still you cannot give any reason for it. But a logician will not give his life for anything because no one would sacrifice his life just for some syllogism, for some process of logic.

Galileo was the first to say that the Earth goes around the Sun, that the Sun does not go around the Earth. This was a logical conclusion and was absolutely correct, but Christianity opposed it. Rome was against it and the whole network of Christianity around the world was not ready to accept Galileo's discovery, because it is written in the Bible that the Sun goes around the Earth. People around the world had been believing that the Sun goes around the Earth – and it does seem to be that way. The Sun rises in the East in the morning and sets in the West in the evening and then again it rises in the East: the Sun seems to be going around the Earth. Even after Galileo, all the languages of the world have continued using the same words, *sunrise* and *sunset*. But the Sun neither rises nor sets, only the Earth turns. The Sun stays where it is, it does not rise or set and the Earth goes around it.

When Galileo said this for the first time he proved it logically, but the Pope summoned him and told him, "You had better ask for forgiveness, otherwise your life is finished." So Galileo had to kneel down and ask for forgiveness.

This has been a very difficult thing to understand, and intelligent people since then have been wondering: did a genius like Galileo become afraid of losing his life? But I think that Galileo was not afraid of losing his life, he could have given his life – but why should one be ready to sacrifice his life for such a trivial reason? What difference does it make whether the Earth goes around the Sun or the Sun goes around the Earth? Why should Galileo have sacrificed his life over such a stupid thing?

This discovery of Galileo's was not from his heart, it was from his head. He must have realized, "Why should I lose my life over whether the Earth goes around the Sun or not?" I know that Galileo was a wise man. If he had been a stupid man he would have been ready to die – because only a stupid person will die for logic. Logic doesn't have much value. Why should one sacrifice his life just for a mathematical conclusion? Life is much more valuable than this.

But a man can give up his life even for a little love. Love possesses the total being and logic catches hold of only a small part of the intellect. Nobody has sacrificed life for the sake of an argument. And if you cannot sacrifice life for something, it means that the thing is not more valuable than life. From many experiences in life, love is the only experience for which a person can sacrifice his life. Love is more valuable than life, but love is illogical.

People have given their lives for God. Many people have become martyrs for God, they have quietly given their lives. They didn't hesitate for a moment to give their lives because, for them, God is love.

This is why Tertullian says, "There is no logical reason to believe that there is a God, impossible to believe, but still I believe God is." This has something to do with the heart. This is a kind of love affair. This conviction is arising from some depth which is far beyond the intellect.

Now we will enter the sutra.

> *"The ultimate reality cannot be known through speech, through mind or through the eyes."*

*The ultimate reality cannot be known through speech...* You can try your best to explain it but it cannot be understood through words. You may explain it very skillfully, very explicitly; you may appeal to the mind in such a way that it cannot be argued against and people will have to agree with you because they have no argument. Still, their hearts will remain unconvinced; someone may defeat your intellect but he cannot touch your heart. A great logician may destroy all your beliefs, you may be defeated, but even then your heart may not agree. The heart will go on saying, "I don't agree." The heart cannot be convinced by logic. Logic can be defeated or it can be victorious, but the heart cannot be convinced in this way. The trust of the heart cannot be created through logic.

Robert G. Ingersoll has written somewhere in his letters that you can convince a person by logic only when he is already ready to agree. Logic is useless. A person can be convinced only when he was ready to be convinced. You cannot appeal to anyone through logic who is not ready to agree. Logic is shallow, it does not enter the depth of life.

What can speaking do? At the most it can argue, it can entertain, it can be appealing, it can be poetic, it can give you pleasure – but the jump to the realization of the ultimate reality cannot be caused by speaking. There have been many great speakers, and it is not because they did not know the truth; they did, but even then they could not convince anyone to take the jump.

Even Buddha cannot convince you through words. To convince you, to create trust in you for the jump, even Buddha has to first prepare you through silence. He makes you silent, calm and quiet before he starts speaking to you; he cannot prove it through words. That is why Buddha was very clear on this point: he would never just answer people's questions. He would say, "Before I answer, you will have to learn to be silent. Sit silently near me for two or three years and when your silence is total, then I will answer you." But it always happened that when a person's silence was total he would never ask any questions – Buddha had answered him in that silence.

What cannot be said with words can be transmitted in silence. Because silence does not enter the mind, it goes straight to the heart. Words just collide with the head and come back again. Silence, the stream of life flowing through silence, enters your heart without any obstacles. At the most, words are helpful to convince you to be silent; that is their utility. Words can do this much: they can help you to become wordless. Then the work of words is over.

But godliness cannot be attained through words, "*...through mind or through the eyes.*" Mind thinks; the process of thinking is called mind. When you think, ponder, contemplate, that process is called mind. But you have to understand this aspect of thinking clearly: you can think only about that which you already know. How can you think about something that you don't know? You can think only about the known. How can you think about that which is not known to you? Thinking is like chewing: as cows and buffaloes eat grass and then go on chewing the cud, so mind also goes on chewing over thoughts. It goes on thinking about that which has already been fed into it, that which is already known to it.

Mind has no relationship with the unknown. It is also not possible, because how can you think about something which you don't know? In a sense thinking is repetition: it is stale, it is never fresh. Thinking is always returning to the past. Thinking is a repetition of memory: whatsoever is in memory is rechewed. But godliness is unknown, you don't know anything about it – how can you think about it? That is why godliness can never have any relation with the mind. As long as the mind is there you are disconnected from godliness; the moment the mind is dissolved you become one with godliness. Mind is the wall, the barrier between you and the ultimate reality.

People come and tell me, "We don't feel like meditating. Our minds don't feel like meditating." I tell them, "Mind will never want to meditate because mind is the enemy of meditation. Mind will find many excuses not to meditate. It will say, 'What are you doing? This is madness! What will happen to you by being silent? If you don't think then you will be lost! It is not right to get caught in these things – protect your rationality, your intellect.'"

Mind will give a thousand and one reasons for not meditating because meditation is the death of mind. Mind dies when you meditate, so the mind will try to protect itself in all possible ways. Your mind finds so many excuses not to meditate. Sometimes these excuses are so trivial and insignificant that one wonders how they could stop a person from meditating.

It is quite natural for the mind to stop you from meditating because it knows that meditation means entering an abyss, and the mind will not return unscathed. Actually, it will simply not survive the journey of meditation. Zen masters call meditation "the state of no-mind."

This sutra is also saying the same thing: the ultimate reality cannot be attained through mind or speech or eyes. You can go on searching through the senses, but the senses can only come into contact with the material. Every sense has its own limit: the eyes can see but cannot hear, the ears can hear but cannot see. But if someone tries to listen with his eyes then he will be in difficulty. The limitation of eyes is that they can see, the limitation of ears is that they can hear, the limitation of the hand is that it can touch and the limit of the nose is that it can smell. One sense can only do one job, it cannot do the work of another sense.

The work of mind is to think, to ponder. Mind can repeat what has been stored in its memory: mind is like a computer, you have to feed it beforehand. First you give it food and then it goes on chewing on it. Now there are amazing computers that can work better than a human mind. What would take years for the most efficient scientist to do a computer can do in seconds. But the difficulty with a computer is that first you have to feed it with data; if you don't feed it then it cannot do anything.

Mind also has to be fed. Suppose you are a Hindu: what is the meaning of being a Hindu? It means that the Hindu religion has been fed into your mind, it means nothing more than that. You are a Jaina or a Christian or a Buddhist – what does it mean? It only means that in your childhood the Jaina religion has been fed into your computer and it goes on thinking only in that way. The Hindu religion has been put into somebody's computer and the Christian religion has been put into someone else's and the person goes on thinking, goes on chewing on the same information and thinks that he is a Hindu or a Christian. Actually he is none of these things. Man is simply born as a human being, everything else has been fed into his mind.

Mind is created by the society. If you are born in a Hindu family but from your very childhood you are left in a Mohammedan family and brought up there, then you will be a Mohammedan, not a Hindu. Then you will bow down to the Koran and you might even feel like burning the Gita. From where do all these ideas come? Others are teaching you all these things. This is why all the religions catch hold of children from a very young age. All the religions want to give religious instructions to young children because once a child escapes from religious teaching, then it will be very difficult to teach him later on. Before the age of seven, when the child's understanding is not yet awakened, everything needs to be filled in his mind. Then he will go on chewing it for his whole life.

If you are a Hindu you will automatically bow down in front of a Hindu temple. This is just mechanical, this is the working of your computer. You have been taught that God lives in this temple. But when you pass by a mosque you will pass by without paying any attention to it. It will not occur to you at all that God is also living there. But someone else will think that God is in the mosque because it has been fed into his computer that Islam is the only true religion.

You are being taught and you go on thinking what is taught to you – but God cannot be taught, there is no way to teach it. This is why you cannot think about God. You might think that someone can think about God, but no: a Hindu thinks about a Hindu God, a Mohammedan thinks about a Mohammedan God, a Christian thinks about a Christian God. And there is no Christian God, no Hindu God; these are just words which have been fed into your mind.

God is beyond words. It is the very existence itself. Nobody can teach it to you, there can be no education for it. This is why there cannot be any school where children can be taught godliness. If it were so easy the whole world would be full of divinity. Science can be taught but religion cannot be taught, this is the difficulty. This is why we can train scientists who can teach physics, chemistry and mathematics, but prayerfulness cannot be taught. But you do teach prayers and this is why all prayers become false.

Love cannot be taught. You can open a school and train people to learn how to love, and if you succeed in it then one thing is certain: those people will never be able to love because love is a thing of the heart and learning happens in the intellect.

This is why often it happens that actors who are professional lovers can never really love. Their love life is very miserable. I know many of them very closely. Whenever actors come to me with their problems it is mostly about their love lives – and people are learning about love from them! They have become experts in acting; they know when and what should be done in the drama and they go on behaving in the same way with their lovers or beloveds. But that is just acting, the heart is not involved. They are experts in acting: they know what should be said, how to sit, how to stand and how to embrace the lover. They know all these techniques, but love is not a technique. Love is absolutely non-technical: it is the opening of the heart.

Tolstoy has written a small story about three saints who lived by the side of a lake. All three were uneducated, but they became very famous and people started coming from faraway distances to see them.

The highest priest of Russia also heard that three holy men were living across the lake but he said, "I don't know them at all and they have never been initiated into the church. How can they be holy men?" But thousands of people were going to see them and were feeling blessed, so he also went to check out the situation.

He went across the lake by boat. The three men were uneducated, rustic; they were sitting under a tree. When the high priest reached there they bowed down to him and touched his feet. The high priest felt reassured that they presented no danger to Christianity.

He asked them, "What do you do? What is your prayer? How do you say it?"

They started looking at each other. The priest asked, "Why don't you speak? What do you say?"

They said, "We don't know much, we are uneducated, nobody has taught us anything. We just say a small prayer." With much hesitation they said, "We ourselves have created a prayer. No one has taught us anything, we have not learned it from anyone."

The priest was feeling very important. He asked, "What is your prayer?" but he thought, "They are *really* rustic."

They humbly replied, "It is such a small prayer that we feel shy to say it. We have heard that God is a trinity, so we have made our own prayer."

Christians believe in the trinity: God the father, his son Jesus, and in between, the Holy Ghost. Just as we in India believe in the trimurti: Shankara, Vishnu and Brahma.

They said, "After some contemplation we have created this

prayer: 'You are three, we are also three – have mercy on us.'"

The priest shouted, "Stop this! Do you call this a prayer? Prayer must be authorized by the church. It has to be accepted by the church, so I will teach you how to pray. You have to remember it and start this new prayer from today on."

They said, "You are so kind – please teach us." So he taught them a long prayer of the church.

They said, "Excuse us, we are uneducated. We will not be able to remember such a long prayer, so please make it a little shorter and more simple."

The priest said, "It can neither be shortened nor simplified. This is the authentic prayer, and for those who do not say this prayer the gates of heaven will remain closed."

Then they asked him to repeat it one more time so they could remember it. The priest repeated the prayer, but they asked the priest to repeat it again one more time. They tried to repeat it and they bowed down to the priest and thanked him. The priest, feeling very happy, went back to the boat.

While he was returning in the boat he saw something like a whirlwind following him on the water. He became afraid because he could not understand what was happening. But soon it became clear that all three men were coming, running over the water. The priest was stunned – they were walking on the water! They went near and grabbed hold of the priest and said, "Please repeat the prayer one more time – we have forgotten it. We are poor and uneducated people!"

The priest said, "You please forgive me, because your own prayer is the right one. You should continue with it: 'You are three, we are also three – have mercy on us.'"

Love is a happening of the heart. There is no organized system for it. There is no method, no mantra, no technique for it. Love is a feeling of the heart. Prayerfulness is also a feeling of the heart – there is no way to teach prayerfulness. People are becoming irreligious because all the religions on earth are trying to teach it and nobody can become religious through teaching. That is why this sutra says: *"The ultimate reality cannot be known through speech, through mind or through the eyes."* The eyes have no capacity to see the invisible. They are made to see the visible, and the ultimate reality is not visible. Mind is not capable of understanding the unknown. The known is its limit and the ultimate reality is unknown. Words cannot express that which is known in silence. Words can express only what is known through words and the ultimate reality is known only in silence.

The second part of the sutra is really amazing:

*"Who but the one who says, 'it is' can know it?"*

One who can easily say, "it is" – not only say it but also experience that it is; one whose heart says, "it is," without any reason, without any logic, without any proof from the senses, without any thinking in the mind, without any learning through words – who else but such a one can know it?

But how can one reach to this state? The phenomenon becomes very difficult because if one feels: "it is," then it is simple, but if one does not feel this then what is to be done?

Nothing can be done positively, something can only be done negatively. If you feel: "it is," if such a trust has been born in you, if you feel its existence and your heart is throbbing with "it is," then it is okay – then the path is very easy.

But if you don't feel godliness this way… Only one person in a hundred thousand can feel it so easily. Most people don't feel the existence of godliness; this is why they try to find arguments and proofs for it. They look for guides and gurus who can tell them or prove that it is and who can show them the path.

People come to me and say, "Show us God." They want me to put it in their hands and say, "This is it, see it, take it" – as if God is a thing. They say, "Unless you show it to us we will not believe it." Then it is very difficult. They say, "Unless you show us…" and all the scriptures say that you cannot experience it unless you trust; just a belief of the mind is not enough to experience it. There are great scholars in this world who believe with their minds, but even they cannot experience it. Only the one who has a trusting heart…

Then what is to be done? Those who can trust, trust. So let's forget about them; they are not to be taken into account, they are the exceptions. But most people cannot trust. So what can be done about them? Should logical arguments be given to them to prove that godliness exists? All the arguments that have been given until now have proved useless because no argument can prove anything, and a non-trusting mind can refute all arguments.

If argument is the criterion for victory, then certainly the non-trusting person will win and the trusting one will lose. In life it is trust that wins, but in an argument it is doubt, mistrust, that always wins.

No trusting person has ever been able to defeat a doubter in an argument. You will be surprised to know this. People who trust don't say this, but I am telling you that no trusting person has ever won an argument against a doubter. He cannot win because his trust is beyond logic – how can he win? The doubter can prove that the ultimate reality does not exist because all your arguments based on trust can be refuted.

The arguments of all the theists in the world are old, conventional, outdated; there is nothing new in them. Their main argument is that there must be someone who has created this world. But then the atheist can argue, "If everything must be created, then who has created God?" Then the trouble begins because then there must be another God above God. Then it is an infinite regression and there is no end to it.

You can reach any conclusion and the atheist will always ask the same question: "Who created it?" If you say that the universe needs a creator but God does not need a creator, the atheist will argue that if God does not need any creator then why can't the world also exist without a creator? This argument is very obvious: if you believe that there is something which is uncreated, then what is the problem in accepting that this world also is uncreated? The theist seems to be very dishonest: he says that God is not created, but for the world he does not apply the same rule; he is using a double standard.

But the atheist says that this world is visible. And if you cannot do without a principle, then it is better to have this principle: that the world is also uncreated. Your God is invisible, so what is the need to drag him into the matter? And since you do accept that God is an uncreated phenomenon – which proves that uncreated phenomena are possible in the first place – so why can't this world also exist without a creator? The theist has no answer to this.

The fact is that a real theist, an authentic theist, religious person, does not try to argue. It is only the scholars pretending to be theists who go on arguing about the existence of God, and they go on being defeated by the atheists and the materialists. No so-called theist can ever defeat an atheist. Logic is meaningful only to the materialist, not to the real theist. The real spiritual person has no relationship to logic. And if you try to fight in someone else's territory you are bound to be defeated.

But in real life the man of trust wins and the man of doubt loses. Not a single atheist has attained to the realization of a Gautam Buddha, not a single atheist could experience the grace of a Mahavira, not a single atheist could know the compassion of a Jesus, not a single atheist could dance like a Krishna. In life the atheist is defeated, but he cannot be defeated intellectually because there he is far ahead. Now the question is: what is to be gained even if you win this argument?

People come to me and I tell them, "I have no objection to your being an atheist. But what are you getting out of being an atheist? I want to know this. If you are getting great peace or great bliss or some other unique experience, then even I will pray that your atheism should grow. Then you are on the right path and you should go on moving on it."

But they say, "No, there is no bliss, there is no peace. Life is full of misery and anguish – but still, there is no God." I tell them, "Think it over. Maybe your life is a misery because of your denial of godliness. Because for those who have trusted its existence, their life is full of bliss. Now it is up to you to decide whether you want logic or bliss in your life. Do you want to have joy in your life or some mathematical principle? If you are satisfied with this mathematical principle then it is perfectly okay to go on believing that there is no divine. But if this brings no satisfaction to you then you will have to seek and search for it. You will have to transform yourself so that you will be able to feel its presence."

Then what is the path? What is the way out for people who cannot easily experience godliness? The first thing is that they should not focus on mind and logic, they should focus on life: they should concern themselves with what they are attaining in their lives.

If a thirsty man is standing on the bank of a river, you tell him to drink water from the river and then his thirst will be quenched. But if instead of drinking the water he wants to know the logic: "How can water quench my thirst? What is the proof for it? Water is made of hydrogen and oxygen and neither hydrogen nor oxygen can quench my thirst. When neither of these two can quench my thirst then how can the mixture of the two quench my thirst? And from where does the capacity to quench thirst come? No, you are mistaken, you are under some illusion." This man will die of thirst standing there on the bank of the river! His logic is right, but if people were to drink water only after satisfying their arguments then they would all have died of thirst long before.

But people don't care about logic when they are thirsty, they just drink water and quench their thirst. They say, "We are not concerned about the logic of how the thirst is quenched, we are only concerned with quenching the thirst. It does not matter which element in the water quenches the thirst, we only know that the thirst is quenched by drinking water."

You should worry about your own life, which is full of anguish, misery and pain. The man who is living a life that is full of godliness has become free of anguish, misery and pain – his life is full of music, dance, a fragrance. If that fragrance and music can become an attraction to you, only then can the atheistic, doubting approach in your life start to disappear and the feeling of the existence of godliness, of "it is" arise.

To me an atheist is suicidal. He is suicidal because he is denying himself all that will allow the flower of his life to bloom – and the whole history of mankind is the proof of this. In life, the greatest atheist is defeated by the most insignificant theist.

A great thinker and atheist like Bertrand Russell is nothing compared to Ramakrishna. Yes, in logic Ramakrishna Paramhansa will certainly be defeated by Bertrand Russell. No argument will convince Russell and he can refute everything that Ramakrishna proposes – but this is not the important thing at all. If Ramakrishna and Russell were to stand side by side, then Russell's life would seem to be colorless. There is no juice flowing in it, there is only a deep sadness in it. There is a radiance, a cheerfulness and a special energy in Ramakrishna which seems to come from some greater source.

If we consider only the intellect, then atheism and doubt are meaningful. But if we are looking at life, then very soon we will arrive at the feeling that godliness is – and you should always consider life first.

A young woman wanted to take sannyas two days ago, but she was hesitating; she was in two minds about whether or not to take sannyas. Everyone is in two minds, split. People are always hesitant to take a new step.

I told that young woman, "You have lived without sannyas for twenty-five years. If you don't take sannyas then you will remain as you are. You have the experience of twenty-five years without sannyas but you have no experience of sannyas. Sannyas is a new door. There is a possibility of something happening there. At the most, nothing will happen – but even now nothing is happening. The worst is that nothing will happen, but nothing has happened in these twenty-five years anyway so there is nothing to lose! But there is a possibility and a hope of something happening by taking this new step. And to hesitate to change a path on which nothing has happened until now is absolutely foolish. If something had happened then there would be no question about choosing the new path; then you should continue with the old path. But if nothing has happened then you should have the courage to change for the new."

But people go on with the old path without giving a single thought to the fact that nothing has happened on it. People are walking on old, well-trodden paths not only for twenty-five years, but maybe for twenty-five lifetimes – and nothing has happened. You are listening to your mind for many lifetimes; now you are wasting this life also for the sake of intellect and mind. You should move away from this path and also try out the dense forest paths which are not of the mind.

The paths of the intellect are well-paved. They are straight and paved and there are milestones on them. You can be certain of where you are standing, where you are going and from where you are coming. But to either side of these paths there are dense forests of life where springs of water are hidden; fragrant flowers and the songs of birds. These paths are not paved or straight and there are many dangers and much to fear; there is none of the security of the known and paved path. There are no crowds there which have always been with you before. There you are alone, but there is the possibility of an opening into the depths of life. There is the fear of getting lost, but there is also the possibility of arriving because no one has ever arrived by traveling on a paved path.

The paved path is neat and clean and you can walk on it comfortably; the crowd is always with you so there is no fear and you are never lonely – but that path will not take you anywhere because it is circular. It goes around a few times and comes back to the same point from whence it began. You don't add anything to your life by following it. A person who begins to realize this about life will soon reach to the state where, without any reasoning, without any argument, without any proof, he can say "it is."

> *"Who but the one who says 'it is' can know it?*
>
> *"One must first be rooted in the trust that it is. Then one must allow this reality to become ever more refined."*

First there should be a heartfelt feeling that godliness is and then the fragrance of this divine reality will start transforming your life. It should pull you, it should become your love. Only then something can happen, only then can transformation happen. Then you can stake your whole life on it. Again, a small glimpse – then you can gamble and accept the challenge. You are then ready to live your life according to it, you are ready to dissolve yourself into it.

But the feeling: "it is," and the first glimpse of it, are possible only for those who live life in its totality and who don't give importance only to the intellect. They watch their own lives – is there misery or is there bliss?

In fact, you can take misery and bliss as the touchstones; go on checking on it. If there is misery in your life, then whatsoever path you are following is wrong; it does not matter if logically it is right or wrong. If your life is miserable then whatsoever you are thinking, your whole pattern of thinking, is wrong. You are on the wrong track. If there is bliss in your life then I say that whatsoever path you are following is right without even asking you about it – because bliss is the consequence of a right path and misery is the consequence of a wrong path.

Western thinkers like Sartre say that life is misery. Buddha has also said that life is misery – but Buddha has said this with a different intention. He has said that the life *which you are living* is misery, the way you are living is misery, and you can wake up and reach to a point where life is no longer a misery. Sartre's words are the same as Buddha's – that life is misery – but Buddha's purpose is totally different.

Sartre says that life is misery, that there is no way to change it and there is nothing beyond it; this is all that life is, this is the be-all and end-all of it, there is nothing beyond it, misery is existential. But why does Sartre emphasize so much that misery is existential? Only one's own life can be the criteria: you cannot enter another person's life, but you know your own life. If my own life is misery, then I will apply this to all; I will generalize it and say that all of life is misery.

All your statements come out of your individual experience, but you expand it and generalize it for everyone. If my life is miserable then I will assume that the whole world is in misery.

A miserable person sees misery everywhere. Even the moon in the sky will seem to be sad. When there is misery within you, you will feel surrounded by pain, by misery, by suffering. But Sartre never thought that he was wrong to think that life is anguish and misery. We have seen that Krishna's life is not anguish, we have seen that Buddha's life is not anguish. We have seen that Lao Tzu's life did not have even a distant echo of misery, it was pure bliss. Among us there have lived a few people who were in utter bliss – but Sartre will say that they are in an illusion. It is very interesting that Sartre is not ready to believe that his own anguish could be his illusion, but he thinks that Krishna's bliss is an illusion.

But I tell you that even if misery is real, even then it is worth exchanging it for an illusory bliss. What is the point of clinging to real misery? Even if the bliss is illusory, it is still worth choosing it. And once someone chooses bliss then he will know that it is the misery that is illusory and not the bliss. But this is possible only through experience; without experience there is no way.

*"One must first be rooted in the trust that it is. Then one must allow this reality to become ever more refined. To the*

> *meditator who embraces this trust in the reality of godliness, the true nature of godliness will effortlessly be revealed in the purity of his heart."*

After the first happening, slowly, slowly the second phenomenon will happen by itself. But if there is no seed, how can the tree grow? Without sowing any seed people wait for it to sprout and become a tree with flowers and fruits. And when there are no fruits they cry and weep that there is no tree – but they have never sown the seed, and without sowing it they are waiting for the tree to grow.

An atheist is like the person who waits to see the ultimate reality of life without sowing the seed. A theist is more scientific in this: first he sows the seed and then he waits. He takes care of the seed and one day his waiting brings fruits. It will take time for the seed to break and sprout and grow, but one who has sown the seed can go on waiting, howsoever long it may take. But if the seed has been sown then there is a hope and a possibility that it may become a tree.

The seed is this feeling that godliness is – you sow this feeling and take care of it because there is much disturbance all around for it. Someone may put a stone on it and it will be difficult for it to sprout; someone may prevent it from being watered and then it will not grow. Even if it grows, animals are all around and can eat it so a fence has to be put around it.

This feeling of "it is" has to be taken care of in the same way as you take care of a seed. There is danger all around. Anyone can say, "What are you doing? – there is no such thing as godliness!" And you also don't know so the feeling is very fragile, anyone can destroy it. If you hear someone speaking very loudly you also become convinced that he must be right.

The founder of the university where I studied was a world-famous advocate, Dr. Harisingh Gaur. He used to tell his students to always carry their large reference law books to court because the magistrate would feel intimidated looking at them and the other advocates would also become a little afraid. He would say, "You will also feel more courageous if you have these books with you. If your client's case is according to law, then try to prove your point by quoting the law books as much as possible. Instead of trying to prove that your client is right, you should just argue by reading out quotations from the law books."

His students used to ask, "Suppose our client is wrong according to the law, then what should we do?"

He would say, "Then you should speak as loudly as possible and bang on the table with all your strength, because your attitude and your banging will create an impression that you are right. A man in the wrong will speak hesitantly: he is afraid, his voice will quiver."

Be aware that in life there are many people around whose attitude thumps on the table when they speak: they speak so loudly that you become stunned. And you think that they must be right because they are speaking so loudly. Your sprout is very small, or maybe you have just sown the seed in the earth and someone says, "There is no such thing as godliness." Then you dig in the earth and start looking to see if the seed you have sown is actually there or if you are under some illusion. But if you dig the earth up again and again to look for the seed, it will not be able to sprout.

There are people all around you and you should not be concerned with what they are saying. Just see what they are, then they will not be able to harm you. Don't just listen to what they say – look into their lives, don't be worried about their words. Then nobody can harm you, your seed will be safe.

People who have not sown any seed have no fear: they move around fearlessly because they don't have anything worth protecting. But one who has sown the seed has to be a little bit cautious; he has to be committed to sitting near the seed and taking care of it. This is why in the beginning he may even feel that he is not so free to move around. He has to wait and care for it. Be aware of people who wander around and say anything they want without any fear; they have not sown anything, they can afford to wander around. They don't have anything to protect and they also have nothing to lose.

A man of trust must be continuously aware of the delicate flow of life that is sprouting in his heart – he has to take care that it is not destroyed. Trivial gossip can destroy it just as if the gossip were stones. And many people around you are very much interested in destruction: they feel powerful when they destroy something. People who have not known anything go on saying all sorts of things.

If someone starts meditating, then anyone from his family or any one of his friends or acquaintances, or even a stranger, can say that there is no value in meditation – as if they have ever meditated, as if they have experienced meditation. If someone says anything about meditation, find out how much he has meditated. You don't usually just accept what others say about many things in life, but about meditation you believe them without any question.

If a person says that a certain medicine is not right for an illness then you immediately ask him, "What qualification do you have? Are you a doctor, an MD, an MBBS, an ayurvedic doctor, a *hakim*, a homeopath?" and if he says, "No, I don't have any degrees; there is no need for me to study for those degrees, but I know that this medicine is not going to help," then you know that there is no need to listen to this man. But even if a fool says something about meditation you immediately start wavering and thinking, "Maybe I am doing something stupid." You don't ask him whether he has ever meditated or not.

Buddha has told his bhikkus, his disciples, again and again that if they want to find something out about meditation, they should always ask only meditators; otherwise they can be led astray. In this world people are so egoistic that no one is ready to accept that he does not know but everyone is eager to give advice.

Only one thing is available for free on this earth, and that is advice. Whether you ask for it or not, people are always ready to give you free advice. It is available in abundance. They even go to your house and knock at your door to give their advice. But you never ask if the person who is advising you has experienced anything, from what source is he speaking – how deep is his meditation, how deep is his love, how much has he experienced the reality of existence? So don't listen to what people say: you should first consider their state of being.

> *"When all desires in the heart of the seeker are dissolved at the root, the seeker will become immortal. He will know godliness, the ultimate reality, to be here.*
>
> *"When all the knots in the heart are completely untied, the seeker will become immortal in his present body. This is the eternal teaching."*

There are two things to be understood. First, the seeker becomes immortal when all the desires in his heart are destroyed from their very roots. Why? Why does a mortal being become immortal by the disappearance of desires? There is a reason for it.

Man, by his very nature, is immortal: only desire is mortal, only desires die. Being never dies, only desires die. But when the desires die you feel that *you* are dying, that *you* are finished. You are so full of desires that you don't know yourself to be anything other than your desires.

There was a great thinker in Bengal. His name was Ishwarchandra Vidyasagar. He has written a memoir. Ishwarchandra was a great scholar so the viceroy's council wanted to honor him. But he used to wear a dhoti and a kurta, like an ordinary, poor Bengali – he was a simple man. His friends told him that it would be disrespectful and would not look proper if he went to the viceroy's council dressed like that, so they arranged for better clothes worthy of the occasion. They said that one should be dressed grandly when one presents himself before the viceroy.

Ishwarchandra agreed to this and he also felt it was right, but in his heart of hearts he was a little worried about changing his dress just to receive the honor. He thought that he would look ridiculous all dressed up, standing there before the viceroy, but he could not gather the courage to speak out. He went for an evening walk the day before he was to go to the viceroy's council. He was very worried about the next day.

Just by his side a Mohammedan gentleman dressed up in *sherwani* and holding a cane in his hand was walking slowly and gracefully. A servant came running to the Mohammedan and said, "Mir Sahib, your house is on fire! Come quickly!" He said, "Okay," but his pace of walking remained the same.

Ishwarchandra was surprised to see this and wondered whether he had heard the right message or not.

The servant also became nervous and said, "Mir Sahib, this will not do, please walk faster! The house is on fire!"

The Mohammedan gentleman said, "There is no reason for me to hurry until and unless *I* am on fire. The house is on fire, but I am not burning. And why should I change my lifelong pace just because my house is burning? And why are you so upset? Is anything of yours burning?"

Even Ishwarchandra became troubled, although nothing of his was burning. The other fellow at least was a servant in that house. His heart started beating fast even though he had nothing to do with the house. He was amazed about this man. Just then a thought came: "This man is not ready to change his pace in spite of his house being on fire, and I have agreed to change my clothes unnecessarily."

The next day he went to the viceroy in his usual poor clothes. His friends were surprised to see him like that. Later on they asked him why he had not changed his clothes and he said, "That man changed my life – his house was on fire and he did not change his pace of walking. He said, 'Unless I am on fire, nothing matters. There is no need to hurry.'"

Your desires die, you do not die. But you are so identified with your desires. Your house is on fire, not you – but you are so much attached to your house that you feel that you are burning. And then you really burn…

Desires are mortal. When a man is dying his fear is not of death, because he can never die; he is afraid that all of his desires are dying, all his hopes are being shattered and whatever he had planned for the future will now be impossible to fulfill. Whatever he has arranged for in the past to bear fruits in the future, all those trees are crumbling down. Now everything is finished.

This sutra is right in saying that the seeker becomes immortal when all his desires disappear. The seeker is already immortal, but his attachment to the desires gives him the illusion that he is mortal. Whoever you are, you become caught in the illusion by being identified with it.

When does desire die? Desire cannot die unless the trust in the reality of godliness first arises within you. Desires exist in you because essentially you want to have bliss in your life – and there is no bliss in your life as it is. What is desire? Desire is your search for bliss, your dreams, your ambition for bliss. And life is full of misery, hence desire.

This misery has to be dropped, and misery can be dropped in two ways. The first is that you try to fulfill your desires in the hope that your misery will disappear – but this is an illusion. In fact your misery never disappears. This is the way of the materialist. The materialist believes that his misery will disappear through the fulfillment of his desires. But the way of religiousness is that desires will disappear when you attain to bliss. Try to understand this. The argument of the materialist is that he will find bliss when he fulfills his desires; the argument of the religious man is that when he has known bliss his desires will disappear. The man of religion feels that if there is bliss within him then his desires will disappear; desires were there only because misery was there.

If within yourself you find what you have desired, then naturally desire will disappear. If you find what you have been searching for within you, then why would you search on the outside? You follow a path because the goal is somewhere else, there, where you have to reach. But no one has ever reached any goal by following his desires. Whenever anyone has found anything, it has always been within himself.

As this feeling of remembrance of godliness, the feeling of the existence of godliness, that it is, becomes deeper and deeper and as your bliss grows, your desires will go on disappearing. And with the disappearance of desire, death also will disappear.

*"When all the knots in the heart are completely untied, the seeker will become immortal in his present body. This is the eternal teaching."* This is the second thing: when all the knots in the heart are completely undone… Indian seers have always compared the heart to a flower. Usually your heart is like a closed bud which has not yet opened – and the way you are living, perhaps it will never open. It has become almost dead. Perhaps the petals have lost their capacity, or there is not enough juice in the flower to open the petals, or there is not enough light for the flower to open. It is lifeless, it is withering.

In Yoga they have talked about the two states of all the chakras, or energy centers. The chakras of an ordinary person who is full of desires are like a withered bud hanging upside down and the branch is also hanging downward because of the withered bud. This is the state of the ordinary, worldly man's energy centers.

These buds become fresh and alive again as the energy rises upward and as the vital energy starts circulating in your tree of life. These buds become alive and throbbing. The direction of the flower's growth changes and the energy that is moving upward starts opening the petals of the bud. And one day all the flowers of life blossom within you.

As long as your life energy is flowing downward your buds

will remain just buds. When the energy moves upward then the buds will become flowers. As long as there is desire, the energy will flow downward because desire is the downward flow. When desire disappears the energy will move upward. All the ego in the heart, all the knots and the clinging and bondages simply disappear. The heart becomes a flower in full bloom.

And when the fragrance of this blooming flower spreads, man becomes immortal in this body. This does not mean that the body will not die: *only* this body will die, but the one who lives within will never die. To attain to this immortality, it is not necessary to die – one can experience this immortality while living in this body.

*"This is the eternal teaching."* Yama is saying that this is the eternal teaching, this is what the enlightened ones have always been saying. Those who have known this have helped others to know it. But this truth cannot be known through speech, through the mind or through the senses. This truth can be known only through a deep feeling in the heart that it is, by entering this feeling deeply. Going into the depths of this feeling is trust, is religiousness. And the one who dives into this depth and keeps going deeper into it, as this trust deepens more and more, as the journey turns more and more within, the realization of your immortality grows deeper in this very body.

And as desire disappears you become the immortal, the deathless one, while you live in this body.

Now get ready for meditation.

17

# Don't Be Afraid of Losing Yourself

*"There are one hundred and one nadis, energy channels, from the heart. Only one goes toward moordha, the crown of the head, and it is called sushumna. By moving into the higher realms through this channel, man becomes immortal. If this does not occur, at the moment of death the other one hundred energy channels will be the cause of endless births and rebirths.*

*"Divine being, knower of all inner thoughts and feelings, only the size of the tip of a thumb, is eternally seated in the heart of man. The seeker must courageously know it to be separate from the body, like the kernel of a coconut shell. He must know it to be the elixir of deathlessness, the immortal essence."*

*Imbibing this wisdom and thus receiving the science of the soul and the methods of Yoga from Yama, the Lord of Death, Nachiketa became the deathless one. Unfettered by desire, he became one with existence, the ultimate reality.*

*All who realize this science of the soul will also become free of desire and of death. They too will know the ultimate reality.*

*"There are one hundred and one nadis, energy channels, from the heart. Only one goes toward moordha, the crown of the head, and it is called sushumna. By moving into the*

> *higher realms through this channel, man becomes immortal. If this does not occur, at the moment of death, the other one hundred energy channels will be the cause for endless births and rebirths."*

Yoga has a special science of its own concerning energy channels, but modern physiology does not agree with it. Scientists have not found the energy channels described by Yoga anywhere inside the human body, and the channels which they have found are not in agreement with the ones mentioned by Yoga. Yogis have made a lot of effort in this, especially yogis that have been educated in the West. Also physicians and physiologists who know Yoga have tried their best to find some similarity between the energy channels of Yoga and the ones discovered by modern science, but their effort could not succeed because it is based on a basic misunderstanding. It will be good if we can understand this misunderstanding.

The energy channels that Yoga has spoken about are not of the physical body, hence they cannot be found in this physical body. And the people who try to prove the similarity between the energy channels of the physical body and the energy channels of Yoga are not doing Yoga any good; they are harming it because Yoga is talking about another body altogether – the subtle body, the energy body which is hidden within the body. It is not gross, it is subtle. By *subtle* is meant that it is made of energy; it is the energy body. Russian scientists have called it "bio-electricity": it is their name for this energy body.

There is a body of electricity hidden within the physical body, and now science has proved it. It is this electricity body which moves the physical body. A great experiment was done in Russia by a scientist and photographer who has developed a new kind of photography known as Kirlian photography. He took photographs of the energy bodies of people, of animals and plants. Just as an X-ray takes pictures of your bones, in the same way Kirlian has developed a method which takes pictures of the energy body. And when this energy body finds a route into the one hundred-and-first energy channel, the flow of that energy creates an aura around the head of that person.

You must have seen the auras shown in pictures around the heads of Krishna, Buddha, Mahavira and Christ: this aura cannot be seen by the physical eyes. But when the life energy enters the one hundred-and-first energy channel, which Yoga calls the *sushumna nadi*, an aura of electricity is formed all around the head. Every living being has this aura, but it is visible only to those who have entered meditation. As one becomes more and more silent, one is able to see other people's auras. Every living being has an aura around him, and this aura shows the inner state of the person.

Kirlian says that a disease will enter this electrical body before moving into the physical body, and it takes six months for this to happen. For example, if you are going to become ill with tuberculosis, then first your energy body will be sick and then after six months your physical body will be affected. The journey from the energy body to the physical body takes six months. Kirlian says that when this bio-electricity can be photographed a person can be treated even before he becomes ill.

This is one of the greatest discoveries of the modern age. It is more difficult to make a person healthy again after he has already become sick; but now, before the physical body becomes sick it can be treated. And the person is not even aware that he is going to get sick in six months' time. But the energy body starts showing the signs: it becomes dull, its energy becomes low, just like a light bulb becomes dim and pale when the current of electricity drops.

When a man is healthy the electricity of his body radiates; it is vibrating with its full force. But when he is about to get ill his energy diminishes, the flow of electricity in the body becomes less, and after six months the physical body will be affected by this. But if you can know about it beforehand you can be treated before you get ill. Before the patient knows he is sick he will be free of it.

In Russia, there has been much research in the last twenty-five years. When a bud blossoms into a flower, its hidden energy body has already flowered many hours before. The eyes cannot see that blossoming energy body but Kirlian can take photos of it because he has invented a very sensitive film. The physical body of the bud blossoms into a flower many hours after its energy body has blossomed. When Kirlian takes a photo of a rosebud, it shows the blossomed energy body of the roseflower. Later on, when the bud blossoms into a flower, it will be exactly the same as the photo of the blossomed energy body of the flower.

When it is describing the channels, Yoga is talking about the energy body. It has no direct connection with this physical body, though the physical body will be affected by it. Whatever changes take place in the energy body will also affect the physical body. This is why a yogi can predict his death six months in advance; we have heard this many times, but now Kirlian has proved the time of six months scientifically.

The experience of Yoga is that six months before death the electrical energy becomes very low: it flickers and brings the news that the physical body can live for only six months more. Six months before death a dying man will no longer be able to see the tip of his nose. When you cannot see the tip of your own nose then know well that after six months you will not be here anymore – and Kirlian also agrees with this.

A few things have to be understood about the nose. The nose on your face is the symbol for your ego: it shows whether a person is egoistic or humble. Just by studying the nose of a person you can see much about him. Six months before death the ego begins to dissolve, and this is why the energy body of the nose starts to disappear. The first thing to disappear in the whole body is the energy body. Then it becomes difficult to see the tip of your nose because then the nose is there just like an empty shell.

The nose is the symbol for the ego. People say, "He has his nose up in the air," or "His nose is out of joint." These expressions have some deep meaning; nothing comes into usage without a reason. On your face, it is your nose which has the personality: if your nose is removed then the whole personality of your face will be lost. And no two people ever have the same nose. Just as the thumbprints of two people are never the same, the noses of two people are never the same. It is the subtle ego that makes the difference.

Just inside this physical body there is an energy body and this energy body is always with you. In your last incarnation, when you died your physical body was left behind but your astral body – the subtle body or the electrical or energy body, or whatsoever name you want to give to it – became free of the physical body. And it is this astral body which has entered a new womb.

The astral body dissolves only when a person has attained to enlightenment. This is why there is no possibility of another birth after the astral body has dissolved; then you *cannot* enter a new body. There is a bridge of electrical current between this astral body and the physical body: when that is broken then you cannot enter a new body. When an ordinary man dies only his physical body dies. When an enlightened one dies his energy body also dies. With the death of the energy body consciousness becomes free of the body and there is no longer any possibility of entering a new body. A person will enter a new body according to the energy he carries at the time of his previous death.

You must have heard about a well-known saying which is very meaningful, because when people believe in a certain thing for thousands of years it is certain that there is some truth, some wisdom hidden in it. You may have heard that when an enlightened one dies, as his life-breath goes out it breaks a hole in the crown of his skull. His energy leaves through the top of his head. A sexual person who is full of lust will leave his body through his sex center. All deaths happen through different points and at different levels in the body. Not all people die in the same way. Just as all people don't live in the same way, they also don't die in the same way. We are unique in life and in death also we are all different.

When Hindus saw that the death of an enlightened one happens through the top of the skull, they started breaking a hole in the skulls of their dead. The son will break a hole with a stick in the skull of his dead father on the funeral pyre. But this is only a symbol because to break the skull of the dead father makes no sense: it is meaningless because his life-breath has already left him. But the ritual has remained because the death of an enlightened person happens spontaneously through the top of the skull; he leaves his body through there and merges with existence.

Every son wants his father also to attain to that ultimate state, so he breaks a hole in the father's skull. But to break a hole in the skull of a dead body that is burning on the funeral pyre has no meaning. It will make no difference if the skull has been broken open by you. Only when the energy moves to the head, to the seventh center on its own, will death happen through the skull. And the next birth is decided by the center through which the life-breath of the person has gone out at death. There is a whole science that has to do with choosing a new womb.

Yoga says that there are one hundred and one energy channels in the heart: one hundred energy channels take you into the world and one energy channel leads you to liberation. These one hundred energy channels are one hundred paths. The journey into different births happens through different energy channels; the next birth is decided by the energy channel through which the life-breath has gone out at the time of death. And there is only one energy channel through which one will not enter a womb again, where life reaches to higher dimensions. The name for that one channel is *sushumna*. The essence of the whole of Yoga is to find how the life energy can move into this energy channel, how the life energy can rise upward and enter *sushumna*, which will liberate the seeker from all ties with the outer world.

Usually your energy is focused in the sex center. Nature needs it to be there. Nature is not concerned with *you*, it is more concerned with the continuation of life. Your life or death are not a concern for nature: the concern is that your children and their children should live on. Nature is not interested in the individual, its concern is with your offspring, that life should continue. This is why sex has such a powerful pull. You try hard in a thousand and one ways, but still the sexual urge possesses you. Nature has put so much energy into this center that you become simply helpless. Sexual desire takes over, it just gets hold of you and you are carried away by it.

All your energy is accumulated at the sex center and this energy usually flows only downward, into sex. This flow of energy has to be re-directed. There are two opposite directions for the flow of energy: one is toward the head which we call *sahasrar,* and the other toward the sex center which we call the *muladhar*. These are the two poles. The energy is accumulated at the *muladhar*: it has to rise to the *sahasrar* and the channel through which it will travel upward is called the *sushumna-nadi.* The energy will rise up higher and higher. This rising of energy is very scientific. When the energy begins to rise, the personality, the appearance, and the behavior of a person will start to change. The personality will change according to where the energy is located.

For example, a small child does not know anything about sex. Sexual energy is lying dormant in him but the sex center has not yet become active. As he becomes sexually mature the sex center will become active and his whole mind, his personality, his behavior will be full of sexuality. He will be constantly obsessed with sex; thinking, waking or sleeping, he will be surrounded by sexual desire. His only interest will be in sex. What has happened? There is suddenly such a great change in the personality!

This is why children become very restless and troubled between the ages of fourteen and eighteen. They themselves don't understand what is going on with them. This period is a very restless one. They cannot talk about it to anyone and nobody explains anything to them. So many changes are happening in them and their minds are so much obsessed with sex that they cannot even think of anything else. All this happens because the sex center is becoming active.

The moment the *sahasrar* becomes active, a similar phenomenon again happens: the person becomes full of godliness in the same way as he had become full of sex when the sex center became active. When the energy reaches the *sahasrar* one starts seeing only godliness in everything. Nature rules you at the sex center and godliness possesses you at the *sahasrar* center. The question is, how can this energy rise up to the *sahasrar*?

The first thing is that whenever the sex urge arises, with your eyes closed, contract the sex organ upward. When you feel the energy is moving downward toward sex, contract the sex organ upward and imagine only one thing: that the energy which was affecting the sex center is now rising upward. You will be surprised to see that after experimenting for a few days, whenever the urge for sex arises, if in that moment you contract the sex organ totally upward, the sex center will become empty of energy. You will find that a hot energy has started rising upward through your spine; it will be a clear experience of heat flowing upward. Sometimes the heat is so obvious that if another person touches your spine he will feel that some fire is moving upward in you.

This is the usefulness of *shirshasana*, the headstand posture: whenever the sex urge arises you can contract the sex organ inward and upward and stand on your head. Then it will be easier for the sex energy to move to the *sahasrar*. It is natural for any energy to flow downward, just as water naturally flows downward. If you are in the *shirshasana* posture and you pull the energy upward the energy will start flowing toward the head.

*Shirshasana* is not just an exercise, it is a profound experiment with celibacy. If you can connect the *sahasrar* with the sex energy, then in a few days you will find that something new has started happening in your head. Some flow has started, as if a flood has come. Every nerve, every cell will be vibrating. You will hear a sort of humming inside your head, as if the silence is making a sound, as if there is a hive of bees humming in your head.

This sound, this humming in the head, is a very good sign. It means that the energy has entered the head. Your work was to bring the energy to the head; then your *sahasrar* will blossom on its own. As soon as the bud starts receiving energy it starts to open. And as soon as it opens the nectar showers, bliss showers.

It is such an unknown experience, like nothing that has been experienced before – such bliss has never been known before. Then you are on this earth but you do not walk on this earth. Others see your feet on this earth, but your feet are not on it. Everything becomes so light that the earth's gravitation simply disappears. It is as if you have taken flight in the sky. There is some truth in the stories of yogis levitating; occasionally they have been factual. But one thing is certainly true: when the energy enters the *sahasrar* through the *sushumna*, you suddenly feel that you have risen above the earth.

If this phenomenon happens while you are meditating, then with your eyes closed you will feel that you have risen several inches above the ground. When you open your eyes you will find yourself sitting on the ground, that you have not risen at all, because the body which has risen is the energy body. But sometimes this flow is so powerful that even the physical body rises, although this rarely happens. But the energy body rises continuously whenever someone's energy enters into the *sahasrar*.

There is a woman in Europe who levitates four feet above the ground just by sitting silently. Thousands of photographs have been taken of her. All types of scientific experiments have been done, but it is beyond their understanding because to rise above the ground is a very unique phenomenon. The earth pulls us down with great force, so this is against the laws of gravitation. When this woman was asked about what she was doing she said, "I don't do anything. I just sit silently and I go on becoming more and more silent. As soon as the moment of silence comes when there is no thought, suddenly I find myself floating above the ground." She rises four feet upward!

Hundreds of people have levitated many times – but the rising of the physical body does not have much value, it is only a show. The rising of the inner body is of great value because when this inner body rises all the influences of the earth on you are destroyed.

The influences of the earth are very deep. As I have said, your body is made up of many compounds, made of all the chemical elements from the earth, and the gravity of earth is constantly pulling you down. The earth's gravity is pulling down not only things, but also your mind and your personality. When your energy rises upward you become like a balloon, you become so light that the earth cannot pull you down.

Just as there is the principle of gravitation, in Yoga there is the principle of grace, of levitation. Gravitation pulls you downward, but there is a magnetic force which pulls you upward. But it depends on your inner state whether you will be influenced from above or below. If your energy is at the lower center you will be influenced from below; if your energy is at the higher center you will be influenced from above.

Whenever the sex urge arises, close your eyes and contract your sex organ inward and imagine that the energy is moving upward. The sex center will relax immediately and you will feel something crawling up your spine, as if some ants are crawling up the spine or some hot liquid is flowing upward. When this happens, feel happy about it and accept it with gratitude. Do as many experiments as you can to pull energy upward. If you cannot do the headstand then you can at least lie down at a sloping angle with your head pointing downward, or you can arrange your bed in such a way that your head is on a slightly lower level than the rest of the body. Lying down in that position you can feel that energy is moving upward. As the energy moves up your thoughts will be less, or as your thoughts become less your energy will rise upward – both of these phenomena are connected.

Hatha yoga tries to move energy upward and Raj yoga tries to stop thoughts, but both are traveling in the same direction. Hatha yoga is concerned with energy rising upward; hence the *shirshasana*, the headstand, *mudras*, gestures through which the energy can be drawn upward and *bandhas*, contraction methods which pull energy up. Hatha yoga is not concerned with thoughts: it says that if the energy rises upward, thoughts will cease on their own. Raj yoga is not concerned about the energy; it says that if thoughts cease the energy will rise on its own. These two are interrelated phenomena; one can start from any point. If you are body-oriented then Hatha yoga is your way, and if you are mind-oriented then Raj yoga is your way. Except for these two there is no other way – either make your mind empty or withdraw your energy and pull it upward.

Remember, there is a natural law that says nature fills any vacuum. Wherever there is a vacuum, energy rushes to fill it up. It is like when you fill a pitcher from the river, a vacuum is created and water rushes immediately from all sides to fill it up. This is how the rains come after the hot season: the air becomes thin because of the summer heat, the air starts rising and creates vacuums in the space and the rain-filled clouds rush to fill those vacuums. Do you think that someone brings the clouds? No, it is the vacuum which pulls them. Wherever there is too much heat vacuums are created and the clouds rush to fill them. Nature abhors a vacuum.

If you empty your mind you are creating an empty space and the energy will start rising upward. Raj yoga is the experiment of emptying the mind. Hatha yoga does not worry about the mind; it says bring the energy upward and thoughts will disappear on their own.

Here we are experimenting with both ways simultaneously: it is a combined process of both Hatha yoga and Raj yoga. In the first three stages of meditation you are bringing the energy upward through Hatha yoga, and in the fourth stage you make your mind empty through Raj yoga. If both processes are experimented with together, results will start to happen very quickly. The speed will be doubled because you are emptying the mind and also bringing the energy upward. The sound *hoo* is a direct hit on the sex center so that the energy will start moving upward.

And the sex center can be hit in two ways. The first way is when you are attracted toward the opposite sex. When you see a beautiful man or woman, then there is a slight reaction in your sex center. This is why human beings have insisted on wearing clothes, because without clothes your sex urge would become obvious in many ways.

In the West, especially in America, in nudist clubs where nude men and women meet and play together, a strange experience is coming to light which no one could have expected. We assume that in general, women are more hesitant to go naked, they will feel shyer. But in the nudist clubs all around the world, it has become clear that women don't hesitate to be nude; it is the men who find it difficult. And this phenomenon is in agreement with yoga.

A man will hesitate because his sexual desire will be immediately visible when he is nude. A woman's desire is not so obvious in her body. So a man is afraid to be nude. Covered with clothes, he appears to be a civilized gentleman. Otherwise every beautiful woman excites him and this affects not only his mind, but also his sex organ. It is immediately affected – a little thrill in the mind and the sex organ reacts to it. A man's sex organ immediately shows that he is sexually excited. He may try to turn his eyes away, he may avoid looking at the woman, but it will make no difference. And this is a very important thing, that he can deceive all parts of his body but he cannot deceive his sex organ.

This is the most authentic part of your body. You can keep your eyes open when you want to close them or you can close them when you want to open them. You can make your eyes function in the opposite way, but you cannot do this with your sex organ. If it has become full of sex then you cannot do anything about it, and if it is not excited with sex then also you cannot do anything. The sex organ is automatic; it has so much energy that it functions on its own.

The experience in all the nudist clubs is that the man is afraid of being naked, he hesitates, while the woman is not at all afraid of being naked because her body is negative, passive. Her sex organ is already hidden, she does not need to hide it. Nothing about what is happening inside of her shows on the outside. Since the woman's sex is receptive it does not become aroused until it is brought to arousal. The man is sexually aggressive, he is already aroused; just a small spark is needed to awaken his sexual desire. The man has invented clothes to cover, to hide his sexuality.

Whenever you feel that your sex organ has become active and has become full of energy, immediately close your eyes, contract the sex mechanism inward and imagine that the energy is rising upward. Or you can trigger the sex center with the sound *hoo*. One trigger comes from the outside from a person of the opposite sex – that is an outer trigger; it will make the energy flow outward. The other trigger can be given inside with this sound and it will move the energy to the inside and raise it upward. The *hoo* sound hits exactly on the sex center. You can do this and experience it for yourself.

Many friends tell me that when they make the sound *hoo* they often start feeling very sexual. It is natural, because the sex center is being triggered. Don't be worried about this sexual urge, don't pay any attention to it. Even if it happens it does not matter: you just go on hammering on it and soon you will find that the sex organ has become relaxed and the energy has started moving upward. This is why I say that in the third stage of the meditation, use the *mahamantra hoo*. In the first stage the breathing is so intense that the energy becomes heated up. It melts, it is no longer frozen.

In the second stage, all your madness has to be thrown out,

and along with the madness, sexuality is also thrown out. You may not be aware that when you start moving your body in the second stage, most of these movements are related to your sexuality. Your body begins to move as if you are making love. Your body begins to shake in the same way; the *mudras*, your body postures and gestures are all sexual. And this is perfectly good because it will help you to throw sexuality out of the mind.

Then the third stage of meditation is hammering with the sound *hoo*. After sexuality has been thrown out and the inner fire has become liquid, then the hit of the sound *hoo* will immediately start moving the energy upward.

Some friends who are meditating here are continuously experiencing that during the meditation they immediately start to do *shirshasana*, the headstand, without knowing what is happening. The fact is that when the sex energy starts moving upward, in that moment, to stand on your head is the most natural posture for the body. In that moment there is no other position better than this. The headstand can be very helpful if you know how to use it. And if you can do the fourth stage of the meditation in *shirshasana* the results will be very deep and fast. You can do the first three stages standing, and after the first three stages do the headstand, stand on your head. The whole fourth stage can be done in *shirshasana*, remaining still and silent. The energy that is moving upward can now move even faster.

> *"There are one hundred and one nadis, energy channels, from the heart. Only one goes toward moordha, the crown of the head, and it is called sushumna. By moving into the higher realms through this channel, man becomes immortal. If this does not occur, at the moment of death the other one hundred energy channels will be the cause for endless births and rebirths.*

> *"Divine being, knower of all inner thoughts and feelings, only the size of the tip of a thumb, is eternally seated in the*

*heart of man. The seeker must courageously know it to be separate from the body, like the kernel of a coconut shell. He must know it to be the elixir of deathlessness, the immortal essence."*

This sutra is saying that the divine lives in everyone, that it is present in everyone – that one of its hands has already reached inside you.

When you dig a well and water flows into it, the flowing of the water means that the source has already reached the well. The presence of the water means that the well is connected with the distant source. So as you go on drawing water from the well fresh water goes on flowing into it.

Each person is like a well. Every human being is connected with the whole, with the infinite source, but he is like a well that has not yet been dug, or where the mud has not yet been removed. The source of water is within us, but in between there is a great layer of earth. One who breaks open or uncovers that layer and looks within himself will reach to that source of water that is connected with the source. It is connected with the infinite. This is why I always tell you after meditation to express the bliss that you have. You should release it, express it, because the more you express it the more it will grow. It is connected with the source and there is no end to it.

Try to understand this essential principle: if you hold misery in, it will grow, it will stagnate and become poisonous. If it is thrown out, if all of it is thrown out, then it is finished. Bliss is absolutely opposite to misery: if you express it, it grows, and if it is suppressed it shrinks. It is like a well which becomes miserly and does not allow its water to go out: it will stagnate and become dirty, it will lose its cleanliness. Slowly, slowly its sources will become closed because they will not be needed anymore; they will become covered with stones and dust. If water is never drawn out of a well then the well will dry up, its connection with the source will cease. The more fresh water is drawn from the well, the more water will rush in from the springs. Because of this constant flow of water the springs will become bigger and turn into many more springs.

If you suppress bliss it will disappear, if you suppress misery it will grow. Throw misery out and it will shrink and express your bliss and it will grow because their natures are opposite. This is why I say to you never to hide your misery – in the second stage of the meditation you are throwing out the misery – but never suppress your bliss. In the fifth stage you are expressing the bliss, and the more you express it the more it will flow and fill you within.

Kabir has said, "Give your bliss with both hands!" It is just like a boatman who throws water out of his boat with both hands – in the same way, when you are full of bliss, give it out. And the more you give it the more you will receive.

You have forgotten how to express bliss – you laugh as if you are crying. It has become impossible for you to dance. Even when I tell you to dance you just shake a little. Such poverty – as if the capacity for expression has been lost. It is as if you have become closed from everywhere. No one has allowed you to laugh or to cry, to dance or to sing; the celebration in your life has been destroyed.

From the very childhood you try to destroy the child's celebration in life. Every older person wants every child to behave like a grown-up. This is how all sources of bliss are cut. Your present level of energy cannot completely shake you, and unless this happens you will never experience that treasure that is hidden within you. It needs to be drawn out, it needs to be pulled out and expressed, it needs to be made visible from every cell of your body. Your concern should be how to make it flow from everywhere. It should overflow!

Dance is very valuable for the meditator – and if a meditator cannot dance, then who else can dance? And don't be miserly in it because what is hidden within you should not remain hidden.

Godliness is hidden in everyone, but you have to recognize that it is separate from your body. The two are standing side-by-side, they are joined; they are standing so close to each other that you have forgotten that godliness is separate from your body. You have become identified with the body, and your body's nearness to godliness has created this identification. Gurdjieff used to say that there is only one thing worth doing, and that is to break our identification. The realization should happen that you are separate from the body. This identification with the body is the root cause of all suffering.

Someone went to Sheik Farid and said, "We have heard that Mansoor was laughing even when his hands and feet were being cut off. We just can't believe it. How can anyone laugh when his hands and feet are being cut off? But we have heard that he was smiling. Even when he was dying, he was happy. Even after he died he had a smile on his face. This doesn't seem to be true. It's like a tale, a made-up story; we can't believe it."

There were a few coconuts nearby, so Sheik Farid took a coconut and gave it to the man and told him, "Break it and bring the kernel to me. But make sure that the kernel does not break, it should remain intact."

The man shook the coconut; it was unripe and the coconut water was shaking in it. He said, "Excuse me, but this kernel cannot be taken out whole. It will break because it is soft and the kernel is still attached to the outer shell."

So Farid gave him another coconut and said, "Try to bring this kernel to me intact, without breaking it." He shook the coconut and the kernel was moving in it. He said, "Now it is possible because the kernel has become separated from the outer shell."

Farid said, "Good, now leave both coconuts here. There is no need to do anything more. Mansoor was like the dry coconut: his kernel and his shell were separate. But you are like the raw coconut: your kernel and your outer shell are joined together. This is why when somebody hurts your outer shell, your kernel also gets hurt. Mansoor's shell was cut off and even then his kernel was unhurt. That's why he was smiling, laughing. Actually, he was saying, "Foolish people! I am not the one that you are cutting up, I am not the one that you are killing. You cannot kill *me*. You are very foolish. You are knocking down my house, but not me."

Mansoor was smiling when his feet were cut off, and he washed his hands with his blood as if he was doing *wazu*, the ritual of washing your hands before doing *namaz*, the Mohammedan prayer. People said, "We have never heard of anyone doing *wazu* with blood."

Mansoor said, "Why not? Only those who cannot do *wazu* with blood do it with water." He was happy and smiling; he was taking the whole thing as a game.

Somebody said, "You are laughing! Do you think this is a game? Your feet have been cut off. Now your hands will be cut off and soon your eyes will be taken out!"

Mansoor was executed by cutting off each part of his body. The death of Jesus was easy: he was simply crucified. But Mansoor's body was cut off piece by piece, and he was still alive when his limbs were being cut off one by one.

Mansoor said, "I have already left the body that you are destroying, so now there is no way for pain. If you had cut me up in the past I would have felt the pain because I was attached to this body – I was identified with the body."

This sutra says:

> *"The seeker must courageously know it to be separate from the body, like the kernel of a coconut shell. He must know it to be the elixir of deathlessness, the immortal essence."*

> *Imbibing this wisdom and thus receiving the science of the soul and the methods of Yoga from Yama, the Lord of Death, Nachiketa became the deathless one. Unfettered by desire, he*

*became one with existence, the ultimate reality.*

*All who realize this science of the soul will also become free of desire and of death. They too will know the ultimate reality.*

I have again shared with you what Yama shared with Nachiketa, and what has happened to Nachiketa can also happen to you. But you have to do something; just listening is not enough. Whatsoever you have heard, take a few steps in that direction, make some effort to live it. Certainly it will happen, this is my promise. Anyone who has sincerely made the effort has never missed. But if you don't take any step nothing will ever happen. You have to travel; the journey cannot be made just by thinking about it. Don't worry that your feet are not strong enough. You should not worry that you can take only one step at a time and "How will I manage this long journey to godliness?" Lao Tzu has said that a journey of ten thousand miles begins with one step – only one step. Nobody can take two steps at a time. So we are all the same in this way, we are all equal. In this there is no difference between us: only one step can be taken at a time.

There is a Chinese story about a man who lived near a very famous mountain which was known for its natural beauty. People felt blessed to climb it. He kept on thinking that one day he would go there, because it was only a distance of ten miles. One day he realized that his whole life was passing by without going there, so one night he decided to go.

It was a dark night, so he lit his small lamp and started out at about two or three o'clock in the early morning with the hope of reaching there by sunrise. But as soon as he reached the boundary of his village he started thinking, "The light of my lamp is barely reaching five or six steps ahead of me, and the darkness is ten miles long. So how can I make this long, dark journey with only this small lamp? I will certainly get lost in the darkness." So he sat down brooding over this.

Just in that moment a monk was passing by. He asked the man, "Why are you sitting there so sadly? What is the matter with you?"

The man said, "For years I was thinking about going to the mountain and today I started the journey. But my lamp is so small and the light is not enough!"

The monk told him, "Get up and come with me. When you walk four steps the light will go four steps ahead of you. Don't get lost in calculation, just walk and see. Ten miles is nothing! You can walk for ten thousand miles with this little lamp. Do you think that the whole ten thousand miles needs to be lit at one stretch? Four steps worth of light are enough for walking. Your earthen lamp is enough for your needs. But don't just sit and brood!"

Instead of wasting time thinking, use this time for making efforts, use it for meditation – then the goal is not far away. And I can assure you of this because the one that you are seeking is hidden within you. You are born immortal but you live believing in death. This illusion can shatter in one second – or it may not shatter for many lives – it all depends on you.

If you want to search deeply and intensely, with a strong determination, there is no obstacle. There will be only one barrier: the more intensely you search, the more you will lose yourself. Don't be afraid of this, because no one can find himself unless he first loses himself. The one who loses himself *deserves* to find himself. Only one who is courageous enough to die will become worthy of immortality. You have to lose yourself: that is the price.

Many people want to know godliness but they are not ready to give themselves. They don't want to give anything, they want it for free. This is why there is only talk, and life is wasted, and time passes, and days come and go, nights come and go, years pass, and man goes on dying.

You have to put yourself at stake. Anything less than that will not do.

...Nachiketa became the deathless one. Unfettered by desire, he became one with existence, the ultimate reality. All who realize this science of the soul will also become free of desire and of death. They too will know the ultimate reality. You too can – like Nachiketa, you also have come here searching. You also can leave here attaining the same thing as Nachiketa. The same can happen to you as happened to him. If you can be as innocent, as full of trust, with such an unwavering longing for the truth and not be diverted by small greeds; if you have the courage to stake the whole world even if it you were given the ownership of it; if you have the patience, if all of these qualities come into your life even a little, then what happened to Nachiketa can also happen to you.

This will be the last meditation of this camp – put your total energy into it. First, wait for two minutes...

[*Osho continues for the Western, English speakers present*]

This will be the last session of meditation in this camp. Bring your total energy to it. The only problem is that you are always divided: a part of you meditates, the other part remains uninvolved – and that remaining part becomes the barrier. The part cannot meditate unless the whole comes into it. The part is impotent, only the whole is potent. Unless your totality is challenged, unless you take a jump as a total being leaving nothing behind, with no withholding, unless this wholeness comes into meditation, your energy will be wasted, your time will be wasted – nothing will happen out of it.

One woman seeker comes to me every day and she says, "One day has passed and the explosion has not happened yet." This morning she came again! She is very innocent, childlike – her eyes were filled with tears and she said, "The last day has come and the explosion has not happened yet!"

The explosion is not something outer that happens to you; the explosion is something inner. It is not something which is going to happen to you; rather, you are going to happen to it. The explosion is not an outer incident, it is inner. If it is not happening it means you are not totally in the meditation. The moment you are totally in it the explosion is bound to happen. There can be no doubt about it.

But you never bring your totality: you jump, you dance, you scream, you do the mantra, but always with the part, with a fragment of your mind.

This will be the last session: bring your totality, take a jump! And when you meditate this evening, don't allow any fragment of your being to stand outside. Become one, become one unit and I promise: the explosion is bound to happen.

Create the cause and the effect will follow. You can go on expecting, but expectations won't do. If it is not happening it means you are not totally in it, just superficially. You do it but just superficially; only the surface is touched, the center remains untouched. And don't be worried that what has not happened in the whole camp, how is it going to happen on the last day? It may happen! You may have boiled to ninety-nine degrees – only one degree more, and the explosion. But a one hundred degree effort is needed.

Now get ready.

# About Osho

Osho defies categorization. Mystic and scientist, a rebellious spirit whose sole interest is to alert humanity to the urgent need to discover a new way of living. To continue as before is to invite threats to our very survival on this unique and beautiful planet.

His thousands of talks cover everything from the individual quest for meaning to the most urgent social, political and environmental issues facing society today. Osho's books are not written but transcribed from audio and video recordings of his extemporaneous talks to international audiences. And he tells them, "Remember: whatever I am saying is not just for you...I am talking also for the future generations."

Osho has been described by *The Sunday Times* in London as one of the "1000 Makers of the 20th Century" and by American author Tom Robbins as "the most dangerous man since Jesus Christ." *Sunday Mid-Day* (Mumbai) has selected Osho as one of ten people – along with Gandhi, Nehru and Buddha – who have changed the destiny of India.

About his own work, Osho has said that he is helping to create the conditions for the birth of a new kind of human being. He often characterizes this new human being as "Zorba the Buddha" – capable both of enjoying the earthy pleasures of a Zorba the Greek and the silent serenity of a Gautama the Buddha.

Running like a thread through all aspects of Osho's talks and meditations is a vision that encompasses both the timeless wisdom of all ages past and the highest potential of today's (and tomorrow's) science and technology.

Osho is known for his revolutionary contribution to the science of inner transformation, with an approach to meditation that acknowledges the accelerated pace of contemporary life. His unique OSHO Active Meditations® are designed to first release the accumulated stresses of body and mind, so that it then becomes easier to experience a stillness and thought-free relaxation which can be taken into daily life.

Two autobiographical works by the author are available:
*Autobiography of a Spiritually Incorrect Mystic,*
St Martins Press, New York (book and eBook)
*Glimpses of a Golden Childhood,* (book and eBook)
OSHO Media International, Pune, India

# OSHO International Meditation Resort

Each year the Meditation Resort welcomes thousands of people from more than 100 countries. The unique campus provides an opportunity for a direct personal experience of a new way of living – with more awareness, relaxation, celebration and creativity. A great variety of around-the-clock and around-the-year program options are available. Doing nothing and just relaxing is one of them!

All of the programs are based on Osho's vision of "Zorba the Buddha" – a qualitatively new kind of human being who is able *both* to participate creatively in everyday life *and* to relax into silence and meditation.

**Location**

Located 100 miles southeast of Mumbai in the thriving modern city of Pune, India, the OSHO International Meditation Resort is a holiday destination with a difference. The Meditation Resort is spread over 28 acres of spectacular gardens in a beautiful tree-lined residential area.

**OSHO Meditations**

A full daily schedule of meditations for every type of person includes both traditional and revolutionary methods, and particularly the OSHO Active Meditations®. The daily meditation program takes place in what must be the world's largest meditation hall, the OSHO Auditorium.

**OSHO Multiversity**
Individual sessions, courses and workshops cover everything from creative arts to holistic health, personal transformation, relationship and life transitions, transforming meditation into a lifestyle for life and work, esoteric sciences, and the Zen approach to sports and recreation. The secret of the OSHO Multiversity's success lies in the fact that all its programs are combined with meditation, supporting the understanding that as human beings we are far more than the sum of our parts.

**Cuisine**
A variety of different eating areas serve delicious Western, Asian and Indian vegetarian food – most of it organically grown especially for the Meditation Resort. Breads and cakes are baked in the Resort's bakery.

**Night life**
There are many evening events to choose from – dancing being at the top of the list! Other activities include full-moon meditations beneath the stars, variety shows, music performances and "meditations for daily life."

**Facilities**
At the Meditation Resort you can buy all your basic necessities and toiletries in the Galleria. In addition, the Multimedia Gallery sells a large range of OSHO media products. For those who enjoy shopping, Pune provides all the options, ranging from traditional and ethnic Indian products to all of the global brand-name stores.

**Accommodation**
You can choose to stay in the elegant rooms of the OSHO Guesthouse, or for longer stays on campus you can select one of

the OSHO Living-In programs. Additionally there is a variety of nearby hotels and serviced apartments.

www.osho.com/meditationresort
www.osho.com/guesthouse
www.osho.com/livingin
Facebook: osho.international.meditation.resort

# OSHO Books (English)

OSHO books are available as printed books and in eBook format, and most of them in audio format too. If a book is not available in one format, you can look up and buy it in another format.

**Early Talks**
The Art of Living
Astrology
Breaking All Boundaries
Compassion and Revolution
Dimensions beyond the Known
The Eternal Quest
From Sex to Superconsciousness
The Great Challenge
Hidden Mysteries
I Am the Gate
The Independent Mind
Into the Void
Keys to a New Life
New Dimensions of Yoga
The Psychology of the Esoteric
Religion's Expiration Date
The Search for Peace
Woman and Rebellion
Work Is Love Made Visible

**Meditation**

And Now and Here
Body/Mind Balancing (Book & Audio)
Falling In Love with Darkness
In Search of the Miraculous
The Inner Journey
Just a Small Step
Meditation: The Art of Ecstasy
Meditation: The First and Last Freedom
The Path of Meditation
The Perfect Way
Silence: The Message of Your Being
Three Steps to Awakening

**Buddha and Buddhist Masters**

The Book of Wisdom
The Dhammapada: The Way of the Buddha (Vols 1-12)
The Diamond Sutra
The Discipline of Transcendence (Vols 1-4)
The Heart Sutra

**Indian Mystics**

As if a Tree Starts Running (Yari)
The Beloved, Vols 1 & 2 (Baul Mystics)
Bliss (Shiva)
Die O Yogi Die (Gorakh)
Enlightenment: The Only Revolution (Ashtavakra)
Geeta Darshan Vol. 1 (Adhyaya 1-2)
Geeta Darshan, Vol.2 (Adhyaya 3)
Krishna: The Man and His Philosophy
The Last Morning Star (Daya)
Showering without Clouds (Sahajo)
The Song of Ecstasy (Adi Shankara)
The True Name (Vols 1&2) (Nanak)

**Kabir**
The Divine Melody
Ecstasy: The Forgotten Language
The Fabric of Life
The Fish in the Sea Is Not Thirsty
The Great Secret
The Guest
The Path of Love
The Revolution

**Western Mystics**
The Art of Dying *(Hasidism)*
Come Follow to You, Vols 1-4 *(Jesus)*
Guida Spirituale *(Desiderata)*
The Hidden Harmony *(Heraclitus)*
I Say Unto You, Vols 1 & 2 *(Jesus)*
The Mustard Seed *(Jesus)*
The New Alchemy: To Turn You On (Mabel Collins)
Philosophia Perennis, Vols 1 & 2 *(Pythagoras)*
Reflections on Kahlil Gibran's The Prophet
Theologia Mystica *(Dionysius)*
The True Sage *(Hasidism)*
The Voice of Silence (Mabel Collins)
Zarathustra: A God That Can Dance
(Nietzsche's *Thus Spake Zarathustra*)
Zarathustra: The Laughing Prophet
(Nietzsche's *Thus Spake Zarathustra*)

**Sufism**
Just Like That
The Perfect Master, Vols 1 & 2
The Secret
Sufis: The People of the Path, Vols 1 & 2
Unio Mystica, Vols 1 & 2
Until You Die

The Wisdom of the Sands, Vols 1 & 2

**Tantra**
The Book of Secrets (Vigyan Bhairav Tantra)
The Tantra Experience (Saraha)
Tantra: The Supreme Understanding (Tilopa)
Tantric Transformation (Saraha)

**The Upanishads**
Behind a Thousand Names (Nirvana Upanishad)
Finger Pointing to the Moon (Adhyatma Upanishad)
Flight of the Alone to the Alone (Kaivalya Upanishad)
The Heartbeat of the Absolute (Ishavasya Upanishad)
I Am That (Isa Upanishad)
The Message beyond Words (Kathopanishad)
Philosophia Ultima (Mandukya Upanishad)
The Supreme Doctrine (Kenopanishad)
That Art Thou (Sarvasar Upanishad, Kaivalya Upanishad, Adhyatma Upanishad)
The Ultimate Alchemy, Vols 1 & 2 (Atma Pooja Upanishad)
Vedanta: Seven Steps to Samadhi (Akshaya Upanishad)
The Way beyond Any Way (Sarvasar Upanishad)

**Tao**
The Empty Boat (Chuang Tzu)
The Secret of Secrets (The Secret of Golden Flower)
Tao: The Golden Gate, Vols 1 & 2 (Ko Hsuan)
Tao: The Pathless Path, Vols 1 & 2 (Lieh Tzu)
Tao: The Three Treasures, Vols 1-4 (Lao Tzu)
When the Shoe Fits (Chuang Tzu)

**Yoga (Patanjali)**
Yoga: The Science of the Soul, Vols 1-10
-The Path of Yoga (Vol.1)

-The Heart of Yoga (Vol.2)
-Yoga: The Mystery beyond Mind (Vol.3)
-The Alchemy of Yoga (Vol.4)
-Yoga: A New Direction (Vol.5)
-Essence of Yoga (Vol.6)
-Yoga: The Science of Living (Vol.7)
-Secrets of Yoga (Vol.8)
-Yoga: The Path to Liberation (Vol.9)
-Yoga: The Supreme Science (Vol.10)

**Zen and Zen Masters**
Ah, This!
Ancient Music in the Pines
And the Flowers Showered…
And the Grass Grows By Itself…
A Bird on the Wing
Bodhidharma: The Greatest Zen Master
The Buddha: The Emptiness of the Heart
Christianity, the Deadliest Poison and Zen,
the Antidote to All Poisons
Communism and Zen Fire, Zen Wind
Dang Dang Doko Dang
The First Principle
God Is Dead: Now Zen Is the Only Living Truth
The Great Zen Master Ta Hui
Hsin Hsin Ming: The Book of Nothing
I Celebrate Myself: God Is No Where, Life Is Now Here
Kyozan: A True Man of Zen
The Language of Existence
Live Zen
The Miracle
Nirvana: The Last Nightmare
No Mind: The Flowers of Eternity
No Water, No Moon
One Seed Makes the Whole Earth Green

The Original Man
Returning to the Source
The Search: Talks on the 10 Bulls of Zen
A Sudden Clash of Thunder
The Sun Rises in the Evening
Take it Easy
This. This. A Thousand Times This
This Very Body the Buddha
Turning In
The White Lotus
Yakusan: Straight to the Point of Enlightenment
The Zen Manifesto: Freedom from Oneself
Zen: The Diamond Thunderbolt
Zen: The Mystery and the Poetry of the Beyond
Zen: The Path of Paradox, Vols 1-3
Zen: The Quantum Leap from Mind to No-Mind
Zen: The Solitary Bird, Cuckoo of the Forest
Zen: The Special Transmission

**Osho: On the Ancient Masters of Zen**
Dogen: The Zen Master
Hyakujo: The Everest of Zen – With Basho's haikus
Isan: No Footprints in the Blue Sky
Joshu: The Lion's Roar
Ma Tzu: The Empty Mirror
Nansen: The Point of Departure
Rinzai: Master of the Irrational

**Responses to Questions**
Be Still and Know
Beyond Enlightenment (Talks in Mumbai)
Beyond Psychology (Talks in Uruguay)
Come, Come, Yet Again Come
The Diamond Sword
From Bondage to Freedom

From Darkness to Light
From Death to Deathlessness
From Ignorance to Innocence
From Misery to Enlightenment
From Personality to Individuality
From the False to the Truth
From Unconsciousness to Consciousness
The Goose Is Out
The Great Pilgrimage: From Here to Here
The Invitation
Light on the Path (Talks in the Himalayas)
My Way: The Way of the White Clouds
Nowhere to Go but In
The Osho Upanishad (Talks in Mumbai)
The Path of the Mystic (Talks in Uruguay)
The Razor's Edge
Sermons in Stones (Talks in Mumbai)
Socrates Poisoned Again After 25 Centuries (Talks in Greece)
The Sword and the Lotus (Talks in the Himalayas)
Transmission of the Lamp (Talks in Uruguay)
Walk without Feet, Fly without Wings and Think without Mind
The Wild Geese and the Water
Yaa-Hoo! The Mystic Rose
Walking in Zen, Sitting in Zen
Zen: Zest, Zip, Zap and Zing

**Osho's Vision for the World**
The Golden Future
The Hidden Splendor
The New Dawn
The Rebel
The Rebellious Spirit

**The Mantra Series**
Hari Om Tat Sat
Om Mani Padme Hum
Om Shantih Shantih Shantih
Sat Chit Anand
Satyam Shivam Sundaram

**Personal Glimpses**
Books I Have Loved
Glimpses of a Golden Childhood
Notes of a Madman

**Interviews with the World Press**
The Man of Truth: A Majority of One

**Meetings with Individuals**
Above All Don't Wobble
Hammer on the Rock

**Quotation Books**
Gold Nuggets
More Gold Nuggets
Words From A Man of No Words

**Letters and Writings**
A Cup of Tea
Earthen Lamps
Flowers of Love
Life Is a Soap Bubble
Love Letters to Life
Seeds of Wisdom

For any information about OSHO Books, please contact:

**OSHO Media International**
17 Koregaon Park, Pune – 411001, MS, India
Phone: +91-20-66019999 Fax: +91-20-66019990
E-mail: distribution@osho.net
Website: http://www.osho.com

# For More Information

The official website of OSHO International is www.OSHO.com

www.OSHO.com/AllAboutOSHO is a comprehensive portal to all things OSHO.

www.OSHO.com/AllAboutOSHO<br>
www.OshoTimes.com<br>
shop.OSHO.com<br>
iOSHO.OSHO.com<br>
YouTube: OSHO/OSHOinternational<br>
Twitter: OSHO<br>
Instagram: OSHOinternational<br>
Facebook: OSHO.international<br>
Facebook: OSHO.international.meditation.resort